Freedom in the World

Freedom in the World

*Political Rights and Civil Liberties
1987-1988*

Raymond D. Gastil

With contributions by

Thomas D. Anderson
Michael Coppedge
Larry Diamond
Milton Friedman
Fred Glahe
Juan J. Linz

Seymour Martin Lipset
Wolfgang Reinicke
Leonard R. Sussman
Frank Vorhies
Harmon Zeigler

FREEDOM HOUSE

The Library of Congress has cataloged this serial title as follows:

Freedom in the world / Raymond D. Gastil.—1978–   —
New York : Freedom House, 1978–
v. : map ; 25 cm.-(Freedom House Book)
Annual.
Includes bibliographical references and index.
ISSN 0732–6610=Freedom in the world.
1. Civil rights—Perodicals. I. Gastil, Raymond D. II. Series.
JC571.F66   323.4'05—dc 19   82–642048
AACR 2   MARC-S
Library of Congress   [8410]
ISBN 0–932088–22–8 (pbk. : alk. paper)
ISBN 0–932088–23–6 (alk. paper)

Distributed by arrangement with

UPA, Inc.
4720 Boston Way
Lanham, MD 20706

3 Henrietta Street
London WC2E 8LU England

CONTENTS

Contents

MAPS AND TABLES

PREFACE

Americans have many foreign policy interests. For most citizens our economic and security relations are foremost, and our foreign policy is directed primarily to securing these interests. However, in the long run the future of our country will only be secured in a free and democratic world. From this perspective achieving this world is both a vital interest of Americans and a vital interest of all peoples. To help us in understanding where we are in the struggle to achieve this world and to keep the relevance of this issue before the public, Freedom House has supported the Comparative Survey of Freedom since 1972.

This yearbook marks the sixteenth year of the Comparative Survey and the tenth edition in this Freedom House series of annual publications. Previous yearbooks, in addition to focusing on the Comparative Survey, have emphasized different aspects of freedom and human rights. The first yearbook, the 1978 edition, examined basic theoretical issues of freedom and democracy and assessed the record of the Year of Human Rights. The second yearbook reported extensively on a conference devoted to the possibilities of expanding freedom in the Soviet Union. The 1980 yearbook considered international issues in press freedom, aspects of trade union freedom, the struggle for democracy in Iran, elections in Zimbabwe, and the relationship between human rights policy and morality. The 1981 yearbook contained essays and discussions from a Freedom House conference on the prospects for freedom in Muslim Central Asia.

The 1982 yearbook emphasized a variety of approaches to economic freedom and its relation to political and civil freedom. The 1983-84 yearbook addressed the problems of corporatism, and the health of democracy in the third world. It also incorporated the papers and discussions of a conference held at Freedom House on supporting democracy in mainland China and Taiwan. We returned in the 1984-85 yearbook to the themes of the definition of freedom and the conditions for the development of freedom that were first addressed in the 1978 yearbook. It also looked at the particular problem of developing democracy in Central America. The 1985-86 yearbook considered America's role in the worldwide struggle for democracy, and reported the results of a conference on supporting liberalization in Eastern Europe. The 1986-87 yearbook offered a number of essays on the nature and value of liberal democracy, as well as comparative discussions of democracy in several countries. These discussions should be seen as a supplement to the theoretical essays in the 1978 yearbook.

This year the ratings and tables produced by the Survey are augmented by a table of social and economic statistical comparisons that many will find useful to compare with the freedom ratings. The discussion of criteria and definitions at the beginning of the 1987-88 yearbook again includes the checklist for political rights and civil liberties. Among current issues, the struggle between openness and censorship is considered in this year's review of constraints on freedom of expression. We also present a round table discussion of how the United States might improve its support of democracy. The discussants were a small group of people from outside the United States directly involved in the struggle for freedom in their own countries. This year it was decided to bring to our readers' attention something of the variety and scope of the work of researchers outside Freedom House that is closely related to the Survey or its themes. Papers include: two recent surveys of comparative political and civil rights (which are interesting to compare with the Survey), two brief efforts to correlate Survey ratings with development, and excerpts from an extensive effort to examine the relationships between economic systems, freedom, equality, and economic or social development. The final paper is a comprehensive report on factors in democratic development from the group conducting perhaps the leading research effort in this area.

We acknowledge, once again, the contribution made by the advisory panel for the Comparative Survey. The panel consists of: Robert J. Alexander, Richard W. Cottam, Herbert J. Ellison, Seymour Martin Lipset, Lucian W. Pye, Leslie Rubin, Giovanni Sartori, Robert Scalapino, and Paul Seabury. We also express our appreciation to those foundations whose grants have made the Survey and the publication of this yearbook possible. Substantial support has again been given by the J. Howard Pew Freedom Trust; their continuing confidence has been a key factor in achieving the Survey's goal of raising the level of understanding of freedom in the world. All Freedom House activities are also assisted by the generous support of individual members of the organization as well as trade unions, corporations, and public foundations that contribute to our general budget. No financial support from any government—now or in the past—has been either solicited or accepted.

We gratefully acknowledge the research and editorial assistance of Jeannette C. Gastil in producing this yearbook.

PART I

The Survey in 1986

FREEDOM IN THE COMPARATIVE SURVEY:

DEFINITIONS AND CRITERIA

Freedom, like democracy, is a term with many meanings. Its meanings cover a variety of philosophical and social issues, many of which would carry us far beyond the discussion of political systems with which the Comparative Survey of Freedom has been principally concerned. Unfortunately, linguistic usage is such that the meanings of freedom infect one another, so that a "free society" may be taken to be a society with no rules at all, or a free man may be taken to be an individual with no obligations to society, or even another individual. This global sense of individual freedom leads many Americans to scoff at the idea that theirs is a free society. Not primarily concerned with politics, most Americans apply the word "free" to their personal relationships, sensing correctly, but for our purposes irrelevantly, the necessity to work at a job, or to drive at a certain speed on the highway. To these individuals, "freedom" sounds like a wonderful goal, but hardly a goal that their society has achieved. Yet freedom, when addressed in a narrow political sense, is the basic value, goal, and, to a remarkable degree, attainment of successful democratic regimes.

Freedom as independence is important to the Survey, but this too is not a primary basis of judgment. When the primary issue for so many countries in the colonial era was to become free from a colonial or occupying power, "freedom" meant that a country had emerged from control by another state, much as the United States had achieved freedom in the 1780s. This sense of freedom was applied to the term "the free world" after World War II because the Soviet Union forced satellization on so many countries of Eastern Europe. By contrast those beyond this sphere were said to be free. In this sense Spain was part of the free world, but at the time only in its relative independence. Still, for a people to accept rule by leaders of their own nationality rather than by foreign leaders is an aspect of political freedom—self-determination is a democratic right. But the fact, for example, that the dictators of Haiti have been Haitians has done little for the freedom or democratic rights of their people.

Since democratic freedoms and human rights are often considered together, it has often been assumed that the Survey of Freedom is equivalent to a survey of human rights. However, in spite of the considerable overlap of the two, concern for democracy and concern for human rights are distinct. A free people can deny human rights to some of their number, and they can certainly deny human rights to others. Thus, the Japanese tendency to exclude foreigners, and to discriminate against those who come to Japan, is unfortunate but does little to affect its democracy. If people are beaten cruelly in the jails of Arkansas, this too is a violation of human rights, but the ill-treatment may both be passively approved by the people of the state and be of little consequence for those requirements for free speech and nonviolent pluralism necessary for the expression of political democracy.

One concern that many have felt with the human rights movement has been its tendency to proliferate as "rights" an ever-lengthening list of desirabilia, a list that mixes general principles of natural rights with the particular concerns of modern intellectuals. This weakens the proposition that there are basic natural rights that all peoples in all places and times should feel incumbent upon themselves and their societies. It also leads to an increasing opposition between expanding democratic freedoms (that is, the ability of a people to decide its own fate) and expanding human rights.

In the Survey, freedom or democracy is taken to mean "liberal democracy." It is surprising how many well-informed persons believe that since the "German Democratic Republic" also uses the term democracy in its label, we must include regimes of this type within our definition. It would be like saying that since the German fascists called their party "National Socialist," discussions of socialism must use definitions that would include the Nazis. Words can be appropriated to many uses, and no one can stop the appropriation, but when an extension of meaning adds little but confusion, and begins to call black white, it should be rejected.

In rejecting the Marxist-Leninist or extreme leftist usage of the word democracy, as in "people's democracy," we do not mean to imply that there is not a range of acceptable meanings of "democracy" that must be taken into account in any survey of democratic freedoms. We have explicitly addressed in previous volumes of the Survey the question of how "economic freedom" might be defined.[1] Our conclusion was that a system was free primarily to the extent that the people were actually given a choice in determining the nature of the economic system. Therefore, a system that produces economic equality, if imposed, is much less democratic than a more unequal system, if freely chosen. Of course, questions must always be asked about the extent to which a system is freely chosen by any people. Economic measures such as land reform in a poor peasant economy may play a significant fact in improving the ability of people to take part in the political process fairly, and thereby choose the economic strategies that they desire.

The Comparative Survey was begun in the early 1970s as an attempt to give a more standardized and relativized picture of the situation of freedom in the world than could be provided by essays of individuals from different backgrounds that had formed, and in part still form, Freedom House's annual review of the condition of freedom in the world. My own experience had been that the world media and, therefore, informed opinion often misevaluated the level of freedom in countries with which Westerners had become particularly involved. In many countries oppressions were condemned as more severe than they were in comparative terms. On the other hand, the achievements of the postwar period in expanding freedom were often overlooked. Many small countries had quietly achieved and enjoyed democracy with relatively little media attention. The most oppressive states were those about which there was the least news in the media. Although these imbalances are still present, it is possible that some improvement in the presentation of the state of freedom in the world has resulted from the development of these Surveys.

The Comparative Survey of Freedom was hardly the first survey. There had been a number of other surveys. Bryce had listed the number of democracies in the world in about 1920.[2] An extensive cross-comparison of societies on social and cultural variables was published in the early sixties by Banks and Textor.[3] Based on an analysis of qualitative and quantitative data for all nations in the period 1960-62, the authors ranked and categorized polities on a wide variety of indices. These included economic

5

development, literacy, and degree of urbanization, as well as political and civil rights. Since the authors' purpose was ultimately to discover correlations among the variables, their indices were more specific than those used in the Comparative Survey. They were interested primarily in presenting detailed information on items such as the nature of the party system, the presence or absence of military intervention, the freedom of opposition groups to enter politics, or the freedom of the press.

The next major effort, by Robert Dahl and colleagues at Yale, was much closer in intent to the Comparative Survey.[4] In updating Banks and Textor's work they placed all significant states along a variety of scales relating to democracy. The resulting scales were then aggregated into scales representing the two fundamental dimensions of "polyarchy" according to Dahl: opportunities for political opposition and degree of popular participation in national elections. Dahl's lists of polyarchies and near-polyarchies were very similar to our lists of free states. A similar rating of democratic systems was developed about the same time by Dankwart Rustow.[5] In both cases, and especially that of Rustow, there seemed to be an overemphasis on the formal characteristics of participation in elections and too little regard for the civil liberties that must complement elections if they are to be meaningful. Nevertheless, the resulting lists were very similar to those produced a few years later in the first Comparative Survey of Freedom, as are the lists of higher ranking states in analyses of human rights conditions.[6] (In Part II, below, two recent attempts to rate the freedom of countries by means analogous to the Survey are presented.)

The essential difference between the Comparative Survey and the other attempts of the last generation has been its annual presentation of the evidence and rankings, as opposed to what are essentially one-shot presentations. The latter often represent much more detailed study, but they suffer from the lack of experience with repeated judgments and changes over a period of years that has served to improve the Comparative Survey.

In many ways more comparable to the Survey are the annual reports on human rights to Congress of the State Department's Bureau of Human Rights and Humanitarian Affairs.[7] Presenting detailed information on the state of human rights in every country, the reports consider political and civil liberties as well as other issues. They are, of course, influenced by America's foreign policy concerns, but with this caveat they are remarkably informative. Improving in coverage and comparability are also the annual reports of Amnesty International.[8] Amnesty's concerns in the area are much narrower, but information on Amnesty's issues—execution, political imprisonment, and torture—often has a wider significance. Both of these efforts have now become basic sources of information for the Comparative Survey.

The purpose of the Comparative Survey, then, is to give a general picture of the state of political and civil freedoms in the world. By taking a consistent approach to the definition of freedom, distinctions and issues that are often overlooked are brought out. In particular, its comparative approach brings to the reader's attention the fact that the most publicized denials of political and civil liberties are seldom in the most oppressive states. These states, such as Albania and North Korea, simply do not allow relevant information to reach the world media. There may or may not be hundreds of thousands in jail for their beliefs in North Korea: few care because no one knows.

Besides giving a reference point for considering the performance of independent countries, by its existence the Survey stands for the importance of democracy and freedom in an often cynical world. Too often, Westerners believe that democracy is impossible outside of a few Western countries, and consign the rest of the world to perpetual despotism. The story of the struggle for democratic freedoms is a much more complicated one, and needs to be told. In a sketchy manner the Survey records the advances and retreats of democracy, and alerts the world to trends that should be resisted and those that should be supported.

The Categories of the Survey

The two dimensions of the Survey are political rights and civil liberties. **Political rights** are rights to participate meaningfully in the political process. In a democracy this means the right of all adults to vote and compete for public office, and for elected representatives to have a decisive vote on public policies. **Civil liberties** are rights to free expression, to organize or demonstrate, as well as rights to a degree of autonomy such as is provided by freedom of religion, education, travel, and other personal rights.

7

Political rights and civil liberties are rated on seven-point scales, with (7) the least free or least democratic and (1) the most free. With no exact definition for any point on these scales, they are constructed comparatively: countries are rated in relation to other countries rather than against absolute standards. The purpose of the rating system is to give an idea of how the freedoms of one state compare with those of others. Different persons with different information, or even with the same information, might compare countries differently. But unless the results of such comparisons are wildly different, there should be no concern. For example, if the Survey rates a country a (3) on political rights, and another person, accepting the criteria of the Survey, rates it a (4), this is an acceptable discrepancy. If judgments of two persons should turn out to be more than one point off, however, then either the Survey's methods are faulty, or the information of one of the judges is faulty.

The generalized checklist for the Comparative Survey is outlined in the accompanying Checklist for Freedom Ratings. The following discussion of some checklist items is keyed to the tabular presentation of the checklist.

Discussion of Political Rights

(1-2) Political systems exhibit a variety of degrees to which they offer voters a chance to participate meaningfully in the process. Let us briefly consider several levels of political participation and choice.

At the antidemocratic extreme are those systems with no process, such as inherited monarchies or purely appointive communist systems. Little different in practice are those societies that hold elections for the legislature or president, but give the voter no alternative other than affirmation. In such elections there is neither the choice nor possibility—in practice or even sometimes in theory—of rejecting the single candidate that the government proposes for chief executive or representative. In elections at this level the candidate is usually chosen by a secretive process involving only the top elite. More democratic are those systems, such as Zambia's, that allow the voter no choice, but suggest that it is possible to reject a suggested candidate. In this case the results may show ten or twenty percent of the voters actually

CHECKLIST FOR FREEDOM RATINGS

POLITICAL RIGHTS

1. Chief authority recently elected by a meaningful process

2. Legislature recently elected by a meaningful process

   Alternatives for (1) and (2):

   a. no choice and possibility of rejection
   b. no choice but some possibility of rejection
   c. government or single-party selected candidates
   d. choice possible only among government-approved candidates
   e. relatively open choices possible only in local elections
   f. open choice possible within a restricted range
   g. relatively open choices possible in all elections

3. Fair election laws, campaigning opportunity, polling
   and tabulation

4. Fair reflection of voter preference in distribution of power
   — parliament, for example, has effective power

5. Multiple political parties
   — only dominant party allowed effective opportunity
   — open to rise and fall of competing parties

6. Recent shifts in power through elections

7. Significant opposition vote

8. Free of military or foreign control

9. Major group or groups denied reasonable self-determination

10. Decentralized political power

11. Informal consensus; de facto opposition power

CIVIL LIBERTIES

12. Media/literature free of political censorship

    a. Press independent of government
    b. Broadcasting independent of government

13. Open public discussion

14. Freedom of assembly and demonstration

15. Freedom of political or quasi-political organization

16. Nondiscriminatory rule of law in politically relevant cases

    a. independent judiciary
    b. security forces respect individuals

17. Free from unjustified political terror or imprisonment

    a. free from imprisonment or exile for reasons of conscience
    b. free from torture
    c. free from terror by groups not opposed to the system
    d. free from government-organized terror

18. Free trade unions, peasant organizations, or equivalents

19. Free businesses or cooperatives

20. Free professional or other private organizations

21. Free religious institutions

22. Personal social rights: including those to property, internal and external travel, choice of residence, marriage and family

23. Socioeconomic rights: including freedom from dependency on landlords, bosses, union leaders, or bureaucrats

24. Freedom from gross socioeconomic inequality

25. Freedom from gross government indifference or corruption

voting against a suggested executive, or, rarely, rejecting an individual legislative candidate on a single list. In some societies there is a relatively more open party process for selecting candidates. However the list of preselected candidates is prepared, there is seldom any provision for serious campaigning against the single list.

The political system is more democratic if multiple candidates are offered for each position, even when all candidates are government or party selected. Popular voting for alternatives may exist only at the party level—which in some countries is a large proportion of the population—or the choice may be at the general election. Rarely do such systems extend voter options to include choice of the chief authority in the state. Usually that position, like the domination by a single party, is not open to question. But many legislators, even members of the cabinet, may be rejected by the voters in such a system, although they must not go beyond what the party approves. Campaigning occurs at this level of democracy, but the campaigning is restricted to questions of personality, honesty, or ability; for example, in Tanzania campaigning may not involve questions of policy. A further increment of democratic validity is effected if choice is possible among government-approved rather than government-selected candidates. In this case the government's objective is to keep the most undesirable elements (from its viewpoint) out of the election. With government-selected candidates there is reliance on party faithfuls, but self-selection allows persons of local reputation to achieve office. More generally, controlled electoral systems may allow open, self-selection of candidates for some local elections, but not for elections on the national scale. It is also possible for a system, such as that of Iran, to allow an open choice of candidates in elections, but to draw narrow ideological limits around what is an acceptable candidacy.

Beyond this, there is the world of free elections as we know them, in which candidates are both selected by parties and self-selected. It could be argued that parliamentary systems, such as are common outside of the United States, reduce local choice by imposing party choices on voters. However, independents can and do win in most systems, and new parties, such as the "Greens" in West Germany and elsewhere, test the extent to which the party system in particular countries is responsive to the desires of citizens.

(3) In most of the traditional western democracies there are fair election laws, at least on the surface. This is not true in many aspiring democracies. Senegal, for example, did not allow opposition parties to join together for the last general election, a regulation the government seems determined to maintain. Since effective oppositions often emerge from coalitions, this regulation is a useful device for preventing fragmented opposition groups from mounting a successful challenge. At least until recently, election laws in Egypt and South Korea have been devised so that the size of the majority of the governing party is artificially inflated after its victory.[9] This is a useful device where there is a danger of excessive fragmentation leading to majorities too weak to govern, but it seems in these cases to be intended to reduce the size of the opposition.

Political scientists dispute whether it is fairer to allow people to contribute to candidates as they like, or whether the government should disburse all campaign funds. Obviously, if the former system is allowed there will be advantages for the more wealthy. However, if the latter is allowed there will be advantages for those who already have power, since governmental disbursement systems must allow funds to be spent in accordance with past patterns (and impoverished campaigns favor incumbents who initially are better known). If outcomes of elections were determined simply by the amounts spent, then depending on government financing would support a quite unchanging vote distribution. One example of this tendency on a restricted scale is the use of the public media for electioneering, usually by giving the parties, or candidates, or at least the major parties and candidates, specified and equal time on television or radio.

Perhaps the most common accusation against the fairness of elections is the extent to which the government takes advantage of the resources of office to defeat its opponents. Incumbents and government officials can often issue statements and make appearances related to the campaign that are not strictly described as campaigning. "News," whatever its origin, is likely to favor incumbents simply because as long as they are incumbents their actions are more newsworthy. Other practices that continue in the less-advanced democracies, but were common in all democracies until recently, are various forms of "vote buying," whether this be by actually distributing money, the promise of large projects, or the promise of future positions to well-placed influentials in critical districts. The use of government equipment such as jeeps and helicopters has often been alleged in campaigns in the third world, such as those of Congress (I) in India or of Barletta in Panama in 1984.

Few democracies are now seriously plagued by direct manipulation of votes, except occasionally on the local level. However, new democracies and semidemocracies are plagued both by such manipulations and equally by accusations that they have occurred. Elections recently in Bangladesh, Guyana, Panama, and Mexico have been marred by such accusations, and with justification. One test of a democracy is the extent to which it has effective machinery in place to prevent flagrant cheating. Such methods generally include genuinely neutral election commissions and poll watchers from all major parties to observe the voting and tabulation of results.

Given the advantages of the incumbents, and thereby generally the government and its party, any campaigning rules that restrict the campaign are likely to affect opposition candidates or parties most severely. The very short campaigns prescribed by many democratic systems might seem unfair to Americans—yet many countries have a fully competitive system with such limited campaigns (probably because their strong parties are, in effect, continuously campaigning). More serious are restrictions placed on campaigning or party organization, such as Indonesia's restriction of opposition party organization to the cities.

(4) Even though a country has a fair electoral process, fair campaigning, and meaningful elections, it will not be a functioning democracy unless those elected have the major power in the state. The most common denial of such power has come through the continued domination of the political system by a monarch or a self-selected leader, as in Morocco or Pakistan. Another common denial of real parliamentary power is occasioned by the continued direct or indirect power of the military—or military and king as in Thailand. In Latin America it is common even in otherwise functioning democracies for the military services not to be effectively under the control of the civilian and elected government. By tradition, ministers of defense in most Latin American countries are appointed from the military services rather than being civilians as is the practice in more mature democracies. In countries such as

Guatemala and El Salvador, the problem has gone beyond that of the military not being under civilian control. In such cases, at least until recently, an economic elite has been unwilling to let elected governments rule. Such an elite may directly and indirectly struggle against its opponents through violent internal warfare outside the control of the system—although elements of the system may be used to implement the desires of these shadowy rulers.

(5) In theory it should be quite possible for democracy to be perfected without political parties. Certainly the founding fathers of the American Republic did not think parties were necessary. The leaders of many countries that have moved from liberal democratic models to single parties argue for the necessity to reduce the adversarial spirit of parties; they claim to be able to preserve democracy by bringing the political struggle within the confines of one party. However, in practice policy is set in single parties by a small clique at the top; those in disfavor with the government are not allowed to compete for office by legal means— indeed, they are often ejected from the single party all together, as in Kenya.

The conclusion of the Survey is that while parties may not be necessary for democracy in very small countries such as Tuvalu, for most modern states they are necessary to allow alternatives to a ruling group or policy to gain sufficient votes to make a change. Therefore, the existence of multiple parties is important evidence for the existence of democracy, but is not absolutely conclusive. We are waiting for demonstrations of the ability of one-party or nonparty systems to achieve democracy. (Nepal's experiment with a nonparty system is worth watching in this connection.)

"Dominant Party" structures such as those of Malaysia or Singapore allow oppositions to mobilize to the extent that they can publicize alternative positions and effectively criticize government performance, but not to the extent that they represent a realistic threat to the group in power. Controls over campaigning, expression of opinion, patronage, and vote manipulation, as well as "punishment" of areas that vote against the government are methods used in such systems to make sure that the governing party remains in power.

(6-7) An empirical test of democracy is the extent to which there has been a recent shift in power occasioned through the operation of the electoral process. While it is true that the people of a country may remain relatively satisfied with the performance of one party for a long period of time, it is also true that a party in power may be able over time to entrench itself in multiple ways to such a degree that it is next to impossible to dislodge it by legit-imate means. For a time in the first years of the Survey there was the suspicion that the social democratic party of Sweden had accomplished this. However, in 1976 social democratic domination was ended after forty-four years. The extent of democratic rights can also be empirically suggested by the size of an opposition vote. While on rare occasions a governing party or individual may receive overwhelming support at the polls, any group or leader that regularly receives seventy percent or more of the vote indi-cates a weak opposition, and the probable existence of undemo-cratic barriers in the way of its further success. When a govern-ment or leader receives over ninety percent of the vote this indicates highly restrictive freedom for those opposing the system: over ninety-eight percent indicate that elections are little more than symbolic.

(8) A free, democratic society is one that governs itself through its own official processes. The two most blatant means of denying the control of a society by its elected leaders are military or foreign control. Since control of violent force is a basic requirement of all governments, when those who directly have this power begin to affect the political process, this aspect of government is turned on its head. The traditional democracies have long since been able to remove the military from power; at the opposite extreme are purely military regimes, as in much of Africa. A few countries remain under a degree of foreign control or influence. For example, in Europe, Finland, and to a lesser extent Austria, must remain neutral because of the pressure of the Soviet Union. Mongolia and Afghanistan are under direct Soviet occupation.

There are many vague accusations that one or another country is under military or foreign control. In this spirit the United States is said to be "ruled" by a military-industrial complex or Mexico is said to be under American control. But there is simply too much evidence that these "controllers" are frequently ignored

15

or slighted for such accusations to be taken too seriously. To a degree every country in the world is influenced by many others— large and small. (While smaller countries generally have less power of self-determination than larger countries, for most issues the power of the individual voter in the smaller states to control his life through the ballot is likely to be greater than that of people in larger countries.) The Survey's position in regard to both of these kinds of "outside" control is to record only the most flagrant cases, and to not enter the area of more complex interpretations.

(9) A democratic polity is one in which the people as a whole feel that the process is open to them, and that on important issues all individuals can be part of a meaningful majority. If this is not true, then the democratic polity must either divide, or devise methods for those who feel they are not part of the system to have reserved areas, geographical or otherwise, in which they can expect that their interests will be uppermost. In other words there must be either external or internal self-determination. Most democracies are relatively homogeneous. But even here, without some forms of elected local or regional government, people in some areas will feel crushed under a national majority that is unable to understand their particular problems or accept their values. Federal democracies, such as India or the United States, have devised elaborate methods for separate divisions of the country to be in important degrees self-governing. The problems of over-centralization in Europe have recently been addressed by countries such as France, Spain, and the United Kingdom, but in the case of Northern Ireland, current subdivisions or political boundaries continue to make a section of the people feel like foreigners in their own land.

(10) The question of self-determination is closely related to the extent to which political power has been decentralized. Since it would be possible for a country to have an elaborate degree of decentralization and still hand down all the important decisions from above, we must test empirically the extent to which persons or parties not under control of the center actually succeed politically. The fact, for example, that Japanese-Americans are able to play a leading role in Hawaiian politics, or that the Scots nationalists are able to achieve a significant vote in Scotland suggest an authentic devolution of political power.

(11)   Finally, the Survey wants evidence for the extent to which the political decision process depends not only on the support of majorities at the polls, but also on a less adversarial process involving search for consensus among all groups on issues of major public interest. A democracy should be more than simply a society of winners and losers. The most common way for this to be demonstrated is for the opposition to be taken into account in major decisions and appointments, even when it does not have to be consulted in terms of the formal requirements of the system. Recently, the extreme unwillingness of the government and opposition—or the president and legislature—to accomodate to the interests of the other in Ecuador has reduced its politics to a struggle of warring camps.[10] Obviously, this test of informal power is particularly important in judging the degree of success of one-party "democracies" that base their claim to legitimacy on their willingness to achieve national consensuses.

Discussion of Civil Liberties

(12) The potential checklist for civil liberties is longer and more diffuse than that for political rights. While many civil liberties are considered in judging the atmosphere of a country, primary attention is given to those liberties that are most directly related to the expression of political rights, with less attention given to those liberties that are likely to primarily affect individuals in their private capacity.

At the top of the list are questions of freedom for the communications media. We want to know whether the press and broadcasting facilities of the country are independent of government control, and serve the range of opinion that is present in the country. Clearly, if a population does not receive information about alternatives to present leaders and policies, then its ability to use any political process is impaired. In most traditional democracies there is no longer any question of censoring the press: no longer are people imprisoned for expressing their rational views on any matter—although secrecy and libel laws do have a slight affect in some democracies. As one moves from this open situation, from ratings of (1) to ratings of (7), a steady decline in freedom to publish is noticed: the tendency increases for people to be punished

17

for criticizing the government, or papers to be closed, or censorship to be imposed, or for the newspapers and journals to be directly owned and supervised by the government.

The methods used by governments to control the print media are highly varied. While pre-publication censorship is often what Westerners think of because of their wartime experience, direct government ownership and control of the media and post-publication censorship through warnings, confiscations, or suspensions are more common. Government licensing of publications and journalists and controls over the distribution of newsprint are other common means of keeping control over what is printed. Even in countries with a degree of democracy, such as Malaysia, press controls of these sorts may be quite extensive, often based on an ostensible legal requirement for "responsible journalism." Control of the press may be further extended by requiring papers to use a government news agency as their source of information, and by restricting the flow of foreign publications.[11]

Broadcasting—radio or television—are much more frequently owned by the government than the print media, and such ownership may or may not be reflected in government control over what is communicated. It is possible, as in the British case, for a government-owned broadcasting corporation to be so effectively protected from government control that its programs demonstrate genuine impartiality. However, in many well-known democracies, such as France or Greece, changes in the political composition of government affects the nature of what is broadcast to the advantage of incumbents. The government-owned broadcasting services of India make little effort to go beyond presenting the views of their government.

In most countries misuse of the news media to serve government interests is even more flagrant. At this level, we need to distinguish between those societies that require their media, particularly their broadcasting services, to avoid criticism of the political system or its leaders, and those that use them to "mobilize" their peoples in direct support for government policies. In the first case the societies allow or expect their media, particularly their broadcasting services, to present a more or less favorable picture; in the second, the media are used to motivate their peoples to actively support government policies and to condemn or destroy those who oppose the governing system. In

18

the first, the government's control is largely passive; in the second it is directly determinative of content.[12]

The comparison of active and passive control by government brings us to the most difficult issue in the question of media freedom—self-censorship. It is fairly easy to know if a government censors or suspends publications for content, or punishes journalists and reporters by discharge, imprisonment, or worse; judging the day-to-day influence of subtle pressures on the papers or broadcasting services of a country is much more difficult. Perhaps the most prevalent form of government control of the communications media is achieved through patterns of mutual assistance of government and media that ensure that, at worst, reports are presented in a bland, non-controversial manner—a common practice in Mexico and Pakistan.

Some critics believe that most communications media in the West, and especially in the United States, practice this kind of censorship, either because of government support, or because this is in the interest of the private owners of the media. In the United States, for example, it is noteworthy that National Public Radio, financed largely by the state, is generally much more critical of the government in its commentaries than are the commercial services. The critics would explain this difference by the greater ability of commercial stations to "police" their broadcasts and broadcasters. The primary explanation, however, lies in the gap between the subculture of broadcasters and audience for public radio and the subculture of broadcasters and especially audience for commercial stations.[13]

(13) Open public discussion is at least as important a civil liberty as free communications media. The ultimate test of a democracy is the degree to which an atmosphere for discussion in public and private exists free of fear of reprisal by either the government or opposition groups. Even in the relatively free communist society of Yugoslavia people are still being imprisoned for the expression of critical opinions in private.[14] Certainly Iranians have had to be careful in recent years not to express too openly opinions that go against the prevailing ideology.

(14-15) Open discussion expressed through political organization, public demonstration, and assemblies is often threatening to

19

political incumbents. There are occasions in which such assemblies may be dangerous to public order and should be closely controlled or forbidden. But in many societies this hypothetical danger is used as a pretense to deny opposition groups the ability to mobilize in support of alternative policies or leaders. In Malaysia, for example, the government's denial of public assembly to the opposition has been one of the main ways to restrict the ability of the opposition to effectively challenge the rule of the government.[15] Obviously, denial of the right to organize freely for political action is the most generalized form of the attempt to prevent the effective mobilization of opposition to government policies. Control over political organization is a distinguishing characteristic of one-party states, but many multiparty states place limits on the kinds or numbers of political parties that may be organized. Controls over extremist parties that deny the legitimacy of democratic institutions, such as many fascist or communist parties, are understandable—still, they represent limits on freedom. Political and civil freedoms overlap closely on the right to political organization. The distinction is between denying the right to participate in elections and denying the right to organize to present alternative policies or arguments for and against change in other ways.

(16) A democratic system is not secured unless there is a legal system that can be relied on for a fair degree of impartiality. The electoral process, for example, needs to be supervised by electoral commissions or other administrative systems that ultimately can be checked or overruled by the judicial system. People accused of actions against the state need to have some hope that their cases will be tried before the courts of the society and that the process will be fair. One of the tests that the author often applies to a country is whether it is possible to win against the government in a political case, and under what conditions. A reliable judicial system requires a guarantee of the permanence of judicial tenure, particularly at the highest levels, as well as traditions of executive noninterference developed over a period of years. Of course, in no society are all trials fair or all judges impartial; but in this respect there are vast differences between democracies and nondemocracies.

A significant but less striking difference exists between the ways in which security services treat the public in democracies and nondemocracies. Since the people of a democracy are the sponsors of the system,[16] in theory the security services are their hired employees, and these employees should treat them with the utmost respect. However, because of the nature of the task of police and army, and their monopoly over force, in larger societies, at least, this relationship is often forgotten. Even in full-fledged democracies many security services have a reputation, for example in France or certain parts of the United States, of treating people with carelessness and even brutality. But it is clearly true that to the degree that security forces are the employees, even in theory, of a smaller group than the people as a whole, then their behavior will be even less "democratic."

(17) Certainly democracy requires that people be free from fear of the government, especially in regard to their politically related activities. To this degree, the emphasis of organizations such as Amnesty International on the extent of imprisonment, execution, or torture for reasons of conscience is closely related to any measurement of democracy. Oppressive countries imprison their opponents, or worse, both to silence the particular individuals, and to warn others of the dangers of opposing the system. Recently, exile and disappearances have been used as a further deterrent. "Disappearance" is generally a form of extra-judicial execution, often carried out in support of the ruling system. Such terrorism may or may not be directly under the orders of government leaders. These practices underscore the fact that a great deal of such internal state terrorism does not involve the normal legal process; frequently opponents are incarcerated through "detentions" that may last for years. In the Soviet Union and some other communist countries, the practice of using psychiatric institutions to incarcerate opponents has been developed on the theory that opposition to a people's state is itself a form of mental illness.

It is important in this regard to distinguish between the broader category of "political imprisonment" and the narrower "imprisonment for reasons of conscience." The former includes all cases that informed opinion would assume are related to political issues, or issues that can be defined politically in some states (such as religious belief in communist or some Islamic societies).

21

It includes those who have written articles that the regime finds offensive as well as those who have thrown bombs or plotted executions, or even caused riots, to dramatize their cause. Since clearly the latter actions cannot be accepted by any government, all states, at whatever level of freedom, may have some "political prisoners." But if we take the category of political prisoners and separate out those who appear to have not committed or planned, or been involved in supporting acts of violence, then we have the smaller category of "prisoners of conscience." Their existence must be counted against the democratic rating of any country. This is not to say that the existence of prisoners of conscience who have been involved in violence cannot also be taken in many countries as an indication that a system may not be sufficiently responsive to demands expressed nonviolently—too often there may be no effective means to express opposition without violence. The distinction between prisoners by reason of conscience and political prisoners is in practice often blurred by the outsider's difficulty in deciding whether particular incarcerated individuals have or have not committed or planned acts of violence. Nevertheless, by looking at the pattern of a regime's behavior over a period of years it is possible to estimate the degree to which a regime does or does not have prisoners of conscience.

Anti-dissident terror undertaken by groups that support the general system of a country but are not, or may not be, under government control is often difficult to evaluate in determining a country's rating. In the case where the terrorism is carried out by the security services, or their hired hands, we can either assume that these services are no longer controlled by the civilian administration, and to this extent the system cannot be called free, or that the civilian administration actually approves of the actions. In cases where the terror stems from parties or cliques outside of this structure, which to some degree has been the case in El Salvador, then the judgment has to be based on a finer balance of considerations.

(18-20) Democracies require freedom of organization that goes far beyond the right to organize political parties. The right of individuals to organize trade unions, or to organize cooperatives, or business enterprises are certainly basic rights that may be limited only with great care in a free society. The right of union or peasant organization has been particularly significant because it allows large groups of ordinary people in many societies to balance, through numbers, the ability of the wealthy to concentrate power. However, in some societies, such as those of western Africa, the ability of medical, bar, and academic associations to mobilize or maintain alternatives to ruling groups has been of equal importance. Democracies require freedom of organization because there must be organized, countervailing power centers in a society—which is one definition of pluralism—if a society is going to maintain free institutions against the natural tendency of governments to aggregate power.

(21) It is for this reason that religious freedom, in belief and in organization, has been particularly important for the defense of freedom in a more general sense. Religious institutions have been able to maintain opposition strength in societies as different as those of Poland and Chile. A strong religious institution can build a wall around the individual dissident that a government will be loathe to breach for the sake of imposing its order. In countries such as Argentina or Philippines the organized church and organized unions have gone a long way toward insuring a society able to resist the encroachments of government. The question is not whether a particular established organization, such as the church, is itself favorable toward democracy. It is rather whether there are organizational structures willing and able to exist independently of government direction. Without such countervailing organizational power, it is unlikely that significant civil liberties can be maintained against government pressure.

(22) Civil liberties also include personal and individual social rights, particularly those that are likely to most directly affect the ability of people to withstand the pressures of the state. Especially important are those to property, travel (including emigration), and to an independent family life. The right to property does not necessarily mean the right to productive property, but it does mean the right to property that can provide a cushion against government pressures such as dismissal from a position, that will make possible private publications, or other activity that cannot be financed unless people have more than subsistence incomes. The ability of an individual to travel, particularly to

leave the country, is of great importance to dissidents or potential dissidents. It allows them additional sources of support and an additional refuge should the effort to improve conditions in their own country fail. An independent family offers another type of emotional haven that makes possible independent thinking and action. Opposition to Mao during the 1960s in China became almost impossible when individuals could no longer trust even spouses and children not to inform on their activities. The complete isolation of the individual, even in the midst of a crowded life, is the ultimate goal of oppressors.

(23-24) Civil liberty requires, then, that most people are relatively independent in both their lives and thoughts. It implies socioeconomic rights that include freedom from dependency on landlords, on bosses, on union leaders, or on bureaucrats. The kind of dependencies that the socioeconomic system imposes on individuals will vary from society to society, but widespread dependencies of these kinds are incompatible with democratic freedoms. This implies that there should be freedom from gross socioeconomic inequality. It should be noted that we are not saying that democracy requires that incomes or living standards be equalized. But we are saying that if inequalities are too great, if a small group of very wealthy lives in the midst of a large number of very poor individuals, it is likely that relations of dependency will develop that will make impossible the unfettered expression of opinion or a free and uncoerced vote.

(25) Finally, there would seem to be an indirect requirement that the civil liberties of a democracy include freedom from the extremes of government indifference and corruption. These conditions make it impossible for the people affected to feel that they are in any important sense the sponsors of their political system. Such indifference and corruption also implies that the mechanisms of democracy in the state are simply not working. If there is a continued record of disregard for the interests of the people, and yet the representatives of the people are not replaced by the electoral or judicial process, the system is not working. Such indirect tests are necessary for a rating system that is based in large part on regular monitoring of press reports from around the world.

Status of Freedom

After countries are rated on seven-point scales for levels of political rights and civil liberties, these ratings are summarized in terms of overall assessments as **free, partly free,** and **not free.** This categorization is interpreted to mean that the list of operating democracies in the world is made up of those countries given the summary status of "free." Terms such as "free" and "not free" are only to be understood as relative expressions of the degree of political and civil liberties in a country. Use of the Status of Freedom rating necessarily places in the same category countries that are actually quite far apart in terms of their democratic practices—such as Poland or South Africa at the less-free edge of partly free and Thailand or or Mexico at the more free.

The Survey is based on library research, updated by a more or less continuous flow of publications across the author's desk. Once the basic nature of the political system and its respect for civil liberties is established, following the flow of information either confirms or disconfirms this general picture, as well as recording any changes that may occur. It also has had the effect since the beginning of the Survey in 1972 of refining the author's sensitivity to those conditions and indicators that go with different levels of democratic rights.

The use of general descriptions and a flow of information is particularly useful because the Survey is based on evidence of democratic or nondemocratic behavior by the governments of countries in regard to their own peoples. Because interest in human rights and democracy is often centered in the legal community, many students or analysts in this area concentrate their attention on changes in laws or legal structures. Even Amnesty International takes the position that the numbers imprisoned or executed in a country is a less important indicator of change than change in the law in regard to these practices.[17]

The criticism is often made that the Survey ignores many "human rights," such as the right to adequate nutrition. This criticism can be addressed on several levels. Most appropriate is the remark that the Survey is of political and civil freedoms and not of human rights. (In philosophical terms neither freedom nor democracy are properly understood as including all "goods" and only goods.") The Survey is seriously concerned with some of the social and economic group of "rights." Clearly, some social and economic rights, such as the right to the freedom of workers or of businessmen to organize, are considered basic rights by the Survey. It is our feeling that some of the other proposed rights, including some of those implied by the Universal Declaration of Human Rights, involve social priorities that societies have a right to decide for themselves through the political process. In order to give people maximum freedom to develop their societies in terms of their needs and desires as they understand them, it is important that the list of rights be reduced to the minimum that allows them to make this determination.

The objection that the Survey should take more seriously "economic rights" in the narrower sense of economic freedom has been addressed in the 1982 and 1983-84 Freedom in the World volumes. As was mentioned in the beginning of this Chapter, the conclusion was that the basic economic right of all democracies was for the people to have an authentic and repeated opportunity to choose the economic system they desired. Their choice might range from libertarian to any one of a number of forms of socialist. To this we added that to be effective this economic freedom of choice must be based on some relative equalities in power; the absence of dependency that is included in the checklist above as a requisite civil liberty in a democracy must be generally present for economic freedom to be meaningful.

We have, of course, always been concerned with the relationships that might exist between needs variables, such as medical care, nutrition, or education, and the political and civil liberties with which we are concerned. It is important to see if there are any necessary relationships between freedom and standards in these areas, or whether the existence of civil and political liberties enhances the meeting of such needs by a society. Table 9 below offers the reader a chance to look empirically at some of the relations that exist. The papers in Part IV address the question in more causal or theoretical terms.

If more resources were available for assistance and on-site investigations, the Surveys could be greatly improved. They began, and have continued to be, a generalized attempt to improve the informed public's picture of the world. In spite of their limitations, some political scientists, economists, and sociologists have used the yearly Surveys as a source of data for correlation analyses of related variables. They are useful because they represent the only annual attempt to compare the level of democratic rights in all the countries in the world. (For further discussion of the Survey see Freedom in the World: 1986-87, pages 79-96.)

NOTES

1. See R. D. Gastil, **Freedom in the World: 1982** (Westport: Greenwood Press, 1982), especially the article by Lindsay Wright, and **Freedom in the World: 1983-84.** For further discussions of the definitions of freedom and democracy from the viewpoint of the Survey see the relevant discussions in **Freedom in the World** 1978, 1984-85, and 1986-87.

2. James Bryce, Viscount, **Modern Democracies** 2 vols. (Macmillan, 1924).

3. Arthur Banks and Robert Textor, **A Cross-Polity Survey** (Cambridge: MIT Press, 1963).

4. Robert Dahl, **Polyarchy: Participation and Opposition** (New Haven: Yale University Press, 1971), pages 231-49.

5. Dankwart A. Rustow, **A World of Nations** (Washington: Brookings Institution, 1967).

6. For example, Charles Humana, **World Human Rights Guide** (New York: Facts on File, 1986).

7. For example, United States Department of State, **Country Reports on Human Rights Practices for 1986,** Department of State (Washington, 1987).

8. **Amnesty International Report, 1983** (London: Amnesty International, 1983).

9. On Senegal see **Africa Research Bulletin,** December 1983, page 7050; on Egypt, **Middle East,** July 1984, page 22.

10. See **Latin American Weekly,** November 20, 1986, June 18, 1987, November 29, 1987.

11. **Keesing's Contemporary Archives,** 1984, pages 32782-85; **Far Eastern Economic Review,** September 20, 1984, pages 40ff. Compare also the discussion by Leonard Sussman, in Part III, below.

12. William Rugh, **The Arab Press: News Media and Political Process in the Arab World** (Syracuse: Syracuse University Press, 1979).

13. For an attempt to suggest the relatively greater importance of sub-cultural as opposed to class or other interests in determining the opinions of people in our society see R. D. Gastil, "'Selling Out' and the Sociology of Knowledge," **Policy Sciences,** 1971, 2, pages 271-277.

14. **Amnesty Action,** January 1985.

15. See, for example, **Far Eastern Economic Review,** August 23, 1984.

16. Alfred Kuhn, **The Logic of Social Systems** (San Francisco: Jossey-Bass, 1975), pages 330-61.

17. **Amnesty Action** January 1, 1985, page 7. Here it is suggested that improvement in human rights is seen less in changes in the numbers imprisoned or killed in a country than in changes in its laws, such as laws against torture or imprisonment without trial.

SURVEY RATINGS AND TABLES FOR 1987

A spirit of change and openness blew through the communist world in 1987. A trend that had begun much earlier in Eastern Europe and China, the moderation of avowedly Marxist-Leninist regimes extended at last to the Soviet Union itself. It was only the beginning of a process that at best will have many reversals and hesitancies. Some apparent change may be only tactical maneuvering by communist leaders attempting to deceive Western leaders or publics—or their own peoples. But even if some Marxist leaders began with tactics, the liberalizations that have already occurred are likely to have important and beneficial consequences, both for the communist states and those many third world states that have taken aspects of communist doctrine as their own. Freedom is infectious, particularly when it has become the standard of advanced societies.

The Tabulated Ratings

The accompanying Table 1 (Independent States) and Table 2 (Related Territories) rate each state or territory on seven-point scales for political and civil freedoms, and then provide an overall judgment of each as "free," "partly free," or "not free." In each scale, a rating of (1) is freest and (7) least free. Instead of using absolute standards, standards are comparative. The goal is to have ratings such that, for example, most observers would be likely to judge states rated (1) as freer than those rated (2). No state, of course, is absolutely free or unfree, but the degree of freedom does make a great deal of difference to the quality of life.[1]

In political rights, states rated (1) have a fully competitive electoral process, and those elected clearly rule. Most West European democracies belong here. Relatively free states may receive a (2) because, although the electoral process works and the elected rule, there are factors that cause us to lower our rating of

TABLE 1

FREEDOM RATINGS: INDEPENDENT STATES

	Political Rights[1]	Civil Liberties[1]	Status of Freedom[2]
Afghanistan	7	7	NF
Albania	7	7	NF
Algeria	6	6	NF
Angola	7	7	NF
Antigua & Barbuda	2	3	F
Argentina	2	1	F
Australia	1	1	F
Austria	1	1	F
Bahamas	2	3 ·	F
Bahrain	5	5	PF
Bangladesh	4	5	PF
Barbados	1	1	F
Belgium	1	1	F
Belize	1	1	F
Benin	7	7	NF
Bhutan	5	5	PF
Bolivia	2	3	F
Botswana	2	3	F
Brazil	2	2	F
Brunei	6	5	PF
Bulgaria	7	7	NF
Burkina Faso[4]	7	6	NF
Burma	7	7	NF
Burundi	7	6	NF
Cambodia	7	7	NF
Cameroon	6	6	NF
Canada	1	1	F
Cape Verde	5 ·+	6	PF ·+
Central African Rep.	6 +	6	NF
Chad	6 +	7	NF
Chile	6	5	PF
China(Mainland)	6	6	NF
China(Taiwan)	5	4 +	PF
Colombia	2	3	F
Comoros	6	6	NF

	Political Rights[1]	Civil Liberties[1]	Status of Freedom[2]
Congo	7	6	NF
Costa Rica	1	1	F
Cote d'Ivoire[3]	6	5	PF
Cuba	6	6	NF
Cyprus(G)	1	2	F
Cyprus(T)	2	3	F
Czechoslovakia	7	6	NF
Denmark	1	1	F
Djibouti	6	6	NF
Dominica	2	2	F
Dominican Republic	1	3	F
Ecuador	2	3	F
Egypt	5	4	PF
El Salvador	3	4	PF
Equatorial Guinea	7	7	NF
Ethiopia	6 +	7	NF
European Community	2	1	F
Fiji	6 -	5 -	PF -
Finland	1 · +	2	F
France	1	2	F
Gabon	6	6	NF
Gambia	3	3 +	PF
Germany(E)	7	6	NF
Germany(W)	1	2	F
Ghana	7	6	NF
Greece	2	2	F
Grenada	2	1 · +	F
Guatemala	3	3	PF
Guinea	7	6 ·	NF
Guinea-Bissau	6	7	NF
Guyana	5	5	PF
Haiti	6 -	5 -	PF
Honduras	2	3	F
Hungary	5	4 · +	PF
Iceland	1	1	F
India	2	3	F
Indonesia	5	6	PF

	Political Rights[1]	Civil Liberties[1]	Status of Freedom[2]
Iran	5	6	PF
Iraq	7	7	NF
Ireland	1	1	F
Israel	2	2	F
Italy	1	1	F
Jamaica	2	2 · +	F
Japan	1	1	F
Jordan	5	5	PF
Kenya	6	6 −	NF −
Kiribati	1	2	F
Korea(N)	7	7	NF
Korea(S)	4	4 +	PF
Kuwait	6	5	PF
Laos	7	7	NF
Lebanon	6 · −	5 · −	PF
Lesotho	5	6 · −	PF
Liberia	5	5	PF
Libya	6	6	NF
Luxembourg	1	1	F
Madagascar	5	5	PF
Malawi	6	7	NF
Malaysia	3	5	PF
Maldives	5	6	PF
Mali	7	6	NF
Malta	1 +	2 · +	F · +
Mauritania	6 +	6	NF
Mauritius	2	2	F
Mexico	4	4	PF
Mongolia	7	7	NF
Morocco	4	5	PF
Mozambique	6	7	NF
Nauru	2	2	F
Nepal	3	4	PF
Netherlands	1	1	F

	Political Rights[1]	Civil Liberties[1]	Status of Freedom[2]
New Zealand	1	1	F
Nicaragua	5	5 +	PF
Niger	7	6	NF
Nigeria	6 · +	5	PF · +
Norway	1	1	F
Oman	6	6	NF
Pakistan	4	5	PF
Panama	5 ·	5 −	PF
Papua New Guinea	2	2	F
Paraguay	5	6	PF
Peru	2	3	F
Philippines	2 +	2	F +
Poland	5 +	5	PF
Portugal	1	2	F
Qatar	5	5	PF
Romania	7	7	NF
Rwanda	6	6	NF
St. Kitts-Nevis	1	2 · −	F
St. Lucia	1	2	F
St. Vincent	1 ·	2	F
Sao Tome & Principe	7	7	NF
Saudi Arabia	6	7	NF
Senegal	3	4	PF
Seychelles	6	6	NF
Sierra Leone	5	5	PF
Singapore	4	5	PF
Solomon Islands	2	2	F
Somalia	7	7	NF
South Africa	5	6	PF
Spain	1	2	F
Sri Lanka	3	4	PF
Sudan	4	5	PF
Suriname	4 +	4 +	PF +
Swaziland	5	6	PF
Sweden	1	1	F

33

	Political Rights[1]	Civil Liberties[1]	Status of Freedom[2]
Switzerland	1	1	F
Syria	6	7	NF
Tanzania	6	6	NF
Thailand	3	3	PF
Togo	6	6	NF
Tonga	5	3	PF
Transkei	5	6	PF
Trinidad & Tobago	1	1 ∙ +	F
Tunisia	6	5	PF
Turkey	2 +	4	PF
Tuvalu	1	1	F
Uganda	5	4	PF
USSR	7	6 +	NF
United Arab Emirates	5	5	PF
United Kingdom	1	1	F
United States	1	1	F
Uruguay	2	2	F
Vanuatu	2	4	PF
Venezuela	1	2	F
Vietnam	6 +	7	NF
Western Samoa	4	3	PF
Yemen(N)	5	5	PF
Yemen(S)	6	7	NF
Yugoslavia	6	5	PF
Zaire	6 +	7	NF
Zambia	5	5	PF
Zimbabwe	5 −	6	PF

Notes to the Table

1. The scales use the numbers 1-7, with 1 comparatively offering the highest level of political or civil rights and 7 the lowest. A plus or minus following a rating indicates an improvement or decline since the last yearbook. A rating marked with a raised period (∙) has been reevaluated by the author in this time; there may have been little change in the country.

2. F designates "free," PF "partly free," NF "not free."

3. Formerly designated Ivory Coast

4. Formerly Upper Volta.

the effective equality of the process. These factors may include extreme economic inequality, illiteracy, or intimidating violence. They also include the weakening of effective competition that is implied by the absence of periodic shifts in rule from one group or party to another.

Below this level, political ratings of (3) through (5) represent successively less effective implementation of democratic processes. Mexico, for example, has periodic elections and limited opposition, but for many years its governments have been selected outside the public view by the leaders of factions within the one dominant Mexican party. Governments of states rated (5) sometimes have no effective voting processes at all, but strive for consensus among a variety of groups in society in a way weakly analogous to those of the democracies. States at (6) do not allow competitive electoral processes that would give the people a chance to voice their desire for a new ruling party or for a change in policy. The rulers of states at this level assume that one person or a small group has the right to decide what is best for the nation, and that no one should be allowed to challenge that right. Such rulers do respond, however, to popular desire in some areas, or respect (and therefore are constrained by) belief systems (for example, Islam) that are the property of the society as a whole. At (7) the political despots at the top appear by their actions to feel little constraint from either public opinion or popular tradition.

Turning to the scale for civil liberties, in countries rated (1) publications are not closed because of the expression of rational political opinion, especially when the intent of the expression is to affect the legitimate political process. No major media are simply conduits for government propaganda. The courts protect the individual; persons are not imprisoned for their opinions; private rights and desires in education, occupation, religion, and residence are generally respected; and law-abiding persons do not fear for their lives because of their rational political activities. States at this level include most traditional democracies. There are, of course, flaws in the liberties of all of these states, and these flaws are significant when measured against the standards these states set themselves.

Movement down from (2) to (7) represents a steady loss of the civil freedoms we have detailed. Compared to (1), the police and courts of states at (2) have more authoritarian traditions. In some

TABLE 2

FREEDOM RATINGS: RELATED TERRITORIES

	Political Rights[1]	Civil Liberties[1]	Status of Freedom[2]
Australia			
Christmas Island	4	2	PF
Cocos Island	4	2	PF
Norfolk Island	4	2	PF
Chile			
Easter Island	5	5	PF
Denmark			
Faroe Islands	1	1	F
Greenland	1	1	F
France			
French Guiana	3	2	PF
French Polynesia	3	2	PF
Guadeloupe	3	2	PF
Mahore (Mayotte)	2	2	F
Martinique	3	2	PF
Monaco[4]	4	2	PF
New Caledonia	2 +	2	F
Reunion	3	2	PF
St. Pierre & Miq.	2	2	F
Wallis and Futuna	4	3	PF
Israel			
Occupied Territs.	5	5	PF
Italy			
San Marino[3]	1	1	F
Vatican City[3]	6	4	PF
Netherlands			
Aruba	1	1	F
Neth. Antilles	1	1	F
New Zealand			
Cook Islands	2	2	F
Niue	2	2	F
Tokelau Islands	4	2	PF
Portugal			
Azores	2	2	F
Macao	3	4	PF
Madeira	2	2	F

	Political Rights[1]	Civil Liberties[1]	Status of Freedom[2]
South Africa			
Bophuthatswana[4]	6	5	PF
Ciskei[4]	6	6	NF
SW Africa (Namibia)	6	5	PF
Venda[4]	6	6	NF
Spain			
Canary Islands	1	2	F
Ceuta	2	3	F
Melilla	2	3	F
Switzerland			
Liechtenstein	3	1	F
United Kingdom			
Anguilla	2	2	F
Bermuda	2	1	F
B. Virgin Islands	2	1	F
Cayman Islands	2	2	F
Channel Islands	2	2 · −	F
Falkland Islands	2	2	F
Gibraltar	1	2	F
Hong Kong	4	2	PF
Isle of Man	1	1	F
Montserrat	2	2	F
St. Helena	2	2	F
Turks and Caicos	2	2	F
United States			
American Samoa	2	2	F
Belau[5]	2	2	F
Guam	2 · +	2	F · +
Marshall Islands[5]	2	2	F
Micronesia (F.S.M.)[5]	2	2	F
Northern Marianas	1	2	F
Puerto Rico	2	1	F
Virgin Islands	2	2 ·	F
France-Spain (condominium)			
Andorra[3]	3	3	PF

Notes to the Table

1-2. See Notes, Table 1.

3. Nominally independent, these states are legally dependent on another country (or countries in Andorra's case) in such areas as foreign affairs, defense, customs, or services.

4. The geography and history of these "homelands" cause us to consider them dependencies.

5. Now in transition; high degree of self-determination.

cases they may simply have a less institutionalized or secure set of liberties, such as in Portugal or Greece. Those rated (3) or below may have political prisoners and generally varying forms of censorship. Too often their security services practice torture. States rated (6) almost always have political prisoners; usually the legitimate media are completely under government supervision; there is no right of assembly; and, often, travel, residence, and occupation are narrowly restricted. However, at (6) there still may be relative freedom in private conversation, especially in the home; illegal demonstrations do take place; and underground literature is published. At (7) there is pervading fear, little independent expression takes place even in private, almost no public expressions of opposition emerge in the police-state environment, and imprisonment or execution is often swift and sure.

Political terror is an attempt by a government or private group to get its way through the use of murder, torture, exile, prevention of departure, police controls, or threats against the family. These weapons are usually directed against the expression of civil liberties. To this extent they surely are a part of the civil liberty "score." Unfortunately, because of their dramatic and newsworthy nature, such denials of civil liberties often become identified in the minds of informed persons with the whole of civil liberties.

Political terror is a tool of revolutionary repression of the right or left. When that repression is no longer necessary to achieve the suppression of civil liberties, political terror is replaced by implacable and well-organized but often less general and newsworthy controls. Of course, there is a certain unfathomable terror in the sealed totalitarian state, yet life can be lived with a normality in these states that is impossible in the more dramatically terrorized. It would be a mistake to dismiss this apparent anomaly as an expression of a Survey bias. For there is, with all the blood, a much wider range of organized and personal expression of political opinion and judgment in states such as India, or even Guatemala, than in more peaceful states such as Czechoslovakia.

In making the distinction between political terror and civil liberties as a whole we do not imply that the United States should not be urgently concerned with all violations of human rights and perhaps most urgently with those of political terror. Again it must be emphasized that the Survey is not a rating of the relative desirability of societies—but of certain explicit freedoms.

A cumulative judgment of "free," "partly free," or "not free" is made on the basis of the foregoing seven-point ratings, and an understanding of how they were derived. Generally, states rated (1) and (2) will be "free"; those at (3), (4), and (5), "partly free"; and those at (6) and (7), "not free." A rating of (2),(3) places an independent country in the "free" category; a rating of (6),(5) places it in the "partly free."

It has long been felt that the Survey has paid too little attention to the material correlates, conditions, or context of freedom or non-freedom. While we have argued elsewhere that there is no one-to-one relation between wealth and freedom, and that history has diffused freedom along with economic wealth more than one has produced the other, the relationship remains important. For more on this relationship, see Table 9 in this chapter and Part IV.

The reporting period covered by this Survey (November 1986 to November 1987) does not correspond with the calendar of short-term events in the countries rated. For this reason the yearly Survey may mask or play down events that occur at the end of the year.

The Survey is aware that many of its judgments of what is or is not an independent country are questioned. The principle that we have used is a pragmatic one that combines several criteria. A country exists independently to the extent that persons from a central core of people identified with that country more than any other country rule in the name of their country through control of its territory, or at least what they define as the central area of that territory. It helps if a country, in the modern world, has some historical and geographical continuity. But historical existence in the past, such as that of Lithuania or Georgia in the USSR, or Tibet in China, is not enough to make the Survey's list. Whether a country's leaders are actually in control, or "rule" is also defined loosely. Many doubt, for example, the existence of a separate country of Transkei—and for good reason. However, the Survey believes that the independence or separateness of Transkei is comparable to that of Swaziland, Lesotho, Mongolia, Laos, or, in a different sense, Afghanistan or Lebanon. The separateness of the other homeland states is less clear, if only marginally.

RATING COUNTRIES BY POLITICAL RIGHTS

Most
Free

1

Australia	Dominican Rep.	Luxembourg	Spain
Austria	Finland	Malta	Sweden
Barbados	France	Netherlands	Switzerland
Belgium	Germany (W)	New Zealand	Trinidad &
Belize	Iceland	Norway	Tobago
Canada	Ireland	Portugal	Tuvalu
Costa Rica	Italy	St. Kitts-Nevis	United Kingdom
Cyprus (G)	Japan	St. Lucia	United States
Denmark	Kiribati	St. Vincent	Venezuela

2

Antigua & Barb.	Cyprus (T)	Israel	Philippines
Argentina	Dominica	Jamaica	Solomons
Bahamas	Ecuador	Mauritius	Turkey
Bolivia	Greece	Nauru	Uruguay
Botswana	Grenada	Papua	Vanuatu
Brazil	Honduras	New Guinea	
Colombia	India	Peru	

3

El Salvador	Guatemala	Nepal	Sri Lanka
Gambia	Malaysia	Senegal	Thailand

4

Bangladesh	Morocco	Sudan	Western Samoa
Korea (S)	Pakistan	Suriname	
Mexico	Singapore		

5

Bahrain	Iran	Paraguay	Transkei
Bhutan	Jordan	Poland	Uganda
Cape Verde	Lesotho	Qatar	United Arab
China (Taiwan)	Liberia	Sierra Leone	Emirates
Egypt	Madagascar	South Africa	Yemen (N)
Guyana	Maldives	Swaziland	Zambia
Hungary	Nicaragua	Tonga	Zimbabwe
Indonesia	Panama		

6

Algeria	Cote d'Ivoire	Lebanon	Syria
Brunei	Cuba	Libya	Tanzania
Cameroon	Djibouti	Malawi	Togo
Central	Ethiopia	Mauritania	Tunisia
African Rep.	Fiji	Mozambique	Vietnam
Chad	Gabon	Nigeria	Yemen (S)
Chile	Guinea-Bissau	Oman	Yugoslavia
China	Haiti	Rwanda	Zaire
(Mainland)	Kenya	Saudi Arabia	
Comoros	Kuwait	Seychelles	

7

Least
Free

Afghanistan	Burundi	Ghana	Niger
Albania	Cambodia	Guinea	Romania
Angola	Congo	Iraq	Sao Tome &
Benin	Czechoslovakia	Korea (N)	Principe
Bulgaria	Equatorial	Laos	Somalia
Burkina Faso	Guinea	Mali	USSR
Burma	Germany (E)	Mongolia	

RATING COUNTRIES BY CIVIL LIBERTIES

Most **Free** **1**	Argentina Australia Austria Barbados Belgium Belize	Canada Costa Rica Denmark Grenada Iceland Ireland	Italy Japan Luxembourg Netherlands New Zealand Norway	Sweden Switzerland Trinidad & Tob. Tuvalu United Kingdom United States
2	Brazil Cyprus (G) Dominica Finland France Germany (W) Greece	Israel Jamaica Kiribati Malta Mauritius Nauru	Papua New Guinea Philippines Portugal St. Kitts-Nevis St. Lucia	St. Vincent Solomons Spain Uruguay Venezuela
3	Antigua & Barb. Bahamas Bolivia Botswana	Colombia Cyprus (T) Dominican Rep. Ecuador	Gambia Guatemala Honduras India	Peru Thailand Tonga Western Samoa
4	China (T) Egypt El Salvador Hungary	Korea (S) Mexico Nepal Senegal	Sri Lanka Suriname Turkey Uganda	Vanuatu
5	Bahrain Bangladesh Bhutan Brunei Chile Cote d'Ivoire Fiji Guyana	Haiti Jordan Kuwait Lebanon Liberia Madagascar Malaysia Morocco	Nicaragua Nigeria Pakistan Panama Poland Qatar Sierra Leone Singapore	Sudan Tunisia United Arab Emirates Yemen (N) Yugoslavia Zambia
6	Algeria Burkina Faso Burundi Cameroon Cape Verde Cen. Afr. Rep. China (M) Comoros Congo	Cuba Czechoslovakia Djibouti Gabon Germany (E) Ghana Guinea Indonesia Iran	Kenya Lesotho Libya Maldives Mali Mauritania Niger Oman Paraguay	Rwanda Seychelles South Africa Swaziland Tanzania Togo Transkei USSR Zimbabwe

7
Least
Free
	Afghanistan
	Albania
	Angola
	Benin
	Bulgaria
	Burma
	Cambodia
		Chad
		Equatorial
		  Guinea
		Ethiopia
		Guinea-Bissau
		Iraq
		Korea (N)
			Laos
			Malawi
			Mongolia
			Mozambique
			Romania
			Sao Tome &
			  Principe
				Saudi Arabia
				Somalia
				Syria
				Vietnam
				Yemen (S)
				Zaire

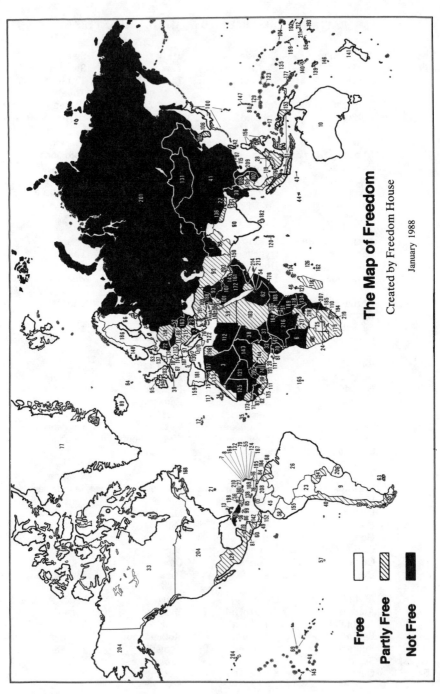

The Map of Freedom

Created by Freedom House

January 1988

Free

Partly Free

Not Free

Free States

8	Antigua & Barbuda
9	Argentina
10	Australia
11	Austria
13	Bahamas
16	Barbados
18	Belgium
19	Belize
23	Bolivia
25	Botswana
26	Brazil
33	Canada
45	Colombia
49	Costa Rica
51a	Cyprus (G)
51b	Cyprus (T)
53	Denmark
55	Dominica
56	Dominican Republic
58	Ecuador
66	Finland
67	France
73	Germany (W)
76	Greece
78	Grenada
86	Honduras
89	Iceland
90	India
94	Ireland
96	Israel
97	Italy
99	Jamaica
100	Japan
104	Kiribati
114	Luxembourg
122	Malta
126	Mauritius
135	Nauru
137	Netherlands
141	New Zealand
148	Norway
53	Papua New Guinea
155	Peru
156	Philippines
159	Portugal
166	St. Kitts-Nevis
167	St. Lucia
169	St. Vincent
177	Solomons
181	Spain
186	Sweden
187	Switzerland
195	Trinidad & Tob.
199	Tuvalu
203	United Kingdom
204	United States
206	Uruguay
208	Venezuela

Related Territories

4	Amer. Samoa (US)
7	Anguilla (UK)
138a	Aruba (Ne)
12	Azores (Port)
17	Belau (US)
21	Bermuda (UK)
27	Br. Vir. Is. (UK)
34	Canary Isls. (Sp)
36	Cayman Isls. (UK)
157a	Ceuta (Sp)
39	Channel Isls. (UK)
48	Cook Isls. (NZ)
63	Falkland Is. (UK)
64	Faroe Isls. (Den)
75	Gibraltar (UK)
77	Greenland (Den)
80	Guam (US)
95	Isle of Man (UK)
113	Liechtenstein (Sw)
117	Madeira (Port)
123	Marshall Isls. (US)
127	Mayotte (Fr)
157b	Melilla (Sp)
129	Micronesia (US)
132	Montserrat (UK)
138	Ne. Antilles (Ne)
139	New Caledonia (Fr)
145	Niue (N.Z.)
147	No. Marianas (US)
160	Puerto Rico (US)
165	St. Helena (UK)
168	St. Pierre-Mq. (Fr)
170	San Marino (It)
198	Turks & C. (UK)
210	Virgin Isls. (US)

Partly Free States

14	Bahrain
15	Bangladesh
22	Bhutan
28	Brunei
35	Cape Verde Is.
40	Chile
42	China (Taiwan)
98	Cote d'Ivoire
59	Egypt
60	El Salvador
65	Fiji
71	Gambia
81	Guatemala
84	Guyana
85	Haiti
88	Hungary
91	Indonesia
92	Iran
101	Jordan
106	Korea (S)
107	Kuwait
109	Lebanon
110	Lesotho
111	Liberia
116	Madagascar
119	Malaysia
120	Maldives
128	Mexico
133	Morocco
136	Nepal
142	Nicaragua
144	Nigeria
151	Pakistan
152	Panama
154	Paraguay
158	Poland
161	Qatar
173	Senegal
175	Sierra Leone
176	Singapore
179	So. Africa
182	Sri Lanka
183	Sudan
184	Suriname
185	Swaziland
190	Thailand
193	Tonga
194	Transkei
196	Tunisia
197	Turkey
200	Uganda
202	United Arab Emirates
140	Vanuatu
212	W. Samoa
213	Yemen (N)
215	Yugoslavia
217	Zambia
218	Zimbabwe

Related Territories

5	Andorra (Fr-Sp)
24	Bophuthatswana (South Afr)
43	Christmas Is. (Austral)

Not Free States

1	Afghanistan
2	Albania
3	Algeria
6	Angola
20	Benin
29	Bulgaria
205	Burkina Faso
30	Burma
31	Burundi
102	Cambodia
32	Cameroon
37	Central African Republic
38	Chad
41	China (Mainland)
46	Comoros
47	Congo
50	Cuba
52	Czechoslovakia
54	Djibouti
61	Equatorial Guinea
62	Ethiopia
70	Gabon
72	Germany (E)
74	Ghana
82	Guinea
83	Guinea-Bissau
93	Iraq
103	Kenya
105	Korea (N)
108	Laos
112	Libya
118	Malawi
121	Mali
125	Mauritania
131	Mongolia
134	Mozambique
143	Niger
150	Oman
163	Romania
164	Rwanda
171	Sao Tome & Principe
172	Saudi Arabia
174	Seychelles
178	Somalia
188	Syria
189	Tanzania
191	Togo
201	USSR
209	Vietnam
214	Yemen (S)
216	Zaire

Related Territories

44	Cocos Isls. (Austral)
57	Easter Is. (Ch)
68	French Guiana (Fr)
69	French Polynesia (Fr)
79	Guadeloupe (Fr)
87	Hong Kong (UK)
115	Macao (Port)
124	Martinique (Fr)
130	Monaco (Fr)
146	Norfolk Is. (Aus)
149	Occupied Trs. (Isr)
162	Reunion (Fr)
180	SW Africa (Namibia) (SA)
192	Tokelau Isls. (NZ)
	Vatican (It)
211	Wallis and Futuna (Fr)

Related Territories

219	Ciskei (SA)
207	Venda (SA)

Declines in Freedom in 1987

There were no countries in which there was a major change in rating or status of freedom in 1986. However, 1987 recorded several important setbacks. Most decisive and unexpected was the destruction of democracy in **Fiji** by its military forces, supported by a majority of its conservative, traditional Fijian chiefs. Fijian democracy often had been held up as an example of successful third world democracy, and of the ability of ethnically mixed populations to make an ethnic representational system work. However, the elements of explosion had been building up for years: an economically and professionally successful class of Fijian citizens of Indian origin had come to make up half of the population. Slightly outnumbered, the native Fijians had been allowed by the unique Fijian democratic system to dominate both the government and the military. To native Fijians was also reserved most of the land; an operating system of government by traditional chiefs also functioned as a supplement to parliamentary government.

It was against this background that in May 1987 a coalition of opposition forces, led by a native Fijian, but dominated ethnically by members of the Indian ethnic community, won a fair election, and proceeded to form a government. Feeling threatened by this change of power, and the shifts in the constitution many native Fijians felt it implied, a military leader overthrew the parliamentary system. As the summer proceeded moderate forces worked toward a new political system that would embed even greater rights for the native Fijians. Yet the native Fijians were in no mood for moderation. As a compromise was about to be achieved, Colonel Rabuka intervened again, dismissed the governor-general, and took the country out of the commonwealth. Return to some form of democracy is promised, but for now the country and the media have been forced into silence or neutrality, rights of assembly and demonstration are curtailed, parliament is dissolved. In most respects Fiji is saddled with a repressive military regime.

The decline of freedom in **Kenya** marked the latest stage in a slow erosion of freedoms over the last several years. There is no longer the appearance of independence within the single ruling party. It has increasingly become a crime, leading to jail or torture, to express opinions critical of the government, or to distribute leaflets opposing the system. The media are no longer free; and repressions of university students and faculty are common. Statements by major regime opponents are either repressed or not reported.

Events in **Panama** also marked a further slide downward. Revelations about the military leadership and its interference in past elections and investigations sparked massive demonstrations against the government and the leader of the defense forces. These were met with ever more intimidating force. By fall there was no longer an operating opposition newspaper, and all media were operating under narrow restrictions. Occasional opposition statements still managed to be issued; and highly critical statements against the leadership are publicly made, especially by Church leaders. Arrests of opponents, however, were generally for only a few days.

Haiti was unable to overcome its legacy of poverty and despotic rule and establish the democratic system promised by a constitution approved by referendum. The violent, anarchical suppression of the election, the electoral commission, and many who spoke up or tried to vote marked a retreat in both political and civil liberties. Whether the ultimately responsible military government can hold credible elections in the near future appears doubtful.

Movements downward elsewhere were more marginal. A libel suit and accusation of sedition against an opposition leader suggested a cooler democratic atmosphere in **St. Christopher (Kitts) and Nevis.** The government's ability to rule in **Lebanon** declined further, under the combined pressures of external forces and internal factional armies. Its ability to command reliable security forces, as well as its ability to tax, have by now almost evaporated. After its recent coup **Lesotho** has not managed to reestablish the guarantees of civilian government—the government remains unable to explain the mysterious deaths of opponents. In **Zimbabwe,** opposition parties have been all but banned.

Advances in Freedom

Nineteen eighty-seven saw many advances in Freedom. In the communist world, the most significant advance was that in civil liberties in the **USSR.** Many long-term political prisoners were released. Discussion of political issues became more open in the government's primary media, while in more elite or specialized publications and discussion groups a wide variety of issues were addressed with a new frankness. On a more advanced level, freedom of discussion, organization, and access continued to develop in **Poland** and **Hungary.** Poland is a quietly embattled state. Out of the struggle has come an increasing tacit recognition of the rights of the people against the state. Few prisoners of conscience remain. The government is faced by an intransigent church and population that insists on its own organizations and publications, even in the face of government proscriptions. A judicial system is beginning to develop in which private cases can even be made against government representatives. The government now recognizes that there is, indeed, an opposition, just as it has long recognized that it cannot control what goes on in the churches. Many in the West fail to realize that Hungary has not had political prisoners for some time, and that travel into and out of the country has become a recognized and generally observed right. Foreign publications are readily available. There is little opposition media or organization, but opinion reflecting a range of positions on economic and political affairs is now commonly available in the controlled media.

In the third world, Marxist-Leninist states, or states modeled in part on their forms, have moved toward greater freedom. Discussion has been slightly more open in **Vietnam**, while legislative elections have allowed for at least restricted choice and some aspects of campaigning. **Nicaragua** has allowed the major opposition newspaper to resume publication; the Catholic radio station has also returned to the air, although under restrictions. The release of political prisoners appears problematic. **Cape Verde** now has an assembly with non-party members, and quite open discussion. There are few, if any, political prisoners. In spite of its poor human rights record, a constitutional referendum in **Ethiopia** and subsequent assembly elections with choice among candidates were both more than dictated exercises. Popular consultations on the constitution led to changes in the final draft.

In Africa, **Nigeria** has gradually moved back toward a freer and more consensual society. Media freedoms have again expanded as a definite plan has been outlined for yet another return to

democracy. Local elections should be held in December, 1987.
Mauritania saw local elections that allowed for the return to the
political process of many of the factions and leaders that had been
excluded in recent years. The government of **Chad** managed to
incorporate a variety of leaders from the many factions that have
battled over its poverty in recent years; internal violence has been
largely replaced by common action against an external enemy.
Recent elections in the **Central African Republic** have been
relatively non-coercive and have allowed some choice. A well
publicized political trial has been held openly and with apparent
fairness. Election procedures and the choice offered voters also
improved this year in **Zaire**. The near-democracy of **Gambia** saw
an election with open and free campaigning and a credible result.

This was the year to recognize that democracy has returned to
the **Philippines**. A referendum and legislative elections confirmed
the results of the earlier election of Mrs. Aquino and reestablished
a functioning democratic system. The subsequent ability of the
government to overcome, or live with, the threat from the military,
while in the midst of a serious guerrilla war suggested that the
revived system might succeed. In the same area, Nationalist
China (Taiwan) moved forward through a successful multiparty
election in December, 1986, and a subsequent expansion of civil
liberties. Most political prisoners were freed. The media became
notably more open—there were even journalistic reports from the
mainland. The people were also given at least a limited right to
visit the mainland.

Turkey's legislative elections in late 1987, following a major
referendum, marked the recovery of political freedoms for most
Turks—the large Kurdish minority remained without any rights of
self-determination, however. An agreement of the two major
parties, and the subsequent victory of the opposition made the
democracy of **Malta** more convincing than it had been recently.
In the Caribbean an overwhelming and unique victory by the
opposition in **Trinidad and Tobago** proved that this country
offered a freer democratic environment than had been assumed.
Control over violence and a more civil atmosphere of discussion
has improved the conditions for democracy in **Jamaica**. **Grenada**
seemed to have essentially completed its move back to full
independence and a functioning democratic system. **Suriname**
extended both its political and civil liberties as its people

accepted a new constitution and rejected military rule in the course of a decisive legislative election. Whether the new system will be allowed to function democratically is still in question, but the strength of the civil bureaucracy, as well as labor and political organization are reassuring.

Among related territories, the quality of political activity and expression in **Guam** increasingly conforms to the democratic patterns of Micronesia as a whole. In French **New Caledonia**, a period of political ferment and a sequence of elections or referendums has confirmed the desire of the great majority of residents to maintain political ties with France—however unjust this may seem to many of the island's original inhabitants.

Other Changes and Trends

In the developed world the year saw a continued advance in the diversity and availability of information. Monopoly government control over broadcasting has continued its decline in Western Europe. The government's control over expression in **Greece** was significantly reduced by the establishment of private radio stations with a commitment to opposition viewpoints in major cities.

The American news media were again full of stories of freedom or its denial that did not, for one reason or another, affect the Survey. The struggle for freedom was intense in Afghanistan, South Africa, Chile, and Paraguay. Yet, on review, the ratings of the Survey in these cases remained reasonable comparatively. In Afghanistan, this was, of course, because the Survey's rating was already at 7-7, the lowest in the system. The freedom of the news media declined in **South Africa,** but the diversity of opinion that continually makes its way to the surface there, the legal and illegal demonstrations, the extent and variety of opposition organization, and the plurality of independent and often combative institutions, including the universities and courts, make a lower rating inappropriate.

Two danger signals from Asia should be specially noted. In **India's** contententious and often violent democracy, the government's apparent support for a variety of labor and legal actions against a major newspaper were worrisome. In **Malaysia's** part-democracy the arrest of many leading political and

TABLE 5
Most Significant Changes: 1986 to 1987

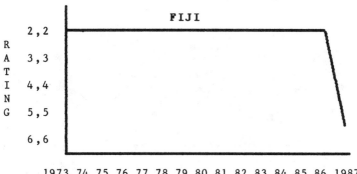

FIJI

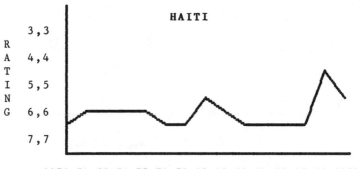

HAITI

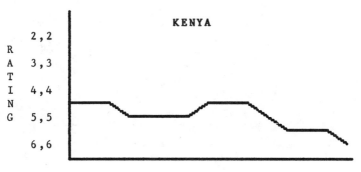

KENYA

Survey: 1987

KOREA (S)

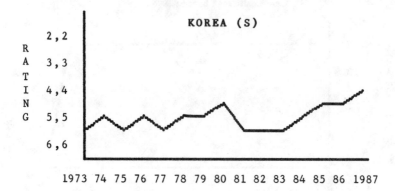

LEBANON

MALTA

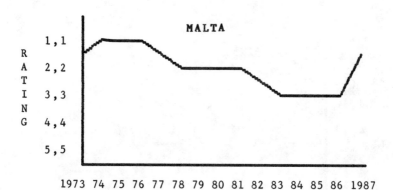

50

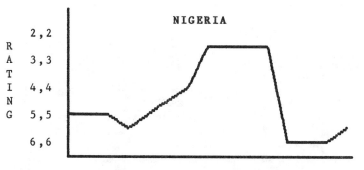

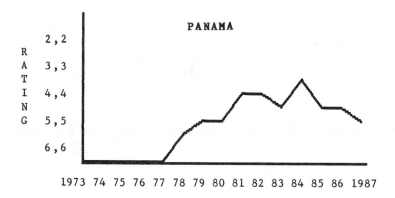

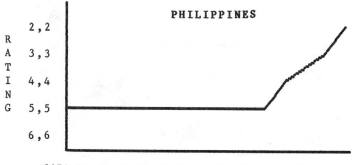

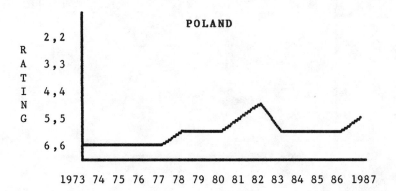

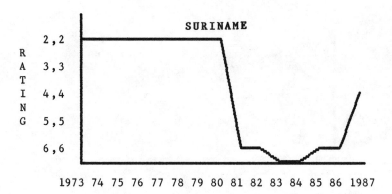

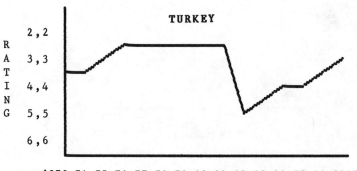

intellectual figures from several parties constituted a flagrant attempt to silence critics. If maintained, the move presages a serious decline in freedom.

The Record of Gains and Losses: 1973-1987

Table 5 relates the most important of this year's changes in country ratings to the recent record of the countries involved. In this regard "important" must be a partly subjective judgment, but it certainly excludes those changes in ratings that resulted from the analyst's judgment or method of rating.

Table 6 allows the reader to roughly trace the course of freedom since the Survey began. It should be noted that changes in information and judgment since 1973 make many ratings not strictly comparable from year to year. Nevertheless, the table reflects the direction of trends in each country.

Since the Survey began, the world has experienced a number of gains and losses of freedom, either immediate or prospective. Most generally, there has been an advance of Soviet communism in Southeast Asia after the fall of South Vietnam, and at least its partial institutionalization in South Yemen, Ethiopia, and the former Portuguese colonies of Africa. In the Americas an imminent danger of the spread of communism has arisen in Nicaragua, and an erstwhile danger in Grenada. Perhaps equally significant has been the amelioration of communism in many areas. While mainland China is still a repressive society, it has increased freedom through the support of private initiative, through more open discussion in some areas, and through the sending of thousands of students overseas. While Poland suggests the immediate limits of change, nearly every country in Eastern Europe is freer today than it was at the beginning of the 1970s. Recently, this trend has been extended to the Soviet Union.

In Western Europe gains for democracy in Spain, Portugal, and Greece were critical to its continual advancement everywhere. After the setback in Chile, gains have been achieved in many parts of Latin America. Argentina, Bolivia, Brazil, Dominican Republic, Ecuador, Honduras, Peru, and Uruguay reestablished democratic institutions. Several countries that the Survey listed as "free" at the beginning may now be more authentically free. Colombia is an

TABLE 6

RATINGS OF COUNTRIES SINCE 1973

Country	73	75	77	78	79	80	81	82	83	84	85	86	87
Afghan-istan	4	7	7	7	7	7	7	7	7	7	7	7	7
	5	6	6	6	7	7	7	7	7	7	7	7	7
	PF	NF	NF	NF	NF	NF	NF	NF	NF	NF	NF	NF	NF
Albania	7	7	7	7	7	7	7	7	7	7	7	7	7
	7	7	7	7	7	7	7	7	7	7	7	7	7
	NF	NF	NF	NF	NF	NF	NF	NF	NF	NF	NF	NF	NF
Algeria	6	6	6	6	6	6	6	6	6	6	6	6	6
	6	6	6	6	6	6	6	6	6	6	6	6	6
	NF	NF	NF	NF	NF	NF	NF	NF	NF	NF	NF	NF	NF
Angola[3]	7	6	6	7	7	7	7	7	7	7	7	7	7
	6	4	6	7	7	7	7	7	7	7	7	7	7
	NF	PF	NF	NF	NF	NF	NF	NF	NF	NF	NF	NF	NF
Antigua & Barbuda[3]	2	2	2	2	2	2	2	2	2	2	2	2	2
	3	3	3	2	2	2	2	2	3	3	3	3	3
	F	F	F	F	F	F	F	F*	F	F	F	F	F
Argentina	6	2	6	6	6	6	6	6	3	2	2	2	2
	3	4	5	6	5	5	5	5	3	2	2	1	1
	PF	PF	NF	NF	NF	NF	NF	NF	PF	F	F	F	F
Australia	1	1	1	1	1	1	1	1	1	1	1	1	1
	1	1	1	1	1	1	1	1	1	1	1	1	1
	F	F	F	F	F	F	F	F	F	F	F	F	F
Austria	1	1	1	1	1	1	1	1	1	1	1	1	1
	1	1	1	1	1	1	1	1	1	1	1	1	1
	F	F	F	F	F	F	F	F	F	F	F	F	F

Notes to the Table

*. Indicates year of independence.

1. Ratings are from the Jan/Feb issues of Freedom at Issue through 1982. The ratings for 1983, 1984, and 1985 are based on 1983-84 and subsequent yearbooks. The three lines are political rights, civil liberties, and status of freedom.

2. Ratings for 1974 and 1976 may be obtained from Table 6, 1985-86 yearbook.

3. Until 1975 Angola, Mozambique, and Guinea-Bissau (formerly Portuguese Guinea) were evaluated together as Portugal Colonies (A), while Sao Tome and Cape Verde were Portugal (B). Until 1978 Antigua, Dominica, and St. Lucia were considered together as the West Indies Associated States (and Grenada until 1975). The Comoros and Djibouti (Territory of the Afars and Issas) were considered as "France: Overseas Territories" until 1975. Until 1975 Kiribati and Tuvalu were considered together as the Gilbert and Ellice Islands. Cyprus was regarded as a unit until 1981.

4. 1973 ratings for South Africa were white: 2,3,F and black: 5,6,NF.

5. Ratings for North Vietnam for 1973-1976 were 7,7,NF; those for South Vietnam were 4,5,PF for 1973-75, 7,7,NF for 1976.

Table 6 (continued)

Country	73	75	77	78	79	80	81	82	83	84	85	86	87
Bahamas	2	1	1	1	1	1	1	1	2	2	2	2	2
	2	2	2	2	2	2	2	2	2	2	2	2	3
	F	F	F	F	F	F	F	F	F	F	F	F	F
Bahrain	6	4	6	6	6	6	5	5	5	5	5	5	5
	5	4	4	4	4	4	4	5	5	5	5	5	5
	NF	PF	PF	PF	PF	PF	PF	PF	PF	PF	PF	PF	PF
Bangla- desh	2	4	7	6	4	3	3	3	6	6	5	4	4
	4	4	4	4	4	3	3	4	5	5	5	5	5
	PF	PF	PF	PF	PF	PF	PF	PF	PF	PF	PF	PF	PF
Barbados	1	1	1	1	1	1	1	1	1	1	1	1	1
	1	1	1	1	1	1	1	1	1	2	2	1	1
	F	F	F	F	F	F	F	F	F	F	F	F	F
Belgium	1	1	1	1	1	1	1	1	1	1	1	1	1
	1	1	1	1	1	1	1	1	1	1	1	1	1
	F	F	F	F	F	F	F	F	F	F	F	F	F
Belize	2	1	1	1	1	1	1	1	1	2	1	1	1
	2	2	2	2	2	2	2	2	2	1	1	1	1
	F	F	F	F	F	F	F	F	F	F	F	F	F
Benin (Dahomey)	7	7	7	7	7	7	7	7	7	7	7	7	7
	5	6	7	7	7	6	6	6	6	7	7	7	7
	NF	NF	NF	NF	NF	NF	NF	NF	NF	NF	NF	NF	NF
Bhutan	4	4	4	4	4	5	5	5	5	5	5	5	5
	4	4	4	4	4	5	5	5	5	5	5	5	5
	PF	PF	PF	PF	PF	PF	PF	PF	PF	PF	PF	PF	PF
Bolivia	5	6	6	6	5	3	7	7	2	2	2	2	2
	4	5	4	4	3	3	5	5	3	3	3	3	3
	PF	NF	PF	PF	PF	PF	NF	NF	F	F	F	F	F
Botswana	3	2	2	2	2	2	2	2	2	2	2	2	2
	4	3	3	3	3	3	3	3	3	3	3	3	3
	PF	F	F	F	F	F	F	F	F	F	F	F	F
Brazil	5	4	4	4	4	4	4	4	3	3	3	2	2
	5	4	5	5	4	3	3	3	3	3	2	2	2
	PF	PF	PF	PF	PF	PF	PF	PF	PF	PF	F	F	F
Brunei	6	6	6	6	6	6	6	6	6	6	6	6	6
	5	5	5	5	5	5	5	5	5	6	5	5	5
	NF	NF	NF	NF	NF	NF	NF	NF	NF	NF	PF	PF	PF
Bulgaria	7	7	7	7	7	7	7	7	7	7	7	7	7
	7	7	7	7	7	7	7	7	7	7	7	7	7
	NF	NF	NF	NF	NF	NF	NF	NF	NF	NF	NF	NF	NF
Burkina Faso	3	6	5	5	2	2	6	6	6	7	7	7	7
	4	4	5	4	3	3	5	5	5	5	6	6	6
	PF	PF	PF	PF	F	F	PF	PF	PF	NF	NF	NF	NF
Burma	7	7	6	7	7	7	7	7	7	7	7	7	7
	5	5	6	6	6	6	6	6	7	7	7	7	7
	NF	NF	NF	NF	NF	NF	NF	NF	NF	NF	NF	NF	NF

Table 6 (continued)

Country	73	75	77	78	79	80	81	82	83	84	85	86	87
Burundi	7	7	7	7	7	7	7	7	6	7	7	7	7
	7	7	6	6	6	7	6	6	6	6	6	6	6
	NF	NF	NF	NF	NF	NF	NF	NF	NF	NF	NF	NF	NF
Cambodia	6	6	7	7	7	7	7	7	7	7	7	7	7
	5	6	7	7	7	7	7	7	7	7	7	7	7
	NF	NF	NF	NF	NF	NF	NF	NF	NF	NF	NF	NF	NF
Cameroon	6	6	7	6	6	6	6	6	6	6	6	6	6
	4	4	5	5	5	6	6	6	6	7	7	6	6
	PF	PF	NF	NF	NF	NF	NF	NF	NF	NF	NF	NF	NF
Canada	1	1	1	1	1	1	1	1	1	1	1	1	1
	1	1	1	1	1	1	1	1	1	1	1	1	1
	F	F	F	F	F	F	F	F	F	F	F	F	NF
Cape Verde Isls.[3]	5	5	6	6	6	6	6	6	6	6	6	6	5
	6	5	6	6	6	6	6	6	6	7	7	6	6
	NF	PF*	NF	NF	NF	NF	NF	NF	NF	NF	NF	NF	PF
Central Afr. Rp.	7	7	7	7	7	7	7	7	7	7	7	7	6
	7	7	7	7	7	6	6	5	5	6	6	6	6
	NF	NF	NF	NF	NF	NF	NF	NF	NF	NF	NF	NF	NF
Chad	6	6	7	7	6	7	6	7	7	7	7	7	6
	7	7	6	6	6	6	6	6	6	7	7	7	7
	NF	NF	NF	NF	NF	NF	NF	NF	NF	NF	NF	NF	NF
Chile	1	7	7	7	6	6	6	6	6	6	6	6	6
	2	5	5	5	5	5	5	5	5	5	5	5	5
	F	NF	NF	NF	NF	PF	PF	PF	PF	PF	PF	PF	PF
China (M)	7	7	7	6	6	6	6	6	6	6	6	6	6
	7	7	7	6	6	5	6	6	6	6	6	6	6
	NF	NF	NF	NF	NF	NF	NF	NF	NF	NF	NF	NF	NF
China (T)	6	6	5	5	5	5	5	5	5	5	5	5	5
	5	5	5	4	4	5	6	5	5	5	5	5	4
	NF	NF	PF	PF	PF	PF	PF	PF	PF	PF	PF	PF	PF
Colombia	2	2	2	2	2	2	2	2	2	2	2	2	2
	2	2	3	3	3	3	3	3	3	3	3	3	3
	F	F	F	F	F	F	F	F	F	F	F	F	F
Comoros[3]	4	2	5	4	5	4	4	4	4	5	6	6	6
	4	2	3	3	4	4	5	5	4	5	6	6	6
	PF	F	PF	PF	PF	PF	PF	PF	PF	PF	NF	NF	NF
Congo	7	5	5	7	7	7	7	7	7	7	7	7	7
	7	6	6	6	6	7	7	6	6	6	6	6	6
	NF	PF	PF	NF	NF	NF	NF	NF	NF	NF	NF	NF	NF
Costa Rica	1	1	1	1	1	1	1	1	1	1	1	1	1
	1	1	1	1	1	1	1	1	1	1	1	1	1
	F	F	F	F	F	F	F	F	F	F	F	F	F
Cuba	7	7	7	7	6	6	6	6	6	6	6	6	6
	7	7	6	6	6	6	6	6	6	6	6	6	6
	NF	NF	NF	NF	NF	NF	NF	NF	NF	NF	NF	NF	NF

Table 6 (continued)

Country	73	75	77	78	79	80	81	82	83	84	85	86	87
Cyprus(G)[4]	2	4	3	3	3	3	3	1	1	1	1	1	1
	3	4	4	4	4	4	3	2	2	2	2	2	2
	F	PF	PF	PF	PF	PF	PF	F	F	F	F	F	F
Cyprus(T)[4]								4	4	4	3	2	2
								3	3	3	3	3	3
								PF	PF	PF	PF	F	F
Czecho-	7	7	7	7	7	7	7	7	7	7	7	7	7
slovakia	7	7	6	6	6	6	6	6	6	6	6	6	6
	NF	NF	NF	NF	NF	NF	NF	NF	NF	NF	NF	NF	NF
Denmark	1	1	1	1	1	1	1	1	1	1	1	1	1
	1	1	1	1	1	1	1	1	1	1	1	1	1
	F	F	F	F	F	F	F	F	F	F	F	F	F
Djibouti[3]	4	4	3	2	2	3	3	3	5	5	6	6	6
	4	3	3	2	3	4	4	5	6	6	6	6	6
	PF	PF	PF	F*	F	PF	PF	PF	NF	PF	NF	NF	NF
Dominica[3]	2	2	2	2	2	2	2	2	2	2	2	2	2
	3	3	3	2	3	2	2	2	2	2	2	2	2
	F	F	F	F	F*	F	F	F	F	F	F	F	F
Dominican	3	4	4	4	2	2	2	2	1	1	1	1	1
Republic	2	2	3	2	2	3	3	3	2	3	3	3	3
	F	PF	PF	PF	F	F	F	F	F	F	F	F	F
Ecuador	7	7	6	6	5	2	2	2	2	2	2	2	2
	3	5	5	5	3	2	2	2	2	2	3	3	3
	PF	NF	PF	PF	PF	F	F	F	F	F	F	F	F
Egypt	6	6	5	5	5	5	5	5	5	4	4	5	5
	6	4	4	4	5	5	5	6	5	4	4	4	4
	NF	PF	PF	PF	PF	PF	PF	PF	PF	PF	PF	PF	PF
El	2	2	3	3	4	5	6	5	4	3	2	3	3
Salvador	3	3	3	3	4	3	4	5	5	5	4	4	4
	F	F	PF	PF	PF	PF	PF	PF	PF	PF	PF	PF	PF
Eq.	6	6	6	7	7	7	7	7	7	7	7	7	7
Guinea	6	6	7	7	7	6	6	6	6	6	7	7	7
	NF	NF	NF	NF	NF	NF	NF	NF	NF	NF	NF	NF	NF
Ethiopia	5	6	7	7	7	7	7	7	7	7	7	7	6
	6	5	6	7	7	7	7	7	7	7	7	7	7
	NF	NF	NF	NF	NF	NF	NF	NF	NF	NF	NF	NF	NF
Fiji	2	2	2	2	2	2	2	2	2	2	2	2	6
	2	2	2	2	2	2	2	2	2	2	2	2	5
	F	F	F	F	F	F	F	F	F	F	F	F	PF
Finland	2	2	2	2	2	2	2	2	2	2	2	2	1
	2	2	2	2	2	2	2	2	2	2	2	2	2
	F	F	F	F	F	F	F	F	F	F	F	F	F
France	1	1	1	1	1	1	1	1	1	1	1	1	1
	2	2	1	1	2	2	2	2	2	2	2	2	2
	F	F	F	F	F	F	F	F	F	F	F	F	F

Survey: 1987

Table 6 (continued)

Country	73	75	77	78	79	80	81	82	83	84	85	86	87
Gabon	6	6	6	6	6	6	6	6	6	6	6	6	6
	6	6	6	6	6	6	6	6	6	6	6	6	6
	NF	NF	NF	NF	NF	NF	NF	NF	NF	NF	NF	NF	NF
Gambia	2	2	2	2	2	2	2	3	3	3	3	3	3
	2	2	2	2	2	2	2	4	4	4	4	4	3
	F	F	F	F	F	F	F	PF	PF	PF	PF	PF	PF
Germany (East)	7	7	7	7	7	7	7	7	7	7	7	7	7
	7	7	7	7	6	7	6	7	7	6	6	6	6
	NF	NF	NF	NF	NF	NF	NF	NF	NF	NF	NF	NF	NF
Germany (West)	1	1	1	1	1	1	1	1	1	1	1	1	1
	1	1	1	1	2	2	2	2	2	2	2	2	2
	F	F	F	F	F	F	F	F	F	F	F	F	F
Ghana	6	7	7	6	6	4	2	2	6	7	7	7	7
	6	5	5	5	4	4	3	3	5	6	6	6	6
	NF	NF	NF	PF	PF	PF	F	F	NF	NF	NF	NF	NF
Greece	6	2	2	2	2	2	2	1	1	1	2	2	2
	6	2	2	2	2	2	2	2	2	2	2	2	2
	NF	F	F	F	F	F	F	F	F	F	F	F	F
Grenada	2	2	2	2	2	4	5	6	7	5	2	2	2
	3	4	4	3	3	5	5	5	6	3	3	2	1
	F	PF*	PF	F	F	PF	PF	NF	NF	PF	F	F	F
Guatemala	2	4	4	4	3	3	5	6	6	5	4	3	3
	3	3	3	4	4	5	6	6	6	6	4	3	3
	F	PF	PF	PF	PF	PF	PF	NF	NF	PF	PF	PF	PF
Guinea	7	7	7	7	7	7	7	7	7	7	7	7	7
	7	7	7	7	7	7	7	7	7	5	5	5	6
	NF	NF	NF	NF	NF	NF	NF	NF	NF	NF	NF	NF	NF
Guinea-Bissau	7	6	6	6	6	6	6	6	7	6	6	6	6
	6	6	6	6	6	6	6	6	6	6	6	7	7
	NF	NF*	NF	NF	NF	NF	NF	NF	NF	NF	NF	NF	NF
Guyana	2	4	3	3	4	4	4	5	5	5	5	5	5
	2	3	3	3	3	4	4	4	5	5	5	5	5
	F	PF	PF	PF	PF	PF	PF	PF	PF	PF	PF	PF	PF
Haiti	7	6	6	7	7	6	6	7	7	7	7	5	6
	6	6	6	6	6	5	6	6	6	6	6	4	5
	NF	NF	NF	NF	NF	NF	NF	NF	NF	NF	NF	PF	PF
Honduras	7	6	6	6	6	6	4	3	3	2	2	2	2
	3	3	3	3	3	3	3	3	3	3	3	3	3
	PF	PF	PF	PF	PF	PF	PF	PF	PF	F	F	F	F
Hungary	6	6	6	6	6	6	6	6	6	6	5	5	5
	6	6	6	5	5	5	5	5	5	5	5	5	4
	NF	NF	NF	NF	NF	NF	NF	NF	NF	PF	PF	PF	PF
Iceland	1	1	1	1	1	1	1	1	1	1	1	1	1
	1	1	1	1	1	1	1	1	1	1	1	1	1
	F	F	F	F	F	F	F	F	F	F	F	F	F

Table 6 (continued)

Country	73	75	77	78	79	80	81	82	83	84	85	86	87
India	2	2	2	2	2	2	2	2	2	2	2	2	2
	3	3	5	2	2	2	3	3	3	3	3	3	3
	F	F	PF	F	F	F	F	F	F	F	F	F	F
Indonesia	5	5	5	5	5	5	5	5	5	5	5	5	5
	5	5	5	5	5	5	5	5	5	6	6	6	6
	PF	PF	PF	PF	PF	PF	PF	PF	PF	PF	PF	PF	PF
Iran	5	5	6	6	6	5	5	6	6	5	5	5	5
	6	6	6	5	5	6	5	6	6	6	6	6	6
	NF	NF	NF	NF	PF	PF	PF	NF	NF	PF	PF	PF	PF
Iraq	7	7	7	7	7	7	6	6	6	7	7	7	7
	7	7	7	7	6	7	7	7	7	7	7	7	7
	NF	NF	NF	NF	NF	NF	NF	NF	NF	NF	NF	NF	NF
Ireland	1	1	1	1	1	1	1	1	1	1	1	1	1
	2	2	1	1	1	1	1	1	1	1	1	1	1
	F	F	F	F	F	F	F	F	F	F	F	F	F
Israel	2	2	2	2	2	2	2	2	2	2	2	2	2
	3	3	3	3	2	2	2	2	2	2	2	2	2
	F	F	F	F	F	F	F	F	F	F	F	F	F
Italy	1	1	2	2	2	2	1	1	1	1	1	1	1
	2	2	1	1	2	2	2	2	2	1	1	1	1
	F	F	F	F	F	F	F	F	F	F	F	F	F
Ivory Coast	6	6	6	6	6	6	6	5	5	6	6	6	6
	6	6	5	5	5	5	5	5	5	5	5	5	5
	NF	NF	NF	NF	NF	PF	PF	PF	PF	PF	PF	PF	PF
Jamaica	1	1	1	2	2	2	2	2	2	2	2	2	2
	2	2	3	3	3	3	3	3	3	3	3	3	2
	F	F	F	F	F	F	F	F	F	F	F	F	F
Japan	2	2	2	2	2	2	1	1	1	1	1	1	1
	1	1	1	1	1	1	1	1	1	1	1	1	1
	F	F	F	F	F	F	F	F	F	F	F	F	F
Jordan	6	6	6	6	6	6	6	6	6	5	5	5	5
	6	6	6	6	6	6	6	6	6	5	5	5	5
	NF	NF	NF	NF	NF	NF	NF	NF	NF	PF	PF	PF	PF
Kenya	5	5	5	5	5	5	5	5	5	6	6	6	6
	4	4	5	5	5	4	4	4	5	5	5	5	6
	PF	PF	PF	PF	PF	PF	PF	PF	PF	PF	PF	PF	NF
Kiribati	2	2	2	2	2	2	2	2	1	1	1	1	1
	2	2	2	2	2	2	2	2	2	2	2	2	2
	F	F	F	F	F*	F	F	F	F	F	F	F	F
Korea (N)	7	7	7	7	7	7	7	7	7	7	7	7	7
	7	7	7	7	7	7	7	7	7	7	7	7	7
	NF	NF	NF	NF	NF	NF	NF	NF	NF	NF	NF	NF	NF
Korea (S)	5	5	5	5	5	4	5	5	5	5	4	4	4
	6	6	6	5	5	5	6	6	6	5	5	5	4
	NF	PF	NF	PF	PF	PF	PF	PF	PF	PF	PF	PF	PF

Table 6 (continued)

Country	73	75	77	78	79	80	81	82	83	84	85	86	87
Kuwait	4	4	6	6	6	6	6	4	4	4	4	6	6
	4	3	5	4	3	4	4	4	4	4	4	5	5
	PF	PF	NF	PF	PF	PF	PF	PF	PF	PF	PF	PF	PF
Laos	5	5	7	7	7	7	7	7	7	7	7	7	7
	5	5	7	7	7	7	7	7	7	7	7	7	7
	PF	PF	NF	NF	NF	NF	NF	NF	NF	NF	NF	NF	NF
Lebanon	2	2	4	4	4	4	4	4	5	5	5	5	6
	2	2	4	4	4	4	4	4	4	4	4	4	5
	F	F	PF	PF	PF	PF	PF	PF	PF	PF	PF	PF	PF
Lesotho	7	5	5	5	5	5	5	5	5	5	5	5	5
	4	4	4	4	4	5	5	5	5	5	5	5	6
	NF	PF	PF	PF	PF	PF	PF	PF	PF	PF	PF	PF	PF
Liberia	6	6	6	6	6	6	6	6	5	6	5	5	5
	6	3	4	4	4	5	6	6	5	5	5	5	5
	NF	PF	PF	PF	PF	PF	NF	NF	PF	PF	PF	PF	PF
Libya	7	7	7	7	6	6	6	6	6	6	6	6	6
	6	7	6	6	6	6	6	7	6	6	6	6	6
	NF	NF	NF	NF	NF	NF	NF	NF	NF	NF	NF	NF	NF
Luxem-bourg	2	2	2	1	1	1	1	1	1	1	1	1	1
	1	1	1	1	1	1	1	1	1	1	1	1	1
	F	F	F	F	F	F	F	F	F	F	F	F	F
Madagascar (Malagasy Rep.)	5	5	6	5	5	6	6	6	5	5	5	5	5
	3	4	5	5	5	6	6	6	6	6	6	5	5
	PF	PF	NF	PF	PF	NF	NF	NF	PF	PF	PF	PF	PF
Malawi	7	7	7	7	6	6	6	6	6	6	6	6	6
	6	6	6	6	6	7	7	7	7	7	7	7	7
	NF	NF	NF	NF	NF	NF	NF	NF	NF	NF	NF	NF	NF
Malaysia	2	3	3	3	3	3	3	3	3	3	3	3	3
	3	3	4	4	3	4	4	4	4	5	5	5	5
	F	PF	PF	PF	PF	PF	PF	PF	PF	PF	PF	PF	PF
Maldives	3	3	4	4	5	5	5	5	5	5	5	5	5
	2	2	4	4	5	5	5	5	5	5	5	6	6
	PF	PF	PF	PF	PF	PF	PF	PF	PF	PF	PF	PF	PF
Mali	7	7	7	7	7	7	7	7	7	7	7	7	7
	6	6	7	7	7	6	6	6	6	6	6	6	6
	NF	NF	NF	NF	NF	NF	NF	NF	NF	NF	NF	NF	NF
Malta	1	1	1	2	2	2	2	2	2	2	2	2	1
	2	1	2	2	2	2	3	3	4	4	4	4	2
	F	F	F	F	F	F	F	F	PF	PF	PF	PF	F
Mauri-tania	6	5	6	6	6	6	7	7	7	7	7	7	6
	6	6	6	6	6	6	6	6	6	6	6	6	6
	NF	NF	NF	NF	NF	NF	NF	NF	NF	NF	NF	NF	NF
Mauritius	3	3	2	2	2	2	2	2	2	2	2	2	2
	2	2	2	2	4	4	4	3	2	2	2	2	2
	F	F	F	F	PF	PF	PF	F	F	F	F	F	F

Table 6 (continued)

Country	73	75	77	78	79	80	81	82	83	84	85	86	87
Mexico	5	4	4	4	4	3	3	3	3	3	4	4	4
	3	3	4	4	4	3	4	4	4	4	4	4	4
	PF	PF	PF	PF	PF	PF	PF	PF	PF	PF	PF	PF	PF
Mongolia	7	7	7	7	7	7	7	7	7	7	7	7	7
	7	7	7	7	7	7	7	7	7	7	7	7	7
	NF	NF	NF	NF	NF	NF	NF	NF	NF	NF	NF	NF	NF
Morocco	5	5	5	4	3	3	4	4	4	4	4	4	4
	4	5	5	3	4	4	4	5	5	5	5	5	5
	PF	PF	PF	PF	PF	PF	PF	PF	PF	PF	PF	PF	PF
Mozam-bique3	7	6	7	7	7	7	7	7	7	6	6	6	6
	6	6	7	7	7	7	7	7	6	7	7	7	7
	NF	NF	NF	NF	NF	NF	NF	NF	NF	NF	NF	NF	NF
Nauru	2	2	2	2	2	2	2	2	2	2	2	2	2
	2	2	2	2	2	2	2	2	2	2	2	2	2
	F	F	F	F	F	F	F	F	F	F	F	F	F
Nepal	6	6	6	6	6	5	3	3	3	3	3	3	3
	5	5	5	5	5	4	4	4	4	4	4	4	4
	NF	NF	NF	NF	NF	PF	PF	PF	PF	PF	PF	PF	PF
Nether-lands	1	1	1	1	1	1	1	1	1	1	1	1	1
	1	1	1	1	1	1	1	1	1	1	1	1	1
	F	F	F	F	F	F	F	F	F	F	F	F	F
New Zealand	1	1	1	1	1	1	1	1	1	1	1	1	1
	1	1	1	1	1	1	1	1	1	1	1	1	1
	F	F	F	F	F	F	F	F	F	F	F	F	F
Nicaragua	4	5	5	5	5	5	5	6	6	5	5	5	5
	3	4	5	5	5	5	5	5	5	5	5	6	5
	PF	PF	PF	PF	PF	PF	PF	PF	PF	PF	PF	PF	PF
Niger	6	7	7	7	7	7	7	7	7	7	7	7	7
	6	6	6	6	6	6	6	6	6	6	6	6	6
	NF	NF	NF	NF	NF	NF	NF	NF	NF	NF	NF	NF	NF
Nigeria	6	6	6	5	5	2	2	2	2	7	7	7	6
	4	4	4	4	3	3	3	3	3	5	5	5	5
	PF	PF	PF	PF	PF	F	F	F	F	NF	NF	NF	PF
Norway	1	1	1	1	1	1	1	1	1	1	1	1	1
	1	1	1	1	1	1	1	1	1	1	1	1	1
	F	F	F	F	F	F	F	F	F	F	F	F	F
Oman	7	7	6	6	6	6	6	6	6	6	6	6	6
	6	6	6	6	6	6	6	6	6	6	6	6	6
	NF	NF	NF	NF	NF	NF	NF	NF	NF	NF	NF	NF	NF
Pakistan	3	3	4	6	6	6	7	7	7	7	4	4	4
	5	5	5	4	5	6	5	5	5	5	5	5	5
	PF	PF	PF	PF	PF	NF	NF	NF	NF	NF	PF	PF	PF
Panama	7	7	7	6	5	5	4	4	5	4	6	6	5
	6	6	6	5	5	5	4	4	4	3	3	3	5
	NF	NF	NF	NF	NF	PF	PF	PF	PF	PF	PF	PF	PF

Table 6 (continued)

Country	73	75	77	78	79	80	81	82	83	84	85	86	87
Papua New	4	3	2	2	2	2	2	2	2	2	2	2	2
Guinea	2	2	2	2	2	2	2	2	2	2	2	2	2
	PF	PF	F	F	F	F	F	F	F	F	F	F	F
Paraguay	4	5	5	5	5	5	5	5	5	5	5	5	5
	6	5	6	6	5	5	5	5	5	5	5	6	6
	PF	PF	NF	NF	PF	PF	PF	PF	PF	PF	PF	PF	PF
Peru	7	6	6	6	5	5	2	2	2	2	2	2	2
	5	6	4	4	4	4	3	3	3	3	3	3	3
	NF	NF	PF	PF	PF	PF	F	F	F	F	F	F	F
Philip-	4	5	5	5	5	5	5	5	5	4	4	4	2
pines	6	5	5	5	5	5	5	5	5	4	3	2	2
	PF	PF	PF	PF	PF	PF	PF	PF	PF	PF	PF	PF	F
Poland	6	6	6	6	6	6	6	5	6	6	6	6	5
	6	6	6	5	5	5	4	4	5	5	5	5	5
	NF	NF	NF	NF	PF	PF	PF	PF	PF	PF	PF	PF	PF
Portugal	5	5	2	2	2	2	2	2	1	1	1	1	1
	6	3	2	2	2	2	2	2	2	2	2	2	2
	NF	PF	F	F	F	F	F	F	F	F	F	F	F
Qatar	6	6	5	5	5	5	5	5	5	5	5	5	5
	5	5	5	5	5	5	5	5	5	5	5	5	5
	NF	NF	PF	PF	PF	PF	PF	PF	PF	PF	PF	PF	PF
Romania	7	7	7	7	7	7	7	7	7	7	7	7	7
	6	6	6	6	6	6	6	6	6	7	7	7	7
	NF	NF	NF	NF	NF	NF	NF	NF	NF	NF	NF	NF	NF
Rwanda	7	7	7	7	6	6	6	6	6	6	6	6	6
	6	5	5	5	5	6	6	6	6	6	6	6	6
	NF	NF	NF	NF	NF	NF	NF	NF	NF	NF	NF	NF	NF
St.Kitts-	2	2	2	2	2	2	2	2	2	1	1	1	1
Nevis[3]	3	3	3	3	3	3	3	3	3	1	1	1	2
	F	F	F	F	F	F	F	F	F*	F	F	F	F
St.Lucia[3]	2	2	2	2	2	2	2	2	2	1	1	1	1
	3	3	3	3	3	3	3	2	2	2	2	2	2
	F	F	F	F	F	F*	F	F	F	F	F	F	F
St.Vincent	2	2	2	2	2	2	2	2	2	2	2	2	1
	2	2	2	2	2	2	2	2	2	2	2	2	2
	F	F	F	F	F	F*	F	F	F	F	F	F	F
Sao Tome &	5	5	5	6	6	6	6	6	7	7	7	7	7
Principe[3]	6	5	5	5	5	6	6	6	7	7	7	7	7
	NF	PF	PF	NF	NF	NF	NF	NF	NF	NF	NF	NF	NF
Saudi	6	6	6	6	6	6	6	6	6	6	6	6	6
Arabia	6	6	6	6	6	6	6	6	7	7	7	7	7
	NF	NF	NF	NF	NF	NF	NF	NF	NF	NF	NF	NF	NF
Senegal	6	6	6	5	4	4	4	4	4	3	3	3	3
	6	5	4	3	3	3	4	4	4	4	4	4	4
	NF	NF	PF	PF	PF	PF	PF	PF	PF	PF	PF	PF	PF

Table 6 (continued)

Country	73	75	77	78	79	80	81	82	83	84	85	86	87
Sey- chelles[3]	3 2 PF	2 2 F	1 2 F*	6 3 PF	6 4 PF	6 5 PF	6 6 NF	6 6 NF	6 6 NF	6 6 NF	6 6 NF	6 6 NF	6 6 NF
Sierra Leone	4 5 PF	6 5 PF	6 5 PF	5 5 PF	6 5 PF	5 5 PF	5 5 PF	5 5 PF	5 5 PF	4 5 PF	5 5 PF	5 5 PF	5 5 PF
Singapore	5 5 PF	5 5 PF	5 5 PF	5 5 PF	5 5 PF	5 5 PF	5 5 PF	4 5 PF	4 5 PF	4 5 PF	4 5 PF	4 5 PF	4 5 PF
Solomons	4 2 PF	4 2 PF	2 2 F	2 2 F	2 2 F*	2 2 F	2 2 F	2 2 F	2 2 F	2 3 F	2 3 F	2 2 F	2 2 F
Somalia	7 6 NF	7 6 NF	7 7 NF	7 7 NF	7 7 NF	7 7 NF	7 7 NF	7 7 NF	7 7 NF	7 7 NF	7 7 NF	7 7 NF	7 7 NF
South Africa[4]		4 5 PF	4 5 PF	5 6 PF	5 6 PF	5 6 PF	5 6 PF	5 6 NF	5 6 PF	5 6 PF	5 6 PF	5 6 PF	5 6 PF
Spain	5 6 NF	5 5 PF	5 3 PF	2 2 F	2 3 F	2 2 F	2 3 F	2 3 F	1 2 F	1 2 F	1 2 F	1 2 F	1 2 F
Sri Lanka	2 3 F	2 3 F	2 3 F	2 2 F	2 3 F	2 3 F	2 3 F	2 3 F	3 4 PF	3 4 PF	3 4 PF	3 4 PF	3 4 PF
Sudan	6 6 NF	6 6 NF	6 6 NF	6 5 NF	5 5 PF	5 5 PF	5 5 PF	5 6 PF	5 5 PF	6 6 NF	6 6 NF	4 5 PF	4 5 PF
Suriname	2 2 F	2 2 F	2 2 F	2 2 F	2 2 F	2 2 F	7 5 NF	7 5 NF	7 6 NF	7 6 NF	6 6 NF	6 6 NF	4 4 PF
Swaziland	4 2 PF	6 4 PF	6 4 PF	6 4 PF	6 5 PF	5 5 PF	5 5 PF	5 5 PF	5 5 PF	5 6 PF	5 6 PF	5 6 PF	5 6 PF
Sweden	1 1 F	1 1 F	1 1 F	1 1 F	1 1 F	1 1 F	1 1 F	1 1 F	1 1 F	1 1 F	1 1 F	1 1 F	1 1 F
Switzer- land	1 1 F	1 1 F	1 1 F	1 1 F	1 1 F	1 1 F	1 1 F	1 1 F	1 1 F	1 1 F	1 1 F	1 1 F	1 1 F
Syria	7 7 NF	6 7 NF	6 6 NF	5 6 PF	5 6 PF	5 6 PF	5 6 NF	5 6 NF	6 7 NF	6 7 NF	6 7 NF	6 7 NF	6 7 NF
Tanzania	6 6 NF	6 6 NF	6 6 NF	6 6 NF	6 6 NF	6 6 NF	6 6 NF	6 6 NF	6 6 NF	6 6 NF	6 6 NF	6 6 NF	6 6 NF

Table 6 (continued)

Country	73	75	77	78	79	80	81	82	83	84	85	86	87
Thailand	7	5	6	6	6	4	3	3	3	3	3	3	3
	5	3	6	5	4	3	4	4	4	4	4	3	3
	NF	PF	NF	NF	PF	PF	PF	PF	PF	PF	PF	PF	PF
Togo	7	7	7	7	7	7	7	7	7	6	6	6	6
	5	6	6	6	6	6	6	6	6	6	6	6	6
	NF	NF	NF	NF	NF	NF	NF	NF	NF	NF	NF	NF	NF
Tonga	4	5	5	5	5	5	5	5	5	5	5	5	5
	2	3	3	3	3	3	3	3	3	3	3	3	3
	PF	PF	PF	PF	PF	PF	PF	PF	PF	PF	PF	PF	PF
Transkei			6	6	5	5	5	5	5	5	5	5	5
			5	5	5	6	6	6	6	6	6	6	6
			NF*	NF	PF	PF	PF	PF	PF	PF	PF	PF	PF
Trinidad	2	2	2	2	2	2	2	2	1	1	1	1	1
& Tobago	3	2	2	2	2	2	2	2	2	2	2	2	1
	F	F	F	F	F	F	F	F	F	F	F	F	F
Tunisia	6	6	6	6	6	6	6	5	5	5	5	6	5
	5	5	5	5	5	5	5	5	5	5	5	5	6
	NF	NF	NF	NF	NF	PF	PF	PF	PF	PF	PF	PF	PF
Turkey	3	2	2	2	2	2	5	5	4	3	3	3	2
	4	3	3	3	3	3	5	5	5	5	5	4	4
	PF	F	F	F	F	F	PF	PF	PF	PF	PF	PF	PF
Tuvalu3	2	2	2	2	2	2	2	2	1	1	1	1	1
	2	2	2	2	2	2	2	2	2	2	2	1	1
	F	F	F	F	F*	F	F	F	F	F	F	F	F
Uganda	7	7	7	7	7	6	5	5	4	4	5	5	5
	7	7	7	7	7	6	5	5	5	5	4	4	4
	NF	NF	NF	NF	NF	NF	PF	PF	PF	PF	PF	PF	PF
USSR	6	6	7	7	7	6	6	6	6	7	7	7	7
	6	6	6	6	6	6	7	7	7	7	7	7	6
	NF	NF	NF	NF	NF	NF	NF	NF	NF	NF	NF	NF	NF
United Arab Emirates	7	6	5	5	5	5	5	5	5	5	5	5	5
	5	5	5	5	5	5	5	5	5	5	5	5	5
	NF	NF	PF	PF	PF	PF	PF	PF	PF	PF	PF	PF	PF
United Kingdom	1	1	1	1	1	1	1	1	1	1	1	1	1
	1	1	1	1	1	1	1	1	1	1	1	1	1
	F	F	F	F	F	F	F	F	F	F	F	F	F
United States	1	1	1	1	1	1	1	1	1	1	1	1	1
	1	1	1	1	1	1	1	1	1	1	1	1	1
	F	F	F	F	F	F	F	F	F	F	F	F	F
Uruguay	3	5	6	6	6	6	5	5	5	5	2	2	2
	4	5	6	6	6	6	5	5	4	4	2	2	2
	PF	PF	NF	NF	NF	NF	PF	PF	PF	PF	F	F	F
Vanuatu	4	4	3	3	3	3	2	2	2	2	2	2	2
	3	3	3	3	3	3	3	3	4	4	4	4	4
	PF	PF	PF	PF	PF	PF	F*	F	PF	PF	PF	PF	PF

Table 6 (continued)

Country	73	75	77	78	79	80	81	82	83	84	85	86	87
Venezuela	2	2	1	1	1	1	1	1	1	1	1	1	1
	2	2	2	2	2	2	2	2	2	2	2	2	2
	F	F	F	F	F	F	F	F	F	F	F	F	F
Vietnam[5]			7	7	7	7	7	7	7	7	7	7	6
			7	7	7	7	7	7	6	6	7	7	7
			NF	NF	NF	NF	NF	NF	NF	NF	NF	NF	NF
Western Samoa	4	4	4	4	4	4	4	4	4	4	4	4	4
	2	2	2	2	2	2	3	3	3	3	3	3	3
	PF	PF	PF	PF	PF	PF	PF	PF	PF	PF	PF	PF	PF
Yemen (N)	4	5	6	6	6	6	6	6	6	5	5	5	5
	4	4	5	5	5	5	5	5	5	5	5	5	5
	PF	PF	NF	NF	NF	NF	NF	NF	NF	NF	PF	PF	PF
Yemen (S)	7	7	7	7	7	6	6	6	6	6	6	6	6
	7	7	7	7	7	7	7	7	7	7	7	7	7
	NF	NF	NF	NF	NF	NF	NF	NF	NF	NF	NF	NF	NF
Yugoslavia	6	6	6	6	6	6	6	6	6	6	6	6	6
	6	6	6	5	5	5	5	5	5	5	5	5	5
	NF	NF	NF	NF	NF	NF	NF	NF	PF	PF	PF	PF	PF
Zaire	7	7	7	7	7	6	6	6	6	6	7	7	6
	6	6	6	6	6	6	6	6	6	7	7	7	7
	NF	NF	NF	NF	NF	NF	NF	NF	NF	NF	NF	NF	NF
Zambia	5	5	5	5	5	5	5	5	5	5	5	5	5
	5	4	5	5	5	5	6	6	6	5	5	5	5
	PF	PF	PF	PF	PF	PF	PF	PF	PF	PF	PF	PF	PF
Zimbabwe	6	6	6	6	5	4	3	3	4	4	4	4	5
	5	5	5	5	5	5	4	5	5	5	6	6	6
	NF	NF	NF	NF	PF	PF	PF	PF	PF	PF	PF	PF	PF

65

example. (El Salvador and Guatemala probably should not have been listed as free in 1973. El Salvador may be as free today.)

African democracy has not fared well during these years. In many areas there has been a noticeable decline, especially in countries such as Ghana, Nigeria, Burkina Faso (Upper Volta), and Kenya in which great hopes were placed in the 1970s. In sub-Saharan Africa only Senegal seems to have made progress, and this remains limited. While there has been a very modest resurgence of free institutions in Middle Eastern countries such as Jordan or Egypt, the destruction of Lebanon's democracy will be hard to make up. Further east, India has hung on tenaciously to its freedoms. The people of Sri Lanka have lost freedoms; those of Thailand and Nepal have made some hopeful progress. Now in Southeast Asia, in the arc from Philippines to Korea, there has been a remarkable turn away from authoritarian institutions and toward democracy. We can only hope it continues.

During this period many new democratic states successfully emerged—in the South Pacific from Papua New Guinea to the east, and among the islands of the Caribbean. Yet 1987 saw the crown of this development in the Pacific—Fiji—succumb to an all too familiar military intervention in the name of ethnicity.

Elections and Referendums

Evidence for political freedom is primarily found in the occurrence and nature of elections or referendums. Therefore, as a supplement to our ratings we summarize in the accompanying Table 7 the national elections that we recorded for independent countries since late 1986. One or more elections from earlier in 1986 are included because they were overlooked in last year's annual. The reader should assume that the electoral process appeared comparatively open, fair, and competitive, unless our remarks suggest otherwise; extremely one-sided outcomes also imply an unacceptable electoral process. Voter participation figures have been omitted this year because they are often unobtainable, and when obtainable, highly questionable. Many states compel their citizens to vote; in others it is unclear whether voter participation figures refer to a percentage of those registered or of those of voting age.

TABLE 7

NATIONAL ELECTIONS AND REFERENDUMS

Country Date	Type of Election	Results and Remarks
Albania 2/1/87	legislative	"everyone" voted; only vote against party held invalid
Algeria 2/26/87	legislative	choices allowed within party; 15% of ballots spoiled
Argentina 9/16/87	legislative	opposition wins nationally and regionally in fully open process
Australia 7/11/87	legislative	government margin thinned; 95% vote in compulsory voting system
Bahamas 6/19/87	legislative	government wins easily amid accusations of unfair practices
Central African Rep. 7/31/87	legislative	one party; but choice and little coercion
Comoros 3/22/87	legislative	opposition effectively excluded from rigged exercise
Denmark 9/8/87	legislative	setback for government
Djibouti 4/24/87	general	single list wins, but minor dissent allowed

67

Country Date	Type of Election	Results and Remarks
Egypt		
4/6/87	legislative	government wins overwhelmingly; opposition activity restricted
10/5/87	referendum	referendum on presidency; all parties endorse incumbent
Ethiopia		
2/1/87	referendum	constitution approved easily (but 18% allowed to vote against it)
6/14/87	legislative	limited choice allowed within one-party system
Fiji		
4/12/87	legislative	opposition coalition wins (later annulled by coup)
Finland		
3/15-16/87	legislative	conservative renaissance; communists continue decline
Gambia		
3/11/87	legislative	80% participate; government wins, but opposition gains
Germany (West)		
1/25/87	legislative	government coalition wins; minor partner gains
Haiti		
3/30/87	referendum	constitution approved by large majority
11/29/87	presidential	voting cancelled in mid-course by regime that seemed to endorse violence

Country Date	Type of Election	Results and Remarks
Iceland 4/25/87	legislative	mixed result leads to broad coalition; women's party gains 10% of vote
Indonesia 4/23/87	general	government wins overwhelmingly in controlled process
Ireland 2/17/87	legislative	opposition wins narrowly
Italy 6/14/87	legislative	essentially unchanged; socialists gain at expense of communists
11/7-8/87	referendum	voters approve five complicated measures on nuclear energy and judges
Kiribati 3/12-19/87	legislative	84% participation; roughly even split
5/12/87	presidential	president wins reelection, but eligibility disputed
Korea, South 10/27/87	referendum	massive support for new constitution
Malawi 5/27/87	legislative	single party; slight choice
Malta 5/9/87	legislative	grand compromise makes fair and relatively nonviolent election possible; opposition wins narrowly

Survey: 1987

Country Date	Type of Election	Results and Remarks
Mauritius 8/30/87	legislative	government returned to power in open election
Mongolia 6/22/86	legislative	99.9% approve single list
Nauru 12/6/87	legislative	even division; opposition takes over
1/24/87	legislative	president regains majority
New Zealand 8/16/87	legislative	government (Labour) wins handily
Niger 6/14/87	referendum	97% approve constitution; opposition essentially not allowed
Papua New Guinea 6/13-7/4 /87	legislative	heavily contested; confused result; parties evanescent; PM ultimately regains post
Philippines 2/2/87	referendum	constitution (and president) approved overwhelmingly after intense campaign
5/11/87	legislative	amorphous group of "presidential supporters" takes nearly all seats
Portugal 7/19/87	legislative	governing party wins majority for first time; 72% vote; also election to European parliament

Country Date	Type of Election	Results and Remarks
Poland		
11/29 /87	referendum	voters fail to support government's economic and political plans
St. Lucia		
4/6/87	legislative	government wins by hairthin margin
4/30/87	legislative	new election fails to increase margin; government accepts
Somalia		
12/23/86	presidential	99.9% unopposed exercise
South Africa		
5/6/87	legislative	white-only franchise; government support increases
Suriname		
11/2/87	referendum	constitution approved by large majority
11/25/87	legislative	massive support for old political parties; rejection of military rule
Switzerland		
4/5/87	referendum	overwhelming approval of new restrictions on refugees
10/18/87	legislative	little change; social democrats decline; greens rise
Trinidad and Tobago		
12/15/86	legislative	opposition sweeps election; first change in government since independence

Country Date	Type of Election	Results and Remarks
Transkei 9/25/86	legislative	high turnout; government wins easily, but opposition gains
Togo 12/21/86	presidential	99% vote, and 99.9% approve
Tonga 2/18–19/87	legislative	choice and turnover; but those elected have little power
Turkey 9/6/87	referendum	voters narrowly support lifting ban on former politicians
11/29/87	legislative	fair and open process; government wins, but old parties make partial comeback
United Kingdom 6/11/87	legislative	government wins handily; third party fades
Vietnam 4/19/87	legislative	controlled; but some choice and campaigning
Yemen, South 10/28–30/86	legislative	controlled one party; but some independents elected
Zaire 9/6/87	legislative	limited choice; improved procedures

Although we seldom include non-national elections, they are occasionally more significant than national elections. Recent regional elections in India, France, and Italy come to mind. The reader's attention should also be drawn to the number of referendums that occurred during the year. There seems to be a definite tendency toward letting citizens more directly influence their government through this means.

Political-Economic Systems and Freedom

The accompanying Table 8 (Political and Economic Systems) fills two needs. It offers the reader additional information about the countries we have rated. For example, readers with libertarian views may wish to raise the relative ratings of capitalist countries, while those who place more value on redistributive systems may wish to raise the ratings of countries toward the socialist end of the spectrum. The table also makes possible an analysis of the relation between political and economic forms and the freedom ratings of the Survey. Perusal of the table will show that freedom is directly related to the existence of multiparty systems: the further a country is from such systems, the less freedom it is likely to have. This could be considered a trivial result, since a publicly competitive political system is one of the criteria of freedom, and political parties are considered evidence for such competition. However, the result is not simply determined by our definitions: we searched for evidence of authentic public competition in countries without competitive parties, and seldom found the search rewarded. Both theoretical and empirical studies indicate the difficulty of effective public political opposition in one-party systems.

The relation between economic systems and freedom is more complicated and, because of our lack of emphasis on economic systems in devising our ratings of freedom, is not predetermined by our methods. Historically, the table suggests that there are three types of societies competing for acceptance in the world. The first, or traditional type, is marginal and in retreat, but its adherents have borrowed political and economic bits and pieces from both the other types. The second and third, the Euro-American and Sino-Soviet types, are strongest near their points of

73

TABLE 8

POLITICAL SYSTEM:	Multiparty			Dominant-Party
	centralized		decentralized	
ECONOMIC SYSTEM: **Capitalist** inclusive	Antigua & Bar. F Bahamas F Barbados F Belize F Colombia[4] F Costa Rica F Cyprus (G) F Cyprus (T) F Dominica F Dom. Rep.[4] F El Salvador[1/3] PF	Iceland F Ireland F Japan F Luxembourg F Mauritius F New Zealand[3] F St.Lucia F St.Vincent[3] F Spain[3] F Suriname[1] PF	Australia F Belgium F Canada F Germany(W)[3] F Lebanon PF St.Kitts-Nev. F Switzerland F United States F	Malaysia PF
non- inclusive	Ecuador F Guatemala[1] PF Honduras[1/4] PF	Thailand[1] PF	Botswana F Papua New Guinea F Solomons[2] F	Gambia[4] PF Liberia[1] PF Transkei PF
Capitalist- Statist inclusive	Argentina F Grenada F Italy F Jamaica[3] F Korea (S)[1] PF	Panama[1] PF South Africa PF Sri Lanka PF Turkey[1/4] PF Venezuela F	Brazil[3/4] F Trinidad & Tobago F	China(Taiwan) PF Mexico PF
non- inclusive	Bolivia F Morocco[3] PF Pakistan[1/2] PF Peru[4] F	Philippines F	India F Vanuatu PF	Bangladesh[1] PF Indonesia[1/4] PF Iran[2/4] PF Paraguay[1/3/4] PF
Mixed Capitalist inclusive	Austria F Denmark F Finland F France F Greece F Israel F Malta F	Netherlands F Norway F Portugal F Sudan[5] PF Sweden F U.K.[3] F Uruguay F		Egypt[1/3/4] PF Nicaragua PF Senegal[3/4] PF Singapore PF Tunisia[4] PF Zimbabwe[5] PF
Mixed Socialist inclusive				Guyana PF Syria[1/4] NF
non- inclusive				Madagascar[1/2] PF
Socialist inclusive				
non- inclusive	Notes to the Table 1. Under heavy military influence or domination. (All countries in the Nonparty Military column are military dominated.) 2. Party relationships anomalous. 3. Close decision along capitalist-to-socialist continuum. 4. Close decision on inclusive/noninclusive dimension. 5. Noninclusive.			

POLITICAL-ECONOMIC SYSTEMS

One-Party			Non-Party	
socialist	communist	nationalist	military	nonmilitary
		Djibouti NF	Chile[3] PF	Jordan[2/3/4] PF Western Samoa[2/4] PF
Sierra Leone[1] PF		Cameroon[3] NF Comoros NF Gabon NF Ct. d'Ivoire[4] PF Kenya NF Malawi NF	Chad NF Fiji[4] PF Haiti PF Lesotho PF Niger NF Yemen (N) PF	Bhutan[3] PF Maldives PF Nepal[3] PF Swaziland PF Tonga PF Tuvalu F
			Ghana NF Nigeria[3/4] PF	Bahrain PF Brunei PF Kuwait PF Nauru F Qatar PF Saudi Arabia NF Un. Arab Emirs PF
		Zaire[1] NF Central Afr. Rep.[3] NF	Eq. Guinea[3] NF Mauritania NF Uganda[3] PF	Kiribati F Oman NF
Burundi[1/5] NF			Guinea[5] NF	
Libya[1/2/3] NF Seychelles[3] NF	China (M)[3] NF Poland[1] PF Yugoslavia[3] PF			
Burma[1] NF Cape V.I.[3/4] PF Congo[1/3] NF Somalia[1/3] NF Zambia[3] PF		Mali[1] NF Rwanda[1/3] NF Togo[1] NF	Burkina Faso NF	
Algeria[1] NF Sao Tome & Prin.[3/4] NF	Albania NF Bulgaria NF Cuba NF Czecho- slovakia NF Germany(E) NF	Hungary[3] PF Korea (N) NF Mongolia NF Romania NF USSR NF Vietnam NF		
Angola NF Benin[1/3] NF Guinea- Bissau[1/3] NF Iraq[3/4] NF Mozambique NF Tanzania NF Yemen (S)[1] NF	Afghanistan NF Cambodia NF Ethiopia[1] NF Laos NF			

origin, but have spread by diffusion and active propagation all over the world. The Leninist-socialist style of political organization was exported along with the socialist concept of economic organization, just as constitutional democracy was exported along with capitalist economic concepts. In this interpretation, the relation of economic systems to freedom found in the table may be an expression of historical chance rather than necessary relationships. Clearly, capitalism does not cause nations to be politically free, nor does socialism cause them to be politically unfree.[2] Still, socialists must be concerned by the empirical relationship between the rating of "not free" and socialism that is found in tables such as this.

The table shows economies roughly grouped in categories from "capitalist" to "socialist." Labeling economies as capitalist or socialist has a fairly clear significance in the developed world, but its usefulness may be doubted in labeling the mostly poor and largely agrarian societies of the third world in this manner. However, third world states with dual economies, that is, with a modern sector and a preindustrial sector, have economic policies or goals that can be placed along the continuum from socialist to capitalist. A socialist third world state usually has nationalized all of the modern sector—except possibly some foreign investment—and claims central government jurisdiction over the land and its products, with only temporary assignment of land to individuals or cooperatives. The capitalist third world state has a capitalist modern sector and a traditionalist agricultural sector, combined in some cases with new agricultural projects either on family farm or agribusiness models. Third world economies that fall between capitalist and socialist do not have the high taxes of their industrialized equivalents in the first world, but they have major nationalized industries (for example, oil) in the modern sector, and their agricultural world may include emphasis on cooperatives or large-scale land reform, as well as more traditional forms.

The terms inclusive and noninclusive are used to distinguish between societies in which the economic activities of most people are organized in accordance with the dominant system and those dual societies in which fifty percent or more of the population remain largely outside.

States with inclusive capitalist forms are generally developed states that rely on the operation of the market and private provision for industrial welfare. Taxes may be high, but they are not confiscatory, while government interference is generally limited to subsidy and regulation. States classified as noninclusive capitalist, such as Liberia or Thailand, have not over fifty percent of the population included in a capitalist modern economy, with the remainder of the population still living traditionally. In these the traditional economy may be individual, communal, or feudal, but the direction of change as development proceeds is capitalistic.

Capitalist states grade over into capitalist-statist or mixed capitalist-states. Capitalist-statist countries are those, such as Brazil, Turkey, or Saudi Arabia, that have very large government productive enterprises, either because of an elitist development philosophy or major dependence on a key resource such as oil. Government interferes in the economy in a major way in such states, but not primarily because of egalitarian motives. Mixed capitalist systems, such as those in Israel, the Netherlands, or Sweden, provide social services on a large scale through governmental or other nonprofit institutions, with the result that private control over property is sacrificed to egalitarian purposes. These nations still see capitalism as legitimate, but its legitimacy is accepted grudgingly by many in government. Mixed socialist states, such as Syria or Poland, proclaim themselves to be socialist but in fact allow rather large portions of the economy to remain in the private domain.

Socialist economies, on the other hand, strive programmatically to place an entire national economy under direct or indirect government control. States such as the USSR or Cuba may allow some modest private productive property, but this is only by exception, and rights to such property can be revoked at any time. The leaders of noninclusive socialist states have the same goals as the leaders of inclusive socialist states, but their relatively primitive economies or peoples have not yet been effectively included in the socialist system. Such states generally have a small socialized modern economy and a large preindustrial economy in which the organization of production and trade is still largely traditional. It should be understood that the characterizations in the table are impressionistic; the continuum between capitalist and socialist economies is necessarily cut arbitrarily into categories for this presentation.

Political systems range from democratic multiparty to absolutist one-party systems. Theoretically, the most democratic countries should be those with decentralized multiparty systems, for here important powers are held by the people at two or more levels of the political system, and dissent is legitimated and mobilized by opposition parties. More common are centralized multiparty systems, such as France or Japan, in which the central government organizes lower levels of government primarily for reasons of efficiency. Dominant-party systems allow the forms of democracy, but structure the political process so that opposition groups do not have a realistic chance of achieving power. They often face censorship, vote fraud, imprisonment, or other impediments.

The now classical form of one-party rule is that in states such as the USSR or Vietnam that proclaim themselves to be communist. The slightly larger group of socialist one-party states are ruled by elites that use Marxist-Leninist rhetoric, organize ruling parties very much along communist lines, but either do not have the disciplined organization of communist states or have explicitly rejected one or another aspect of communism. A final group of nationalist one-party states adopts the political form popularized by the communists (and the fascists in the last generation), but the leaders generally reject the revolutionary ideologies of socialist or communist states and fail to develop the totalitarian controls that characterize those states. There are several borderline states that might be switched between socialist and nationalist categories (for example, Libya). "Socialist" is used here to designate a political rather than economic system. A socialist "vanguard party" established along Marxist-Leninist lines will almost surely develop a socialist economy, but a state with a socialist economy need not be ruled by a vanguard party. It should be pointed out that the totalitarian-libertarian continuum is not directly reflected by the categorization in this table.

Nonparty systems can be democratic, as in the small island of Nauru, but generally they are not. Nepal's nonparty system is one of the most democratic of attempts to establish such systems. Other nonparty systems may be nonmilitary nonparty systems such as Tonga or Saudi Arabia, or military nonparty systems, such as that in Niger.

TABLE 9

SOCIAL AND ECONOMIC COMPARISONS*

	GNP[1] per Person	Under 5[1] Mortality per 1000	Adult[1] Literacy per 100	Pol/Civ Ratings (1-7)
Afghanistan[3/4]	200	330	24	7/7
Albania	950	52	75	7/7
Algeria	2500	117	50	6/6
Angola[2/3]	500	242	41	7/7
Antigua & Barbuda	2000	32	89	2/3
Argentina	2100	40	96	2/1
Australia	10850	11	100	1/1
Austria	9100	13	100	1/1
Bahamas	7000	30	89	2/3
Bahrain	10500	35	72	5/5
Bangladesh	150	196	33	4/5
Barbados	4600	16	98	1/1
Belgium	9000	13	100	1/1
Belize	1100	23	91	1/1
Benin	270	193	26	7/7
Bhutan	150	206	18	5/5
Bolivia	500	184	74	2/3
Botswana	900	99	71	2/3
Brazil	1900	91	78	2/2
Brunei	20000	14	80	6/5
Bulgaria	5690	21	96	7/7
Burkina Faso	150	245	13	7/6
Burma	180	91	78	7/7
Burundi	230	200	34	7/6
Cambodia	75	216	75	7/7
Cameroon	800	162	56	6/6
Canada	13000	10	100	1/1
Cape Verde	400	95	50	5/6
Central African Rep.	270	232	41	6/6
Chad	80	232	26	6/7
Chile	1800	26	97	6/5
China (Mainland)	370	50	69	6/6

	GNP per Person	Under 5 Mortality per 1000	Adult Literacy per 100	Pol/Civ Ratings (1-7)
China (Taiwan)	2800	9	92	5/4
Colombia	1350	72	88	2/3
Comoros	300	135	48	6/6
Congo	1000	122	63	7/6
Costa Rica	1250	25	94	1/1
Cote d'Ivoire	620	157	43	6/5
Cuba	1600	19	96	6/6
Cyprus (G)	3700	17	89	1/2
Cyprus (T)	na	na	na	2/3
Czechoslovakia	7000	17	100	7/6
Denmark	11000	10	100	1/1
Djibouti	480	257	12	6/6
Dominica	1100	30	80	2/2
Dominican Republic	900	88	77	1/3
Ecuador	1150	92	82	2/3
Egypt	700	136	45	5/4
El Salvador[2]	710	91	72	3/4
Equatorial Guinea	180	223	37	7/7
Ethiopia	130	257	11	6/7
Fiji	1800	34	86	6/5
Finland	10800	8	100	1/2
France	9800	11	99	1/2
Gabon	3500	178	62	6/6
Gambia	250	292	25	3/3
Germany (E)	8000	13	100	7/6
Germany (W)	10900	12	100	1/2
Ghana	380	153	53	7/6
Greece	3900	18	92	2/2
Grenada	900	20	50	2/1
Guatemala	1200	109	55	3/3
Guinea	330	259	28	7/6
Guinea-Bissau	180	232	31	6/7
Guyana	580	41	96	5/5
Haiti	340	180	38	6/5
Honduras	730	116	59	2/3
Hungary[3]	5000	21	99	5/4

	GNP per Person	Under 5 Mortality per 1000	Adult Literacy per 100	Pol/Civ Ratings (1-7)
Iceland	11000	7	100	1/1
India	250	158	44	2/3
Indonesia	540	126	74	5/6
Iran[3]	3500	162	51	5/6
Iraq	1900	100	47	7/7
Ireland	4800	12	100	1/1
Israel	5000	16	95	2/2
Italy	6500	13	97	1/1
Jamaica	1000	25	92	2/2
Japan	11300	9	100	1/1
Jordan	1600	65	75	5/5
Kenya	300	121	59	6/6
Kiribati	460	100	100	1/2
Korea (N)	1000	35	90	7/7
Korea (S)	2100	35	92	4/4
Kuwait	16000	25	70	6/5
Laos	200	170	84	7/7
Lebanon	1600	56	77	6/5
Lesotho	500	144	74	5/6
Liberia	470	215	35	5/5
Libya	8000	130	66	6/6
Luxembourg	13000	11	100	1/1
Madagascar	250	97	68	5/5
Malawi	180	275	41	6/7
Malaysia	2000	38	73	3/5
Maldives	300	91	82	5/6
Mali	140	302	17	7/6
Malta	3400	14	81	1/2
Mauritania	425	223	17	6/6
Mauritius	1100	32	83	2/2
Mexico	2000	73	90	4/4
Mongolia	1000	64	90	7/7
Morocco[2]	650	130	33	4/5
Mozambique[2]	360	252	17	6/7
Nauru	19000	38	99	2/2
Nepal	160	206	26	3/4
Netherlands	9200	10	100	1/1

	GNP per Person	Under 5 Mortality per 1000	Adult Literacy per 100	Pol/Civ Ratings (1-7)
New Zealand	7300	14	100	1/1
Nicaragua[2]	850	104	85	5/5
Niger	200	237	14	7/6
Nigeria	760	182	43	6/5
Norway	13900	10	100	1/1
Oman	7000	172	30	6/6
Pakistan	380	174	30	4/5
Panama	2000	35	88	5/5
Papua New Guinea	720	94	45	2/2
Paraguay	1000	61	88	5/6
Peru	1000	133	85	2/3
Philippines	650	78	86	2/2
Poland[3]	4500	21	100	5/5
Portugal	2000	22	85	1/2
Qatar	18000	43	51	5/5
Romania[3]	3500	31	97	7/7
Rwanda	290	214	47	6/6
St. Kitts-Nevis	1500	36	92	1/2
St. Lucia	1200	22	60	1/2
St. Vincent	900	33	84	1/2
Sao Tome & Principe	320	80	60	7/7
Saudi Arabia[2]	10000	101	30	6/7
Senegal	380	231	28	3/4
Seychelles[2]	2500	20	57	6/6
Sierra Leone	370	302	29	5/5
Singapore	7400	12	86	4/5
Solomon Islands	600	50	50	2/2
Somalia[2]	270	257	12	7/7
South Africa[2/3]	2300	104	46	5/6
Spain	4500	12	95	1/2
Sri Lanka	350	48	87	3/4
Sudan[2]	350	187	25	4/5
Suriname	3000	41	90	4/4
Swaziland	800	182	68	5/6
Sweden	11800	8	100	1/1

	GNP per Person	Under 5 Mortality per 1000	Adult Literacy per 100	Pol/Civ Ratings (1-7)
Switzerland	16000	9	100	1/1
Syria[2]	1600	71	60	6/7
Tanzania[2]	260	183	80	6/6
Thailand	825	55	91	3/3
Togo	250	160	41	6/6
Tonga[2]	1000	28	90	5/3
Transkei	na	na	na	5/6
Trinidad & Tobago	6500	26	96	1/1
Tunisia	1300	110	54	6/5
Turkey	1130	104	74	2/4
Tuvalu	700	40	95	1/1
Uganda[2]	300	178	57	5/4
USSR	7400	29	99	7/6
United Arab Emirates	20000	43	71	5/5
United Kingdom	8500	12	100	1/1
United States[2]	16400	13	96	1/1
Uruguay	1700	32	94	2/2
Vanuatu[2/4]	800	100	10	2/4
Venezuela	3400	45	88	1/2
Vietnam	200	98	90	6/7
Western Samoa	700	50	98	4/3
Yemen (N)[2]	550	210	10	5/5
Yemen (S)[2]	550	210	40	6/7
Yugoslavia[2]	2200	31	90	6/5
Zaire[2]	170	170	61	6/7
Zambia	450	135	70	5/5
Zimbabwe	700	121	75	5/6

Notes to the Table

1. Aside from the Political/Civil ratings based on the Comparative Survey (Table 1), the sources for the table data were UNICEF, **Statistics on Children in UNICEF Assisted Countries** (New York: 1987); UNICEF, **The State of the World's Children** (New York: 1987); Population Reference Bureau, **1987 World Population Data Sheet** (Washington: 1987); **1987 Britannica Book of the Year,** "World Data," pages 577ff. and 812ff.

2. The literacy figure for this country is questionable or incomparable.

3. The GNP for this country is questionable or incomparable.

4. The mortality rates for this country are questionable.

In this yearbook Table 9 (Social and Economic Comparisons) is introduced to help the reader relate the discussion of political and civil liberties to the more standard measures by which countries are compared. The table offers three measures of social and economic health alongside the Survey ratings. The measures are GNP/Capita, under five mortality, and literacy. In gathering the data an attempt was made among a wealth of conflicting data to give a reasonable figure for each country. In many cases the data are doubtful either because the figures have not actually been gathered, or because of political considerations. It seems most unlikely, for example, that the under five mortality rates for North and South Yemen are exactly the same, or those for North and South Korea. But variations among countries with different systems, and at different levels of development, are so extreme that precision is not necessary for understanding, or searching for, the major relationships.

The measures chosen are those that seem to offer the best available quantitative evidence for the presence or absence of economic and social growth on the one hand, and the extension of the results of this growth fairly over a population on the other. If a country with a relatively high GNP/Capita does relatively poorly in providing health services and nutrition for its young (and the under five rate serves as an indicator for performance here), or allows its population to remain unlettered, then we can rightly question the desirability of its institutions. If it is a democracy, we can question whether the formal institutions of democracy are actually working as they should to give the majority of the people a means to pursue their interests. Offering this table here is particularly appropriate, for it offers a background to the discussion of these issues from other viewpoints in Part IV below.

Conclusion

Important gains for freedom were again evident in 1987. In East Asia several societies seemed to vie with one another in their efforts to become a part of the modern world, with its expected respect for political, civil, religious, personal, and economic freedom. The Philippines continued its rapid return to democracy. Taiwan took a major step toward freedom through both political

84

and civil liberalization. South Korea's military leaders and their democratic opponents, faced with the opportunity of the forthcoming Olympic Games and the threat of continuing urban violence, made a strong move to establish a democratic system. Whether they will carry through on their initiatives remains to be seen, but this time, and in this context, there is hope. Freedom did not advance in mainland China this year, but past advances were largely maintained, and the shift to younger, more cosmopolitan leadership was encouraging.

The maintenance of the Chinese advance was supported ideologically by the more general changes that have been infecting Marxist-Leninist regimes almost everywhere. The moderation of oppression in the Soviet Union and Eastern Europe was echoed in many other communist or one-party socialist states. Often changes went no further than verbalisms, or acceptance of more pragmatic economic policies. But this openness to the world seemed to be a herald of other changes. Of course, repression and the terrors of massive human rights violations continued to stalk much of the world, particularly in the Middle East and Africa. And many of the gains that have been made for democracy in the last few years remain endangered, particularly in still fragile, new democracies or near-democracies such as Ecuador, Peru, Brazil, Philippines, Thailand, Honduras, Guatemala, or El Salvador. Missteps in these states would bring the military back to power—as would missteps in the process of bringing democracy to Haiti, Suriname, or South Korea.

On a smaller scale we must also not forget that the year saw the destruction of democracy in Fiji. This not only affected the Fijians, but also the peoples of many other small Polynesian, Melanesian, and Micronesian states with new or emerging democracies. Many people in the South Pacific have looked to Fiji as the state in their region with the most stable and effective institutions, a state that was more able than its neighbors to play an international as well as regional role. The collapse of this role-model cannot be taken lightly.

NOTES

1. For further details on the methods and criteria used in the Survey see the foregoing chapter on definitions and criteria.

2. See Lindsay M. Wright, "A Comparative Survey of Economic Freedoms," in R. D. Gastil, **Freedom in the World: Political Rights and Civil Liberties, 1982** (Westport, Connecticut: Greenwood Press, 1982), pages. 51-90.

PART II

Parallel Surveys of Freedom

CIVIL AND POLITICAL LIBERTIES IN THE WORLD:

A GEOGRAPHICAL ANALYSIS

Thomas D. Anderson*

The amount of freedom enjoyed by individuals varies widely among the countries of the world. This complexity of conditions has many causes, including ideological differences concerning just what constitutes freedom. Disagreement exists even among scholars with similar viewpoints over the problems of how to classify and measure levels of freedom. Such impediments notwithstanding the subject has a broad popular interest and is a common basis for distinguishing one government from another. In order to provide a rational basis for such perceptions I have devised a system that allows all sovereign states to be ranked on the basis of the degree of personal liberty present in each in mid-1986. In a multi-authored volume devoted to the Third World this effort adds yet another perspective and set of comparisons.

The personal liberties treated here are part of a broader concept of human rights. The initial world standard in this regard was the Universal Declaration of Human Rights passed by the United Nations General Assembly on December 10, 1948. This document of thirty articles and thirty sub-articles is comprehensive, yet constitutes merely a statement of worthy principles. Toward the purpose of establishing a legal basis for compliance by all ratifying states it was divided and passed by the General Assembly in the form of treaty provisions in 1976. These two documents are the International Covenant on Civil and Political Rights and the International Covenant on Economic, Social, and Cultural Rights.[1]

---

* This chapter is taken from a forthcoming book, James Norwine and Alfonso Gonzales, eds. The Third World: States of Mind and Being (London: Allen and Unwin, 1988). Dr. Anderson is Professor of Geography at Bowling Green State University.

Controversy regarding human rights issues centers mainly on the relative significance of the content of these two covenants. The emphasis in First World (Western) countries is on the importance of civil and political liberties, whereas Second World (Eastern) and many Third World governments profess a primary concern with economic and social goals. Philosophically the roots are, respectively, with the concept of the natural rights of man versus that of a naturally harmonious society which is the intellectual foundation of Marxism. In short, should government primarily protect individual or collective rights? A recent critique of these two positions from the perspective of East European scholars is by Drygalski and Kwasniewski.[2]

Domestic critics of the Western stance, however, often employ sophisms such as "other cultures have different views of freedom" or "hungry people don't care about civil and political rights." These are ethnocentric arguments that my own geographical research finds unpersuasive, especially when valid examples are not cited. There is, for example, slight evidence that a social justice that does not include individual justice is adopted willingly by most of the world's peoples.

The emphasis here is on the word "willingly". Fundamental to the Western concept of civil and political rights is the notion of choice. Choice in turn encompasses individual decisions expressed periodically in collective fashion (contested elections), a diffusion of government power (checks and balances), and the mutability of the government policy in response to popular will (referendum). Inextricably bound up with the notion of choice are open expression of ideas and unfettered movement. In my view denial of any of these elements constitutes infringement of basic rights regardless of the excuses offered.

Disputes about the central content of human rights can convey the impression that the two segments are antagonistic in purpose. Yet on the assumption that social justice includes the non-discriminatory provision of such needs as food, shelter, employment, education, and old-age security, one finds that it has been achieved in countries that also protect civil and political liberties. Successful examples include but are not limited to New Zealand, Japan, and the Scandinavian countries. On the other hand, governments that proclaim a principal concern with collective rights do no better in social and economic areas and very much worse with respect to civil and political liberties. Examples here are Poland, Cuba, East Germany, North Korea, Libya, and Singapore.

The Democratic Revolution

The classification scheme used here has evolved gradually from one first devised in 1976. The focus is on civil and political liberties, but criteria more concise than those of the United Nations are employed. It is based on the concept of the Democratic Revolution as articulated by Preston E. James. James, in turn, took the term and many ideas from the work of Palmer.[3] Identified are six elements, each of which represent radical changes in the status of the individual relative to the power of the state. Oppression by rulers is an ancient condition of mankind, only its form and justifications have changed in modern times. On the other hand, legally-protected personal rights on a mass scale are little over two centuries old.

James' six elements are as follows: (1) the individual is accorded equal treatment before the law; (2) the individual is protected from arbitrary acts of those in authority; (3) the individual has the right to be represented where taxes are levied or law formulated; (4) the principle of majority rule and use of the secret ballot are accepted; (5) the rights of free access to knowledge and open discussion of policy issues are accepted; (6) the individual can exercise freedom of choice; he has the right to take a job or leave it, to move from one place to another, to express religious convictions in any way he wishes—he possesses a revolutionary new right, the right to resign.[4]

This emphasis on personal rights is not meant to belittle the importance of economic and social needs; their provision is essential to the maintenance of a society. Rather the liberating values of the Democratic Revolution raise the quality of human existence above that of a well-run military unit or slave plantation, indeed, that of an animal farm.

As a response to those who may protest that these are Western European ideas imposed on other cultures, I offer the words of Chief Joseph of the Nez Perce American Indian nation over a century ago:

> Let me be a free man—free to travel, free to stop, free
> to work, free to trade where I choose, free to choose
> my own teachers, free to follow the religion of my
> fathers, free to think and talk and act for myself—and I
> will obey every law or submit to the penalty.[5]

Although the elegant phrasing reflects his own genius, the non-literate Chief Joseph merely expressed the traditional values of his people. It seems clear that the idea that an individual has worth and a right to choose was not a uniquely European concept.

The following indicators were used to apply James' six elements. They derive in part from personal perceptions and in part from Lipset:[6] (1) Did the current national leadership gain power by legal means, and are there one or more recognized sets of leaders attempting to gain office by the same political process?; (2) Is there an accepted legal procedure by means of which current national leaders may be removed from office or their replacements selected upon death or resignation?; (3) Do the public media openly distribute views from domestic and foreign sources that are at variance with official policy, and is news of national events, favorable and unfavorable, freely available inside and outside the country?; (4) Are the inhabitants allowed to move freely within the country and to emigrate and return if they choose? A related aspect is the level of restrictions placed on foreigners who wish to leave or enter the country.; (5) Do the country's courts make rulings against the national government, and are such rulings respected?; (6) Are there present a number of organizations not under direct state control with which inhabitants may openly affiliate if they choose?

The thrust of these indicators is to assess the opportunities for the peaceful transfer of political power, the expression of alternative views, and freedom of movement. These rights were deemed prerequisite to the function of other human rights. Restriction of movement, for example, is what most distinguishes the life of a convict from those not imprisoned. In a related sense, if reporters are not permitted to seek out and publicize details about economic, civil, political, and social conditions, how else is a society to learn about them? Surely government pronouncements are not reliable sources of news. Few North Americans accept at face value all claims by their own public officials. Why then should they not reserve judgment on unverified versions of reality by those in power in other countries?

Based on the elements of the Democratic Revolution and the supplementary indicators listed above, six categories were devised for the classification of all countries. They are:

I. Countries where all elements of individual rights are specified by law and presently are extended to all inhabitants without restriction.

II. Countries where all elements of individual rights are specified by law, but are not extended uniformly to some minorities, often due to residual prejudice.

III. Countries where most of the elements of individual rights are specified by law, but where access by many inhabitants to one or more rights is inhibited by law, custom, or arbitrary authority.

IV. Countries where most of the elements of individual rights are restricted by law, custom, or arbitrary authority, but where at least one such element is available to nearly all inhabitants.

V. Countries where none of the elements of individual rights is available due to law, custom, or arbitrary authority, but where effective political organization provides social and economic stability.

VI. Countries where the status of most inhabitants, with respect to all individual rights, is insecure even where specified by law due to the capricious exercise of absolute authority or a near absence of civil organization resulting from disruptive political, social, or economic conditions.

These categories include two distinctive features. One is the attention to all inhabitants of a state. Many countries contain large numbers of resident aliens. To exclude such people from the political process is a morally and legally defensible practice. But discriminatory treatment in areas of civil liberties was viewed as an infringement of human rights.

A concern for discrimination in ethnically and racially diverse countries also is a part in that the role of tradition was considered. The term custom is used to identify cultural inertia where its presence inhibits the rights of some segments of a society. As has been demonstrated in the United States, Canada, and India, passage of legislation that mandates equal treatment regardless of ethnicity does not necessarily alter established attitudes.

Country Rankings

The ranking of each country was a difficult task. Verified information was used to the greatest extent possible, yet often the final choice rested on intuitive judgment tempered by long experience. Known conditions were balanced and trends considered. In several instances countries with comparable circumstances were placed in different categories based on perceptions of progress or retrogression. An unavoidable shortcoming is the fact that bias-free information for many areas is incomplete or conflicting, and it is contemporary. Even in countries for which data are accurate, a sudden change in policy may alter human rights circumstances.

Information came from a diversity of sources, with newspapers a vital means of monitoring change. The World Factbook issued regularly by the Central Intelligence Agency is a solid resource for background data.[7] Comparable but different ratings systems also were gleaned. These were Humana's World Human Rights Guide[8], the U.S. Department of State's Country Reports on Human Rights Practices[9], and Freedom in the World: Political Rights and Civil Liberties, 1985-86[10]. The latter is prepared annually by Raymond D. Gastil for Freedom House and is of exceptional value for this purpose. My own ratings conform closely with those of Gastil despite differences in criteria and categories. Agreement was not total.

Brief Analysis of Country Ratings

Space permits only selective explanation and analysis. In Scandinavia, for example, Iceland and Denmark are ranked higher than Norway and Sweden not due to superior virtue but because of greater ethnic homogeneity. They have no native Sammi (Lapps). Finland's still lower rank reflects its geopolitical decision to allow Soviet sensibilities to inhibit a full range of political expression. This sort of self-censorship is hardly repression but is not full freedom either.

Most of these countries, often termed collectively the Free World, were placed in Category II in order to highlight imperfections. In nearly all these states widespread civil and political liberties are not shared equally by various racial or ethnic minorities. The unassimilated elements consist of either or both indigenous peoples and recent immigrants.

At the low end of the scale the human condition is as much uncertain as deplorable. Past despots such as Idi Amin and Pol Pot are out of power, but the Soviet invasion of Afghanistan continued. The near anarchy of civil strife in Lebanon seems endless. Personal restraints in countries ranked in Category V may be greater than in Category VI, but they are predictable and are administered efficiently.

Category IV includes a number of obvious dictatorships and feudal monarchies. However, at least one leavening freedom was distinguished in each. In many the key freedom was the right to emigrate and to return. It is the feature that most differentiates Yugoslavia from other communist-ruled East European countries, for example. Apartheid in South Africa is a despicable policy that restricts all races in some way. Nevertheless, a steady flow of people cross its borders in both directions, and opposition figures are both free from prison and quoted in the media.

All communist-governed countries are ranked in the lower half, a decision based on performance. Each practices the Leninist principle of democratic centralism which makes impermissible the espousal of alternative views. The resultant repression effectively rejects all tenets of the Democratic Revolution. On the other hand, Hungary, Poland, and Yugoslavia are ranked higher not because they are less socialist, but because they permit greater personal freedom.

TABLE 10

RANKING OF COUNTRIES BY CIVIL AND POLITICAL LIBERTIES

I.
Austria	Denmark	Luxembourg
Barbados	Iceland	New Zealand*
Costa Rica*	Ireland	Switzerland*

II.
Antigua-Barbuda*	France	Portugal
Argentina	Germany, West	**St. Kitts-Nevis**
Australia	Greece	**St. Lucia**
Bahamas	**Grenada**	**St. Vincent**
*Belgium	Italy	**Solomon Islands**
Belize	**Jamaica**	Spain
Botswana*	Japan	Sweden
Canada	**Kiribati**	**Trinidad-Tobago**
Colombia*	**Mauritius**	**Tuvalu**
Cyprus (G)	**Nauru**	United Kingdom
Dominica	*Netherlands	U.S.A.
Dominican Republic	Norway	**Venezuela**
Fiji	**Papua New Guinea**	

III.
Bolivia	Israel	**Sierra Leone**
Brazil	**Kuwait**	**Singapore**
Comoro Islands*	**Malaysia**	**Sri Lanka**
Cyprus (T)	**Maldives***	**Thailand**
*Ecuador	**Malta**	**Tonga**
El Salvador	**Mexico**	**Tunisia**
Egypt	**Morocco**	**Turkey**
Finland	**Nepal**	*Uruguay
Guatemala	**Panama**	**Vanuatu**
Guyana*	**Peru**	**Western Samoa**
*Honduras	**Philippines**	
India	**Senegal**	

Third and Fourth World countries are shown in darker type.
Ratings are for conditions as of May 20, 1986.
*Indicates that placement in adjacent category was considered.

TABLE 10 (Continued)

IV.
Algeria	Ivory Coast	Saudi Arabia
*Bahrain	Jordan	South Africa
Bangladesh	*Kenya	Sudan
*Bhutan	*Korea, South	Swaziland
Burkino Faso	Lesotho	Syria*
Chile	Liberia	Tanzania*
China (Taiwan)	Madagascar	Transkei
Djibouti*	Malawi*	Uganda
Ghana*	Mozambique*	United Arab Em's.
Guinea	Nicaragua	Yemen, North
Guinea-Bissau*	Nigeria	Yugoslavia
Haiti	Pakistan	Zambia
Hungary	Paraguay	*Zimbabwe
Indonesia	Poland	
Iran	Qatar	

V.
Albania	Cuba	Niger
Angola	Czechoslovakia	*Oman
Benin	Equatorial Guinea	Romania
Bulgaria	*Gabon	Rwanda
Burma	Germany, East	Sao Tome & Prin.
Burundi	Ethiopia*	*Seychelles
Cambodia	Iraq	Somalia
Cameroon	Korea, North	Suriname
Cape Verde	Laos	*Togo
Central African Rep.	*Libya	U.S.S.R.
Chad	Mali	Vietnam
*China	Mauritania	Yemen, South
Congo	Mongolia	Zaire

VI.
Afghanistan
Lebanon

Several generalizations seem appropriate. Of the 165 countries, 81 are ranked in the upper half. Most of these are in Western Europe, the Americas, and the Southwest Pacific. As a continent the peoples of Africa are the least free and those of North America the most free. Indeed, only a few repressive governments were in power in the entire Western Hemisphere in mid-1986. Thirty-one of the countries ranked in the upper half had historic links with the British Empire, a total that does not include Israel, Egypt, or the United Kingdom. With no apology for past British imperialism, clearly its impact included more than just merchants, missionaries, and mischief. Similarly the democracies in West Germany and Japan resulted directly from the policies of Western occupation forces after World War II.

The ranks of some countries calls into question the assumption that functioning democracy demands a highly literate population and an advanced economy. Even though most of the freest societies meet such criteria, many others do not. Striking exceptions are places like Botswana, Papua New Guinea, and the Solomon Islands. Others with somewhat more advanced circumstances are Barbados, Belize, Costa Rica, India, and Venezuela. This evidence suggests that the premise that mass access to civil and political freedoms is a feature only of Europeanized, middle-latitude countries does not accord with reality.[11]

This incomplete and personalized version of the patterns of personal freedom in the world is intended as much to provoke thought as to provide information. Because it rates all sovereign states on the same scale, it highlights diversity within the Third World as well as contrasts between Third World and more advanced countries. Inevitably political events will invalidate some of the assessments shown here. Yet, if this effort fosters greater awareness of the vital human issues involved, it will have achieved its main purpose.

NOTES

1. U.S. Department of State, **Human Rights.** Selected Documents, N. 5 (revised) (Washington, DC: U.S. Government Printing Office, 1978).

2. Drygalski, J. and J. Kwasniewski, "Harmonious Society Versus Conflict-Ridden Society: Marxism and Liberalism," in Adjit Jain, Alexander Matejko, eds. **A Critique of Marxist and Non-Marxist Thought** (New York: Praeger, 1986), pages 259-281.

3. James, P. E., **One World Divided,** 2nd edition (Lexington, MA: Xerox College Publishing, 1974), pages 29-31; Palmer, R. R. **The Challenge,** Vol. I, **The Age of the Democratic Revolution** (Princeton, NJ: Princeton University Press, 1959).

4. James, **One World Divided,** page 2.

5. Chief Joseph, as printed in the **North American Review,** April 1879.

6. Lipset, S., **Political Man: The Social Basis of Politics** (Garden City, NY: Anchor Books, 1963), page 27.

7. Central Intelligence Agency, **The World Factbook** (Washington, DC: U.S. Government Printing Office, 1983).

8. Humana, C., **World Human Rights Guide** (New York: PICA Press, 1984).

9. U.S. Department of State, **Country Reports on Human Rights Practices** (Washington, DC: U.S. Government Printing Office, 1985).

10. Gastil, R. D., **Freedom in the World: Political Rights and Civil Liberties 1985-86** (Westport, Ct.: Greenwood Press, 1986)

11. MacPherson, C.B., **The Life and Times of Liberal Democracy** (New York: Oxford University Press, 1977). Many writers express this attitude but few so clearly as MacPherson, especially pages 6-7.

A SCALE OF POLYARCHY

Michael Coppedge and Wolfgang Reinicke*

The authors have developed a scale based on Robert Dahl's concept of polyarchy that measures the degree to which national
political systems meet the minimum requirements for political
democracy, where real-world "democracies" rather than abstract
ideals are the standard. The Polyarchy Scale is constructed from
five simple indicators of freedom of expression, freedom of
organization, media pluralism, the extent of the suffrage, and the
holding of fair elections. Eighty percent of the nations in the
world are then ranked, without recourse to weighting schemes,
along the scale of eleven types, and all but seven of the remaining
nations are ranked approximately.

To measure Dahl's concept of polyarchy, we constructed a
Guttman scale.[1] Polyarchy is defined as the set of institutional
arrangements that permits public opposition and establishes the
right to participate in politics. In these two respects—public
contestation and inclusiveness—polyarchy is similar to the concept
of democracy.

However, polyarchy is not, and was not intended to be, exactly
equivalent to democracy. The term "democracy" inevitably calls to
mind a host of ideals that no actual political system has ever
approached. But we also refer to certain actual systems as
"democracies," which is often confusing. In order to "maintain the
distinction between democracy as an ideal system and the
institutional arrangements that have come to be regarded as a kind
of imperfect approximation of an ideal," Dahl and Lindblom
introduced the term "polyarchy" to denote the latter.[2]

The concept of polyarchy is also limited to the most basic
institutional requirements for democracy, specifically those that
had been met in most Western European countries by the end of
the First World War. A country can qualify as a full polyarchy even
if it does not allow workplace or communitarian democracy, pro-

---

* Michael Coppedge and Wolfgang Reinicke are doctoral candidates in political science at Yale University.

portional representation, referenda, or party primaries. Further-more, polyarchy does not take into account varying degrees of democracy at different levels of the polity; it is concerned with the national regime only.[3] Finally, no level of socioeconomic equality is required for a country to be fully polyarchic. Political and social scientists working in some traditions of scholarship would include social and economic equality in the definition of democracy, but in Polyarchy, Dahl discusses socioeconomic equality only as a condition that favors the development of polyarchy. So it should be clear that polyarchy reflects political, not social or economic, democracy. Our scale of polyarchy, then, measures the degree to which national political systems meet the minimum requirements for political democracy, where real-world "democracies" rather than abstract ideals are the standard.

Dahl proposed eight "institutional guarantees" of inclusion and public contestation.[4] They are:

1. Freedom to form and join organizations
2. Freedom of expression
3. Right to vote
4. Eligibility for public office
5. Right of political leaders to compete for support
6. Alternative sources of information
7. Free and fair elections
8. Institutions for making government policies depend on votes and other expressions of preference.

He also discussed the possibility of constructing a scale of polyarchy based on these guarantees that would permit comparisons of different countries according to the extent of permissible opposition and the inclusiveness of participation. At the time of Polyarchy's publication, it was not possible to construct a valid measure of polyarchy. Norling and Williams[5] made a valiant attempt to construct a Guttman scale of polyarchy, but they were handicapped by inadequate data.[6] Now the data are much more detailed and complete. Since the early 1980s there have been multiple sources of information on the political systems of every country in the world. Usually these sources provide detail sufficient to rate each country on each of the relevant criteria. The information is surprisingly current: even though our research was done in the summer of 1986, there was enough recent information to make our analysis a snapshot of the mid-1985 situation.

The sources differ in the quality, format, and completeness of the information they provide. A few cover all countries, others omit the smaller ones. A few sources present information in pre-coded variables, others in a descriptive format. Some sources are useful for measuring all of the requirements for polyarchy, while others are useful for only one or a few. Rather than tinkering with a motley assortment of indexes and weighting schemes, we coded the variables ourselves. Fresh coding allowed us to draw on different sources and differently formatted data for each variable and to use single sources in the few cases in which multiple sources were not available. The sources consulted for each variable are listed in Table 11.

TABLE 11

SOURCES CONSULTED FOR CODING VARIABLES

Fair Elections (FAIRELT): Gastil 1986, Statesman's Yearbook 1986, Banks and Textor 1985, Europa 1986a-d; and in some cases, Phillips 1984, Delury 1983, DOS 1986, Watch Committees 1986, Humana 1986, and McHale 1983.

Freedom of Expression (FREXT): Humana 1986, Gastil 1986, DOS 1986, and Watch Committees 1986.

Media Pluralism (ALTINF): Humana 1986, Gastil 1986, DOS 1986, and Watch Committees 1986.

Freedom of Organization (FREORG): Humana 1986, Gastil 1986, DOS 1986; and in some cases Europa 1986a-d, Phillips 1984, Statesman's Yearbook 1986, Banks and Textor 1985, McHale 1983, Delury 1983, and Alexander 1982.

Extension of Suffrage (SUFF): Banks and Textor 1985, Delury 1983, Alexander 1982, McHale 1983, Fukui 1985, and Europa 1986a-d.

Defining and Coding the Variables

All of the variables used in our scale are very simple categorical variables with only three or four categories.[7] Guarantee number 7, "free and fair elections," for example, is measured by FAIRELT, a variable with three possible values:[8]

1. Elections without significant or routine fraud or coercion.
2. Elections with some fraud or coercion.
3. No meaningful elections: elections without choice of candidates or parties, or no elections at all.

We did not code a separate variable for guarantee number 8, "Institutions for making government policies depend on votes and other expressions of preference," because in a more recent reformulation of these criteria, Dahl stipulated that officials who have "control over government decisions about policy," rather than the policies themselves, should depend on votes.[9] This amendment made the eighth guarantee essentially equivalent to number 7, "free and fair elections."

The freedom of organization variable (FREORG) has four categories:[10]

1. Some trade unions or interest groups may be harrassed or banned but there are no restrictions on purely political organization.

2. Some political parties are banned and trade unions or interest groups are harrassed or banned, but membership in some alternatives to official organizations is permitted.

3. The only relatively independent organizations that are allowed to exist are non-political.

4. No independent organizations are allowed. All organizations are banned or controlled by the government or the party.

The variable measuring freedom of expression (FREXT) contains three categories:[11]

1. Citizens express their views on all topics without fear of punishment.

2. Dissent is discouraged, whether by informal pressure or by systematic censorship, but control is incomplete. The extent of control may range from selective punishment of dissidents on a limited number of issues to a situation in which only determined critics manage to make themselves heard. There is some freedom of private discussion.

3. All dissent is forbidden and effectively suppressed. Citizens are wary of criticizing the government even privately.

It was not necessary to construct a variable for number 5, "Right of political leaders to compete for support," because this requirement is implicit in three others—"free and fair elections," "freedom to form and join organizations," and "freedom of expression."

The fourth variable, ALTINF, is a measure of guarantee number 6, "availability of alternative sources of information." This variable preserves its original four categories:

1. Alternative sources of information exist and are protected by law. If there is significant government ownership of the media, they are effectively controlled by truly independent or multi-party bodies.

2. Alternative sources of information are widely available but government versions are presented in preferential fashion. This may be the result of partiality in, and greater availability of, government-controlled media; selective closure, punishment, harassment, or censorship of dissident reporters, publishers, or broadcasters; or mild self-censorship resulting from any of these.

3. The government or ruling party dominates the diffusion of information to such a degree that alternative sources exist only for non-political issues, for short periods of time, or for small segments of the population. The media are either mostly controlled directly by the government or party or restricted by routine prior censorship, near-certain punishment of dissident reporters, publishers, and broadcasters, or pervasive self-censorship. Foreign media may be available to a small segment of the population.

4. There is no public alternative to official information. All sources of information are official organs or completely subservient private sources. The media are considered instruments of indoctrination. Foreign publications are usually unavailable or censored and foreign broadcasts may be jammed.

The indicator of guarantee number 3, the right to vote, is SUFF, which has the following categories:

1. Universal adult suffrage.
2. Suffrage with partial restrictions.
3. Suffrage denied to large segments of the population.
4. No suffrage.

It should be noted that quite a few countries that do not hold elections nevertheless provide for universal adult suffrage. We coded the suffrage variable according the the legal provisions of each country, leaving their interpretation to a later stage of analysis.

It proved impossible to create a separate variable for number 4, "Eligibility for public office," because information on this requirement is still incomplete. However, the information that is available suggests that eligibility for office differs very little from eligibility to vote, so the measurement error resulting from the omission of this guarantee should be very small.

There is little reason to doubt the accuracy of the ratings.[12] Since the variation is large and the categories are broad, few countries fall near a borderline, and in most cases there was a consensus among the sources as to the proper rating. The raw data used in scaling are included in the appendix to this paper.

The Scale and Its Interpretation

Since polyarchy is a two-dimensional concept, we constructed two separate measures. The measure of the dimension of inclusiveness is simply SUFF, the "right to vote" variable. The measure of public contestation is a Guttman scale, which is best understood as an ordered typology ranging from systems with full public contestation (Type 0) to those that allow no contestation (Type 10).[13]

TABLE 12

DISTRIBUTION OF COUNTRIES ON TWO-DIMENSIONAL SCALE OF POLYARCHY

Degree of Public Contestation

Extent of Suffrage

Scale Types		Full	Partial	Very Restricted	None
Full	0	41	0	1	0
	1	10	0	0	0
	2	11	0	0	1
	3	1	0	1	0
	4	14	1	0	0
	5	8	0	0	0
	6	6	0	1	2
	7	15	0	0	4
	8	13	0	0	6
	9	5	0	0	2
None	10	20	0	1	6
	Totals	144	1	4	21

A frequency crosstabulation of the measurements on the two dimensions (Table 12) leads us to question the usefulness of inclusiveness as a criterion for polyarchy. Eighty-five percent of all countries today provide for universal suffrage, whether they hold meaningful elections, approval elections, or no elections at all. Furthermore, all but two of the countries that have less than full suffrage do not have meaningful elections in the first place. These two countries—South Africa and Western Samoa—should not be ranked as high as countries with the same polyarchy scores, but it is much simpler to treat these two cases as anomalies than to create a separate conceptual dimension to take them into account.

However, some readers might feel that it would be worthwhile to keep the inclusiveness dimension in order to distinguish between non-democratic regimes with limited hypothetical suffrage and non-democratic regimes with no hypothetical suffrage at all. We disagree, but the ratings on the suffrage variable are included in the appendix for the benefit of these readers. Dropping the suffrage dimension leaves us with a unidimensional scale of polyarchy that is identical to the scale of public contestation.

One of the advantages of Guttman scaling is reproducibility: if one knows the score of a country on the scale, one can reproduce, or reconstruct, the country's ratings on each of the component variables. (Actually, with the minimum coefficient of reproducibility of .900, one can reproduce ninety percent of the ratings.) This one-to-one correspondence between scores and combinations of characteristics, or "perfect scale types," makes a Guttman scale very easy to interpret. The Polyarchy Scale scores, scale types, and their interpretations are presented in Table 13.

TABLE 13

INTERPRETATION OF POLYARCHY SCALE SCORES

Scale Score*	Scale Type**	Interpretation
0	1 1 1 1	Meaningful fair elections are held, there is full freedom for political organization and expression, and there is no preferential presentation of official views in the media.
1	1 1 1 2	Meaningful fair elections are held, and there is full freedom for political organization and expression, but there is preferential presentation of official views in the media.
2	1 1 2 2	Meaningful fair elections are held and there is full freedom for political organization, but some public dissent is suppressed and there is preferential presentation of official views in the media.
3	1222/2122	(Undefined due to lack of cases.)
4	2 2 2 2	Elections are marred by fraud or coercion, some independent political organizations are banned, some public dissent is suppressed, and there is preferential presentation of official views in the media.
5	3 2 2 2	No meaningful elections are held, some independent political organizations are banned, some public dissent is suppressed, and there is preferential presentation of official views in the media.

(continued)

Table 13 (Continued)

Scale Score*	Scale Type**	Interpretation
6	3 3 2 2	No meaningful elections are held, only nonpolitical organizations are allowed to be independent, some public dissent is suppressed, and there is preferential presentation of official views in the media.
7	3 3 2 3	No meaningful elections are held, only nonpolitical organizations are allowed to be independent, some public dissent is suppressed, and alternatives to the official media are very limited.
8	3 4 2 3	No meaningful elections are held, all organizations are banned or controlled by the government or official party, some public dissent is suppressed, and alternatives to the official media are very limited.
9	3 4 2 4	No meaningful elections are held, all organizations are banned or controlled by the government or official party, some public dissent is suppressed, and there is no public alternative to official information.
10	3 4 3 4	No meaningful elections are held, all organizations are banned or controlled by the government or official party, all public dissent is suppressed, and there is no public alternative to official information.

---

* The scale score is the sum of the four ratings minus four.

** The numbers of the perfect scale type are the ratings expected on the four component variables—FAIRELT, FREORG, FREXT, and ALTINF, respectively.

The most obvious implication of this scale is that polyarchy can be measured, albeit roughly. It is impossible to rank each country one by one on a scale that spans the whole range of polyarchy—non-polyarchy, because as soon as we try to rank countries within types, we encounter a multidimensional reality that does not allow simple comparisons such as rankings.[14] But we can produce an ordered typology with ten to twelve types that apply to many countries at once. This Polyarchy Scale should be very useful for identifying countries that are roughly similar in the degree of polyarchy they possess, and for making broad comparisons of dissimilar types.

This scale is also useful as a checklist: it tells the researcher making comparisons involving polyarchy which characteristics of political systems to pay attention to, and which to ignore. Broadly speaking, someone who is interested in how polyarchic a country is compared to other countries in the world should examine four things: elections, freedom of organization, freedom of expression, and alternatives to official sources of information. The Polyarchy Scale also provides more specific items for a checklist. Success in constructing a scale depends as much on how each variable is divided into categories as it does on selecting the correct variables. Based on the category descriptions for each variable, then, the important things to know in measuring polyarchy are:

1. whether or not elections are held that offer voters a meaningful choice of parties or candidates;

2. whether or not election outcomes are affected by significant fraud or coercion;

3. whether all, some, or no political organizations are banned;

4. if all political organizations are banned, whether some or no nonpolitical organizations are allowed to function independently;

5. whether freedom of expression is complete, non-existent, or somewhere in between;

6. whether the media are pluralistic or government dominated;

7. if the media are pluralistic, whether official views receive preferential or balanced treatment; and

8. if the media are government dominated, whether control is complete or incomplete.

It is equally important to note some of the distinctions that are not useful for measuring polyarchy:

1. elections without choice vs. no elections;

2. one-party states vs. no-party states;

3. exceptional vs. routine suppression of dissent;

4. electoral fraud or coercion that changes the winner of an election vs. fraud or coercion that changes only the margin of victory;

5. in states with full freedom of political organization, full vs. partial freedom of nonpolitical organization.

Each of these five distinctions frustrated our preliminary attempts to construct a scale. Their incompatibility with the other criteria does not mean they are unimportant distinctions for other concepts or issues; it simply means that they vary independently of the more basic components of polyarchy. For example, the first two distinctions listed above were designed to distinguish between authoritarian and totalitarian regimes. Their irrelevance means that equally anti-polyarchic effects can be achieved by different types of non-democratic regimes.

A Ranking of Countries

One problem that frequently arises in scale and index construction is assigning weights to the variables. How important is having a free press compared to having freedom of organization? Do you penalize a country more for having fraudulent elections than you do for sporadic press censorship? Most scaling techniques offer no definitive solutions to these problems. One great advantage of Guttman scaling is that it makes it possible to rank countries without having to decide on the relative weights of the component variables, as long as the countries' ratings match the scale types. That means, for example, that any country that fits type 0 perfectly will always rank higher than any country that fits type 1 perfectly, no matter how the component variables are weighted.

Owing to this special property of Guttman scaling, the Polyarchy Scale produces an unequivocal ranking of 137 of the world's 170 independent nations. For the remaining thirty-three countries that do not fit the scale types perfectly, ranking is more problematic. There is no a priori way to weight the variables in order to decide whether these countries rank above, below, or on par with the countries that have the same scale score and match the scale types.

Nevertheless, we can make a convenient distinction between two types of deviating cases. One group consists of twenty-six countries whose ratings differ only slightly from the corresponding perfect scale type: no rating is more than one category removed from the expected level, and no more than two ratings are off. We call these cases "approximately equivalent variants." Doubling the weight of one of the variables would move these countries only one rank up or down, so their ranks can safely be considered approximately correct. Table 14 below shows the ranking of scale types and variants among the ten scale scores.

The other group consists of anomalies: countries with one or more ratings that are two or more levels removed from the norm, or have three or more odd ratings altogether. The ranks of these countries change more drastically as the variable weights are modified, so that the ranks of anomalies cannot safely be considered approximately correct. Take, for example, the small European principalities of Andorra, Liechtenstein, and Monaco. In media pluralism, freedom of expression, and freedom of organization, they are like Type 0 polyarchies. But the effective leaders of their governments are not elected; they are either born to the office or appointed by other unelected officals. We prefer not to guess where these odd cases should be ranked. Fortunately, there are only a few—Andorra, Liechtenstein, Monaco, Vatican City, and Syria. South Africa and Western Samoa are also considered anomalies because of their restricted suffrage.

Concluding Observations

A quick perusal of Table 14 leads us to make two concluding observations. One is that there were fifty-one full polyarchies (type 0) and near-polyarchies (type 1) in the world in mid-1985, amounting to thirty percent of all independent nations. In terms of population, the extent of polyarchy was more limited, only twenty-one percent. If we had limited our analysis to consolidated regimes only, the proportion would be reduced further still, as we would have had to exclude Argentina, Brazil, Honduras, the Dominican Republic, Ecuador, Peru, Uruguay, and possibly other countries.

Secondly, it would be interesting to update these country ratings annually, in a manner analogous to that of the Comparative Survey of Freedom, to produce a set of polyarchy time series. There is no reason why this cannot be done, since the categories for each variable need not change and most of the sources consulted for the ratings are now updated annually. The need for updating is obvious, since at this writing (July 1987) the positions of the Philippines, Guatemala, South Korea, and perhaps the USSR and several other countries would be different. Researchers who plan to use the ranking should keep in mind that it is a snapshot of political institutions that sometimes change very suddenly.

TABLE 14

COUNTRY RANKINGS ON POLYARCHY SCALE: MID-1985

The series of numbers in parentheses are the combinations of ratings received by the countries in that column. The first digit is the rating on FAIRELT, the second is for FREORG, the third is for FREXT, and the fourth is for ALTINF.

Scale
Score   N   Scale Types (1 1 1 1):

0	41		
		Argentina	Luxembourg
		Australia	Nauru
		Austria	Netherlands
		Barbados	New Zealand
		Belgium	Norway
		Belize	Papua New Guinea
		Brazil	Portugal
		Canada	St. Christopher & Nevis
		Colombia	St. Lucia
		Costa Rica	St. Vincent & the Grens.
		Denmark	San Marino
		Finland	Spain
		France	Sweden
		Germany, West	Switzerland
		Grenada	Trinidad & Tobago
		Honduras	Tuvalu
		Iceland	United Kingdom
		Ireland	United States
		Italy	Uruguay
		Japan	Venezuela
		Kiribati	

1   10   Scale Types (1 1 1 2):

Botswana	Ecuador
Cyprus	Mauritius
Dominica	Solomon Islands
Dominican Republic	

Approximately Equivalent:

Israel, Peru (1 1 2 1)
Fiji (2 1 1 1)

(continued)

Table 14 (Continued)

2   9   Scale Types (1 1 2 2)

Antigua & Barbuda   India
Bahamas   Thailand
Bolivia

Approximately Equivalent:

Vanuatu (1 1 2 3)
Greece, Jamaica (2 1 1 2); Panama (2 2 1 1)

3   0   No cases

4   16   Scale Types (2 2 2 2):

Egypt   Philippines
El Salvador   Singapore
South Korea   Sri Lanka
Malta   Turkey
Mexico

Approximately Equivalent:

Senegal (2 2 1 2)
Malaysia, Nicaragua, Zimbabwe (1 2 2 3)
Maldives, Morocco (3 1 2 2), Lebanon (3 2 2 1)

5   7   Scale Types (3 2 2 2):

Bangladesh   Guatemala
Chile   Liberia

Approximately Equivalent:

Gambia, Indonesia, Guyana (2 2 2 3)

6   9   Scale Types (3 3 2 2):

Jordan   Sudan
Kuwait   Tunisia

Approximately Equivalent:

Lesotho, Madagascar, Pakistan, Paraguay (3 2 2 3)
Bhutan (3 4 1 2)

(continued)

Table 14 (Continued)

7   19   Scale Types (3 3 2 3):

Brunei	Ghana	Suriname
Burkina Faso	Guinea	Swaziland
C. A. R.	Haiti	Taiwan
Chad	Poland	Tonga
Djibouti	Rwanda	Yugoslavia
Gabon	Sierra Leone	Zambia

Approximately Equivalent: Iran (3 2 3 3)

8   18   Scale Types (3 4 2 3):

Bahrain	Congo	Nigeria
Benin	Hungary	Seychelles
Burundi	Ivory Coast	Uganda
Cameroon	Kenya	United Arab Emirates
Cape Verde	Mauritania	North Yemen
Comoros	Nepal	

Approximately Equivalent: Qatar (3 3 2 4)

9   7   Scale Types (3 4 2 4):

Algeria	Tanzania
Equatorial Guinea	Zaire
Oman	

Approximately Equivalent:

Malawi, Niger (3 3 3 4)

10   27   Scale Types (3 4 3 4):

Afghanistan	Germany, East	Mozambique
Albania	Guinea-Bissau	Romania
Angola	Iraq	Sao Tome & Princ.
Bulgaria	Kampuchea	Saudi Arabia
Burma	Korea, North	Somalia
China	Laos	Togo
Cuba	Libya	USSR
Czechoslovakia	Mali	Viet Nam
Ethiopia	Mongolia	South Yemen

Anomalies excluded from the ranking are: Andorra, Liechtenstein, Monaco, Vatican City (3 1 1 1); Syria (3 2 3 4); and South Africa and Western Samoa (1 2 2 2 and 1 1 1 1 with limited suffrage).

NOTES

1. The term "polyarchy" was originally coined in Dahl, Robert A. and Charles Lindblom, **Politics, Economics, and Welfare** (New York: Harper and Brothers, 1953), but was developed most fully in Dahl, Robert A., **Polyarchy: Participation and Opposition** (New Haven: Yale University Press, 1971).

2. Dahl, **Polyarchy,** page 9n.

3. Ibid., pages 10-14.

4. Ibid., page 3.

5. Ibid., Appendix A.

6. As a consequence, they had to exclude from their analysis twenty-one countries that were independent by 1968. Another consequence was that data were missing for a large number of the countries that were included in the analysis, which biased the ranking in favor of the countries about which less was known. Finally, the available data did not match Dahl's criteria for polyarchy very closely. Norling and Williams relied on updated versions of ten variables from Banks and Textor's 1963 Cross-Polity Survey that seemed to be related to the requirements for polyarchy. But they never tested the Banks and Textor variables to see whether they were conceptually valid substitutes for Dahl's eight criteria. Instead, they simply tried to scale the ten variables directly, with results that were optimistically judged "moderately satisfactory." Their coefficient of reproducibility was only .829, even though it was calculated by a controversial method of counting errors that tends to raise the coefficient artificially (McIver, John P. and Edward G. Carmines 1981. **Unidimensional Scaling.** [Beverly Hills: Sage Publications, 1981], pages 42-45).

7. Our original variables had a larger number of categories than the ones described here. During preliminary scaling we discovered that many of the original distinctions were not useful in measuring a country's overall degree of polyarchy. Erasing these distinctions by combining categories left us with the very simple variables that we used in the final scale. The substantive implications of these adjustments are discussed below.

8. The original version of this variable included categories that distinguished between countries that held Soviet-type approval elections (without a choice of candidates) and countries that held no elections at all for effective government officials (for example, Chile). It also distinguished between degrees of fraud or coercion that probably determined the winner of the election, and those that only changed the margin of victory.

9. Dahl, Robert A., **Dilemmas of Pluralist Democracy** (New Haven: Yale University Press, 1982), pages 10-11.

10. This variable began with seven categories, but had to be collapsed into four to produce a scale. This adjustment eliminated two distinctions: that between one-party and no-party states, and that between states that allow freedom of purely political organization but harrass or ban trade unions or other interests groups, and those that guarantee freedom of both political and nonpolitical organization.

11. The original version of FREXT contained two middle categories instead of one, in order to distinguish between exceptional and routine suppression of dissent, where control was nevertheless incomplete.

12. All ratings were assigned initially by one coder consulting multiple sources, as specified in Table 11. For some of the ratings, it was necessary to rely on a single source, but the number of countries affected is small: over ninety-five percent of the ratings are based on more than one source. Where there were superficial disagreements among the sources, the coder tried to read between the lines to see a reality that was compatible with all of the descriptions. Where these differences were unreconcilable, two coders reviewed the sources and jointly agreed on the correct rating, sometimes after consulting additional sources.

13. After collapsing a few categories in the original variables, as described in previous endnotes, we found that it was possible to generate more than one scale that met the minimum criterion of a coefficient of reproducibility of at least .900. The final scale that we present here was chosen because it does the best job of discriminating between countries that are subjectively dissimilar while still meeting the reproducibility requirement (at exactly .900).

14. In technical terms, if we try to construct a more precise scale by increasing the number of categories in each variable so that each institutional guarantee is measured more accurately, the coefficient of reproducibility falls below .900.

References

Alexander, Robert J., ed. 1982. **Political Parties of the Americas: Canada, Latin America, and the West Indies.** Westport, Conn.: Greenwood Press.

Banks, Arthur S., ed. 1985. **Political Handbook of the World.** New York: McGraw-Hill.

Banks, Arthur S. and Robert B. Textor 1963. **A Cross-Polity Survey.** Cambridge: M.I.T. Press.

Dahl, Robert A. 1971. **Polyarchy: Participation and Opposition.** New Haven: Yale University Press.

Dahl, Robert A. 1982. **Dilemmas of Pluralist Democracy.** New Haven: Yale University Press.

Dahl, Robert A. and Charles Lindblom 1953. **Politics, Economics, and Welfare.** New York: Harper and Brothers.

DOS. See United States Government.

Delury, George E., ed. 1983. **World Encyclopedia of Political Systems and Parties.** Harlow, Essex, UK: Longman.

Europa 1986. **The Europa Yearbook.** London: Europa Publications.

Europa 1986a. **South America, Central America and the Caribbean.** London: Europa Publications.

Europa 1986b. **The Far East and Australasia.** London: Europa Publications.

Europa 1986c. **Africa South of the Sahara.** London: Europa Publications.

Europa 1986d. **The Middle East and North Africa: A Survey and Directory of the Countries of the Middle East.** London: Europa Publications.

Fukui, Haruhiro, ed. 1985. **Political Parties of Asia and the Pacific.** Westport, Conn.: Greenwood Press.

Gastil, Raymond L. 1986. **Freedom in the World: Political Rights and Civil Liberties, 1985-1986.** Westport, Conn.: Greenwood Press.

Gorden, Raymond L. 1977. **Unidimensional Scaling of Social Variables: Concepts and Procedures.** New York: Free Press.

Humana, Charles. 1986. **World Human Rights Guide.** New York: Facts on File.

McHale, Vincent E., ed. 1983. **Political Parties of Europe.** Westport, Conn.: Greenwood Press.

McIver, John P. and Edward G. Carmines 1981. **Unidimensional Scaling.** Beverly Hills: Sage Publications.

Phillips, Claude S. 1984. **The African Political Dictionary.** Santa Barbara, Calif.: ABC-Clio.

The Statesman's Year-Book, 1986: Statistical and Historical Annual of the States of the World. London and New York: Macmillan, St. Martin's Press.

United States Government, Department of State. 1986. **Country Reports on Human Rights Practices for 1985.** Washington: United States Government Printing Office.

Watch Committees, The, and Lawyers Committee for Human Rights. 1986. **Critique: Review of the Department of State's Country Reports on Human Rights Practices for 1985.** New York: Fund for Free Expression for the Watch Committees and the Lawyers Committee for Human Rights.

APPENDIX: A SCALE OF POLYARCHY*

COUNTRY	FAIRELT	FREORG	FREXT	ALTINF	SUFF
Afghanistan	3	4	3	4	4
Albania	3	4	3	4	1
Algeria	3	4	2	4	1
Andorra	3	1	1	1	1
Angola	3	4	3	4	3
Antigua & Barbuda	1	1	2	2	1
Argentina	1	1	1	1	1
Australia	1	1	1	1	1
Austria	1	1	1	1	1
Bahamas	1	1	2	2	1
Bahrain	3	4	2	3	4
Bangladesh	3	2	2	2	1
Barbados	1	1	1	1	1
Belgium	1	1	1	1	1
Belize	1	1	1	1	1
Benin	3	4	2	3	1
Bhutan	3	4	1	2	1
Bolivia	1	1	2	2	1
Botswana	1	1	1	2	1
Brazil	1	1	1	1	1
Brunei	3	3	2	3	4
Bulgaria	3	4	3	4	1
Burkina Faso	3	3	2	3	1
Burma	3	4	3	4	1
Burundi	3	4	2	3	1
Cameroon	3	4	2	3	1
Canada	1	1	1	1	1
Cape Verde	3	4	2	3	1
Central African Rep.	3	3	2	3	1
Chad	3	3	2	3	1
Chile	3	2	2	2	1
China	3	4	3	4	1
Colombia	1	1	1	1	1
Comoros	3	4	2	3	1
Congo	3	4	2	3	1
Costa Rica	1	1	1	1	1
Cuba	3	4	3	4	1
Cyprus	1	1	1	2	1
Czechoslovakia	3	4	3	4	1

* As defined above, FAIRELT = fair elections; FREORG = freedom of organization; FREXT = freedom of expression; ALTINF = availability of alternative sources of information; SUFF = the extent of the suffrage; (1) satisfies the criteria most closely; (4) satisfies them least.

COUNTRY	FAIRELT	FREORG	FREXT	ALTINF	SUFF
Denmark	1	1	1	1	1
Djibouti	3	3	2	3	1
Dominica	1	1	1	2	1
Dominican Republic	1	1	1	2	1
Ecuador	1	1	1	2	1
Egypt	2	2	2	2	1
El Salvador	2	2	2	2	1
Equatorial Guinea	3	4	2	4	1
Ethiopia	3	4	3	4	4
Fiji	2	1	1	1	1
Finland	1	1	1	1	1
France	1	1	1	1	1
Gabon	3	3	2	3	1
Gambia	2	2	2	3	1
Germany, East	3	4	3	4	1
Germany, West	1	1	1	1	1
Ghana	3	3	2	3	4
Greece	2	1	1	2	1
Grenada	1	1	1	1	1
Guatemala	3	2	2	2	1
Guinea	3	3	2	3	4
Guinea-Bissau	3	4	3	4	4
Guyana	2	2	2	3	1
Haiti	3	3	2	3	1
Honduras	1	1	1	1	1
Hungary	3	4	2	3	1
Iceland	1	1	1	1	1
India	1	1	2	2	1
Indonesia	2	2	2	3	1
Iran	3	2	3	3	1
Iraq	3	4	3	4	1
Ireland	1	1	1	1	1
Israel	1	1	2	1	1
Italy	1	1	1	1	1
Ivory Coast	3	4	2	3	1
Jamaica	2	1	1	2	1
Japan	1	1	1	1	1
Jordan	3	3	2	2	1
Kampuchea	3	4	3	4	1
Kenya	3	4	2	3	1
Kiribati	1	1	1	1	1
Korea, North	3	4	3	4	1
Korea, South	2	2	2	2	1
Kuwait	3	3	2	2	3
Laos	3	4	3	4	4

COUNTRY	FAIRELT	FREORG	FREXT	ALTINF	SUFF
Lebanon	3	2	2	1	2
Lesotho	3	2	2	3	4
Liberia	3	2	2	2	1
Libya	3	4	3	4	1
Liechtenstein	3	1	1	1	1
Luxembourg	1	1	1	1	1
Madagascar	3	2	2	3	1
Malawi	3	3	3	4	1
Malaysia	1	2	2	3	1
Maldives	3	1	2	3	1
Mali	3	4	3	4	1
Malta	2	2	2	2	1
Mauritania	3	4	2	3	4
Mauritius	1	1	1	2	1
Mexico	2	2	2	2	1
Monaco	3	1	1	1	1
Mongolia	3	4	3	4	1
Morocco	3	1	2	2	1
Mozambique	3	4	3	4	4
Nauru	1	1	1	1	1
Nepal	3	4	2	3	1
Netherlands	1	1	1	1	1
New Zealand	1	1	1	1	1
Nicaragua	1	2	2	3	1
Niger	3	3	3	4	4
Nigeria	3	4	2	3	4
Norway	1	1	1	1	1
Oman	3	4	2	4	4
Pakistan	3	2	2	3	1
Panama	2	2	1	1	1
Papua New Guinea	1	1	1	1	1
Paraguay	3	2	2	3	1
Peru	1	1	2	1	1
Philippines	2	2	2	2	1
Poland	3	3	2	3	1
Portugal	1	1	1	1	1
Qatar	3	3	2	4	4
Romania	3	4	3	4	1
Rwanda	3	3	2	3	1
St. Christopher & Nevis	1	1	1	1	1
St.Lucia	1	1	1	1	1
St. Vincent & Gren.	1	1	1	1	1
San Marino	1	1	1	1	1
Sao Tome & Principe	3	4	3	4	1
Saudi Arabia	3	4	3	4	4

COUNTRY	FAIRELT	FREORG	FREXT	ALTINF	SUFF
Senegal	3	2	1	2	1
Seychelles	3	4	2	3	1
Sierra Leone	3	3	2	3	1
Singapore	2	2	2	2	1
Solomon Islands	1	1	1	2	1
Somalia	3	4	3	4	1
South Africa	1	2	2	2	3
Spain	1	1	1	1	1
Sri Lanka	2	2	2	2	1
Sudan	3	3	2	2	4
Suriname	3	3	2	3	4
Swaziland	3	3	2	3	1
Sweden	1	1	1	1	1
Switzerland	1	1	1	1	1
Syria	3	2	3	4	1
Taiwan	3	3	2	3	1
Tanzania	3	4	2	4	1
Thailand	1	1	2	2	1
Togo	3	4	3	4	1
Tonga	3	3	2	3	1
Trinidad & Tobago	1	1	1	1	1
Tunisia	3	3	2	2	1
Turkey	2	2	2	2	1
Tuvalu	1	1	1	1	1
Uganda	3	4	2	3	4
United Arab Emirates	3	4	2	3	1
United Kingdom	1	1	1	1	1
United States	1	1	1	1	1
Uruguay	1	1	1	1	1
Ussr	3	4	3	4	1
Vanuatu	1	1	2	3	1
Vatican City	3	1	1	1	4
Venezuela	1	1	1	1	1
Viet-Nam	3	4	3	4	1
Western Samoa	1	1	1	1	3
Yemen, North	3	4	2	3	1
Yemen, South	3	4	3	4	1
Yugoslavia	3	3	2	3	1
Zaire	3	4	2	4	1
Zambia	3	3	2	3	1
Zimbabwe	1	2	2	3	1

PART III

Current Issues

OPENNESS AND CENSORSHIP

Leonard R. Sussman*

Suddenly this year, glasnost, the word, was understood on every continent. Though the word has different meanings in the East and West,[1] many forms of glasnost are being tested wherever governments want to use the new technologies of mass communications to mobilize their own citizens, and create abroad a self-designed national image. In Asia, Africa, the Pacific Basin, Latin America, as well as the homeland of the copyright holder, the Soviet Union, this has been the year when governmental censorship expanded its effectiveness, often under the cloak of glasnost.

This may seem a linkage of opposites—equating governmental censorship with glasnost, defined by the Soviets and many Americans as "openness." But glasnost was never designed by Lenin or Gorbachev to mean a plurality of ideas, or the objective reporting of events or personalities. Glasnost is the more effective use of communications to inspire or command support for governmental policies.

Mikhail Gorbachev in **Perestroika** stated his problem clearly:

> The presentation of a "problem-free" reality backfired: a breach had formed between word and deed, which bred public passivity and disbelief in the slogans being proclaimed. It was natural that this resulted in a credibility gap; everything that was proclaimed from the rostrums and printed in newspapers and textbooks was put to question. Decay began in public morals. [Gorbachev added,] We can no longer tolerate stagnation.[2]

For managerial effectiveness, therefore, the "means of production" (all communications media) remain under centralized control. The media are "opened," however, to permit controlled criticism

---

* Leonard R. Sussman is Executive Director of Freedom House.

mainly of marginal aspects of policy or administrative performance; and this almost exclusively on domestic questions. While little criticism of foreign affairs is permitted in the Soviet's glasnost, the term and the policy have had significantly positive effects in foreign relations. The Soviet Union is widely regarded now as having freed its citizens to learn more about their society, and play more of a role in directing future affairs. Actually, no institutional, constitutional, or administrative changes have fundamentally altered Communist Party control over every aspect of a Soviet citizen's life.

It would be misleading to assert that other countries, far removed from the Soviet Union, have consciously employed glasnost to achieve greater control over their mass media. Rather, the "glasnosting" of information in other countries may start from a lesser degree of governmental interference in mass communication, and work down to greater controls. Soviet glasnost began with total control and "opened" to a new level of controlled criticism and exhortation. This mixture of sophisticated controls and crude censorship was visible this year in as widely separated places as Malaysia, Chile, Kenya, South Africa, and China. In these countries, elaborate rationales were given for controlling domestic and foreign journalists. Censorship was not new in these nations, but laws and regulations were imposed to "protect" citizens from irresponsible journalism, or avoid civil disruption. These impositions were generally resisted by the citizens who were to be "protected." But the rationale of providing "safe" public discourse via the mass media seemed to reflect the spirit and limitations of glasnost. Cultural and national traditions dictated different styles of governmental control. All forms, however, reflected the same parentage: the desire of the sovereign to set and limit the range of ideas in public discourse.

In this general climate, censorship thrived this year in many more countries. Old-style controls were harshly imposed in Fiji, Bangladesh, and Paraguay. In three-quarters of the nations, governmental influence over the print and broadcast media continued (see Table 15).

The Ambivalence of Glasnost

The ambivalence of Soviet glasnost was apparent during an afternoon this writer and his son spent in Moscow in July 1987 with the editor of the magazine about to be launched under the name of Glasnost.[3] Sergei Grigoryants had spent ten years in Soviet prisons, mainly for writing unauthorized articles circulated as samizdat. He was last released just five months before we met him. He still bore the physical signs of incarceration and a hunger strike. Yet he was determined to test the limits of glasnost. He knew it would not be easy. Some thirty other writers, many recently released from prisons, would contribute essays, reports and documents which could not be seen in the official press—even under glasnost.

Grigoryants at an open press conference announced he would begin publishing Glasnost and asked the Kremlin for assistance in publishing the magazine. In the absence of official help he would type each copy on onionskin paper, using carbon to duplicate the 55-page issue. High officials refused to grant permission to publish Glasnost, but—a significant tribute to the policy of glasnost—they did not immediately cast Grigoryants and his friends into prison or labor camps. Grigoryants was not yet ready to say that glasnost, the policy, would last. "It's only a beginning," he told us, "but the future of the magazine may indicate the future of glasnost."

On that basis, ambivalence seems to be the Kremlin's policy. Two editors of Glasnost were briefly detained early in October. On October 30, plainclothes officers detained Grigoryants as he left the apartment that serves as the magazine's office. Another editor was also briefly held. Some 70 copies of the magazine were taken by the authorities. TASS, the official news agency, accused the editors of Glasnost of illegally using government printing facilities.

This charge reflects in microcosm the fundamental dilemma the Kremlin must face with regard to the sharing of information. At every level in the restructuring of Soviet society—perestroika, restructuring, is regarded as the key to the Soviet Union's future viability in a post-industrial world—it will be necessary to share information. Photocopiers, such as Grigoryants needed to produce his magazine, are tightly guarded by the authorities. Only specially selected employees may use photocopiers, and they are under direct surveillance of a special department. Such controllers are

TABLE 15

NEWS MEDIA CONTROL BY COUNTRIES

	Generally Free[1]	Partly Free[1]	Generally Not Free[1]	Gov't News Agency[2]	Civil Liberties[3]
Afghanistan			PB	X	7
Albania			PB	X	7
Algeria			PB	X	6
Angola			PB	X	7
Antigua & Barbuda		PB			3
Argentina	PB			X	1
Australia	PB				1
Austria	PB				1
Bahamas	P	B			3
Bahrain			PB	X	5
Bangladesh		PB		X	5
Barbados	P	B			1
Belgium	PB				1
Belize	P	B			1
Benin			PB	X	7
Bhutan			P		5
Bolivia	P	B		X	3
Botswana	P	B			3
Brazil	PB				2
Brunei			PB		5
Bulgaria			PB	X	7
Burkina Faso			PB	X	6
Burma			PB	X	7
Burundi			PB	X	6
Cameroon			PB	X	6
Canada	PB				1
Cape Verde		P	B		6
Cambodia (Kampuchea)			PB	X	7
Central Afr. Rep.			PB	X	6
Chad			PB	X	7
Chile		P	B	X	5
China (Mainland)			PB	X	6
China (Taiwan)		PB			4
Colombia	PB				3
Congo			PB	X	6
Costa Rica	PB				1
Cote d'Ivoire		P	B	X	5
Cuba			PB	X	6
Cyprus (G)	P	B		X	2
Cyprus (T)	P	B		X	3

Notes to the Table

1. P designates print media; B designates broadcast (radio and TV) media. Print media refers primarily to domestic newspapers and news magazines. Countries with undeveloped media or for which there is insufficient information include: Comoros, Djibouti, Kiribati, Rwanda, Solomons, Tuvalu, and Western Samoa.
2. X designates the presence of a government news agency, with or without the availability of private news services.
3. See Table 1, above.

Communications: Openness and Censorship

	Generally Free[1]	Partly Free[1]	Generally Not Free[1]	Gov't News Agency[2]	Civil Liberties[3]
Czechoslovakia			PB	X	6
Denmark	PB				1
Dominica	PB				2
Dominican Rep.	P	B			3
Ecuador	PB (?)				3
Egypt		PB		X	4
El Salvador		PB			4
Equatorial Guinea			PB		7
Ethiopia			PB	X	7
Fiji			PB		5
Finland	P	B			2
France	P	B		X	2
Gabon			PB	X	6
Gambia	PB				3
Germany (E)			PB	X	6
Germany (W)	PB				2
Ghana			PB	X	6
Greece	P	B		X	2
Grenada	P	B			1
Guatemala		PB			3
Guinea			PB		6
Guinea-Bissau			PB		7
Guyana		P	B	X	5
Haiti		P	B		5
Honduras	PB				3
Hungary			PB	X	4
Iceland	PB				1
India	P	B		X	3
Indonesia		P	B	X	6
Iran			PB	X	6
Iraq			PB	X	7
Ireland	PB				1
Israel	PB				2
Italy	PB			X	1
Jamaica	P	B			2
Japan	PB				1
Jordan			PB	X	5
Kenya			PB	X	6
Korea (N)			PB	X	7
Korea (S)		P	B	X	4
Kuwait		P	B	X	5
Laos			PB	X	7
Lebanon		PB		X	5
Lesotho			PB		6
Liberia		P	B		5
Libya			PB	X	6
Luxembourg	PB				1
Madagascar			PB	X	5
Malawi			PB	X	7
Malaysia			PB	X	5

133

Communications: Openness and Censorship

	Generally Free[1]	Partly Free[1]	Generally Not Free[1]	Gov't News Agency[2]	Civil Liberties[3]
Maldives		P	B		6
Mali			P B	X	6
Malta	P	B			2
Mauritania			P B	X	6
Mauritius	P	B			2
Mexico		P B		X	4
Mongolia			P B	X	7
Morocco		P	B	X	5
Mozambique			P B	X	7
Nauru	P B				2
Nepal		P	B	X	4
Netherlands	P B				1
New Zealand	P B				1
Nicaragua		P	B	X	5
Niger			P B	X	6
Nigeria		P B		X	5
Norway	P B				1
Oman			P B		6
Pakistan		P	B	X	5
Panama			P B		5
Papua New Guinea	P B			X	2
Paraguay		P	B		6
Peru	P B				3
Philippines	P B			X	2
Poland		P	B	X	5
Portugal	P B			X	2
Qatar			P B	X	5
Romania			P B	X	7
St.Kitts-Nevis	P B				2
St.Lucia	P B				2
St.Vincent	P	B			2
Sao Tome & Prin.			P B		7
Saudi Arabia			P B	X	7
Senegal		P B			4
Seychelles			P B	X	6
Sierra Leone		P	B	X	5
Singapore		P	B	X	5
Somalia			P B	X	7
South Africa		P	B		6
Spain	P B			X	2
Sri Lanka		P B		X	4
Sudan		P	B	X	5
Suriname		P	B		4
Swaziland			P B		6
Sweden	P B				1
Switzerland	P B				1
Syria			P B	X	7
Tanzania			P B	X	6
Thailand		P B			3
Togo			P B	X	6

	Generally Free[1]	Partly Free[1]	Generally Not Free[1]	Gov't News Agency[2]	Civil Liberties[3]
Tonga		PB			3
Transkei			PB		6
Trinidad & Tobago	PB				1
Tunisia		P	B	X	5
Turkey		P	B	X	4
Uganda		P	B	X	4
USSR			PB	X	6
United Arab Emirs.		P	B	X	5
United Kingdom	PB				1
United States	PB				1
Uruguay	PB				2
Vanuatu		PB			4
Venezuela	PB				2
Vietnam			PB	X	7
Yemen (N)			PB	X	5
Yemen (S)			PB	X	7
Yugoslavia			PB	X	5
Zaire			PB	X	7
Zambia		P	B	X	5
Zimbabwe			PB	X	6

Table Summary for Countries

	General Rating		Print Media		Broadcast Media	
	No.	%	No.	%	No.	%
Free	54	34	55	34	38	24
Partly free	58	36	40	25	31	20
Not free	48	30	65	41	90	56

Governments in three-fourths of the world have a significant or dominant voice in determining what does and what does not appear in the media. This definition of control does not include regulation such as that practiced by the FCC: it means control over newspaper or broadcast content. In some countries particular media (often broadcasting) may be government financed and indirectly government managed like the BBC, but are still largely free of government control of content.

In only one-fourth of the countries are both the print and broadcast media generally free: the press is generally free in one-third. Newspapers tend to be freer than radio or TV.

While this table concentrates on the status of the domestic news media, foreign journalists' access to sources and freedom to transmit news generally reflects the government's treatment of domestic journalists.

Nearly a half century ago there were thirty-nine national news services in twenty-eight countries. Seventy percent of these were at least nominally independent of government (Robert Desmond, The Press and World Affairs, Appleton-Century, 1937). Today there are ninety. The number of government-operated news services has increased rapidly, partly in consequence of recommendations made at UNESCO. Fifty-six percent of the countries have a government news agency: seventy-seven percent of the "not free," sixty-four percent of the "partly free," and twenty percent of the "free" countries. Of nations with the lowest civil liberties rating (7), eighty-nine percent operate government news agencies. National news agencies often use the world news services of the transnational Western media or TASS. They may then decide what world news may be distributed inside the country. Some national news agencies assign themselves the sole right to secure domestic news for distribution inside or outside the country.

135

connected with the KGB. Consequently, the construction and use of photocopiers is regarded as a state secret. If this anachronism continues, progress in science and industry, so ardently sought by Gorbachev, may be seriously hampered.

The content of Glasnost also came under attack. The Moscow evening paper Vechernyaya Moskya headlined a virulently hostile article, "People who shriek from the sidelines." The paper condemned Glasnost for "harping on" old themes of the violations of human rights, political prisoners, psychiatric abuses and freedom to emigrate. Grigoryants did, indeed, write on these themes. They are still relevant issues. No changes have been made in the penal code to end harsh incarceration for "slandering" the state (particularly on trumped-up charges). Most political prisoners assigned to psychiatric hospitals and subjected to inhuman treatments remain in those hospitals.

Grigoryants handed us the first issue of Glasnost from which we published for the first time in English his introduction to the publication.[4] He premised his activity on the insistence of "the nation's leaders" that there must be "radical change." Restructuring for him, however, would be possible "only with the development of democratic practices." Those, such as himself, who had "already spoken and written the truth about life in their society, despite prohibitions and repressions, would find it easier to become a part of this process." That was the hope but not yet the reality. He recognized the danger of "provoking the actions of the reform's opponents." Yet, he said, inaction was for him "unacceptable." He added solemnly, "It is our feeling and conviction that the fate of the nation and the fate of humanity are being decided now, and this forces us to seek our way of participating in the current process of change." Grigoryants then echoed Gorbachev's critique of Soviet information policy, but with a different prescription:

> The need for independent publication is dictated by the fact that the entire print medium in our country is part of that very political, administrative, or economic apparatus which is far from irreproachable and has recently been subjected to open criticism. Since the mass media are part of this apparatus, they do not adequately provide the feedback necessary between society and the leadership, and the media share the blame for

the fact that the nation has come to a pre-crisis situation. Independent informational publications, while not capable of presenting a totally comprehensive and balanced picture of the life in the country for organizational and financial reasons, will nonetheless be a necessary complement to existing press organs, and together with them they will present a sufficiently objective idea about life in our society.[5]

Grigoryants had told us how important it would be for Glasnost to be recognized in the West. Not only would its ideas be conveyed, but the very life of the publication might be saved if the authorities realized that the world was watching. Considerable press attention was given the magazine in the United States and Europe. And in the Soviet Union, by word of mouth and the age-old grapevine, Glasnost gained unusual attention. "Its reception," wrote Grigoryants in the second number, "exceeded our expectations." He acknowledged this was due not so much because the content is unusual, "as because of the very fact of the appearance of an open, unofficial socio-political journal for the first time in seventy years in Russia, and because of the hopes expressed for it." The volume of material submitted to the editor was so great that selections had to be made both in Moscow and in the English edition published in New York by the Center for Democracy.

The ambivalence noted earlier permiated the official response to the magazine. The first deputy to the chairman of Goskomizdat (State Publishing Committee) invited Grigoryants to visit, and told him there were thousands of publications in the country representing state and public organizations, but Glasnost represented no one and therefore would not be registered. Grigoryants was told that since there was no law on the press in the USSR, he was not breaking any law by publishing. He expressed gratitude for that. But he was then interviewed by the deputy chairman of the district executive committee, and the acting district prosecutor. They told him that regulations specify that an editor bears responsibility for the content of published materials and must submit copies of them to Glavit (the chief censoring agency). But—Catch 22—since the publication of Glasnost is not authorized, no censor is assigned to it. There is no one to show it to. Grigoryants commented, "As far as I know, the censors do not work on a pro bono basis."

Issues 2, 3 and 4 of Glasnost carried articles on the destruction of archives in the USSR, the establishment of varied public organizations, the present operations of the KGB, secrecy in the USSR, the right to emigrate, nationality problems, and the press. There were also reports on the release of political prisoners, and some from psychiatric institutions. These are all subjects not covered in the official organs of communications, and all are regarded as highly sensitive.

Perhaps an even more daring challenge was directed to Gorbachev in an open letter addressed to him by Vyacheslav Chornovil, a Ukrainian dissident and former political prisoner. He stated in his 30-page letter that several Ukrainian journalists who have been barred from writing in the press are "legally resuming the publication of the sociopolitical and literary journal Ukrains'kyi visnyk [Ukrainian Herald], which came out [as samizdat] in the difficult conditions of the years 1970-72, and fully meets today's requirements for glasnost."

Chornovil touched the most sensitive nerve of Soviet nationalities policy. He argued that "today the national question, the most important one for a multinational country that has proclaimed itself a union of sovereign socialist states, finds itself in the most obscure blind alley of restructuring." He continued:

Theory (including your speeches at congresses and plenums) is totally devoid of any analysis of the real state of affairs, and the same general phrases about "flourishing and drawing together" that are known still from Stalinist times are repeated, with the same warnings about the inadmissability of preserving national survivals (although in practice one such "survival" that has been banished now for almost 60 years turns out to be, of all things, the national languages of the non-Russian members of the "equal" union).

Chornovil suggests that a special plenum of the Communist Party of the Soviet Union should be convened to examine the nationalities problem, with the same candor that Gorbachev displayed in outlining the country's economic problems in June 1987.

Religious as well as nationality and political groups have produced publications this year. Indeed, some twenty different associations of citizens met in a publicly announced conference at midyear.

Official ambivalence, and worse, was recorded November 8 by Grigoryants announcing new harassment of Soviet human rights activists by the KGB. Soviet officials "tirelessly and repeatedly talk about glasnost, perestroika and democratization, and about the observance of Socialist law," said Grigoryants. But based on personal experience, "the climate remains as before," he said. The absence of political trials this year "inspired some hope in us for an improvement in the political climate." But, he said, "everything has returned to its place and the attitude of the KGB and the police towards us has not changed."

He noted that on October 30 [long celebrated as the Day of the Political Prisoner], the KGB and the police took into illegal preventive detention about 40 people who had intended to take part in a peaceful demonstration in defense of political prisoners. "Crude physical force was used against Sergei Grigoryants, Andrei Shilkov and Kirill Podrabinek," a press release sent to the West stated. It continued, "The state security agencies put a permanent tail" on four persons, Grigoryants himself, and the staff of Glasnost and Ekspress-Khronika, some of whose editors have been incarcerated in mental institutions as well as prisons, according to the release. It reported that security agents on November 1 again attacked Grigoryants and Dmitri Eisner. Their appeal to police for help had "only one effect," said the statement: "Afterwards Eisner was badly beaten once again." A week later, security agents attacked the editor of Ekspress-Khronika, coupled with "anti-Semitic insults and threats to cripple him." Telephones of staff members have been disconnected, or calls interfered with. Mail is not delivered. The statement concluded, "Numerous appeals to agencies that protect rights have achieved no results . . . Those who commit these crimes should bear legal responsibility for them."

Are such incidents the vestigial acts of unreconstructed centurians? Gorbachev seems to imply that, when he writes "many problems have accumulated and it won't be easy to solve them. But change has begun and society cannot now turn back."[6] Can it, or has it already, in the displays of ambivalence throughout the society? Vladimir Bukovsky, one of the best-known Soviet dissidents, believes the Soviet Communist Party, five to seven years from now, "with or without Gorbachev at the helm, will go into reverse gear and reclaim its property." That "property" would include the return of SS-20s aimed at Western Europe, the clampdown of all dissidence, and the forcing of Western bankers and businessmen to cut their losses in the Soviet Union. That is Bukovsky's forecast.[7]

Criticism of glasnost within the Soviet Union has come from Viktor Chebrikov, the head of the KGB, and Egor Ligachev, the ranking party ideologist. He is sometimes regarded as second in command to Gorbachev. Ligachev accused Egor Yakovlev, editor of the Moscow News, of exceeding the boundaries of glasnost. Yakovlev responded that "to clear away the braking mechanism is a painful and complex operation. [L]ike a malignant tumor, this braking mechanism exists inside each one of us: very often in the lack of courage to act according to our own conscience and convictions." On this subject, my son and I in July queried the editor of the English-language edition of Moscow News. We asked him about criticism of his paper. It had published numerous articles previously considered unfit to print. Vladimir Pilchugin told us, "We have enemies not only in New York, but here as well." Another staffman told us there had been a street demonstration against the paper some days earlier.

Pilchugin clearly was pleased with the changes of the past year. Now, he said, he looks out of his window and sees lines of people reading his paper on the display board. Down the street, outside the other papers, nobody. Moscow News prints only 250,000 of its one million copies in Russian, and these go mainly to the intelligentsia in the Moscow area. Yet, said Pilchugin significantly, "I read Pravda [to see the current line], but Pravda reads Moscow News to see how far they can go." "How far?" we asked him. Nobody knows, he said, he must use his own judgment. He showed us quotes from Time and other Western magazines which he has reprinted. But he added quickly, "No anti-Soviet stuff, of course."

Sometimes the innovation in Moscow News is quite subtle, and may appear only in the English edition. During our visit, the current issue reported the American Peace March, presumably organized by the Soviets, from Leningrad to Moscow. A front-page picture showed Americans carrying banners side by side with Soviet citizens. The caption in English carried words that did not appear in the Russian edition (bracketed words are from the English version):

> While our two countries plod disgruntingly [and not
> always forwards] toward mutual understanding, these
> Soviets and Americans were not afraid to walk side by
> side [to the sound of a different drummer].

There were freshly discordant sounds within the Soviet Union.
An organization called "Pamyat," founded in the early 1980s, arran-
ges meetings at which prominent writers, historians, and artists
appear. The organization helps restore historical and cultural
monuments. But "Pamyat" has developed another interest: it
expresses extreme Russian nationalist and anti-Semitic sentiments.
The notorious anti-Semitic forgery, "The Protocols of the Elders of
Zion," has been read aloud at a "Pamyat" meeting. Cassettes of
that session were circulated widely in Moscow. As a result,
"Pamyat" was officially disbanded in 1986, but it continues to meet
while other groups have greater difficulty securing meeting places.
In April 1987, "Pamyat" seized control of the Moscow section of an
official body that preserves historical and cultural monuments.
Supporters of "Pamyat" seem active all over the Soviet Union, des-
pite some press opposition as well as support. "Pamyat" believes
tsarist Russia was an ideal state, that Lenin was a hero done in by
Jewish Old Bolsheviks, and that "Pamyat's" enemies are literally
serving Satan. Unlike other right-wing extremist groups in the
Soviet Union, "Pamyat" has members who are quite influential in
Soviet society. It is believed by researchers at Radio Free
Europe/Radio Liberty, who provided these analyses of "Pamyat",
that people who hold views similar to those of "Pamyat" may represent a majority in the leadership of the Writers' Union, though
clearly a minority in the unions of cinema and theatre workers.[8]

That is the price of freedom, the American Civil Liberties
Union might say in defending a similar group in the United States.
But where freedom does not prevail, the existence and broad
membership of a hate group must be assumed to reflect the studied
ambivalence and some objective of state policy.

Other Drummers, Other Censors

Marching to other drummers, were the censors in the politically
rightist countries of Chile and Paraguay. In both nations aging

dictators were promising elections and referenda, and an eventual "transition" toward democracy. Meanwhile, both regimes harass the press into self-censorship. In Orwellian fashion they employ constitutions and statutes, designed to protect press freedom, in order to restrict undesirable news and publications.

When General Augusto Pinochet ejected the elected government in 1973, all the news media that had supported the previous regime were eliminated and their property confiscated or expropriated. By decree in July 1974, Pinochet converted "acts against the government," including the exercise of free expression or publication or broadcasting, into specified crimes. Another decree the next year stipulated "misuse of publicity" as one way in which the security of the state could be attacked. As punishment, a newspaper or magazine could be suspended from publishing for ten days, and a radio station put off the air for the same time. For more serious breaches, seizure of the "printing machines" was authorized.

The constitution amended in 1980 provides for freedom to disseminate opinion without prior censorship, but makes the disseminator responsible for "crimes or abuses" committed in exercising such liberty. Readers and listeners are also given the right of "rectification," to have a declaration freely carried in the medium that presumably harmed him. These provisions, however, will go into effect in 1990, when Pinochet promises to turn over the government—if no state of siege is in effect. A 1984 law amending the earlier statute on "misuses of publicity" is particularly objectionable because it deprives both the medium and the journalist of the defense of truth, when charged.

Under Pinochet, closure and suspensions of the media have been frequent. Under the state of siege decreed in 1984, prior censorship was imposed. Judicial complaints have been issued against editors and reporters. Though they may be acquitted, they inevitably serve time in prison. Emilio Filippi, a distinguished independent journalist in Santiago, addressed a Freedom House conference there in November. He had suffered imprisonment years earlier. He noted that twenty Chilean journalists are still under police charges. One reporter has been sentenced to spend every night in prison for one and one-half years. Filippi said that the military courts generally act against the press, but civilian courts are sometimes just. There are many press laws, and the courts follow the letter rather than the spirit of the laws. Given the mean spiritedness of the dictatorship, however, that would seem to be a distinction without a difference. Certainly that was so for the three Chilean journalists murdered this year, and three others who received death threats.

During our visit to Chile, a new regulation based on Article 8 of the constitution was being completed. Journalists hesitated to discuss it because the exact terms were not yet formally released. Ignacio Gonzalez Camus, president of the College of Journalists, described the new regulation as "the most serious thing that has happened to the press since September 11, 1973." On that day, some twenty publications and ten radio stations were shut down. Emilio Filippi recalls that when harsh censorship was lifted once before, followed by expected self-censorship, the colonel issuing the new order said, "The more prudent you are, the safer you are; the safer you are, the fewer difficulties you will have; the fewer difficulties you have, the more points you win."

It is still more difficult to win points in Paraguay today under the rule of General Alfredo Stroessner. He seized power thirty-four years ago, and banners in Asuncion support only his candidacy again in 1988. As in Chile, the word goes out, it is the status quo or "chaos." In both countries, many citizens seem far too intelligent to believe that, but the moderate, democratic-minded population is seriously split over minute differences. The armies, moreover, seem unlikely to give up the power and considerable financial gain they have acquired from the regimes. In Paraguay, particularly, the military has been given legal right to profit from the years in uniform, provided the chief of government approves.

Such information does not appear in the Paraguayan press. When the most important daily newspaper, ABC Color, and the most lively radio station, "Radio Nanduti," suggested there were governmental irregularities both media were repeatedly harassed, their owners imprisoned several times, and both shut down permanently. We went to Asuncion in November principally to assist Radio Nanduti. The sign at the entrance to the arrival gate said, "Welcome to the land of peace and prosperity." The state of siege in effect since 1954 had been lifted in April 1987. Secret police photographed press and radio reporters interviewing me at the airport. I had been invited to speak at a press conference at Radio Nanduti later that day. But the government had ruled the conference could be held—but no one could attend!

143

That edict had been applied several times earlier when Nanduti planned seminars at its 250-seat theatre. Such meetings in the past had produced books on democratization. After the station's owner, Humberto Rubin, had been arrested several times on trumped-up charges against his broadcasts, a government-supported mob in April 1986 attacked the building with gunshots and stones. The chanting mob broke every outside window, and screamed epithets at Rubin and his wife. Part of the station's equipment was stolen so that pirates presumed to be supported by the government noisily wiped out Radio Nanduti's broadcast signal. Facing bankruptcy, Rubin shut down the station in January 1987.

We appeared for the press conference, but heavily armed officers blocked the avenue, the side street, and the entrance to the radio station. The courageous Catholic radio station broadcast, live, the blockading of Nanduti. We left the building, were interrogated briefly by the officers, and went to a hotel where we held the press conference. I said that this was an archaic way to treat the flow of ideas. Most of Latin America had given up such draconian acts, I added, because they reflected fear of one's own countrymen, and lack of trust in their good sense. The message was carried by the Catholic radio, and in the one relatively independent newspaper. Next day, driving through Asuncion with Rubin, we stopped at a traffic signal. A truck driver next to us gave Rubin a thumbs-up sign, and added words of encouragement. One must have great admiration for the publisher Aldo Zucilillo, and Humberto and Gloria Rubin. In a land where other newspapers and radio stations may continue in partial freedom, they are totally blacked out—unfree—because they fought for greater freedom than the dictator would allow.

Farther north in the hemisphere, the commandante of Managua engaged another journalist in one of the most unusual acts of press-state concordats ever recorded. President Daniel Ortega of Nicaragua on October 1, 1987, agreed in writing that the daily newspaper La Prensa could be reopened "without any restrictions except those imposed by responsible journalism." That still left a major loophole: who is to determine what is responsible journalism? La Prensa's owner, Violeta Chamorro, widow of the paper's slain editor, had just turned down Ortega's first offer: reopen with prior censorship. Dona Violeta said she would keep the paper closed rather than submit. For four years, starting in 1982, the Sandinistas imposed draconian censorship. On at least 41 occasions La Prensa was unable to publish. On June 26, 1986, the Sandinistas shut down La Prensa completely.

Ultimately, La Prensa decided to accept Ortega's latest offer and publish again. In the joint statement signed October 1, Dona Violeta said the newspaper would "contribute to the climate of peace and understanding the country needs to advance the process of peace and national reconciliation." Perhaps even more interesting may be another document, not yet published at this writing, that will set forth the concerns and views both sides expressed in the dramatic negotiating sessions on September 19. These sessions led to the reopening of La Prensa.

Radio Catolica was also permitted to return to the air, but forbidden to broadcast news. Still shut down by government edict, despite commitments made under the Arias plan for peace in Central America, were twenty-two other radio stations, all nongovernmental television channels, and all the newspapers of the political parties and labor unions. These are essential if the nonviolent, democratic opposition in Nicaragua is to have a fair voice before elections are held—if they are held, as part of the Arias agreement.

Censorship By Complexity

In most of Africa, governments either own the newspapers and radios, or exert unquestioned influence over them. That is not true in Nigeria where a robust newspaper tradition provides diverse, often raucous, views. The present military government has been more permissive than its recent predecessors, but this year it banned for six months the lively newsweekly Newswatch. The magazine had leaked secret information. The government lifted the ban a month early and Newswatch reappeared with a bold cover story headlined, "How powerful is the press?" Inside, the magazine carried eight colorful articles and editorials describing the reason for the banning, and the implications of censorship. The issue also carried letters from abroad congratulating the magazine for persevering. Its verve and freedom seemed unimpaired in the months afterward, but any government shutdown is bound to have some chilling effect.

In South Africa, however, the nature and degree of censorship is quite different from the rest of the continent. There is still the appearance of some press freedom, but that exists mainly for news and information that are not important—either to the government or to the public's understanding of life in that country today. To manage this extensive control of information in a society undergoing revolution, the government has enacted many statutes governing the press and other media. This amounts to censorship by complexity, since an editor must have constant consultation with a lawyer if he is to keep himself and his paper out of court, and publishing.

We visited South Africa in October to attend an international conference on censorship called by The Star, the leading English-language paper, celebrating its hundredth birthday. In conversations with white and black editors, publishers, and reporters, it became clear that the principal effect of the countless regulations was to dry up the sources of information for domestic and foreign journalists functioning in South Africa. Since sources as well as journalists could be convicted for a vast array of offenses, few were taking risks—particularly since even eyewitness accounts could not be published in most instances. This leads to a severe loss of credibility among black readers. Most of the horrendous action takes place in their townships. A black paper such as City Press, edited by the distinguished Percy Qobozo, cannot carry eye-witness accounts of an event in Soweto. Instead City Press must run the version given by the government information office. "An editor in South Africa has a horrendous responsibility," says Qobozo. "He has to walk a virtual minefield every day to try to keep the public informed without having his newspaper shut down."

At the conference, Harvey Tyson, editor of The Star, said that in South Africa today "no real newspaper could ever publish a normal edition without facing prosecution." Therefore, he said, you "ignore the mare's nest of regulations, and do what you have to do."

With such frustration a daily preoccupation, and a black reporter from his newspaper having "disappeared" as we conferees arrived, Tyson invited Stoffel Botha to explain the complex censorship system. Botha, Minister of Information, was frank. He said the creation of a democratic society must be postponed in South Africa as long as the country was threatened by "subversive" forces. Journalists may not like it, he said, but that is the way it is.

Three months earlier, August 28, the latest regulation (R. 123) had been set in place.[9] It established a central directorate for monitoring the press. R. 123 was the sixth major regulation issued under Public Safety Act No. 3 of 1953 which empowers the State President to declare a state of emergency. Two regulations in 1986 and four in 1987 grant the state increasing emergency powers. Two in 1987 (R. 97 and R. 123) specifically control the news media.

As a consequence, the Minister is empowered to determine whether a periodical systematically has "the effect" of promoting or fanning revolution or uprisings in the republic, or has taken other acts "aimed at the overturning of the government by other than constitutional means." The text further widens the net by establishing guilt if a publisher sparks "unrest," or foments "feelings of hatred or hostility" toward public authorities. The regulation attaches guilt to the publication which promotes boycotts, strikes, civil disobedience, and similar acts.

On finding such material, the Minister is authorized to warn a publication of its alleged breaching of the law. If such actions continue, the Minister may ban the publication for up to three months. For most publications in South Africa that is tantamount to forcing the company into bankruptcy, and casting the journalists onto the streets without unemployment insurance or welfare provisions.

This writer discussed these provisions with a white editor of an "alternative" newspaper and the black editor of the only national weekly black newspaper, City Press. Both separately acknowledged that this latest regulation was the most serious hindrance yet to their remaining in journalism.

While the foreign visitors were present, the Information Minister issued his first "warning" to a newspaper—the New Nation, a strongly dissenting journal. It had been assumed the new restrictions were partly designed to close several "alternative" papers. I was told a series of charges had been filed against another "alternative" paper, The Weekly Mail, which later received a warning. Some eight official queries had been made to City Press.

An attorney who helps assure the continued publication of any newspaper in South Africa faces almost an impossible task. He must keep in mind, not only the most complex laws and precedents, but the audience for which the paper is intended (official determinations may vary with the anticipated readers), and the presumed mind-set of the censor. He may decide an article or publication is a threat for entirely subjective or political reasons. Yet the many statutes and regulations must be used by the censor and by publisher's attorney to avoid being outlawed.

The woeful history of South Africa's legislation since 1950 encompasses far more than censorship. All social and political activities which threaten separation of races have been the object of legislation. Yet press law epitomizes this society-wide phenomenon: the state criminalizes after the fact any activity which appears to threaten apartheid. Henceforth, then, the individuals and organizations so engaged are suppressed. As one observer put it to me, "The individuals and organizations are banned or imprisoned or go into exile or just go home or get bored or tired or grow older and, probably, wiser and more cynical. But the law remains on the statute books!"

Consequently, our 1986 edition of Newspaper Man's Guide to the Law, by Lane, Hoffe, Disa and Tathem is 332 pages—yet it does not include the 1987 regulations that create a new set of restrictions and procedures.

Percy Qobozo's words should be taken as he intended, and not as a display of pique over the especially harsh treatment he receives as a black journalist: "White members of the public will suffer more by the blackout of news, because the blacks live in a township where the revolution is occurring. They know by sight and word of mouth what is occurring, but the whites in their secure white suburbs do not." While the intent in South Africa is quite different from the Soviet objective, the systematized dissemination of official information, under the guise of some permissiveness, smacks of glasnost.

The Ambivalence of Freedom

Not only repressive societies are troubled by the communications media. Free countries, where news and information are generally more pervasive, and certainly more independent of government, can create troubles for officials. The retention of state secrets, usually tied to national security, inspires most tension between state and journalists. The tendency to overclassify government documents, out of honest concern for national security, or to preserve political control or avoid embarrassment, affects every democratic bureaucracy. Citizens of some free countries accept state secrecy as a traditional expectation. Other democratic societies—the United States, Canada, and increasingly the United Kingdom—expect continuous struggles by journalists to persuade officials to release more and more hitherto secret caches. Sometimes, when American journalists pry out a secret or serve as the conduit for an insider's leak, there is public objection that openness has gone too far. Such was not the general reaction this year at the revelation of the arms-for-hostages manipulations in Iran and elsewhere by staff members of the National Security Council. The secret dealings with Iranians, arms merchants, and Nicaraguan-contra middlemen broke down not because the cover of secrecy had been blown: The conception of the negotiations had been flawed, and the persona could not produce the results anticipated.

In the United Kingdom, the government's bid for secrecy took a somewhat comic turn. Britain's Law Lords imposed a ban on press coverage of the facts and allegations that appeared in the book, Spycatcher, the memoirs of Peter Wright, formerly a member of MI - 5, the highly secret UK intelligence agency. The catch was, the book had been published in the United States and excerpted in Australia, and was circulating in the UK itself. The press ban hardly restricted the spread of the information, but it did reflect a desire to censor for censorship's sake. Wright had charged, for example, that some thirty British agents spied on and defamed Prime Minister Harold Wilson who served three terms between 1964 and 1976. Three London newspapers nevertheless carried the story, and faced contempt charges. "Our secret agents take an oath to keep secret," said a government spokesman. "What we are trying to do is make certain they stick to that oath."

But then the agent should be pursued, to the extent of the law, and not the press informing the public. The Wilson incidents, now history, should be examined for their implications today. The public has a right to consider the challenge which Wright's book uncovered.

Meanwhile, the House of Commons has been examining the Official Secrets Act. The 76-year-old law needs revision, the Labor Party has held and Prime Minister Thatcher agreed. She hesitated while the Spycatcher controversy persisted. One amendment would retain the protection of defense, international relations and security matters, but repeal the broad prosecutorial power of Section Two. The proposal would require the government to prove that "serious injury" had resulted from a disclosure, and would allow the defendant to argue that he had acted in the national interest. A showdown on this bill may come in 1988.

The Indian government was beset all year by the deep prodding of two independent and largely oppositionist English-language newspapers, The Statesman and the Indian Express. Both papers turned up widespread scandals that enmeshed Prime Minister Rajiv Gandhi and many political leaders around him, and threatened to destabilize his government.

The Statesman published scores of articles, many front-page, with bold headlines; reports from the paper's Washington correspondent, and many scathing editorials crying scandal around the Prime Minister. The issue began with revelations of suspicious payments to Bofors, the Swedish weapons contractor, on deals totalling $1.3 billion. The Statesman charged the Gandhi government was guilty of corruption involving "mind-boggling sums," "illicitly made fortunes salted away abroad and handsome payoffs in every official transaction."[10] There were strong suggestions that a friend of the Prime Minister had violated currency regulations. Several top colleagues of Gandhi left the government.

The Indian Express no less forcefully pressed that long-running story, and also deeply explored allegations of fraud involving a Bombay textile company. When the company was not prosecuted, the Express strongly criticized the government. Not long afterward, hundreds of government agents raided the offices of the Express. "This is a deliberate government attempt to intimidate one of the country's leading newspapers," said the editor of the rival Hindustan Times. The Prime Minister denied he had directed the raids. In November, however, the Gandhi government assumed financial control over the building which houses the Express' offices and press. The Express had been on strike, and could not pay rent on government land. The paper charged the Gandhi government had helped sustain the strike. The Statesman regarded the incident as a warning to any paper that exposes the "misdemeanors of the ruling party."

Altogether, these were the severest attacks on press freedom in India since Raji Gandhi's mother, Indira Gandhi, placed the country's news media under her control in the 1975 Emergency.

In the Philippines, as prevailed prior to Ferdinand Marcos' rule, the very openness of the press under Corazon Aquino has produced a licentious—and thus less credible—press. In this climate, there are stirrings of measures to inhibit the most irresponsible journalists. One radio station was shut down as a signal of concern. Publishers are aware that public perception of widespread irresponsibility could generate support for governmental controls.

Such a warning was issued in Malaysia in 1985 by Prime Minister Mahathir Mohamad. He said then that as the top elected official he could determine what was safe to report in the press, radio and television.[11] In a brief meeting with him then, this writer contended that the public should determine the extent of press responsibility since the government is a party to the state-press relationship. Mohamad moved this year on his warning. On October 28 he shut down three leading newspapers, including the lively English-language daily, The Star. A fourth subsequently was closed, all in the name of avoiding racial antagonism. Among the Star's columnists was the former Prime Minister, Tunku Abdul Rahman, who appealed the revocation of the Star's license to publish. Rahman said, "I think the way it is going the country is heading to dictatorship." He added that the internal security act was meant to deal with communist terrorists, not common citizens.

Late in November, the government moved further: it proposed a bill prescribing bans on publications that alarm public opinion. It would suspend papers that carry articles judged to be against the national interest. There would be prison terms for those who print "false" news. The National Union of Journalists said, "That is the administration's unequivocal repudiation of the freedom of the press, with a very clear message that dissent will not be tolerated."

Expansion of Freedom

It is clear from our accompanying table, and most earlier reports in this essay that the free flow of information, within and between countries, is mainly a function of the degree to which governments own, control, or intervene in the movement of ideas and data. The more governmental influence, the less freedom for the individual citizen to understand what is going on around him. It is a welcome sign, therefore, to report a small but growing trend of governments divesting themselves of news and information media, and welcoming private ownership. Change in ownership by itself does not guarantee improvement in the quality of journalism. But it does provide more diversity than government monopolies offer.

There can be immediate changes that seem to reduce pluralism, as occurred this year in France, but privatization does limit the most powerful political impact, the influence of big government over the communications media. France released government control over 300 radio stations on the FM dial in the Paris area. These were mainly broadcasters representing gay, African, Chinese, and other minorities. Some 96 stations will remain, and the others may resume if they pay the cost. Television channels are also being examined, and a new TV authority created.

Mrs. Aquino has appointed a three-man cabinet committee to study the privatization of People's Television 4, and twenty-four radio stations in the Philippines. A private company formed by the former director-general of the Spanish state radio and television networks will transmit 24-hour TV programs to Spain from overseas. The Madrid government is not questioning the legality of these overseas, private transmissions. In Jamaica, WI, four new privately-owned TV and radio stations were expected to be functioning in 1988. The Portuguese government intends to transfer one of two public television channels to private ownership, and grant new licenses for TV operations by private companies. The United Kingdom expects to substantially expand the number of television channels, as in the United States. These would be funded by advertising or viewer subscription. The Thatcher government seeks to gain from the impending worldwide boom in television. As though to underscore the correlation between press/broadcast freedom and nongovernmental ownership, the government of Malaysia in October rejected all twenty-two applications to set up private radio stations in the country.

UNESCO Marks Time

Neither UNESCO nor the United Nations General Assembly provided new ammunition this year for press-controllers. UNESCO was more concerned all year with replacing its two-term Director General,

Amadou Mahtar M'Bow. He had run afoul of Western journalists (and later their governments) by too strongly supporting developing country demands for a new world information and communication order. This was interpreted for many years as a distinct threat to journalists who do not work for governmental information services. That debate was muted in UNESCO, but carried over to the UN Committee on Information. There, the United States repeatedly stood alone in rejecting resolutions on the information order that, at worst, were convoluted code-phrases long since defanged at UNESCO. That organization in November chose its new DG: Professor Federico Mayor, a biochemist from Spain who had long served as deputy to M'Bow. Mayor promised reforms of UNESCO's administration and programs so that the United States and the United Kingdom would return to the organization. They had left in 1985 and 1986. Mayor did not specify how he would alter UNESCO's communications programs. He would, after all, face a constituency of 158 countries. More than one hundred are developing countries that regard UNESCO as their idea-factory and service agency. It would seem, however, that a freshly arrived DG, facing financial if not intellectual bankruptcy, could persuade his board and secretariat to eliminate those programs which clearly arouse bitter dissension, and have no possible consensual support. In this category are further efforts to define a "new information order," or discuss specific governmental controls over news media. These have been implicitly or explicitly debated as codes of journalistic practice, press "responsibility," or licensing of journalists.

An Unambiguous Declaration

Journalists the world over seemed to have recognized by 1987 that governmental influences over the media of news and information had reached near-crisis proportions. For professional observers who frequently cry crisis, sometimes prematurely, their formally expressed concern for their own roles was somewhat overdue. There were, after all, thirty-four murders of journalists in twelve countries in 1987, about the same as in the previous two years. Another 10 were kidnapped or disappeared this year, 23 were beaten and 41 shot. At least 179 were arrested and 49 expelled from countries from which they were reporting.

With such statistics in mind, and new confirming stories to be told, journalists from thirty-five countries met in London in January to "challenge the censors." The meeting was arranged by the World Press Freedom Committee, and was cosponsored by five other global free-press groups. They agreed to create a "fund against censorship," provide legal aid where possible, and set up a "censorship hotline" to sound the alarm worldwide when censors strike. The Declaration of London formulated at that meeting stated:

> "Journalism has always been a hazardous profession . . . This conference, however, has attested to a more ominous trend: the growing use of brute force by government powers, criminal forces and other interests seeking to intimidate the news media. . . . We are disturbed also by the proliferation of press controls which equate with censorship in all but name . . . While direct prepublication or prebroadcast censorship remains limited, indirect censorship flourishes worldwide. . . . These curbs on the domestic news media are matched by the obstacles erected by many countries to international press coverage. . . . In a world that is becoming increasingly one through new communications technologies, press freedom is indivisible. When censorship applies anywhere, it restricts access of the public everywhere to full knowledge of events. . . . Only through the fullest commitment to a free and unrestricted flow of news gathered by free and independent journalists will we overcome those seeking to blind the world to what is happening in it."

Such objectives will always conflict with the "glasnosting" of news and information, whether contrived in Moscow, Kuala Lumpur, or Pretoria.

NOTES

1. In November 1986 we noted the definition of "glasnost" as primarily "publicity." See "Communications: Revising the Limits of Disclosure," page 102, in Raymond D. Gastil, **Freedom in the World: Political Rights and Civil Liberties: 1986-1987** (Westport, Ct.: Greenwood Press, 1987).

2. Mikhail Gorbachev, **Perestroika** (New York: Harper and Row, 1987), page 22.

3. See Leonard R. Sussman and Mark J. Sussman, "The Birth of Glasnost," in **Freedom at Issue,** September-October 1987.

4. See Leonard R. Sussman, "Glasnost, the Magazine, vs. Glasnost, the Policy," **The Wall Street Journal,** op-ed page, July 31, 1987.

5. The English version of **Glasnost** (published in Moscow) is translated and published in New York City by the Center for Democracy, 358 West 30 Street, New York 10001, at $6 an issue.

6. Gorbachev, **Perestroika,** page 10.

7. Vladimir Bukovsky, "Gorbachev's Glasnost Lies," **Sunday Times** (London), November 1, 1987.

8. Radio Free Europe/Radio Liberty, 342/87.

9. **Government Gazette,** Republic of South Africa, Pretoria, 28 August 1987, Proclamation by the State President, No. R. 123, 1987.

10. Editorial, **The Statesman,** Calcutta, April 12, 1987.

11. For a discussion of Prime Minister Mahathir bin Mohamad's dissertation on press freedom in 1985 see Leonard R. Sussman, "No Detente in International Communications," in Raymond D. Gastil, **Freedom in the World: Political Rights and Civil Liberties, 1985-1986,** (Westport, Ct.: Greenwood Press, 1987).

SUPPORTING DEMOCRATIC DEVELOPMENT:

A DISCUSSION[1]

GASTIL: Our theme for this afternoon is the attempt by the United States to support democracy through private and public means. By supporting democracy we are primarily interested in support in the context of this conference of the National Endowment for Democracy (NED), and less concerned with more general questions such as those of trade or military policy. Each of you might think about aspects of United States' support for democracy in your country that you found particularly helpful, and identify American attempts to support democracy that you have not found helpful. For example, both among Chinese and Americans, support for the development of democracy in China has focused on developing a more open and liberal discussion of issues within China. The central focus of support for democracy in the Soviet Union, on the other hand, has emphasized dissidents—and the problems of imprisonment, torture, or the denial of exit visas. Perhaps there should be an effort to discover the relative accomplishments of these and other approaches. One wonders whether we could support both kinds of emphases in regard to China? Would the more personal, "dissident approach" to China interfere with the gains for liberalization that have been made by other approaches, such as that supported by NED of Liang Heng (founder and editor of The Chinese Intellectual, a quarterly magazine originally intended for Chinese students studying in the West but now circulated within China)?

BRAUMAN: The humanitarian aid policies of the major democracies in nondemocratic countries need to be reevaluated.

Our organization—Medecins Sans Frontieres—has been publicizing over the past eighteen months Ethiopia's misuse of foreign aid. International assistance in Ethiopia has been used to amplify a political project that is an absolute disaster for the country; humanitarian efforts are being used to achieve political goals. The result will be that in the next two or three years we are going to see a new famine, without any doubt, because the government is collectivizing the whole country. Thirty million peasants in Ethiopia are going to be "villagized," as they say in Ethiopia.

The problem is a real one. International assistance should be either under tight control or limited to countries that promote democracy—or at least leave the civil society some space to express itself. This is not the case in Ethiopia.

Apparently there is a large movement in the States to support the civilian population affected by drought and famine in Ethiopia, without any consideration of what are the real causes of their famine. Watching TV this morning, I saw two persons from important humanitarian organizations, Save the Children Fund and Catholic Relief Services, permanent voluntary agencies, saying that now in Ethiopia all the country was green, and that it was absolutely marvelous to see what was happening there. They didn't say one word about forced resettlement and villagization. But if one talked about South Africa and the efforts of the community to develop itself, without mentioning apartheid, there would be a scandal.

Of course, it is easy to develop real humanitarian work in most of Africa. Most African countries, whether democratic or nondemocratic, leave some space to the civil society to express itself.

GASTIL: We often do give pure humanitarian aid to countries whose politics are very antidemocratic, and try to divorce it from political considerations. Is it generally felt by other people here that pure humanitarian aid hurts the democratic effort in general, or is neutral to it, or what? Could it have possible advantages in the long run?

BRAUMAN: I would not make a separation between democratic and antidemocratic. I would make a separation between countries who accept the idea of a civil society and those that deny it. Ethiopia is a totalitarian regime and denies the right of any independent group to express itself as an independent group. Therefore, all groups, whether they are Ethiopian or expatriate groups, are obliged to follow a policy dictated by the government.

I have worked a number of years in Africa and I know that most of the African governments are dictatorships, but they don't deny the right to private social organizations to express themselves. So this is a real difference.

GASTIL: Let's take another example. Let's say there was a large famine in Marxist-Leninist South Yemen. From the point of view of supporting democracy around the world, if the United States were in any way—private or public—to try to provide extensive aid to South Yemen, realizing the government is totalitarian, repressive, and very much like Ethiopia's, do you think this would be something that would hurt our worldwide effort to support democratic development?

ZAVALA: It seems to me that if we believe in democratic principles and values, we have to help. If we have the means to help, we should help whoever has the need of it. Of course, it becomes a problem when, in a case like Ethiopia, the government is not doing what it should, but we should not punish the people of Ethiopia because of their government's actions.

Perhaps the solution would be to try to find if there is a real civil society, as you were saying, to try to help through civic organizations, not through the government, through different groups. In your case, medical doctors.

GASTIL: You mean through groups in-country?

ZAVALA: Groups in-country that are trying to better the situation of the people, and send the aid through these groups instead of the government.

BRAUMAN: I would like to make a brief point about that. Everybody should be aware that there is a new problem facing international charitable aid in some third world countries. A number of governments understand that one of their richest raw materials is hunger, and they fabricate hunger, and then they sell it on the international charity market. That is what is happening now.

If there is no adverse reaction in the international community of those who give money, food, or relief goods, I mean this is going to develop. I am talking about Ethiopia because this is the most incredible example. But we can see the example that Mozambique is raising now. If we are going to encourage the government to create famine and then to sell it and sell it more and more expensively, this will not benefit the population; it will benefit only the dictatorship.

We face a cruel dilemma when we aid a government like Ethiopia's, hoping that some portion of this aid will go to the population. Part of the assistance benefits the population, but only a small part. The rest of the assistance goes to the government and helps them create a new system which is going to favor new famines. The process will go on and on.

GASTIL: What then are your policy recommendations? What should private or government organizations be doing to avoid this result?

BRAUMAN: I think they should be more careful about the way they distribute aid. The international community now accepts the principle of refusing to be blackmailed by hostage taking, as far as individuals are concerned. This should be extended to whole peoples.

A while back the United States decided to suspend aid to Ethiopia unless the deportation and resettlement of the population was stopped. As a result, the Ethiopian government decided to stop. Now the Ethiopian government is resuming the resettlement and villagization operation, but nobody cares. People act as though it is not occurring. The Ethiopian government stopped it under international pressure; now they resume it and there is no international pressure. This means that they are going to be able to do whatever they want with the funds provided by the international assistance in the name of solidarity, and to create the exact opposite of solidarity.

CARDENAL: In offering aid it is necessary to discover a point between total support and conditional support. Sometimes you give too much support. Sometimes when you do act you want to run the show completely; you don't allow a national leadership to grow, to take the responsibility, because the others are making the big decisions. For example, in Nicaragua the U.S. was making the decisions for the Contras. There is a tendency of the United States to try to run the show and make the others marionettes. Then when your people gain power, you concentrate too much on your relations with the government and ignore the opposition.

GASTIL: The United States in most of its aid activities, both private and public, has connections primarily with the government in power at the time, and relatively little, in most instances, with opposition groups. It is a difficult problem to avoid but, nevertheless, there may be more scope for developing relations with the opposition.

MONTEMAYOR: The basic question is how do we find a way whereby aid can be given that will somehow expand the frontiers of democracy. The first step is to analyze each country and then see the possibilities where aid, as an instrument of democracy, could be most effective. And that will imply identifying groups that are democratic in practice. Many groups say they are for democracy, but internally they are totalitarian. So it is not enough to look only at the goals, but the process, as we look at the true nature of the organizations we may wish to help. In some cases acceptable organizations may not exist. But there will be individuals, or perhaps schools, that have to some extent tried to apply democracy in their own work. So we can start with that.

What channels we choose will depend on the political situation. For example, it would be very difficult in Indonesia to go through the trade unions to finance, say, trade union education activities. This would immediately lead to political problems for those involved.

So we must be flexible and innovative. In many countries cooperative groups would be the best place to start, because there is little objection to people increasing incomes. The cooperative is a mechanism whereby you practice economic democracy and whereby people are trained to discuss proposed solutions to their own problems, and perhaps later on this can lead to more political activities.

That is what I mean by being very flexible, and I think very careful also in the positive sense, so that the aid could at least come in. Then as the assisted organization grows and people become more aware of the possibilities, they could expand into other duties.

GASTIL: Certainly NED has an institution-building function in many countries. One might even think of an institution-building function that is little more than an attempt to build institutions that could receive humanitarian aid under difficult conditions. In other words, in a country such as Niger, where we may not have a possibility of giving aid to private organizations within the country because such organizations hardly exist, it would be helpful to long-term U.S. foreign policy as well as the people of Niger for an organization like NED to try to develop some internal structure there. Then in the future, if the U.S. wanted to give humanitarian aid to the country, there would at least be acceptable organizations to receive the aid.

GERSHMAN: An example is Haiti.

BERLANGER: This is what I was waiting for. It is crucial in many poor countries to find human resources that are able to absorb efficiently any international aid. This is true especially in democratic development. Because it is a more political field, aid for democratic development is always subject to the criticism of outside interference. So it is fundamental that you find a structure inside a country with flexibility, leverage, and a certain autonomy. Unfortunately, my experience is that too often an aid organization really wants to have a branch inside a country. So a branch is established and a general manager is sent from abroad. There may be some partnership, but this is not really institution building. I appreciate the possibility that we have had to work with the Endowment in this sense. The major problem for the United States is with large agencies like USAID, as well as some private volunteer organizations that don't have all this flexibility because of their large bureaucracy. They are not able to deal with the people.

Our case was actually not so different from Ethiopia. The first time we approached the Endowment it was under Duvalier. The job we could do at that time wasn't exactly the job that we are doing right now. But we were able to do something positive and affect the Duvalier government.

GASTIL: What were you able to do under the Duvalier government?

BERLANGER: What we have been able to do is to build a network that could offer an alternative to the people. If we had just faced the situation as it was, without trying to build the possibility for the future, we would have concluded that there was nothing to do, aside from isolated help or helping the government.

GASTIL: What about the possibility of strengthening existing institutions that have some kind of defense mechanism against the government? I am thinking, for example, of religious institutions. In Ethiopia it's the only one I can think of that might have a possibility perhaps; of course, in Haiti the religious institution is also important.

Would it have been useful for organizations like NED to think in terms of strengthening the structures of such institutions that could carry some of the weight of this need?

BRAUMAN: Certainly, yes, provided you look into it carefully because, as you know, certain churches are really state-controlled and others are independent. Unfortunately, in Ethiopia again, those churches that got assistance were those whose leaders were nominated by the government.

GASTIL: But aren't there almost always degrees of control, especially in church-state relations?

CHEA: At least in my country, the churches are separated from the state. The activities are for the society, but they are separate. They respect the government and the government respects the activities of the church—Catholic and Protestant. The activities are for the society, but they are separate in this respect.

BERLANGER: I think that in this issue, helping the church would depend on what project is being considered. The church also can be used as a channel for specific projects. But this is not the same thing as institution building. In fact, the church itself is a structure that can be somewhat rigid. In my country, if a church has an interesting project and an aid organization does not have any kind of dogmatism or ideological frame, then they can get cooperation with the church. Basically it can be more effective, instead of trying to put everything through the church directly. This is an important point. We need to discuss the question of using those organizations that are trying to avoid an ideological framework.

CARDENAL: I think that humanitarian aid is not given with the purpose of increasing democracy, but is given as humanitarian aid.

GASTIL: But we don't want our aid to interfere with our attempt to extend at least the basis for democracy.

CARDENAL: But humanitarian aid is not a good example of how to extend democracy. It makes people dependent. You have to give it in case of crisis, of course. That I am for. For humanitarian reasons you have to help. This will not help develop democracy—because the one that gives is going to be the powerful one; the one that receives is becoming more dependent.

Even if there is abuse in the distribution, you have given the help, because at least something is being received by the people. Nonetheless, we have to take care to do the best we can, perhaps through the churches. In Nicaragua we have the "popular churches." If we were to try to distribute food through the Catholic popular church, they might decide to actually let the Sandinistas do the distribution. They would receive the food from your hands, but the real distributors would be the Sandinistas. But this is not a good issue to spend our time on here. We are looking for ways of making people democratic.

BERLANGER: But your humanitarian aid, does it include other things besides food?

CARDENAL: Well, many things, but primarily food.

BERLANGER: It is important to distinguish between what makes people dependent and what does not. If you are providing support for schools or for health, I am not sure that will make the people more dependent. The question of dependence relates to the provision of food. So it is not only a question of dependence; it is a question of affecting the production in a country. To me it doesn't seem really obvious that, if you are helping some people to have more education and better health, you are making them more dependent.

CARDENAL: No. You are not.

VO VAN AI: It is unreal to talk about humanitarian aid in a Communist country because Communist countries are not democratic countries, and if we talk about aid within a Communist country it is as if we were comparing it with a democratic society.

Hanoi has been appealing to Western nongovernmental, church, and humanitarian organizations for humanitarian aid because they say war has destroyed the economy, and now the children are hungry and the economy is in ruins; they need food and money to feed the people.

We know from our own experience and through what we have been doing in Vietnam that no humanitarian aid actually reaches the Vietnamese population. It all goes to support the war effort in Cambodia or other military efforts. In fact, the people benefit in no way whatsoever from any kind of food aid which is sent in from the outside.

So aid, even humanitarian aid, should be parallel with a global strategy for developing democracy in these countries. If we don't seek to exert some kind of pressure, for example, in the case of Vietnam or the Vietnamese government, then it's not possible to help them in a humanitarian way.

For the past century, the Vietnamese people have had no tradition of democracy in their country. From 1955 to 1975 American aid to Vietnam did not go into the hands of the democratic leadership. This is why today Vietnam is under a Communist regime. If the aid given by the Americans before 1975 could have been better handled, in a more democratic way, then the result would not be what it is today.

So I was very moved and impressed to see that during the two days of the conference there is emerging a global strategy and a global concept that would be very helpful to Vietnam in the future.

In Vietnam, we need to elevate the cultural and educational level of the people inside the country, if there are going to be any real changes in the future.

There are underground democratic movements inside Vietnam and these should be supported and aided. One of the ways in which we have been working over the past years is to publish information for circulation inside Vietnam to these movements, so they know what is happening in the world.

That is one of the ways that, although we can't bring them much help, we can bring them hope and support, and that is very concrete aid in Vietnam's situation.

GASTIL: Let me bring a suggestion to this discussion. The Polish expert, Kolakowski, suggested earlier at this conference something that I think has to be taken to heart. That is, there have been and are variations among Communist countries. Poland, for example, is Communist, under one party rule, and yet the Catholic Church has been used as a channel for giving aid to the Polish people directly.

I suspect there are other Communist countries in which smaller efforts could be made through some of the churches. That certainly would not be true in certain countries, and in Vietnam you give us an example.

But couldn't we think of ways in which this situation in Ethiopia, to go back to the earlier example, or Vietnam, could be made to evolve so that methods could be found for helping the people more directly? Wasn't it true, for example, that for a while, people were able to send packages to their relatives in Vietnam? Some of these got through to individuals, didn't they?

VO VAN AI: This is true, yes.

GASTIL: If you can get through to individuals, then there may be other openings. The dilemma for U.S. policy, whether we are talking about a relief organization or the government, is that "this year" people may be starving and people want to do something about it, and these other programs seem very long range. So I think we have to have some answers for immediate problems.

QUESADA: At the time of the Vietnam War the Philippines was involved in helping neighboring countries, I think Laos. The people we sent were soldiers, but they did civic action work—building roads and bridges. I am not sure if it was on a government-to-government basis; probably the U.S. government financed it. We also had what was called "Operation Brotherhood." But again, the Philippine doctors went to neighboring countries to do medical work. Now, looking at the Vietnamese problem, perhaps organizations like NED could work along these lines. For example, the neighbors of a country that needs help would supply the leg work in terms of volunteers, and then perhaps an international or American organization would take care of logistics—materials, or other expenses.

To me this is a very effective way of saying democracy is better than nondemocratic forms of government. When you go to a country and build roads and bridges, without saying this is to promote communism or democracy, but the people know that you come from a democratic country, that perhaps is a different way of promoting things. Sometimes it's better if you go into a country and help people without saying, "I am doing this because I am promoting democracy." Sometimes it's good not to have any labels. But if they know it comes from a foreign country that is democratic, they will say maybe democracy is better.

GASTIL: You are talking about aid proxies. You are saying that, for example, it might be useful to get Filipinos into Vietnam today, to build roads.

MONTEMAYOR: But when political control is total, any physical infrastructure introduced will actually reinforce the political control.

QUESADA: Yes. That's one way of looking at it. But from the host government's perspective it is also a problem. Any offer to help solve their deficiencies might weaken their hold on the people.

So, for example, in the Philippines, we have this problem with wounded Communist soldiers. What do you do with them? They need doctors. Of course our military would not want them to be treated, because after they are treated they go back and shoot the soldiers. The same is true with food aid.

GASTIL: One thing we are trying to do is introduce pluralism into nondemocratic societies. Your idea is interesting because you would be getting people with some democratic experience into a nondemocratic country on a day-to-day basis.

QUESADA: There has to be an exchange of ideas. When volunteers from a neighboring democracy are building roads and bridges, they

167

are going to talk to the people about a lot of other things besides roads and bridges.

RUBIN: What I wanted to request is that, when other international forums like this one we have had in the last two days—and now this private one—are held, Paraguay be included in the discussion, because even when academics talk on this kind of topic, they talk of Chile and go no further. And, subconsciously or unconsciously, we who try to promote and want to practice democracy must not ignore this dictatorship. With our silence we become accomplices.

The policy must be one of confrontation, calling a dictatorship a dictatorship, and not being so soft-spoken about Paraguay. One of the most important means could be reports in the U.S. press. I would ask you colleagues, when you return to your countries, to talk about this topic.

GASTIL: What about the U.S. press? Mr. Quesada's point about proxy workers should be remembered. Would it be useful for publicity about the situation in Paraguay to be emphasized by Argentinian or Brazilian organizations rather than the U.S.?

RUBIN: We are doing that already. But we find it has more of a repercussion when it's published in the New York Times or the Washington Post. If there is a prisoner fasting or someone has been jailed, the impact is greater when it is published on the front page of the New York Times.

ZAVALA: I would like to raise another issue, with all due respect. I have been thinking these two days, and this is in relation to Nicaragua, here you are organizing these beautiful meetings promoting democracy, and the U.S. Congress has passed X amount of money to fund what you are doing, what NED is doing, and you are publishing your freedom survey in New York.

However, when the time comes to try to study democracy in Central America, or in Nicaragua, because of the normal—and I emphasize "normal"—political battles inside the United States, what the United States is doing to establish democracy in Nicaragua is practically zero. It is a big commotion that amounts to nothing.

Why nothing? Because it has become an issue in internal American politics. So this is just the ground work. They think we can go higher, forgetting about the complete case, and think about it in more general terms. What happens when, because of A, B, or C, an issue becomes critical to the extent you have different opinions inside the United States? Then you cannot get together, you cannot have a common policy and still help democracy. You are destroying efforts at democracy.

I don't know whether I made it clear enough. Did I?

GASTIL: You made it clear, but the issues are not too clear in my mind. Where do we go from there?

ZAVALA: From there, the U.S. should have enough appreciation of democracy to avoid this problem. Major issues of freedom should not be allowed to become internal political problems—there should be a bipartisan position right away.

VO VAN AI: It comes back to the same idea, too. I think there is no global strategy. The Soviet Union has a strategic global policy, one that supports struggle movements in the third world. They not only support them with guns and money and all the rest, but they support them in the media, they support them in a consequential way, and they support them right to the bitter end; whereas I think around the table—and I think a lot of democratic movements in different countries feel this—that sometimes you are in the news and sometimes you are not, but the problems are always the same. It is very difficult to keep going in a struggle movement without a global strategic policy.

GASTIL: In certain areas the United States is not going to have a consistent global policy. In military or trade policy, we are not going to have it. But what we could have is a consistent policy in areas where NED is involved. I mean we could have a consistent policy year after year in this more restricted arena.

VO VAN AI: One of the important ways to do that it is with international pressure through the media. Closed societies fear international pressure—they are fragile in that respect. This would be an efficient way of opening closed societies.

To quote an example, in 1985, we filed a human rights complaint against the Vietnamese government in the United Nations. We had a press conference in Geneva last year after we tried to complain, and immediately Hanoi radio came out with a very virulent reaction, saying that Vo Van Ai was a traitor to his country.

Recently, Vietnam's Minister of Interior, when receiving a delegation of Swiss humanitarians, said that he would be closing down all reeducation camps in Vietnam. That was one of the things we had been campaigning for through our human rights complaint—the closing down of reeducation camps, as well as the liberation of political prisoners.

We don't really believe that because he is saying they are going to close the camps means that they will, but it does mean that he is sensitive to that kind of international pressure. They may eventually make concessions if they feel it necessary.

We believe in linkage. So we feel that all countries who have trade relations with Vietnam, in all their dealings with the Vietnamese government, should bring human rights into the discussion, so that human rights would be more respected in the country. It would be a means of pressure when aid is considered.

BERLANGER: We all seem agreed that what NED is doing, as a minimum, is nonpartisan and can be generally accepted in the States. So now, why don't you go on beyond this stage to extend what you are doing? Staying at the present limited level of NED work will eventually affect badly the work they are already doing, which is positive.

Unfortunately, NED is only engaging in very short-term projects. This is not a policy that can make democratic transition viable in countries with an opening to democracy, or produce an opening in countries that do not yet have one.

The NED work we are doing now is positive and significant—as you mentioned, everyone agrees on that, at least those participating in this panel. But up to now we don't see really clearly the engagement, the will to move forward beyond these very limited issues. NED is dealing now with crises, and it doesn't even have the resources to do that. We cannot achieve what we want if we don't engage in long-term work. We have to be able to plan what we are going to do over five or ten years.

GASTIL: You're talking about project commitment times?

BERLANGER: Yes, project commitment times, as an example.

ZAVALA: You mentioned two very good words: to "build institutions." That takes time. And to build the capacity of a people, that takes longer. The effort has to be long term.

QUESADA: Let me raise another issue. All the discussion so far has been in trying to formulate a solution to problems. Maybe we can look at trying to prevent problems.

In the case of the Philippines, this is one of the things that has been bothering me. The Americans are part of the solution to our problem, but I am not really sure they were not part of the problem in the first place.

When I look at Vietnam and Nicaragua, dictatorships seem not to have been encouraged, but certainly at a certain stage were helped by American support.

Senator Bradley pointed out the problem with the attitude that: "If my enemy is his enemy, then he is my friend." And yet one American president said, "he's a son-of-a-bitch, but he's our son-of-a-bitch."

Going back to the Philippine experience, Marcos was elected substantially because of his claim to be the most decorated war hero, and many of the medals were American medals. When he was out of power, some U.S. office declassified information that claimed those medals were fake. It occurred to me that, if the Americans had released this information when Marcos was campaigning for the presidency, maybe he would have lost the election.

So perhaps some effort should be exerted towards preventing the repetition of this cycle, because dictatorship resulting in communism has repeated itself many times. And apparently we don't learn from experience. The only group that benefits, if you want to call that a benefit, from all this is the arms industry. If there were a group within the United States—I don't know if it should be NED or whatever—that would work very hard towards opposing any potential dictatorship in any part of the world, I think you will solve a lot of future problems. In fact, you will prevent problems from being created.

Of course, I realize the United States has a lot of things to concentrate on these days; there are too many things happening. But certainly one little group similar to NED, just concentrating on this—if you could legislate somehow against helping foreign dictatorships from the very beginning, I think a lot of lives would be saved and there would be more peace in many parts of the world.

GASTIL: Let me ask a question on that, which anybody here might respond to. I found a problem in your suggestion. It seems to me the United States can in certain cases make statements or support activities in a country that are counterproductive for the support of democracy either in that country or in surrounding countries.

I was surprised to hear you say that during an election we might have published information about Marcos. I would have thought that would be very much resented by many Filipinos. I would think sometimes that support for a publication in another country, let's say by the United States, would be resented by people.

Is this not true? Is it just not true that people react in this way to U.S. support?

GERSHMAN: You have to make qualifications. There is a difference between the United States government publishing that information and somebody leaking it to the press so that it comes out, which is the way it would happen.

GASTIL: As you know, leaks can also be leaked. You can't necessarily guarantee that it wouldn't come out looking like an American plot.

HAIG: It seems to me that the United States has to get away from supporting an individual or pulling away support from an individual at a point where it is interference. What we should be doing is supporting a process and supporting those institutions that favor the selection of the country's leadership by the people.

In the past we fell into a trap, because of our own security interests, of supporting individuals. And when we couldn't see another individual as an alternative who would continue to benefit us in the way we felt the previous person did, those dictatorships become very unpleasant for us as well.

I think the purpose of the Endowment is exactly what I'm talking about, which is to provide an alternative to always having to support one individual over another individual.

GASTIL: I agree. But there are some people we have supported that I would like some opinions about. For example, in Central America, both in El Salvador and in surrounding countries, what is the reaction to our support for Duarte? That's an individual on whom our hopes in El Salvador are resting. I agree with the institutions, but sometimes practically we get stuck with an individual for good or bad. What about that?

ZAVALA: My feeling is that your support of Duarte has been welcome. Duarte was accepted by practically everyone as the only alternative. He was a very clear choice. It would have been a problem if you had had two Duartes. I mean one Duarte and another Duarte of another party. Then I guess the position would have been to back the process of democratization without getting involved with a particular person.

BERLANGER: I don't think there is any contradiction in supporting Duarte and at times supporting institutions. If you are in the position where supporting one man is the only alternative, that's fine. But does that exclude trying to lay an institutional groundwork? I don't think so.

BRAUMAN: The U.S. has supported a number of democratic leaders over the past few years—in Guatemala and the Philippines—without any negative or counterproductive reaction.

GASTIL: That is what I am asking. Are there any negative reactions?

GERSHMAN: There is an important distinction that has to be drawn between the situation where the individual in a sense represents the democratic cause in that particular situation and the situation where there is a process that represents democracy.

In El Salvador, the victory of Duarte in that particular situation embodied the democratic cause. In Guatemala, it would have been a mistake for the United States to have openly backed

173

Cerezo. It would have undermined the very process they were trying to establish. And in fact, during that election, the United States was scrupulously nonpartisan and there were great suspicions in Guatemala—I was there—that indeed the United States was backing Cerezo.

The American ambassador repeatedly stated that we were not, so much so that when I attended, as part of an observer delegation to the first round of the elections, an embassy briefing for the American observer team, our ambassador refused even to brief the delegation on the eve of the election for fear that someone might take the very statistics they had derived from polling or other sources as influencing the election, and would not say a word.

Where you have a case like Duarte, you will get the kind of bipartisan support in this country and abroad, because it will be known that that is clearly in the interest of democracy.

I am sure that if the United States were to pick a candidate in Haiti today, it would be counterproductive. At the same time, if we support a process, then it's not counterproductive. One just has to make those kinds of distinctions.

Since I have the floor, let me just say two things about the current debate in the United States, which may seem paradoxical.

On the one hand, there is a deep division on certain issues. These are highly partisan and highly charged issues. Nicaragua is obviously one of these issues. There is indeed great suspicion between the different camps in the United States over whether or not the other side is sincere in its support for democracy. There may be one side that thinks the other side is somehow really for communism, and the other side thinks that the opposition is really for some kind of authoritarian dictatorship.

Neither is true. There is a much deeper underlying bipartisan consensus on behalf of democracy than is apparent, but it has to be brought out. Despite the divisiveness of our debate, this bipartisanship is greater today probably than it has been in a very long time. Ironically, the Nicaraguan revolution contributed to that, because before the Nicaraguan revolution, you had—and this is probably oversimplifying it a bit—a debate in our country between liberals who accused the conservatives of supporting authoritarians and authoritarians who accused the liberals of wanting to overthrow authoritarians and replace them with communists.

It was a very simplistic debate, and it did not really reflect well on the positions of either side. What happened with Nicaragua, and the consequences of the Nicaraguan revolution, is that—I believe—many liberals are much more sensitive today than they were in the past to the need for looking at alternatives to authoritarianism; that it is not enough to just get rid of a dictator; one has to look at what will follow—because obviously in Nicaragua, democracy didn't follow—it wasn't enough to get rid of Somoza.

I think there has been a change in liberal thinking. It can be demonstrated that there is much greater sensitivity to that problem today than there was before.

Similarly, on the conservative side, there is much greater sensitivity to the fact that it is necessary to seek alternatives to authoritarianism; that it is not enough to stand with an authoritarian as the bulwark against communism, but, indeed, they have accepted the notion that stable democratic transition is essential to hold back communism. The experience of Nicaragua has shown that standing by a Somoza does not prevent communism from coming into being.

And so you have today, under a conservative administration, rather vigorous advocacy of democratic change and transition, not only in the Philippines and Haiti, but as we've seen at this conference, in Chile and Paraguay. It is not just the people who have come to our conference. We have ambassadors in those countries today who are openly associating with the democratic opposition, who are advocating peaceful democratic transition. I don't believe that could have happened in Nicaragua, even under the Carter administration. I don't think there would have been that consensus.

So you have a coming together of these. If we have an opportunity to build this kind of long-term bipartisan support, what we are trying to do is build on the consensus that does exist, to bring it out even during a period when they may be fighting with each other on other issues. Slowly, but surely, this will happen.

At the same time, we still have a very long way to go. And we are only really beginning. The main institution we are trying to build now is the Endowment, and it is going to take some time to do that. This is a new idea and it takes building it into the culture. This conference was very successful from that standpoint.

And we are also at a period when—and it may be hard to understand this from abroad—there is no money. They are cutting
everything.

When they cut—and I think this was alluded to by Senator
Lugar—the first thing to get cut is the foreign aid account. You
heard Congressman Kastenmeier yesterday appealing for support for
foreign aid. What he meant was that in a budget-cutting period,
the first thing to go is international assistance, because that does
not sell well in home districts.

Right now, there are limited funds, there is budget cutting.
Everything is being frozen or cut back. Most people don't have
the patience to deal with the kinds of issues we have been dealing
with. They are much more interested in their home districts and
what have you. Simply holding our own with the very meager
budget we have now is absolutely essential, looking towards some
future opportunity when some resources may be available, and to
building a constituency for what we are trying to do.

This is the situation facing us right now. I am sure that in
your own situations, you can imagine what it's like because you
probably face similar circumstances with your own governments.

We had a situation just in the last month where Secretary
Shultz actually opposed the State Department authorization bill in
the House of Representatives because the budget level was so far
below what the State Department had requested. We are in a
period of terrible austerity with regard to these kinds of activities,
and until that problem is resolved we are not going to be in a
position to create the kind of institution that can undertake the
long-term support that is necessary to do this job. So you have to
see this as a first stage, and all the rhetoric you heard is
profoundly important, but it is really part of the building process.

GASTIL: Carl, doesn't that mean in a sense that you need to
internationalize the support for democracy? That you need to get
beyond dependence on the U.S.? There is a lot of commonality in
the interests of the democratic countries of the world. Now, if you
could see as part of your goal sort of energizing this larger world,
maybe you can get a more effective effort.

GERSHMAN: That should be done in and of itself, not just because
we have a budgetary problem.

GASTIL: Sure. But I am saying that it seems to be particularly critical now.

ZAVALA: Talking about that, sometimes the idea has come to my mind—perhaps it is not a great idea, but I just drop it on the table—for something similar to the International Monetary Fund.

As you know, the International Monetary Fund is a club. There are certain rules if you want to belong to that club and receive the help it offers.

Would it be possible to have a Democratic International Monetary Fund? Take out the word "monetary." Where, if you want to belong to that club, you have to do this and this and this. Then you are going to receive this and this and this.

Does it make sense?

GERSHMAN: It sounds like you won't have the flexibility that Leopold wants.

BERLANGEN: That is what I was going to say. The problem with international organizations is that they all deal with governments.

BAUMAN: It is an idea that I have been thinking about for years. I don't think it has to be automatically governmental.

Let's take the example of the International Committee of the Red Cross. It is a purely Swiss organization, but has international status. Why shouldn't we set up this type of organization, an international committee for democracy, with general advisers, who would put international pressure on nondemocratic governments, and try to reorient international organizations and international assistance towards those who commit themselves to develop democracy?

HAIG: Are you talking about an organization that would actually distribute funds, or an organization that would, through recommendations to private organizations with resources, help to determine what countries should be helped?

BRAUMAN: It's in between. It would be an international committee.

177

HAIG: Because once you start putting money in there, then what you have is an impossible group of people. It's one thing to have a bipartisan consensus in one country for certain kinds of programs. It is another thing to internationalize it, because everybody is coming from such different perspectives. Perhaps you could get an international commitment towards certain kinds of work in one country or another, and arrange for the work to be done by smaller organizations with a certain amount of autonomy that would have the flexibility to quickly reach agreement, without taking a year to decide on one program.

GASTIL: This is a very interesting suggestion, and I would like to see those who have suggested it, or are interested in it, continue thinking along this line, and correspond with one another in order to develop the idea further.

PLATTNER: Dr. Gastil is also a member of CCD, the Committees for a Community of Democracies, an organization the Endowment has supported. CCD is attempting to build a world organization, an intergovernmental association, as well as national chapters in different countries that would bring in private sector people working toward this goal.

GASTIL: It is not precisely what the discussion has been pointing toward. But it might be one organization that could sponsor and develop the kind of program we have been discussing.

BRAUMAN: The Geneva Conventions work. We know how they are used. At least the ICRC (The International Committee of the Red Cross) is making an effort, and has been making an effort over the century, to make governments respect the Geneva Conventions. More and more governments have signed them.

ANON: Maybe a "Washington Convention on Democracy"?

BRAUMAN: No, I don't think "Washington" would be right, but a convention on democracy would be useful. More and more countries would have to sign it. This international committee would provide advisers and would make overall decisions on fund allocations. It would not manipulate funds like a bureaucracy.

QUESADA: I don't know how many of you here are members of the Rotary Club, but this is already being done with the Rotary Club, except that it's for hunger and similar causes. Rotary members contribute to an international foundation headed by an international board of directors. So you have situations where, for example, a country might have a total contribution of, let's say, $10,000 a year and will not receive anything as far as benefits, and another country will probably have a contribution of $1,000 a year and will get $750,000 worth of benefits.

Now, the international board decides who gets what. So the way I see it, it is already working, except that the purpose is different. But it is a private organization. It is based right here in the United States. That could probably be a model.

BERLANGEN: One advantage of an international organization of this kind is that it might avoid the criticism that the main needs are going unfilled. When you are an institution like the Endowment, people in the countries aided are bound to say—when you enter the political field—that this is interference with the government. But if it were an international organization, this criticism would be muted. Certainly there would be advantages, but how would it be funded?

GASTIL: It is getting late. The discussion has brought out many new ideas that should be followed up and could prove to be very useful. I want to thank you all for your presence and participation.

NOTE

1. This chapter reports on a forum held in Washington, D.C., on May 19, 1987, subsequent to a general international conference, The Challenge of Democracy, sponsored by the National Endowment for Democracy. The following recent recipients of aid from the Endowment took part:

Leopold Berlanger, Jr.
President, Institut International
d'Haiti de la Recherche et du Development

Rony Brauman, Medecins Sans Frontieres, France

Roberto Cardenal Chamorro, Costa Rica

Current Issues: NED Discussion

Penelope Faulkner
Vice President for International Relations
Que Me (Vietnamese exile organization)

Patricia Guillermo de Chea, President
Centro de Estudios Publicos (CEDEP), Guatemala

Leonardo Q. Montemayor, Secretary General
Federation of Free Farmers, Philippines

Mariano S. Quesada, Organizing Chairman
MORALE, Philippines

Mrs. Humberto Rubin
Radio Nanduti, Paraguay

Maria Rosa Segura de Martini, President
Conciencia, Argentina

Vo Van Ai
President
Que Me (Vietnamese exile organization)

Xavier Zavala, Director
Libro Libre, Costa Rica

Also attending were Carl Gershman, Barbara Haig, and Marc Plattner of the National Endowment for Democracy. The forum was moderated by Raymond Gastil of Freedom House.

PART IV

Democracy, Economic Systems, and Development

A STATISTICAL NOTE ON THE GASTIL SURVEY OF FREEDOM

Milton Friedman*

In his recent Survey of Freedom, Raymond Gastil assigns a ranking ranging from 1 to 7 to 167 countries in respect of their so-called "political rights" and "civil liberties," with 1 denoting the highest degree of attainment of each, and 7 the lowest. In addition, for 165 of the 167 countries they provide quantitative estimates of infant mortality and gross national product per capita. They point out the generally significant relation between the qualitative characteristics of the countries and the quantitative character-istics but make no attempt at a detailed statistical analysis. In particular, since the rankings for political rights and civil liberties are highly correlated with one another, they eschew any effort to isolate their separate influence on the quantitative measures. The purpose of this note is to present some statistical calculations bearing on that issue.

In addition to the categories Gastil considers, one other variable is relevant to such an analysis, namely, whether the country in question is one of those that has recently benefited from the effects of OPEC on the price of oil. For example, Qatar, with a GNP per capita of $28,000, has the highest GNP per capita of any of the 165 countries, and Kuwait and the United Arab Emirates are close behind with a recorded figure of $26,000. Clearly, these have very little if any relation to either political rights or civil liberties.

The standard statistical technique for sorting out the separate influences of correlated variables is multiple regression. Accordingly, I calculated two multiple regressions, one for infant mortality and one for GNP per capita, using three independent

*Milton Friedman is Senior Research Fellow at Hoover Institution, Stanford University.

variables: the rankings for political rights and civil liberties, and a dummy variable assigned the value of 1 for the 14 countries that I identified as oil countries, and 0 for all other countries. As dependent variables, I used the natural logarithms of reported infant mortality and GNP per capita, in order to avoid what statisticians call heteroscedasticity, or the wider absolute variability of the observations for high absolute levels than for low ones. One correction that I did not make, but that in principle would be desirable, would be to weight the observations in accordance with the likely accuracy of reported infant mortality and GNP per capita. Population might well serve as as a proxy for the likely degree of accuracy, but I had no such figures readily available and was unwilling to devote the effort required to collect them. In any event, it is my considered opinion that the results would not be materially affected by introducing such a weighting scheme.

With these preliminaries out of the way, the computed equations are as follows:

$$\text{Log IM} = 2.6250 - 0.0380\text{PR} + 0.3417\text{CL} - 0.0335\text{PC},$$
$$\qquad\quad (20.0) \qquad (0.6) \qquad\quad (4.5) \qquad\quad (0.2)$$
$$R^2 = .42 \qquad \text{S.E.E.} = .706,$$

$$\text{LogGNP} = 8.7761 + 0.0839\text{PR} - 0.4913\text{CL} + 2.0790\text{PC},$$
$$\qquad\quad (44.6) \qquad (0.8) \qquad\quad (4.3) \qquad\quad (6.9)$$
$$R^2 = .432 \qquad \text{S.E.E.} = 1.060,$$

where IM stands for infant mortality, GNP for GNP per capita, PR for ranking by political rights, CL for ranking by civil liberties, PC for the dummy variable indicating whether or not an oil country, R^2 for the square of the multiple correlation coefficient corrected for degrees of freedom, and S.E.E. for the standard error of estimate. The numbers in parentheses below the coefficients are the absolute t-values.[1]

In interpreting the results, recall that 1 represents the highest degree of achievement for political rights or civil rights, and 7 the lowest, so that a positive coefficient means that a deterioration in rights or liberties is associated with a rise in infant mortality or GNP per capita, and conversely for a negative coefficient.

I find the results fascinating. When civil liberties are held constant, political rights show no statistically significant association at all with either infant mortality of GNP per capita. On the other hand, when political rights are held constant, there is a highly significant association between civil liberties and both infant mortality and GNP per capita: the greater the extent of civil liberties, the lower the infant mortality and the higher the GNP per capita. Understandably, being or not being an oil country has no determinable effect on infant mortality but clearly does on level of GNP per capita.

Because the dependent variables are logarithms, the coefficients of the independent variables can be interpreted as comparable to percentages. For example, each one unit improvement in the ranking by civil liberties implies a 34% change in infant mortality, and a 49% change in GNP per capita—down for infant mortality and up for GNP for an improvement in ranking, and conversely for a deterioration in ranking. These are clearly major effects.[2]

To avoid misunderstanding, I hasten to repeat the cliche that correlations is not causation. The regression result is consistent with high income leading to a wider range of civil rights and a lower level of infant mortality or with the kind of institutions that favor civil rights leading to high income and low infant mortality or with both being the common effect of some one or more other variables. However, the regression does convincingly reject the hypothesis that political rights, at least as defined in the Survey of Freedom, are in and of themselves a source of either low infant mortality or high GNP per capita. It does establish the proposition that civil liberties, as defined in the Survey of Freedom, are more significantly related to infant mortality and per capita GNP than political rights, whether because of differences in the accuracy of the rankings or for other reasons.

My intention is not to denigrate the importance of political rights as an essential component of what I regard as a "good society." On the contrary, I strongly believe that they are an essential component. But on this evidence, they cannot be regarded as an effective means to other objectives. My purpose is statistical, not ethical.

For the benefit of those who are distrustful of multiple correlation, I append a table for a cross-classification of the non-oil countries by the two rankings giving the number of observations and the average infant mortality and GNP per capita. These are simple arithmetic averages, not the geometric averages that would be the counterpart of my use of logarithms in the multiple correlation. A detailed examination of these two-way tables yields results that are fully consistent with the results of the multiple correlations, and, incidentally, show how misleading the marginal distributions by themselves can be.

NOTES

1. Incidentally, I computed the same equations excluding the oil countries and the oil dummy. The results were essentially identical.

2. In terms of conventional percentages, the percentage change is different for a rise and a fall—e.g., 29% for a decline in infant mortality as the result of a one unit improvement in the ranking, 40% for a rise in infant mortality as a result of a one unit deterioration. The numbers derived from the logarithms are the geometric mean of these two ways of describing the percentage change.

APPENDIX

SURVEY OF FREEDOM: CROSS CLASSIFICATION BY POLITICAL RIGHTS AND CIVIL LIBERTIES; NUMBER, AVERAGE INFANT MORTALITY AND AVERAGE GNP PER CAPITA

POLITICAL RIGHTS	CIVIL LIBERTIES							
	1	2	3	4	5	6	7	TOTAL
	number of countries							
1	20	10	1	0	0	0	0	31
2	0	12	11	3	0	0	0	26
3	0	1	0	5	2	0	0	8
4	0	0	2	2	4	1	0	9
5	0	0	1	2	15	3	0	21
6	0	0	1	0	5	12	6	24
7	0	0	0	0	2	11	19	32
TOTAL	20	23	16	12	28	27	25	151

AVERAGE INFANT MORTALITY

| | | CIVIL LIBERTIES | | | | | | |
POLITICAL RIGHTS	1	2	3	4	5	6	7	TOTAL
1	14	25	68					19
2		35	70	55				52
3		77		117	77			102
4			48	87	70	74		69
5			21	69	103	101		96
6			34		61	83	114	84
7					150	118	107	113
TOTAL	14	32	62	89	92	99	109	73

AVERAGE GNP PER CAPITA

	1	2	3	4	5	6	7	TOTAL
1	9845	4847	1300					7957
2			918	1745				2730
3				420	1650			950
4			825	925	2038	800		1383
5			500	1125	1065	1167		1059
6			1900		2180	1003	608	1187
7					600	1514	908	1097
TOTAL	9845	4623	965	953	1412	1221	836	2805

LIBERTY AND SOCIAL PROGRESS:
A GEOGRAPHICAL EXAMINATION

Frank Vorhies and Fred Glahe*

I. Political Economic Liberty

Over two centuries ago Adam Smith proposed that there was a causal relationship between individual liberty and national well-being. In The Wealth of Nations, he attacked mercantilism and was generally skeptical of government involvement in the economy.

> Every system which endeavors . . . to draw towards a particular species of industry a greater share of capital than would naturally go to it . . . is in reality subversive of the greater system which it means to promote. It retards, instead of accelerating, the progress of society towards real wealth and progress.[1]

Smith saw social progress arising from individual liberty. Autonomous individual actions would spontaneously bring about fruitful social development.

> The natural effort of every individual to better his own condition, when suffered to exert itself with freedom and security, is so powerful a principle, that it is alone, and without any assistance, not only capable of carrying on the society to wealth and prosperity, but of surmounting a hundred impertinent obstructions with which the folly of human laws too often encumbers its operations.[2]

---

*Frank X. Vorhies is Senior Lecturer at the University of the Witswatersrand; Fred R. Glahe is Professor of Economics at the University of Colorado.

Finally, Smith used casual empiricism to support his proposition. Though free nations were not plentiful in his day, he was able to observe the progress of the British colonies in North America.

> Plenty of good land, and liberty to manage their own affairs their own way, seem to be the two great causes of the prosperity of all new colonies.[3]

Is there today an empirical relationship between liberty and social progress? This paper will investigate this question. The next section presents the views of modern supporters of Smith's proposition. Sections III and IV develop indexes of political economic liberty and social development, respectively. Section V investigates the empirical findings and addresses some policy implications of the results. The last section summarizes the study and makes recommendations for future research.

II. Liberty and Development

During modern times many have promoted Smith's understanding of liberty. Notable liberal scholars include Ludwig von Mises, Friedrich A. Hayek, Milton Friedman, and James Buchanan. The latter three are recipients of the Nobel Prize in Economics. Like Smith, they emphasize the importance of economic liberty for social progress.

Ludwig von Mises adopts an essentially economic view of liberty. Market production and exchange are anarchistic. This economic anarchy, a social order without government intervention, constitutes individual liberty.

> What gives individuals as much freedom as is compatible with life in society is the operation of the market economy. The constitutions and bills of rights do not create freedom. They merely protect the freedom that the competitive economic system grants to individuals against the encroachments on the part of police power.[4]

> [F]reedom in the external life of man [is] that he is independent of the arbitrary power of his fellows. Such freedom is no natural right. It does not exist under

primitive conditions. It arose in the process of social development and its final completion is in the work of mature Capitalism.[5]

For Milton Friedman economic liberty also means autonomous human interaction.

> The essential feature of a market economy is . . . that it . . . provides individuals with an effective support for personal freedom. . . . So long as effective freedom of exchange is maintained, . . . it enables people to cooperate voluntarily in complex tasks without any individual being in a position to interfere with any other.[6]

However, Friedman further emphasizes that "economic freedom is also an indispensable means toward the achievement of political freedom." Political freedom is necessary to insure "the absence of coercion of one man by his fellow man." Economic liberty and liberal government are compliments.

Hayek and Buchanan have thoroughly studied the necessary institutional features of liberal government. It must be limited and it must be democratic. Unlimited government will threaten economic liberty.

> The thesis . . . is that a condition of liberty in which all are allowed to use their own knowledge for their purposes, restrained only by rules of just conduct of universal application, is likely to produce for them the best conditions for achieving their aims; and that such a system is likely to be achieved and maintained only if all authority, including that of the majority of the people, is limited in the exercise of coercive power by general principles to which the community has committed itself.[7]

Mises explains that government must also be democratic "to make peace, to avoid violent revolutions." Political instability is costly in terms of both lives and wealth.

Democratic institutions make the will of the people effective in political matters, by ensuring that its rulers and administrators are elected by the people's votes. Thus are eliminated those dangers to peaceful social development which might result from any clash between the will of the rulers and public opinion.[8]

Liberty has political and economic dimensions. Alternative political, as well as economic, systems should have an impact on social progress. Moreover, political and economic liberty are mutually reinforcing. Those nations with the highest levels of both economic liberty and political liberty should exhibit the highest level of social development. Can this claim be empirically investigated?

III. A Political Economic Liberty Index

At least four major rankings of political liberty exist. These are the annual **Survey of Freedom** by Raymond D. Gastil (1985), the **Cross-National Time-Series Data Archive** by Arthur Banks (1971), the **World Handbook of Political and Social Indicators** by Charles Taylor et al (1972 and 1983), and the **Dimensionality of Nations Project** by Rudolph Rummel (1976). All have good and bad features.[9]

The ranking used in this survey is Raymond Gastil's annual **Survey of Freedom** (1985). It consists of annual rankings of over 160 nations on two seven-point scales, political rights (POL) and civil liberties (CVL). Political rights are essentially the rights to determine who governs. Civil liberties are essentially freedoms of expression.

In each scale, a rating of (1) is freest and (7) least free.

In political rights, states rated (1) have a fully competitive electoral process and those elected clearly rule. . . . Relatively free states may receive a (2) because, although the electoral process works and the elected rule, there are factors that cause us to lower our rating of the effective equality of the process. . . . Below this level, political ratings of (3) through (5) represent successively less effective implementation of democratic processes. . . . States at (6) do not allow competitive electoral processes that would give the people a chance to voice their desire for a new ruling party or for a change in policy. . . . At (7) the political despots at the top appear by their actions to feel little constraint from either public opinion or popular tradition.

Turning to the scale for civil liberties, in countries rated (1) publications are not closed because of the expression of rational political opinion. . . . No major media are simple conduits for government propaganda. The courts protect the individual; persons are not imprisoned for their opinions. . . . Movement down from (2) to (7) represents a steady loss of . . . civil freedoms. . . . Those rated at (3) or below have political prisoners and generally varying forms of censorship. . . . States rated at (6) almost always have political prisoners; usually the legitimate media are completely under government supervision; there is no right of assembly. . . . At (7) there is pervading fear, little independent expression takes place even in private, almost no public expressions of opposition emerge in the police-state environment, and imprisonment or execution is often swift and sure.[10]

Kenneth Bollen has investigated the possibility of bias in the survey. He concludes that "some nations may have been incorrectly rated on Gastil's measures. However, none of the criticism of which I am aware have demonstrated a systematic bias in all of the ratings." He also contends that the measures "show moderate to high degrees of reliability."[11] As a measure of political liberty, the Survey of Freedom is workable.

David Banks observed that the survey is inefficient. "Naturally, one expects these two ratings to be generally similar. But Spearman's rho, a measure of association for ordinal variables, shows the ratings are almost perfectly redundant."[12] Taking twelve-year averages of political liberties and civil rights the simple correlation is 0.966. A simple regression of these two averaged rankings reveals an R-squared of 0.934. In short, one rank may be enough.

Though the two measures are highly correlated, Gastil is attempting to convey different information by them. To capture this information a measure of political liberty (POL LIB) is constructed from the average of political rights and civil liberties. This average has itself been averaged over a twelve year period, 1973-1984. For clarity of exposition we have ordered this and other data so that the higher number is the more desirable. In the case of political liberty we have also converted the ranking to a 1 to 5 scale. A rank of 5 reflects the highest level of political liberty.

Gastil also classifies nations by their economic system. He has five categories: Socialist, Mixed Socialist, Capitalist-Statist, Mixed Capitalist, and Capitalist. We have ranked these 1 to 5, respectively.

> Socialist economies . . . strive programmatically to place an entire national economy under direct or indirect government control. States . . . may allow some modest private productive property, but this is only by exception, and rights to such property can be revoked at any time.

> Mixed Socialist states . . . proclaim themselves to be socialist but in fact allow rather large portions of the economy to remain in the private domain.

> Capitalist-Statist nations . . . have very large government productive enterprises, either because of an elitist development philosophy or major dependence on a key resource such as oil. Government interferes in the economy in a major way in such states, but not primarily because of egalitarian motives.

> Mixed Capitalist systems . . . provide social services on a large scale through governmental or other nonprofit institutions, with the result that private control over

property is sacrificed to egalitarian purposes. These nations still see capitalism as legitimate, but its legiti- macy is accepted grudgingly by many in government.

[Capitalist states] rely on the operation of the market and on private provision for industrial welfare. Taxes may be high, but they are not confiscatory, while government interference is generally limited to subsidy and regulation.[13]

Like all other orderings validity and reliability are concerns. For the purposes of this study Gastil's classification scheme (ECN LIB) must suffice. A more thorough ranking of economic liberty appears to be lacking in the literature.

With a ranking of political liberty and a ranking of economic liberty it is possible to construct a composite index of liberty. Following Smith, Mises et al, the two liberties are multiplicative rather than additive. It is the combination of the two that ought to bring about social progress. Accordingly the two rankings have to be multiplied to create a Political Economic Liberty Index (LIB). A rank of 25 reflects the highest level of liberty.

IV. A Social Development Index

We constructed an index of social development from the comparative national statistics in the 1986 Britannica Book of the Year. These comprehensive data sets are compiled from many sources including the annual Statistical Yearbook of the Council for Mutual Economic Assistance, the annual World Development Report and World Bank Atlas from the World Bank, the Government Finance Statistics Yearbook and the International Finance Statistics from the International Monetary Fund, annual Economic Surveys of the Organization for Economic Cooperation and Development, many publications including the Statistical Yearbook from the United Nations, and the annual World Factbook from the U.S. Central Intelligence Agency. These data are as reliable as is humanly possible. The editors comment:

> Every effort has been made to obtain the best combination of comparability and up-to-datedness from available sources, and, when the completeness of a country's published data permitted, to analyze it further for better agreement in coverage, scope, and datedness.[14]

We selected four indicators of the level of social development. These are the gross national product per capita (GNP CAP), average life expectancy (LIF EXP), the adult literacy rate (ADL LIT), and the infant survival rate (INF SRV). Though others exist, four are adequate to construct an index. Following the work of David Morris we constructed a weighted index.[15] Morris constructed a Physical Quality of Life Index (PQLI) by equally weighting the levels of life expectancy, adult literacy, and infant survival. Since publication the PQLI has been widely acknowledged.[16]

In an attempt to capture not only the quality of social development, but also the opportunities of social development we have added GNP to the PQLI. As a first approximation the four indicators have been equally weighted. In the Social Development Index (DEV) a rank of 100 would reflect the highest level of development.

V. Global and Regional Perspectives

In keeping with the causal relationship between liberty and development as proposed by Smith et al simple regressions may be considered, using the Political Economic Index as the independent variable (X) and the Social Development Index as the dependent variable (Y). Of course, cross-sectional correlation does not strictly imply causation. Nonetheless, the correlations themselves are interesting.

For purposes of this investigation the R-squared and the t statistic are enough. These are reported in Appendix A below. The 150 most populated countries make up the world set. The regional groups are constructed from the set.

Is there a relationship between political economic liberty and social development? For the world the answer is a weak yes.

With an R-squared of 0.275 other factors obviously are important for determining the level of social development. However, the t statistic is 7.488. This indicates that the relationship is significant at the 0.995 confidence level. In short, for the world the level of liberty may have a small, but significant influence on a nation's level of social development.

What about the relationship in various regions of the world? This question is pertinent in part because current U.S. foreign policy is committed to raising the level of democracy in particular nations as a means for improving that nation's prospects for social progress. It is also pertinent because national leaders, like individuals, often judge conditions by comparison to their neighbors. We have investigated five regions.

Africa as a region has the poorest levels of social development. The two least developed countries in the world, Ethiopia and Somalia, are in Africa. Purely due to oil, Libya, which has a world rank of 58, has the highest level on the continent. South Africa has a world rank of 73 and is ranked 3 in Africa.

The United States government has engaged in diplomatic, military, and economic actions to pressure both Libya and South Africa to improve their levels of political liberty. Libya is rank 121 in the world and 38 in Africa. South Africa is ranked 88 and 20 respectively.

Will an increase in liberty bring about more development in these two nations? If the experience of their neighbors is a guide, the answer is no. The R-squared for Africa is 0.039 and the corresponding t statistic is 1.377. Liberty and development are simply not statistically related in Africa.

Though Latin America is more developed than Africa and is generally also liberal, the relationship between the two is equally statistically insignificant. The R-squared of 0.032 and the t of 0.893 indicate that improving political economic liberty is not associated with improving social development. What implications does this have for an American pro-democracy foreign policy?

The least liberal country in the region, Cuba, is ranked 5 in development. The most liberal country in the region, Costa Rica, is only ranked 12. In the middle Nicaragua has a liberty rank 16 and a development rank of 19. Moving Nicaragua's political system towards Costa Rica and away from Cuba will not assuredly improve its potential for social progress. Other factors must also be considered.

In the Middle East are some of the most developed nations in the world. These include the United Arab Emirates, Qatar, and Kuwait with world ranks of 5, 12, and 17, respectively. Their oil revenue overrides their relatively weak indicators of life expectancy and adult literacy. However, like Africa and Latin America, the Middle East exhibits no significant relationship between liberty and development.

With an R-squared of 0.136 and a t of 1.432 policies to improve liberty may not result in improved social development. For example, whether Lebanon adopts the political models of Israel or Syria may not determine its rate of social progress. Oil and perhaps superpower alliances are more important than the liberty of the nation's political system.

Is there a relationship between liberty and development in East Asia? The answer is yes. With an R-squared of 0.475 liberty appears to be an important factor for determining the level of social development. The t statistic is 3.428. This indicates that the relationship is significant at the 0.995 confidence level.

Much discussion has been made about the totalitarian market nations in East Asia. However, the most developed, Japan, is also the most liberal. The least developed nations in the region are Burma, Laos, and Cambodia. These are totalitarian and socialist. If the People's Republic of China, ranked regionally at 11 for both indexes, wishes to develop it would do best to use Japan as its model.

With an R-squared of 0.513 and a corresponding t statistic of 5.288 liberty and development go hand-in-hand on the European continent. The policy implications are straightforward. The road to social development in Europe is liberty.

The most developed nation in Eastern Europe is East Germany. It has a world rank of 23 and a regional rank 15. Dictatorial socialist nations in Africa and Latin America may aspire to East Germany's success. If East Germany wishes to improve its relative position, it must aspire to the success of Western Europe. United States support for improved human rights in the East are meaningful in the regional context.

VI. Conclusion

The empirical investigations indicate that for the world political economic liberty has a small, but significant relationship with the level of social development. By investigating regional groups, it is clear that policies to increase liberty will not necessarily bring about desired results. In Africa, Latin America, and the Middle East liberty appears to have no relationship with development. On the other hand, in East Asia and Europe there is a significant relationship between liberty and development.

More is involved in the level of social development and the prospects for social progress than the degree of political economic liberty. One possible avenue of further research would be to look not only at the level of liberty, but at the level of respect for liberal institutions. Perhaps not only must markets and democracy exist, but they must also be culturally accepted and supported. The predominant religions and customs may provide insight here.

Concerning this paper's investigation of the relation between liberty and development, better data and alternative analyses may provide new results. In particular, there is need to develop a Survey of Market Liberty similar to the political surveys by Gastil. Also, regressions of pooled cross-sectional data do not adequately address the direction of causality as proposed by Smith et al. Pooled time-series data need to be collected and new regressions run.

What the current data does indicate for policy purposes is that certain regions of the world may not take liberty seriously. Based on their own and their neighbor's experiences, liberty is not the obvious road to social progress. Or inversely social progress is not the obvious road to liberty. A United States foreign policy to promote capitalism and democracy will not be universally understood and accepted.

NOTES

1. Adam Smith, **An Inquiry Into the Nature and Causes of the Wealth of Nations** (New York: Modern Library, 1937), page 650.

2. Ibid., page 508.

3. Ibid., page 538.

4. Ludwig von Mises, **The Anti-Capitalist Mentality** (South Holland, Illinois: Libertarian Press, 1972), pages 99-100.

5. Ludwig von Mises, **Socialism: An Economic and Sociological Analysis** (Indianapolis: Liberty Classics, 1981), page 171.

6. Milton Friedman, "Capitalism and Freedom" **New Individualist Review,** 1 (April 1961), pages 3-10. The indented quote and the continuation of the paragraph contain quotes from pages 4 through 10.

7. Friedrich A. Hayek, **Law, Legislation and Liberty: Rules and Order** (Chicago: University of Chicago Press, 1973), page 55.

8. Mises, **Socialism,** pages 61, 400.

9. Raymond D. Gastil, **Freedom in the World, 1984-1985** (Westport, Conn.: 1985); Arthur Banks, **Cross National Time-Series Data Archive** (Cambridge, MA: M.I.T. Press, 1971); Charles Taylor et al, **World Handbook of Political and Social Indicators** (New Haven: Yale University Press, 1972 and 1983), first edition (1972) co-authored by Michael C. Hudson, second (1983) by David Jodice; Rudolph J. Rummel, **Dimensionality of Nations Project** (Ann Arbor, MI: ICPSR Codebooks, 1976); and Kenneth A. Bollen, "Political Rights and Political Liberties in Nations: An Evaluation of Human Rights Measures, 1950 to 1984," **Human Rights Quarterly,** 8,4 (1986), pages 567-591.

10. Gastil, **Freedom in the World,** pages 13-21.

11. Bollen, "Political Rights and Political Liberties," pages 585-586, 588.

12. David L. Banks, "The Analysis of Human Rights Data Over Time." **Human Rights Quarterly,** 8,4, (1986), pages 654-680.

13. Gastil, **Freedom in the World,** pages 52-56.

14. **Britannica Book of the Year** (Chicago: Encyclopaedia Britannica, 1986), page 612.

15. David Morris Morris, **Measuring the Condition of the World's Poor: The Physical Quality of Life Index** (New York: Pergamon Press, 1979).

16. Jan S. Hogendorn, **Economic Development** (New York: Harper and Row, 1987), page 38.

APPENDIX A*

STATISTICAL CORRELATIONS OF SOCIAL DEVELOPMENT AND POLITICAL ECONOMIC LIBERTY

Y: SOCIAL DEVELOPMENT INDEX (0 - 100)
X: POLITICAL ECONOMIC LIBERTY INDEX (0 - 25)

WORLD		#OBS.:	150
CONST.:	52.89	ADJ. R2:	0.275
COEFF.:	1.024	t:	7.488

AFRICA		#OBS.:	49
CONST.:	47.63	ADJ. R2:	0.039
COEFF.:	0.315	t:	1.377

LATIN AMERICA		#OBS.:	26
CONST.:	65.11	ADJ. R2:	0.032
COEFF.:	0.208	t:	0.893

MIDDLE EAST		#OBS.:	15
CONST.:	58.40	ADJ. R2:	0.136
COEFF.:	1.010	t:	1.432

EAST ASIA		#OBS.:	15
CONST.:	59.04	ADJ. R2:	0.475
COEFF.:	1.008	t:	3.428

EUROPE		#OBS.:	28
CONST.:	72.96	ADJ. R2:	0.513
COEFF.:	0.514	t:	5.228

----

*Data tables and other appendices may be obtained from the authors.

THE INTERRELATIONSHIPS OF

FREEDOM, EQUALITY, AND DEVELOPMENT

Harmon Zeigler*

The average personal income in Switzerland is about two hundred times greater than that of Chad. This ratio—between the world's richest and poorest countries—exceeds the comparable distribution of income within any country (excluding the oil exporting Middle Eastern countries). In 1987, the Population Crisis Committee, a research organization concerned with population control, published its Human Suffering Index, a composite index based on such factors as literacy, infant mortality, income, and caloric intake. Switzerland was rated as having the world's best quality of life, while Chad was exceeded in suffering only by Mozambique, Angola, and Afghanistan. International Living, a magazine for travelers, reached a similar conclusion with slightly different data: Switzerland is second best and Chad's poor rating is exceeded only by Angola and the Central African Republic.[1]

Who is to blame for such inequities? Cannot governments "do something"? Why are some countries able to lift themselves from poverty while others are not? Why are the wealthy countries primarily in Europe, Asia, and North America? These questions are not new; they have been asked repeatedly, with answers varying according to predisposition. Marxists believe that, as long as the means of production are in private hands, there can be no genuine growth, no growth that does not enhance the fortunes of the rich and drive the poor deeper into desperate poverty. Supporters of capitalism argue that the profit motive—greed—encourages individuals to acquire wealth: and, as a natural consequence, individual greed leads to collective economic growth and stability.

* The following is excerpted from a chapter in a forthcoming book by Harmon Zeigler. Dr. Zeigler is Philip M. Phibbs Distinguished Professor of Politics and Government, University of Puget Sound.

The major proponents of these disparate philosophies travel the globe preaching to the poor, and African countries are urged to accept capitalism or socialism as a condition for economic aid. The International Bank for Reconstruction and Development, a United Nations affiliate, is a leading propagandist for free enterprise, while the Soviet Union is the most active proponent of socialism. Irrespective of their solutions to the problem of the production and distribution of wealth, the two competing philosophies agree with Marx: politics and economics are inextricably intertwined.

Of course the nations of the world are not easily placed into one of two categories; rather they can be arrayed on a continuum from those with the greatest reliance upon the free market to those with least. Let us consider the following categories:

> Inclusive Capitalist
> Noninclusive Capitalist
> Inclusive Capitalist-Statist
> Noninclusive Capitalist-Statist
> Inclusive Mixed Capitalist
> Noninclusive Mixed Capitalist
> Inclusive Socialist
> Noninclusive Socialist[2]

These economic systems have meaning both in themselves and as devices to achieve other goals. Suppose we believe that collective control of an economy is just, because our morality rejects the ethics of individualism. If we believe in an equal (not necessarily equitable) distribution of income and think capitalism is poorly equipped for redistribution, does it necessarily matter that socialism may not do a better job? Suppose we believe in individual economic freedom and are convinced that those who fail do so because they are lazy. Does it really matter that evidence of systemic failure refutes our belief? In both these cases, we believe in the intrinsic worth of a process. But we should ask the "so what" question even if the answers disappoint us.

There are three components of an economy for which governments generally assume or reject responsibility: growth and stability, equality in income distribution, and budget priorities. All governments strive for economies that enjoy steady growth, are able to withstand "shocks" such as international recessions or shortages in key resources (usually petroleum), and can keep inflation low and employment high.

John Kenneth Galbraith rightly regards income distribution as "one of the major debates in the nonsocialist world."[3] He argues that socialist ideology no longer debates the notion of public ownership of property and, hence, as much levelling as possible has already occurred. Thus the nonsocialist world is the only arena for debating equality. Inequality remains a major focus of classical political theory and its modern practitioners, such as John Rawls.[4] Inequality has also commanded the attention of those who believe it is a cause of violence, and its reduction a fundamental purpose of governments.[5] Much of this debate assumes that socialism, since it is designed to guarantee the populace against extremes of wealth, has done so. Galbraith believes this to be true, as does Charles E. Lindblom, who writes:

> It is in communist provision of . . . some degree of equality in the distribution of income and wealth that the communist claim to approximate the humanitarian vision . . . seems undeniable. On these fronts communist systems have to be credited with great accomplishments, on the whole probably greater than those of the polyarchies [capitalist democracies].[6]

Unfortunately, the world is more complicated than we would prefer if we are to make claims for the ability of different kinds of political-economic systems to deliver on their promises. One of the most obvious complications is wealth.[7] Rich countries can do more than poor ones irrespective of intentions. At the most minimal level, there is not much point in distributing wealth more equitably in a country such as Chad. But how much better off is an average person living in the United Arab Emirates, bloated with oil revenues? If they chose to do so, the oil-rich countries could raise the standard of living of those not directly engaged in oil production, but Chad cannot. Wealth—measured by Gross National Product (the sum of all the goods and services produced in a country in a year) per capita—will figure strongly in any analysis.

Another component of wealth is GNP growth. What kinds of political-economic systems augment growth? In the United States, we have become fascinated by the consistent growth of the Asian countries, principally Japan, Singapore, South Korea, Taiwan, and Hong Kong. At the end of World War II, Japan was in ruins, and personal wealth (GNP per capita) in South Korea and Taiwan was less than that of Ghana or Nigeria. Since then, these countries have experienced more growth than any other segment of the world's population. But economic growth alone is not the best way to assess changes in the economy; we need also to look at rates of inflation and for sharp increases in unemployment. For this reason the index for income growth and stability in the following table combines the rate of GNP growth with the rates of inflation and unemployment.

The most frequently cited goal competitive with equality is freedom. Since few of us, given maximum individual freedom, would voluntarily part with our wealth, state imposed redistribution is required. Leaders of states that intervene directly do so in the belief that they are trading liberty for equality. Although revolutions usually claim to be able to deliver both, a choice of one would appear inevitable. Lindblom writes:

> [Equality has been a] communist aspiration since the nineteenth century, when the pursuit of liberty and equality, which had been taken up during the Enlightenment, went separate ways. Democrats went to the right, seeking liberty. Communists went to the left, seeking equality.[8]

If we must select one and not the other, communism selects equality, capitalism chooses freedom. Much of what we read about politics and the economy assumes that this trade-off is a realistic one. Industrial democracies guarantee much more individual freedom than communist countries. While they occasionally mumble a few phrases about freedom, the leaders of communist nations usually concede that they constrain individual behavior to a degree unthinkable in industrial democracies. So, what about the other half of the bargain: does a society get more economic equality in exchange for less political and economic freedom?

Another important "intervening" variable is a government's spending and budget priorities. Governments that elect to spend most of their money on defense will have little left for improving the lives of their subjects, even if they wished to do so. Public policy is not "pure" choice. Israel and the Arab states spend a great deal on the military because they believe their survival depends on it. For this variable we developed an Index of Social Progress that measures the proportion of available resources spent on education, medical services and welfare as contrasted with defense.

Finally, two measures of the shape of political life are included in our analysis. One is the rate of participation in elections, combined with the legal opportunities for participation; the other is a measure of the party system itself, ranging from competitive two or multiparty systems through de facto one party systems (that is, countries in which only one party actually wins, even though there are some, frequently limited, opportunities for other parties to obtain representation) to political systems with either one legal party or no party at all.

What, then, is the interrelationship among the factors we have described? To find out statistically, we need to put the pieces together in a way that will enable us to take into account the interaction of independent, intervening, and dependent variables. In the following table, we have listed the desired conditions as four dependent variables along the top, and allocated to these variables one independent variable (the economic system) and three intervening variables. The table reports the relationship between the independent variable and the outcomes, taking into account the contribution of the intervening factors. The percentages are the proportion of the variance explained. The greater the variance explained, the more important the independent variable. For example, 55 percent of the variance in income growth and stability is explained by GNP per capita. This table suggests, in fact, that GNP per capita is far more closely related to the four desired conditions than any other variable.

	Income Growth And Stability	Income Equality	Social Progress	Freedom
GNP per Capita	55 %	50 %	32 %	34 %
Participation	5 %	5 %	2 %	-12 %
Party System	-.0001 %	.005 %	12 %	4 %
Economic System	.0008 %	5 %	3 %	-9 %

Democracy: Economic Systems and Equality

Political-Economic Systems and Growth

Although both the free market and socialist polities spend a good
deal of time and money trying to sell their schemes to underdeveloped countries, they have no justification in doing so. The table
suggests that the organization of the economy is unrelated to
income growth or stability. To those who are fond of ruminating
about the wonders of free enterprise, take note of the error of
your ways. Those who believe that "rational planning" is a good
way to insure economic growth should also remain silent. If you
want to predict economic growth, look first to wealth: the rich
grow richer and the poor grow poorer. Wealthy countries provide
a more stable economy than do poor ones; Switzerland's economy
grows more, with more stability, than does Chad's.

Let us consider the following table of the world's best
economies, when ranked in terms of wealth.

	Country	Corporatism	Economic System
1.	Japan	High	Capitalist Inclusive
2.	Switzerland	High	Capitalist Inclusive
3.	Norway	High	Mixed Capitalist Inclusive
4.	West Germany	Medium	Capitalist Inclusive
5.	Austria	High	Mixed Capitalist Inclusive
6.	U.S.A.	Low	Capitalist Inclusive
7.	Finland	Medium	Mixed Capitalist Inclusive
8.	France	Low	Capitalist Inclusive
9.	Netherlands	Medium	Mixed Capitalist Inclusive
10.	Sweden	High	Mixed Capitalist Inclusive

Even though the organization of the economy is unrelated
statistically to income growth and stability, the countries with the
best economies are market-oriented. Central economic planning—
the use of government policies rather than free markets to set
prices, supplies, and the allocation of national effort—is not a
system relied on by the world's most productive economies.

However, the table suggests that government intervention of a
more bureaucratic or organized type, corporatism, is compatible
with highly productive economies. A means of regulating group
conflict, corporatism describes a governmental system with very

close, institutionalized relationships between government bureaucracies and interest groups, with public policies less the result of group conflict than of collaboration between major ("peak") political associations and bureaucracies.[10] The countries generally regarded as having corporatist systems of conflict regulation are Norway, Sweden, Denmark, Austria, and Japan. All are in the top ten except for Denmark (a shade away). This suggests that a market economic system with substantial bureaucratic intervention is compatible with a healthy economy while a more extreme socialist planning model is not. Among the least corporatist governments, only France and the United States make the list. Corporatism need not require a heavy investment of government resources: Japan and Switzerland are vigorously corporatist—in that their bureaucracies guide and direct the market—but their governments do not make major contributions to the GNP.

The top ten countries economically are also thriving democracies (note also the positive relationship in the previous table between political participation and a healthy economy). Democracy does not "cause" growth, but democracy may require a stable economy.

Why Some Nations Remain Poor

For some recent periods (see note 1), the countries with the worst economic performance were:

Country	Economic System
1. Ghana	Capitalist-Statist Inclusive
2. Zaire	Capitalist-Statist Noninclusive
3. Nicaragua	Mixed Socialist Noninclusive
4. Niger	Capitalist Noninclusive
5. Zambia	Mixed Socialist Noninclusive
6. Peru	Capitalist-Statist Noninclusive
7. Bolivia	Capitalist-Statist Noninclusive
8. Chile	Capitalist Inclusive
9. El Salvador	Capitalist Inclusive
10. Jamaica	Capitalist-Statist Inclusive

The reasons for the lack of association between political/economic systems and economic performance should be apparent. Just as there is no obvious pattern among the richest countries, neither is there among the poorer ones. They range from the struggling socialism of Nicaragua to the corrupt and brutal capitalism of Chile. No single system can claim to have solved the problem of wealth and poverty. But the absence of a relationship does not mean that politics does not matter, merely that the institutional structure of a state is not essential to understanding economic growth and stability.

While planned economies are barriers to growth, this is probably due more to the incompetence of government officials than to any inherent flaws in planning. Certainly rapidly expanding economies of Asia do not resemble Western capitalist countries; Japan, Taiwan, Singapore, and South Korea are guided capitalist systems. While they prefer, with some exceptions, not to nationalize, they are disinclined to allow private business to do whatever it chooses.

Both European and Asian corporatist states stress public-private sector cooperation. There is more governmental guidance in Asia, more fine-tuning of capitalist economies largely run by private sectors. The intervention generally takes the form of market manipulation. There is more government tinkering with tax incentives for the development of new products, for example. Since Asian countries lagged behind European industrial democracies, there was more need for such incentives. Given the commitment to the use of the market, with implementation and compliance largely in private hands, Asian corporatist systems, much like their European counterparts, stress close coordination between public bureaucracy and private business. Chalmers Johnson writes:

> This cooperation is achieved through innumerable, continuously operating forums for coordinating views and investment plans, sharing international commercial intelligence, making adjustments to conform to the business cycle or other changes in the economic order to maintain international competitive ability, and spreading both the wealth and the burdens equitably.[11]

Asian corporatist systems differ from European ones not so much in the commitment to collaboration between bureaucracies and interest groups, but in the diversity and range of groups given legitimacy and in the relationship between bureaucracies and political parties.

As these Asian nations continue their economic progress, they demonstrate the compatibility of rational planning and advancing economies. Among industrially developed nations, while the heavy-handed planning of the Eastern bloc has demonstrated that the days of its utility are passed, less severe forms of intervention are routine. In France, for example, the state, even when its elected leaders are in favor of "privatization," has always been a major player in the game of economics. France's most easily recognized product, Renault automobiles, is produced by a nationalized industry that receives direct governmental subsidies of about one and a half billion francs annually. Airbus, the European corporation that manufactures commercial aircraft, receives direct government subsidies from three European countries.

Political-Economic Systems and Equality

Rich countries are more equal than poor countries. Countries that deliberately set about the task of reducing extremes of wealth and poverty are no more successful than those that leave it alone. The failure of governmental systems to influence income distribution is important, because economic growth is not identical to economic development. Rather than growth just for growth's sake, most people look to economic advancement as an opportunity to improve the quality of life. Hence wealth concentrated in the hands of a tiny elite does little good. A country may have a per capita income of $20,000 but an unfair income distribution, so that the benefits of capital are lost. This is rarely the case. Brunei, an oil rich nation on the Borneo coast, enjoys a GNP per capita of about $22,000. However, virtually all of this money is controlled by the ruling family, leaving the average resident as impoverished as those in countries with a per capita income less than one-fourth of Brunei's. It is especially important that countries approaching or passing the take-off stage include as many people as possible in their ascent.

There are many ways to measure income distribution, and each has strengths and weaknesses. One common way is to examine the portion of the total available income acquired by the top ten or twenty percent of the income-earning population, and comparing this proportion to that earned by an equal number at the bottom of the income ladder. The ratio between these two provides a rough measure of income distribution. If the top decile earns, say 30 percent of all income, and the bottom decile earns 5 percent, the ratio is 6 to 1. Another popular method for estimating income distribution is the Lorenz Curve. The number of income recipients are plotted along an axis in terms of cumulative percentages. Another axis plots the income received, it too measured cumulatively. The deviation from the "line of equality" is the actual distribution of income. The Gini Coefficient, named for Conrado Gini, an Italian statistician who wrote in 1912, measures the ratio between the actual area within a Lorenz Curve, and the total area in which it lies. Yet another more complex measure, developed by Michael Don Ward in the United States, improves upon the Gini Index.[12] Ward tries to eliminate the major flaw of the Gini Index, its inability to distinguish between different forms of inequality. A distribution skewed toward the bottom would yield the identical score to one with a distribution skewed toward the top. Ward adds to the Gini Index a number of valuable measures not immediately linked to income, such as social mobility and the relation of poverty to affluence. We use Ward's measure here.

Countries with the most equitable distribution of income are:

Country	Economic System
1. Switzerland	Capitalist Inclusive
2. U.S.A.	Capitalist Inclusive
3. Italy	Capitalist-Statist Inclusive
4. Czechoslovakia	Socialist Inclusive
5. Austria	Mixed Capitalist Inclusive
6. Belgium	Capitalist Inclusive
7. Hungary	Socialist Inclusive
8. USSR	Socialist Inclusive
9. United Kingdom	Mixed Capitalist Inclusive
10. Poland	Mixed Socialist Inclusive

Countries with the least equality in incomes are:

	Country	Economic System
1.	Liberia	Capitalist Noninclusive
2.	Burkina Fasso	Mixed Socialist Noninclusive
3.	Bolivia	Capitalist-Statist Noninclusive
4.	Algeria	Socialist Inclusive
5.	Ecuador	Capitalist Noninclusive
6.	Zaire	Capitalist-Statist Noninclusive
7.	Indonesia	Capitalist-Statist Noninclusive
8.	Somalia	Mixed Socialist Noninclusive
9.	South Yemen	Socialist Noninclusive
10.	Cameroon	Capitalist Noninclusive

Nothing distinguishes the most equal nations: there are capitalist and socialist countries represented on the list. Whether a country sets about the task of income distribution deliberately as an "official" ideology, whether it says nothing about income distribution, or whether it seeks to soften the impact of the market by establishing a strong state presence are of no matter. The same can be said for the least equal nations. No form of government has a monopoly here either. The more equal nations are wealthier than the least equal ones, as the foregoing tables suggest. The important point is that no form of government has achieved equality in income distribution, including those whose ideology demands equality.

The point is important, for many restrictions that socialist governments impose on freedom are in the name of equality. According to Marxist theory, with the socialist revolution, the state collectivizes all means of production, transforming "surplus value" (private profit) into surplus product controlled by the state. Part of the surplus is used to pay wages, the other to pay a "social wage" (services provided by the state). Although the final stage in the evolution of communism, "from each according to his abilities, to each according to his needs," implies an absence of any but the most insignificant differential, socialist governments have not applied the theorem as strictly as they might. There are wage differentials, but they are not as great as in market economies, and there are minimum guaranteed incomes. An opera star or top party leader might earn forty times as much as an unskilled worker, a ratio less excessive than in capitalist countries. With all income paid by the government, there is little opportunity for anybody to strike it rich. What is different about socialist economies is the absence of abject poverty and egregious wealth.

The salary of a Russian entertainer, like the salary of any other employee, is fixed by a formula. There are no Beatles or Rolling Stones; no Reggie Jacksons, no "self made" people such as Microsoft's Bill Gates, who at the age of thirty-one became America's youngest billionare. The absence of conspicuous consumption and deadly poverty exists because of a universal salary structure.

Cuba has had one of the most exhaustive plans for income distribution. Workers were placed into five major occupational groups: (1) "productive workers" (blue-collar workers, both skilled and unskilled), (2) white-collar service employees, (3) administrative and clerical workers, (4) technicians and professionals with university training, and (5) executives (administrators). Within each category are grades from 1 to 9. This categorization is much like that of any public civil service and, since the state was managing the economy, an expanded civil service seemed an appropriate way to go about income distribution. All would not be paid equally, but all would be paid according to a schedule. Additionally, extra effort (as in overtime), extra risk (hazardous jobs), or a high rate of success (exceeding quotas) carried bonuses. Cuba had tried to replace material incentives with moral ones, especially during Che Guevera years, but this has been abandoned. Wage scales were reintroduced, and even authors' royalties, abolished during the heady days of ideological obsession, were allowed once again (the government pays by the page according to the author's prestige).[13]

In the USSR Lenin's "New Economic Policy" produced a mixed or transitional system. While nationalizing basic industry, Lenin included aspects of free enterprise capitalism. Prices were to be determined by laws of supply and demand, and wages in small industrial units and on farms were to be determined by the market. Other wages were subject to protracted haggling. Lenin initially believed that the pay of party officials should not exceed that of competent workmen; in 1919 the party decreed a mere 1.75 differential (ratio) of the highest to the lowest paid workers. But with the emergence of the New Economic Policy, an occupation scale became effective including 17 ranks with an 8 to 1 ratio of highest to lowest. An attempt at narrowing the gap was rejected by Stalin who, first among Soviet theoreticians, declared that Marxism and egalitarianism were incompatible: "Equalitarianism has nothing in common with Marxist socialism." Stalin was belligerent in declaring that socialism, as a transition phase between capitalism and communism, should pay according to one's work (from each according to his abilities). Only in a utopian communist society would one receive according to need. Broad distinctions, between manual and "mental labor," for example, have been layered with minute distinctions ("chief doctors and other leaders in medicine"). The "official" ratio is now 13 to 1, far less than the actual ratio of highest to lowest wage.

Money is less important in socialist societies. Many services for which money is demanded in market economies are supplied by the state; even when payment is required, it frequently does not reflect true market value. Rent, for example, is a fraction of what it is in any major capitalist city, and subway fare is a few pennies. With chronic shortages, availability becomes more important than money. Who cares about rent when apartments are rationed, at a bureaucratically determined size (square feet per person), with waiting lists running into the next decade? About one-third of the apartments in Moscow are communal living arrangements with two or more families sharing kitchen and bathroom facilities.

Roy Medvedev explains:

> Privileges tend to arise where there are shortages. Certain products are . . . available for practically the whole population while others are produced in limited quantity which can satisfy only a small part of the demand. Under the Soviet price system, shortages either mean enormous queues or else distribution takes place via some other channel—personal contacts, nomenklatura privilege, or, worst of all, bribery. . . . New kinds of goods and services are constantly appearing but inevitably become scarce almost at once, which means that only a few people can enjoy them.[14]

We will consider the few shortly, but for now we focus on the many, the masses without contacts or, more importantly, without party membership.

The actual price of goods in the Soviet Union is quite low, since prices are controlled and subsidized. But the average Russian works about three times as long for the same goods as do Americans. The average Soviet wage is about $3,800 a year. The average compact car costs about $12,700 and a color television set costs about $1,100. An apt comparison is with the German Democratic Republic (East Germany) and Czechoslovakia, major socialist allies of the Soviet Union. Their overall economic performance is inferior to the Soviet Union's, but their GNP per capita is about $2,000 more. Average citizens are thus able to spend more for consumer goods than in the USSR.

The orthodox Marxist view holds that class divisions are rooted in private property. Since private property exists at best as a minor component of the economy, there can be no classes. Obviously there are. The solution to the problem of privilege in the classless society is the notion of "positional differentiation." This arcane phrase is meant to describe inequalities based upon one's status with respect to the resources of production. The "intelligentsia," a formally acknowledged status, can legitimately earn more than manual laborers, especially since their relationship is "non-antagonistic," as compared with the deadly contest between bourgeoisie and workers in capitalist society. Additionally, even the distinction according to one's position in production is a transitional phase on the way to pure socialism.

In any case, no amount of personal wealth provides the access to material goods offered by Party membership in most communist countries. The "new class" has appropriated for itself as many of the amenities of life as is possible in stagnant economies. Irrespective of any differences in earning capacity based on an occupational hierarchy, there is such a sharp cleavage between the Party minority and the non-Party majority that this basic distinction partially eradicates all other potential divisions.[15] In a socialist economy, ownership of the means of production is vested in the Party. Therefore, whereas the actual composition of the ruling class may vary, there is a ruling class and it is not the proletariat. The Party, the "vanguard of the proletariat," is becoming less representative of the class over which it assumed guardianship. One-fourth of the Party membership consists of college graduates, as compared with only about fifteen percent of the total population. The highly educated are significantly overrepresented.[16]

The irony is that this situation results from the Marxist belief that in order for a classless society to emerge market forces must be subjected to political control. But control of the means of production enhances the power of the Party and the bureaucracy. Centrally planned economies have merely substituted one elite for another.

The Party nomenklatura is the framework through which privilege is dispensed. The nomenklatura, a list of ranks, consists of those positions filled directly by the Party or with Party approval. There are about twenty-three million people in the USSR with nomenklatura jobs (about nine percent of the total population). A continuation of old czarist table of ranks, the nomenklatura class provides a state registry of the elite. There are three levels of nomenklatura, with the most privileged being those directly appointed by the Politburo and Central Committee of the Party.[17] Perhaps one million (two million including families and relatives) people hold these much sought after "plums." The cabinet ministers, directors of the various parts of the Academy of Sciences, editors of the Party publications, Party bosses in the Republics, deputy ministers, high ranking military leaders, and key ambassadors are the most visible examples of this privileged class. The nomenklatura class makes distributions of real wealth, as opposed to reported income, more tentative than in the West. There are many ways in which the nomenklatura class can "rise above many of the shortages, lines, dirt, and frustration that make life onerous . . ."

Private stores for the nomenklatura class are at three levels of opulence. The "Bureau of Passes," on Granovsky Street in Moscow, is the most infamous example of the "members only" shopping opportunities for the elite. The Central Committee, the staff, and families of members and staff can shop here. While few outsiders have been inside the "Bureau of Passes," it is said to be an all-purpose shopping center, with clothes comparable to those in European department stores, and food or wine comparable to those of American supermarkets.

The "restricted outlet," or "restricted distribution" stores are a step down. These are either special sections of public stores, such as GUM, the large department store on Red Square, or home delivery services. They service the staff of major cabinet ministries, the KGB, and directors of various state owned industries.

There are about one hundred such restricted distribution stores. Normally, no money changes hands. Shoppers have a specified quota marked on their identification cards.

Finally, the Beryozka shops are open to anyone with hard (Western) currency. They are popular with tourists who have these currencies, and are frequented by artists, musicians, athletes, members of diplomatic staffs—those likely to travel. Additionally, "certificate rubles" are issued to Soviet citizens who have earned money abroad. They are supposed to be changed back into rubles, but are generally traded at 8 to 1 for regular rubles on the black market; they are also good in the Beryoskas.

Special apartments are provided either free or for nominal rent to those just below the Central Committee, high military officers, or internationally known entertainers. For those who can shop at Granovsky Street, an additional opportunity is available—the dacha, the second vacation home outside the city. There are two kinds of dachas: the state owned ones that are free, and the privately owned ones. The private ones are better, but neither can be purchased unless official approval is given; they can be reclaimed at any time.

For the average citizen medical attention is free, and prescription drugs are very cheap. However, the quality of medical attention is not very good. The hospitals are overcrowded and dirty, and the level of skill inadequate. Much is made of the fact that most Russian physicians are women; less is said about their level of payment, about 100 rubles a month, less than factory workers. It is not surprising that the high-level nomenklatura do not frequent regular public hospitals. The Ministry of Health maintains a "Fourth Directorate," a special network of clinics. The right to register with these hospitals comes with the job. At the apex is the Central Committee's own hospital, which rivals Western ones in the technology of treatment and physical environment.

The existence of privilege in the world's first communist society should not be taken to mean that the USSR is much different from the capitalist countries. The very fact that income distribution in the USSR is similar to that of industrial democracies is the more important point. As we have seen, the Soviet Union has pursued elite advantage with vigor, while simultaneously establishing a floor for poverty. Except for the elite, life is grim, but nobody starves, nobody is denied medical attention, nobody is unemployed, and there are no "street people." Of course the housing of most Russians is below the standard we would expect to find among families living in poverty in the United States, and unemployment is eliminated by creating "jobs" for which there is little justification (such as attendants on every floor of a hotel, innumerable street sweepers, and transportation conductors).

A Comparison with the United States

In the United States, income is marginally more equitably distributed than in the Soviet Union. Income distribution is fairly constant. The lowest 20 percent of income earners receives 4.7 percent of available income, while the highest 20 percent receives 42.7 percent. Income earned by the top group has been gradually decreasing since the great depression of 1929 (it was 54.4 percent then). However, in the last decade, the income proportion earned by this group has been inching upward. The economic situation of the bottom group rarely changes. The largest increase has been among those in the middle-income groups; they now receive about 52 percent of all income, compared with 33 percent in 1929. Another dramatic change is the income of the top five percent; their share has declined from 30 percent to 15.8 percent. In terms of real dollars, the lowest quintile earns about $11,000 while the highest quintile earns about $33,000 dollars; the top 5 percent earns about $76,000 dollars.

The major difference is that money talks in the United States. "The essential feature of capitalist society is not privilege, but money; in real socialist society, it is not money but privilege."[18] Anybody with the money can blow it all in the Cartier shop on Madison Avenue in New York or on Rodeo Drive in Los Angeles. The market creates American Beryoskas. In the Soviet Union, internal passports limit travel; it is impossible to stay in a city more than a few days without such a passport. In the United States, travel is open, but frequent travel to major cities is too expensive for most people. In the Soviet Union, medical care is readily available to all who need it, but its quality is medieval; in the United States, about 37 million people have no medical insurance and receive about the same kind of care as does the average Soviet citizen. In the Soviet Union, virtually no one is homeless; in the United States, the "street people" phenomenon shows just how insensitive capitalism can be. But for the average American, housing is vastly superior to that in the USSR. In the Soviet Union, travel abroad is restricted to entertainers, athletes, and government or party officials; in the United States, foreign travel is restricted to those who can afford it.

The best predictors of individual wealth are family background, education, and inheritance.[19] The policy preferences of various adminstrations appear to have little to do with income distribution. For example, progressive taxation has not redistributed income. Although we feed ourselves on the rags-to-riches myth, very few people escape the earning opportunities of their social class. Middle-upper to upper class families value education; education raises incomes. As more people get better jobs, inequality is diminished. But as long as social class predicts who will graduate, economic rewards will be unequal and linked to social status.

The following comparison of the occupational status of fathers and sons shows how much mobility actually exists:

Son's Current Occupation

Father's Occupation	White Collar		Manual		Farm
	upper	lower	upper	lower	
Upper White Collar	52	16	13	15	1
Lower White Collar	42	20	15	22	1
Upper Manual	29	13	27	29	1
Lower Manual	23	12	24	41	1
Farm	18	8	23	37	15

Source: Thomas R. Dye, Power and Society (Monterey: Brooks/Cole, 1987), page 74.

A majority of the sons of upper white-collar fathers were themselves in upper white-collar occupations, but the rest of those sons descended to less prestigious occupations than their fathers' (downward mobility). At the other end of the scale, only 41 percent of the sons of lower manual workers ended up in the same kind of job. This means that nearly 60 percent of those sons rose to more prestigious occupations than their fathers' (upward mobility). Overall, there appears to be more upward than downward mobility in the United States. Compared to other industrial democracies, the United States is "normal." Upward mobility exceeds downward mobility in the United States, West Germany, Sweden, Japan, France, and Switzerland. Downward mobility exceeds upward mobility in Denmark, the United Kingdom, and Italy.[20]

It is generally believed that there is more upward mobility in centrally planned economies than in market economies because of the opportunity to move up within the manual labor class by acquiring new skills. In command economies, without the freedom to change jobs, there is less risk in investing in job training. In market economies, labor turnover makes the investment risky and hence relatively rare. Substantial majorities of highly skilled workers in Yugoslavia, for example, received their training through in-factory training or part-time attendance at trade schools or "'workers' universities."[21] Consequently, unlike the United States, skilled manual positions are more prestigious than lower white-collar ones. The reversal of the relative status of these job categories makes comparison of mobility precarious, however. In any case, the relatively fluid mobility within the segments of a class has been "bought at a considerable cost to human liberties, and is dependent upon a high degree of centralized political control over economic life."[22]

Even though Americans buy into the survival-of-the-fittest doctrine, they believe some occupations are overpaid. Majorities think that government officials, owners and executives of large corporations, professional athletes, medical doctors, and movie stars or top entertainers earn too much. On the other hand, majorities think that lower-level white-collar workers, elementary and high school teachers, non-unionized factory workers, and university professors are underpaid.[23] This seemingly contradictory belief system is not so hard to understand. Americans believe that inequality is necessary and desirable in principle, but also that some groups of people are treated unfairly.

Commitment to inequality as a consequence of effort elevates those who succeed to a position of deference approaching that of the Soviet nomenklatura class. Business leaders are the object of adoration in aggressively free market, individualist societies, just as party officials are, at least officially, held in high regard in collectivist ones:

> Businessmen generally and corporate executives in particular take on a privileged role in government that is, it seems reasonable to say, unmatched by any other leadership group other than government. . . . Because public functions in the market system rest in the hands of businessmen, it follows that jobs, prices, production, growth, the standard of living, and the economic security of everyone all rest in their hands. . . . In the eyes of government officials, therefore, businessmen do not appear simply as the representatives of a special interest. . . . They appear as functionaries performing functions that government officials regard as indispensable.[24]

Those who embody the myths of the society will be powerful, and the only difference is in the keepers of the myth, not in economic inequality. Two countries with profound differences are nevertheless comparable in the distribution of wealth. However, the authority of the Party elite is much greater than the political influence of comparable political elites in the United States and, even given the deference toward business, more politically dominant than the economic elite.[25] The reason is simply the concentration of extraordinary political and economic responsibility and the merger of the two into a cohesive power elite:

> Western societies [have] a pluralistic distribution of power in which various institutional spheres are guaranteed legal autonomy. Socialist societies, on the other hand, have a totalitarian authority structure in which the party monopolizes all decision-making processes and denies independence to any major institution.[26]

Economic Growth and Inequality

When economies improve, do all benefit; does a "rising tide lift all boats?" The problem of growth and equity (which is not the same as wealth and equity) was given its major focus by Simon Kuznets about three decades ago. He proposed a law of income growth and development; as economic growth continues, there is an initial rise in inequality and then a leveling off and ultimately a decline in inequality.[27]

Some of the capitalist societies of Europe and North America seem to have followed this pattern, as have the European centrally planned economies. But the evidence is mixed. What is not in dispute is the grim reality of every day life during the transition to wealth. The Industrial Revolution (the last decade of the eighteenth century and all of the nineteenth), harsh and cruel, produced a sharp and tenacious rise in inequality, especially in England, the leading "developing" nation. Unlike most of Europe, English industrial development did not occur around established cities; rather tiny villages suddenly became swollen by the massive migration from the country. Birmingham, Leeds, and Manchester, formerly bucolic villages, tripled in population and became instant industrial slums because water power, and coal and iron existed in the north, not in London. Life was brutal. It was also nasty, and short. Karl Marx's theories about exploitation and capitalism were developed from his observations of the English working class. Charles Dickens' realistic novels (Great Expectations, Little Dorrit, Oliver Twist) captured popular imagination by describing the brutal, almost unbelievable, squalor of working class life. Under these conditions, it is hardly surprising that infant mortality was half again as much in the north as in London. Conditions were comparable to those in Africa today. The only missing ingredient in Hobbes' dreaded state of nature was the solitary life; for working class English families developed a deeper sense of class loyalty than the European or American working classes.

> By the 1830's the character of the British working class as a tribe apart, with its own values, had matured. These values were highly collectivist . . . with an intolerance towards the eccentric or individualist. . . . And this character was to endure down the generations, along with the bitter ancestral memories passed from father to son to grandson to great grandson.[28]

But evidence that actual income was becoming more skewed toward the rich is, even with Kuznets' own data, unclear. In the United Kingdom, for example, the proportion of income received by the richest 5 percent consistently declined after 1880, both before and after taxes (from 48 percent to 18 percent in 1957).[29] A similar pattern was found in the United States, Germany, Norway, Sweden, Denmark, and the Netherlands. But we do not know the pattern of income development before 1880, presumably the midpoint in development for these countries. It is probable that inequality did indeed increase until about 1880, and then began its decline.

But what of today's underdeveloped countries? The evidence is far from clear, and the data far from uniform. However, the following is an approximation of discernible trends:[30]

Country	Economic Performance	Trends in Inequality
Argentina	poor	Inequality rose
Bangladesh	poor	Inequality rose
Brazil	fair	Inequality rose
Costa Rica	fair	Inequality fell
El Salvador	poor	Inequality rose
India	poor	Little change
Mexico	fair	Inequality rose
Pakistan	fair	Inequality fell
Philippines	fair	Inequality rose
Singapore	good	Inequality fell
Sri Lanka	fair	Inequality fell
Taiwan	good	Inequality fell

There really are no discernible trends, with the exception of the outstanding performance of two Asian countries, Taiwan and Singapore. But inequality also fell in several less impressive economies, Pakistan and Costa Rica. We can say, however, that poor countries rarely reduce income inequalities. Additionally, the case of Taiwan does not support the "things will get worse before they get better" thesis. Inequality fell consistently as wealth increased, and began to level off in the 1980's. Although not much more reduction of inequality can be expected, Taiwan is "in the admirable position of combining rapid economic growth, sharply reduced inequality, and widespread alleviation of poverty."[31] The same can be said for Singapore (but not Korea).

Social Progress, Economic Systems, and Inequality

As mentioned above, social progress may be measured by the proportion of available resources spent for education, medical services, and welfare as opposed to defense. Whereas some of these decisions reflect a deliberate decision, in many cases it is simply a matter of having no money to spend on anything. The nations with the lowest scores on the Index are: Ethiopia, Chad, Uganda, Burundi, Tanzania, Pakistan, Zimbabwe, Nigeria, Niger, and Upper Volta (Burkina Faso). Little else need be said. These very poor countries are barely able to sustain a legitimate government. Of considerably greater interest are the ten highest scorers. Ranging from the best to the tenth best, they are: Denmark, Norway, Austria, the Netherlands, Sweden, New Zealand, Austria, Ireland, Belgium, and Finland. These are the European welfare states, but they are not invariably among the richest. Ireland, Belgium, Austria, and New Zealand are relatively impoverished. Ireland, with a GNP per capita half that of the other leaders spends what money it has on education, medical services, and welfare.

None of the major contestants in the global struggle between communism and capitalism appear on the list of the leaders; the USSR and the United States are just about in the middle. Three of the European corporatist countries (Norway, Sweden, and Austria) are among the leaders, but Switzerland and Japan, two strong corporatist countries, are not; and Ireland is a weak corporatist country. No centrally planned economies appear among the leaders. There are several aspiring socialist regimes (Ethiopia and Tanzania) among the ranks of the poor scorers, but surely their form of government is incidental to their poverty. Tanzania's Nyerere wrote of his country's "commitment to the belief that there are more important things in life than the amassing of riches, and [if] the pursuit of wealth clashes with things like human dignity and social equality, then the latter will be given priority."[32] This belief in the trade-off is one of the many ironies surrounding poverty, wealth, and equality. The trade-off is artificial. Tanzania has supplied fewer of the amenities of life than most nations, and little of the equality.

We are led inescapably to Michael Ward's conclusion: ". . .the level of inequality in market economies is roughly identical to that of nonmarket economies."[33]

225

NOTES

1. Population Crisis Committee, "Human Suffering Index", Washington, D.C., the Committee, 1987. **International Living,** January, 1987, pages 6-7. In the following essay, figures for wealth, GNP/capita, and rates of economic growth are based on the World Bank's **World Development Report 1986** (New York: Oxford University Press, 1986).

2. This discussion is based on Raymond D. Gastil, **Freedom in the World** (New York: Greenwood Press, 1987), pages 74-75. (See the discussion of Table 8 above, pages 73-78.)

3. See John Kenneth Galbraith, **The Anatomy of Power** (Boston: Houghton Mifflin, 1983) page 87.

4. John Rawls, **A Theory of Justice** (Cambridge: Harvard University Press), 1971.

5. The following make the argument most completely: Robert Jackman, **Politics and Inequality** (New York: John Wiley, 1975); Bruce Russett, "Inequality and Instability: The Relation of Land Tenure to Politics," **World Politics,** 16 (1964), pages 442-454; and J. Nagel, "Inequality and Discontent: A Nonlinear Hypothesis," **World Politics,** 36 (1974), pages 452-472.

6. Charles E. Lindblom, **Politics and Markets,** (New York: Basic Books, 1979), page 266.

7. Michael Don Ward, **The Political Economy of Distribution,** (New York: Elsevier, 1978), page 181.

8. Lindblom, **Politics and Markets,** page 266.

9. Compare Richard J. Estes and John Morgan, **The Social Progress of Nations** (New York: Praeger, 1984).

10. On corporatism see also Lindsay R. Wright, The Future of Democracy: Corporatist or Pluralist," in R. D. Gastil, **Freedom in the World, 1983-1984** (Westport, CT: Greenwood Press, 1984), pages 73-96.

11. Chalmers Johnson, **MITI and the Japanese Miracle: The Growth of Industrial Policy, 1925-1975** (Stanford: Stanford University Press, 1982), pages 309-312.

12. Ward, **The Political Economy of Distribution,** pages 21 ff.

13. Carmelo Mesa-Lago, **The Economy of Socialist Cuba** (Albuquerque: University of New Mexico Press, 1981), pages 141-174.

14. Roy A. Medvedev, **On Socialist Democracy** (New York: Alfred A. Knopf, 1975), page 229.

15. Frank Parkin, **Class Inequality and Political Order** (New York: Praeger, 1971), pages 138-139.

16. Derived from Jerry F. Hough, **Soviet Leadership in Transition** (Washington: Brookings Institution, 1980), page 28.

17. Mervyn Matthews, **Privilege in the Soviet Union** (London: George Allen and Unwin, 1978), page 34. See also Michael Voslensky, **Nomenklatura** (London: The Bodley Head, 1983), page 184.

18. Voslensky, **Nomenklatura,** page 240.

19. Christopher Jenks, **Who Gets Ahead** (New York: Basic Books, 1977).

20. Seymour Martin Lipset and Reinhard Bendix, **Social Mobility in Industrial Society** (London: Heineman, 1959), page 25.

21. Parkin, **Class Inequality,** page 149.

22. Anthony Giddens, **The Class Structure of the Advanced Societies** (New York: Harper and Row, 1973) page 253.

23. Vassily Aksyonov, **In Search of Melancholy Baby** (New York: Random House, 1987), page 120.

24. Lindblom, **Politics and Markets,** pages 172, 175.

25. Giddens, **Class Structure,** page 253.

26. Parkin, **Class Inequality,** page 140.

27. Simon Kuznets, "Economic Growth and Income Inequality," **American Economic Review** (March, 1955), pages 1-28. Actually, the Kuznets idea—"its going to get worse before it gets better"—is only an assumption, not a firm conclusion.

28. Correlli Barnet, **The Pride and the Fall** (New York: Free Press, 1987), page 190.

29. See Gary Fields, **Poverty, Inequality, and Development** (Cambridge: Cambridge University Press, 1980), page 78.

30. Fields, **Poverty,** pages 88-92.

31. Fields, **Poverty,** page 228.

32. Cited in Shiva Naipaul, **North of South** (London: Penguin, 1982), page 203.

33. Ward, **The Political Economy of Distribution,** page 44.

DEMOCRACY IN DEVELOPING COUNTRIES:

FACILITATING AND OBSTRUCTING FACTORS

Larry Diamond, Juan J. Linz and Seymour Martin Lipset*

The past decade, beginning with the breakdown of Western Europe's last three dictatorships in the mid-1970s, has been a time of great democratic ferment in the world. This ferment has been particularly apparent in the developing world, where it has seen the collapse or withdrawal of most of the "bureaucratic-authoritarian" regimes of South America, the overthrow of long-time personal dictators in countries as diverse as the Philippines, Haiti and Uganda, and rising pressures for democracy in South Korea and Taiwan. As indicated by the military instability in the Philippines, ethnic violence in Sri Lanka, civil wars in Central America, and economic crises in such new democracies as Argentina, Brazil and Peru—not to mention the breakdowns in the early 1980s of Nigeria's Second Republic and Ghana's Third—this democratic progress is tenuous, and considerable movement between democratic, semi-democratic and authoritarian regime forms appears likely in the coming years. From the perspective of three years ago, this very fluidity seemed to us the most compelling reason for studying systematically the conditions for democracy in the less developed countries of the world.

The growth of political and intellectual interest in democracy in developing countries provided a propitious climate for such a study. But, in addition, it seemed to us that there remained huge

---

* Larry Diamond is Senior Research Fellow at the Hoover Institution, Stanford University. Juan J. Linz is Pelatiah Perit Professor of Political and Social Sciences at Yale University. Seymour Martin Lipset is Caroline S.G. Munro Professor of Political Science and Sociology at Stanford University and Senior Fellow at the Hoover Institution.[1]

gaps in our understanding. Previous studies had been limited in important ways: to particular periods of time, particular regions (Europe and/or Latin America), particular processes (breakdowns, transitions), or particular theoretical variables. By contrast, we sought to design a study that would compare the historical experiences of countries throughout Asia, Africa and Latin America, with a shared conceptual orientation and a common, broad set of theoretical concerns. In addition, we sought to examine the entire history of a country's experience with democracy, including the instauration, breakdown and/or consolidation of democracy; periods of democratic persistence, crisis and renewal; experiences with authoritarian rule; and all of the ambivalences and oscillations in between.

With generous support from the National Endowment for Democracy, we enlisted specialists in the history and politics of twenty-six countries in Asia, Africa and Latin America to write case studies of their historical experiences with democratic and authoritarian rule.[2] In addition to reviewing the history, each author was asked to analyze why various political regimes persisted or failed, to explain theoretically the country's overall experience with democracy, and to consider future prospects and perhaps policy implications. Each author was guided in these analytical and theoretical tasks by a flexible but detailed common framework, distilling from the extensive literature a number of propositions about the relationship between cultural, social, economic, political and international factors and the likelihood of stable democracy.

Given the constraints of space we will not define democracy here—other than to indicate that our meaning essentially corresponds empirically to the "free" category in this annual survey of freedom in the world—but rather we refer the reader to some of the standard definitions.[3] Neither will we review here the theories we have drawn upon in organizing the study and interpreting the results.[4] We should note, however, that our concern in this study is to explain not only the democraticness of regimes but also their stability—their persistence and durability over time, particularly through periods of intense conflict, crisis and strain.

The following is a presentation of some of the evidence from our study on the factors that facilitate and obstruct the emergence and maintenance of democracy in developing countries.

Legitimacy and Performance

All governments rest on some kind of mixture of coercion and consent, but democracies are unique in the degree to which their stability depends on the consent of a majority of those governed. So intimately is legitimacy tied to democratic stability that it is difficult to know where definition ends and theorizing begins. Almost as a given, theories of democracy stress that democratic stability requires a widespread belief among both elites and masses that democracy is the best form of government for their society, and hence that the democratic regime is morally entitled to rule.

Legitimacy is in turn related (though not entirely and exclusively) to the effectiveness of regime performance economically and politically. One of the primary reasons for the instability of democratic (and non-democratic) regimes in the Third World has been the combination and interaction of low legitimacy and low effectiveness. Given the low level of development and the strains imposed by modernization, regimes which begin low in legitimacy find it extremely difficult to be effective. Regimes which lack effectiveness, especially in economic growth, tend to continue to be low in legitimacy. Both our own studies and others as well caution against drawing too deterministic a linkage between the economic performance of democratic regimes and the probability of their surviving or breaking down. Nevertheless, it is clear that, over the long term in particular, the effectiveness of democratic regimes in satisfying people's wants heavily effects their stability.

While they have not been immune to problems of recession, inflation and corruption, the more successful democracies in our study have generally experienced relatively steady economic growth, which in turn has strengthened their legitimacy. Some have had the benefit of great natural resources: economic growth has been led in Venezuela by oil, in Botswana by copper and diamonds, in Papua New Guinea by copper mining. But in the long run, sound policies and capable, honest administration are more important to economic performance than a country's natural resource endowments.

Many African countries, for example, have generous mineral endowments. But few have matched the consistent growth performance of Botswana, which averaged 9% real growth in GDP (Gross Domestic Product) annually in the 1970s and a similar rate in this decade following a brief recession. Underlying this performance have been sound policies and effective management. Although government spending and control have expanded rapidly since independence, state policies have not strangled producers of agricultural exports (in this case, the cattle rearers) as they have in much of the rest of tropical Africa. The state has prudently invested in basic infrastructure, and the elite has kept an effective lid on political and administrative corruption. Parastatals have been managed so efficiently that "few require any subsidy and some actually produce a tidy profit"—truly a rare record in Africa. Moreover, efforts have been made to distribute this growth through substantial state investment in education, housing, health and other social services; unusually effective food distribution programs in relief of the drought; and improvement of wages in the formal sector.[5]

Less spectacularly but still significantly, in India, democratic administration and planning have produced economic development and improvement in social well-being. Since independence, India has "experienced a partial renovation of agricultural production leading to self-sufficiency in food, developed a structure of industrialization that produces most products that the country needs, expanded the supply of educated and technical personnel, . . . consistently held down the level of inflation to one of the lowest in the world and in the process ensured a level of self-reliance and payment ability that kept it away from debt crisis."[6] This consistent prudence in economic management and steady improvement in output and capacity is perhaps one of the least appreciated foundations of democratic stability in India. Moreover, while high levels of poverty and inequality persist, and "a number of shadows haunt the economic scene" (most notably the continuing inefficiency of the large public sector), this record of performance has clearly improved the quality of life at the mass level. Since the implementation of "planned development" in 1959, life expectancy at birth has improved from 32 years to 55 years (in 1982).

Similarly in Costa Rica, steady and reasonably well distributed economic growth, by broadly improving living standards over the past three decades, has built up a firm base of democratic legitimacy. This has permitted the regime to weather the severe economic crisis of the 1980s, which necessitated steep austerity measures.

Although the countries treated in our study are economically dependent to varying degrees, their own economic policies and strategies appear to be the more important determinants of economic performance, and can even shape the degree of dependence. This is seen perhaps most clearly in the varying degrees of international indebtedness. Many governments (particularly authoritarian regimes) borrowed heavily during the 1970s to finance grandiose economic expansion plans. As a result, these countries have been saddled with large debt service ratios (that is, external debt service as a percentage of exports). In 1985, these ratios were 26.5% for Brazil, 41.8 for Argentina, 30.6 for Uruguay, 29.5 for Pakistan and 30.8 for Nigeria (where external indebtedness was primarily the legacy of reckless spending and corruption by the civilian Second Republic). By contrast, more cautious strategies kept the debt service ratios down to 9.3% in India, 13.9% in Sri Lanka and 5.4% in Botswana in 1985.[7]

As in politics, it would appear that consistency, prudence and moderation in economic policy are conducive to democratic stability. In Colombia, eclectic, pragmatic, non-doctrinaire economic policies produced steady economic growth with low inflation between 1957 and 1981. Colombia's flexibility and pragmatism, which motivated a relatively early partial reorientation of the economy from import substitution to export promotion, enabled it to avoid some of the "disastrous experiences in import-substitution and sharply 'pendular' policies . . . with their devastating political consequences" in countries like Argentina, Chile, Peru and Uruguay.[8] One of the most pernicious aspects of Argentina's development strategy was that it generated extensive and entrenched economic interests (that is, the owners and workers in the protected, non-competitive industries) determined to fight any change in policy. The resulting deep economic stagnation, in a context of high social mobilization and mobility aspirations, has in turn produced decades of political instability and turmoil. Similar developments accounted in large measure for Uruguay's and Turkey's economic stagnation and decline, which significantly contributed to their democratic breakdowns in 1973 and 1980, respectively.

With regard to economic performance, our evidence underscores the particularly corrosive effects of corruption on the legitimacy of democratic regimes, even more than of authoritarian ones. This is so in part because under conditions of freedom, with competitive elections, an independent judiciary, an opposition in parliament, and a free press, corruption is likely to be more visible than under authoritarianism. Its scale and extension to the whole democratic political class—as has repeatedly occurred in Ghana and Nigeria, for example—delegitimizes the whole political system rather than disqualifying a particular politician or party. As we indicate further below, the prevalence of political corruption throughout the democratic state reduces the political process to a struggle over power rather than policy issues, generating, in turn, cynical and apathetic responses in the electorate (or at least the bulk of it outside patronage networks). Further, such widespread corruption is one of the major arguments used by the military to justify their overthrow of elected governments, even though their own corruption will likely be as great or greater in time.

Political Culture

One important dimension of regime performance is the management of conflict. Here again, democratic regimes require an unusually high degree of effectiveness. As institutionalized systems of competition and conflict, they are especially liable to witness the disintegration of competition into enmity, of conflict into chaos. If political freedom and competition are not to descend into extremism, polarization and violence, there must be mechanisms to contain conflict within certain behavioral boundaries. One of the most important factors in this regard is a country's political culture, that is, the beliefs and values concerning politics that prevail among both the elite and the mass.

It appears that those cases in our study that have been the most strongly and stably democratic also have the most democratic political values and beliefs (although this raises questions of cause and effect that our study cannot clearly settle). In Venezuela, survey data on mass beliefs "show consistently strong support for democracy as a political system," and for such basic democratic principles as the legitimacy of elections and of open opposition and criticism. Moreover, peasants and political leaders alike commonly stress the need for caution, compromise and conciliation in politics.[9] Similarly, survey data in Costa Rica show broad support for democratic institutions among both elites and masses, and a striving toward compromise and consensus. In particular, the political elite disavow violence and respond to protest and confrontation with moderation and conciliation. Costa Rica also manifests unusually high levels of mass political participation, interest and awareness, comparable in many respects to the world's most developed democracies.[10]

Democratic success in the Third World may be traced not only to the growth of democratic values but also to their roots in a country's historical and cultural traditions. From the time of the founding of the Indian National Congress a century ago, "democratic rules of procedure, tolerance of adversaries and reconciliation of conflicting claims became part of the political education of the participants."[11] This liberal tradition was further deepened by Gandhi's emphasis on accommodation, compromise and non-violence. In Botswana, the political culture of "public discussion, community consensus and non-violence" is a major foundation of democratic stability. Holm traces this to the cultural tradition of popular consultation and pursuit of consensus known as the kgotla, which the ruling party has amplified through the practice of discussing "all new policies with the local community in kgotla before any local implementation." Similarly in Papua New Guinea, the traditional "Melanesian ethic" is highly compatible with and supportive of Westminster democracy. The central features of that country's sturdy democratic system, such as "the high degree of competitiveness, the extensive circulation of elites, . . . and the consensual nature of leadership and state power, each manifest the egalitarian, factionalized, exchange-based ethic of the traditional setting."[12]

There is also evidence that the democratic prospect may improve as democratic beliefs and values grow. In Peru, the dramatic increases over the past two decades in democratic values and beliefs, manifested in growing political participation and deeper loyalty to the system (especially among the lower classes), has enabled a second democratic constitutional succession despite economic disaster, guerrilla war, and a first administration so ineffectual it was termed "non-government."[13]

There is also some evidence that ambivalence in a country's political culture is associated with ambivalence in its experience with democracy. Turkey, for example, is torn between a strong consensus on the legitimacy of popular, elective government, and the continuing predeliction (dating back to Ottoman rule) for organic theories of state, which spawn excessive fear of division, intolerance of political opposition and individual deviation, and a tendency to see politics in absolutist terms.[14] The behavioral manifestations of these values have figured prominently in Turkey's democratic breakdowns. Similarly, Nigeria has been torn between a deep and broadly based commitment to political freedom and popular, accountable government, and a weak inclination toward tolerance and accommodation. This has made for political chaos, violence, and democratic breakdown. In both countries, these cultural tendencies have been shaped in part by the overbearing state (see below). In semi-democratic Malaysia, "strong curbs placed on open discussion of political issues are reflective of Malay cultural values, which assume that to do to the contrary will only lead to disaster."[15] Repeated military intervention in Thailand may be linked in part to a military conception of democracy that values "national security, stability and order" over freedom and participation, and dislikes pressure groups and conflict.[16] The violence and instability of democratic politics in post-independence Zimbabwe owe much to a political culture that, despite its appreciation in principle for democratic institutions, bears the scars of the "intolerant, violent and commandist" culture of the liberation struggle.[17]

It is also interesting that strong democratic currents in a country's political culture may make it very difficult for an authoritarian regime to institutionalize its rule. The instability of dictatorial rule in Ghana and Nigeria can be traced in part to the popular commitment to political freedom. Authoritarian rule was never really accepted in the Philippines as a long-term proposition because of that country's commitment to democratic values and traditions, in contrast to Indonesia and Thailand, for example.[18] In Uruguay, the military's failure to perpetuate authoritarian rule was owed in part to "the resilience of the democratic political culture, even among the Armed Forces, and the inhospitable climate for authoritarian discourse."[19]

Social Structure and Socioeconomic Development

The favorable effects of a democratic political culture will be reinforced by social and political structures that minimize the possibility of social and political polarization. In particular, many theories have argued that socioeconomic development changes fundamentally the way individuals and groups relate to the political process. An advanced level of economic development, producing greater economic security and more widespread education, is assumed to reduce socioeconomic inequality and mitigate feelings of relative deprivation and injustice among the lower class, thus reducing the likelihood of extremist politics. Increased national wealth also tends to enlarge the middle class, which has long been associated in political theory with moderation, tolerance and democracy.

The impact of socioeconomic changes, both improvements and declines, on political systems may be seen perhaps most strikingly in Third World authoritarian systems. As our case studies indicate, the most common, and in the long run, probably the most important effect of rapid socioeconomic development under authoritarian rule has been to generate pressures and create social structural conditions more conducive to democracy. At different historical periods and to different degrees, this has been true of Brazil, Costa Rica, the Dominican Republic, Peru, Thailand and South Korea. Beyond mere economic growth, the Peruvian military regime also implemented social reforms that were conducive to democracy. A sweeping land reform program eliminated semifeudal relations, completely ousted the landed aristocracy and created a significant middle peasantry. Trade unions doubled in number and became increasingly politically active, while remaining autonomous from the state. At the same time, General Velasco's reforms also greatly strengthened Peru's industrial bourgeoisie and its professional managerial class. Similarly in South Korea, growth under authoritarian rule was accompanied by social reform and substantial improvement in the welfare of lower income groups, and has stimulated the formation of opposition groups which are demanding greater freedom. Slow or negative growth has, of course, also helped to destabilize and bring down authoritarian regimes, as recently evident in the Philippines and Haiti. Changes made under such conditions do not bode well for the future of democracy.

Evidence from our case studies also supports the proposition that democracy and socioeconomic equality are related. In particular, deep, cumulative social inequalities represent a poor foundation for democracy. Historically, this has been a contributing factor to the instability of democracy in Latin America. Wiarda finds this to be particularly true of the Dominican Republic, where traditions of rigid social hierarchy and steep inequality date back to Spanish colonial rule.[20] Similarly in Peru, peasant laborers on the haciendas historically had very low levels of political efficacy, awareness, and other democratic orientations; the country's discouraging experience with democracy was traceable in part to one of the most glaringly unequal income distributions in Latin America. But with the land reform inaugurated in 1968, increases in political efficacy, trust and other democratic values have been apparent, and the new stratum of "middle peasantry" has since given strong backing to the return to democracy.[21] Hartlyn finds Colombia to be moving in the opposite direction, however, as the inability of the regime to address the "sharp disparities of wealth and income across population groups and regions" has "obstructed the consolidation of democracy." Even more strikingly in Brazil, redressing the enormous inequalities in income and life circumstances (which worsened during the "economic miracle" of the military dictatorship)—what Lamounier terms the challenge of "structural deconcentration"—now looms as a critical and formidable condition for democratic consolidation (and one that is hardly facilitated by Brazil's agonizing burden of international indebtedness).[22]

As suggested by its surprisingly high standing on physical quality of life indicators, Sri Lanka has drawn support for its democratic institutions from its relative limitation and dispersion of socioeconomic inequalities. Costa Rica stands in contrast to most of the rest of Latin America, and especially Central America, in this regard. Since 1948, the legitimacy of democracy in Costa Rica has been strongly buttressed by "increasing popular living standards and decreasing income and wealth inequality," which have given Costa Ricans "the lowest infant mortality and disease rates and the highest literacy, life expectancy and caloric intake of all Central American countries."[23]

Associational Life

Both theory and evidence argue strongly for the importance to stable democracy of autonomous intermediate groups—based on factors such as class, occupation, region, ethnicity, and religion—that can limit state power, provide democratic vitality, leadership and experience and stimulate participation in the formal political arena. In each of the three countries in our study that have enjoyed the most successful experience with democracy in the past few decades—India, Costa Rica and Venezuela—a vigorous network of autonomous and increasingly sophisticated voluntary associations has been an important foundation of democratic stability and robustness.

In Costa Rica, autonomous interest groups developed early and vigorously, first in the form of worker and professional guilds chartered by the state and, later, mutual aid societies and self-help guilds. Today the high level of formal organization is one of the distinguishing features of Costa Rican society. As Booth demonstrates, these organizations—business and producer groups, unions, cooperatives, professional associations, and self-help groups—are primary channels for articulating interests and making demands upon the government.

In India as well, modern associational life developed during colonial rule in the 19th century, in a variety of urban voluntary associations directed to language reform, legal reform, educational modernization, defending freedom of the press, and articulating the rights of women. Later these spread across the country and became vehicles for political protest and organization as well. Today, strong trade unions, student and business associations often align with and strengthen political parties, but they also act autonomously to pursue their own interests.

In Venezuela, a multiplicity of voluntary associations not only balances and limits the power of the state but also supplements the role of political parties in articulating interests, stimulating participation, increasing citizen efficacy and effectiveness, recruiting leaders, and enhancing commitment to the democratic system. In Venezuela, "the operational norms of most associations are modeled on those common in the political system. Competitive elections are standard practice, the rights of opposition are generally respected, and opposition representatives commonly share in group governance through proportional representation. In all these ways, organizational life reflects and reinforces more general political principles."[24]

Where associational life is dense, institutionalized, and auton-omous from state control, it may also undermine authoritarian rule and generate effective pressure for democratization. This was dramatically evidenced last year in the Philippines. There (where 95 percent of the population is Catholic), the Catholic Church was the one institution that Marcos was unable to coopt in his two decades in power, and it proved to be a crucial source of protest against government repression and abuse of power. Associations of lawyers, intellectuals and students also helped to keep democratic aspirations alive and, with crucial segments of the modern business community, joined the Church in the broad popular mobilization that ultimately brought down the Marcos dictatorship. It is noteworthy that throughout Latin America in recent years, the Catholic Church has played a similar role in opposition to political tyranny (not only of the right, but now, in Nicaragua, of the left as well) and in defense of social and political pluralism. Even more than in the Philippines perhaps, the Church in Haiti remained the one institution in the society that the Duvalier dictatorship failed to cow, eliminate or coopt, and so it was able to be a refuge for, and ultimately to encourage, enlighten and help organize, the popular opposition that brought down the regime. Along with the much smaller but still influential Catholic Church, the Protestant denominations in South Korea have also endorsed and given encouragement to the campaign for an end to authoritarian rule there.

One asset of religious institutions in the struggle for political freedom and pluralism is the special moral legitimacy they have almost by definition. But religious institutions may also be advantaged by the fact that they are less explicitly politically self-interested in character than other types of interest groups that seek rewards and resources from the state. Where other non-self-interested types of organizations can be constructed, their impact in defending or campaigning for democracy can be substan-tial. This is the lesson of the Philippine organization, NAMFREL (National Association for the Maintenance of Free Elections), which has had as its sole purpose for four decades the policing of polling places and prevention of electoral fraud, based on a commitment to the democratic system rather than to any particular party. In the 1984 legislative elections, NAMFREL played a key role in limiting electoral fraud and so enabling the opposition to Ferdinand Marcos to realize astonishing gains in the context of authoritarian rule. Subsequently, its vigilance, organization and international reputation for integrity were critical in discrediting the February 1986 presidential "snap election" and so hastening the demise of the Marcos regime.

In Nigeria, efforts to sustain authoritarian rule in the 1970s, and to deepen its repressive character under the military regime of General Buhari (1984-85), were frustrated by the vigilance and organizational strength of the press, the Bar Association, student groups, trade unions, business associations, and intellectuals and opinion leaders. These groups were responsible for the popular mobilization and resistance to authoritarian decrees that helped precipitate Buhari's downfall in a 1985 coup, and they have exerted similar pressure on his military successor for liberal and accountable government. In a somewhat different fashion, in Ghana, the vigor of nonformal associations and modes of economic exchange has made them "alternative loci of power, authority and legitimacy" around which democracy might now be reconstructed from the bottom up.[25]

As a strong and autonomous associational life may buttress or foster democracy, so the absence of a vigorous sector of voluntary associations and interest groups, or the control of such organizations by a corporatist state, may reinforce authoritarian rule and obstruct the development of democracy. Perhaps the classic demonstration of this in our study is Mexico, where the early encapsulation of mass organizations (especially of peasants and workers) by a hegemonic ruling party has been an important foundation of the stability of the authoritarian regime, and where the struggle of labor and other popular movements to break free of corporatist controls is crucial to the struggle for democracy.[26]

Political Institutions

Constitutional and party structures play an important role in shaping the conflict-regulating capacity of democratic systems. While these conditions of political structure are not necessary for stable democracy, nor equivalent in importance to conditions of social structure, they become more significant as the conditions of political culture become less favorable.

One of the stronger generalizations emerging from our study is the danger for democracy of excessive centralization of state power. Where there are major ethnic or regional cleavages that are territorially based, the relationship is by now self-evident and axiomatic: the absence of provisions for devolution and decentralization of power, especially in the context of ethnoregional disparities, feeds ethnic insecurity, violent conflict, and even secessionist pressures. These, in turn, are poisonous to democracy. Currently this phenomenon constitutes a serious challenge to democracy in Peru, where the guerrilla group Sendero Luminoso has mobilized acute feelings of relative deprivation and political alienation in the predominantly Indian Southern highlands, and in Sri Lanka, where a secessionist movement has mobilized the beleaguered Tamils.

Secessionist pressures carry a dual threat to democracies. Unless resolved by political means, through institutions like autonomy, federalism, or—in the extreme—separate statehood, they can lead to the imposition of authority by force and the deterioration or breakdown of democratic rule. Alternatively, a democratic center may be questioned for its inefficiency in creating or its weakness in handling the secessionist crisis, opening the way for military intervention. In differing ways and to differing degrees, these dangers have been present in recent years not only in Peru and Sri Lanka but in India, the Philippines and (to mention a semidemocratic case outside our study) Sudan. Historically, they figured prominently in the failure of Nigeria's first democratic attempt in the 1960s. More generally, the failure to integrate diverse ethnic communities into the national polity, or at least to find some stable formula for accommodating and managing this diversity, has heavily contributed to the temporary breakdown of democracy in Malaysia and to the repeated failure of democratic experiments in Pakistan and Uganda.[27]

An important reason for the failure of the First Nigerian Republic, and the subsequent descent into civil war, was the gross inadequacy of the three-region federal system, which reified the major tripartite ethnic cleavage while assuring one group political hegemony. By contrast, the nineteen-state federal structure in the Second Republic went a long way toward giving Nigeria's many ethnic groups a much greater sense of political security and, also, toward crosscutting ethnicity to some extent. Moreover, as in India—where federalism has functioned, even in a context of virtually continuous one-party dominance, to give opposition parties a stake in the system and to expand access to incorporate new groups—federalism in Nigeria limits the tendency to fixate political ambitions on the center. Although Nigeria's Second Republic failed, polarized ethnic conflict was not a major cause, and the elaborateness of Nigeria's federal provisions helps to explain its recent success in avoiding ethnic polarization.[28]

It is not only to manage ethnic and regional cleavage that decentralization is important to democracy. Centralization of power, by its very nature, tends to undermine democracy. In Colombia, strong presidentialism and increasing centralization of state power have raised the stakes in controlling the executive branch to the point where neither party wants to risk not having a share of it, and hence neither is willing to surrender its mutual consociational stranglehold on the system. In Mexico, centralization and strong presidentialism have been important pillars of one-party domination, and are increasingly viewed as obstacles to democratization and the expansion of participation. In Turkey, state centralization—as reflected in the absence of any tradition of autonomous municipalities and the dependence of municipal and provincial administrations on the central government—has increased the importance of control over the central government, and so reenforced the tendency toward violence and intolerance in the struggle for that control. In Thailand, a highly centralized state bureaucracy manifests cynicism and suspicion of democratic politics. In Senegal, the unresponsiveness to popular concerns and distance from popular reach of a highly centralized state not only fuels a (sometimes violent) resistance movement in the geographically isolated and culturally distant Casamance region, but also undermines the legitimacy of the semi-democratic regime throughout the country.[29] On the other hand, the substantial power of local elected councils over community development and services has been a source of democratic vitality in Botswana. The fact that opposition parties have been able to win control of some of these councils (even some of the most important ones) has mitigated somewhat the effect of continuing one-party dominance at the center, and so enhanced commitment to the system.

Another important feature of the institutional landscape is the party system. We find some evidence for the proposition that the fewer the number of parties (down to an ideal of two) and the broader their social and ideological character, the greater the likelihood of stable democracy. But this depends on how the party system articulates with social cleavages. Of the five most stable democratic systems in our study, two (Venezuela and Costa Rica) have two-party systems composed of broad, multiclass parties; two (India and Botswana) have one-party dominant systems in which the ruling parties incorporate and aggregate a wide range of ethnic and social interests; and one (Papua New Guinea) has a moderate multi-party system in which no party is dominant. In Venezuela, the heterogeneity of the parties reinforces the autonomy of the party leaders, "helping them resist demands from any particular sector," and partially explains the "leadership's success in making pacts and coalitions and selling them to the party faithful."[30] The frequent alternation of the two parties in the presidency has been a prominent feature of stable democracy in Costa Rica. But in both these countries, the success of the two-party system is also associated with the absence of deep social cleavages that, if identified with the party bases, could threaten polarization. Democratic stability for periods of time can also be traced in part to the stability and broad, multiclass character of the essentially two-party systems in Colombia and Uruguay, but when the former proved unable to adapt and the latter became ideologically polarized, these systems became threatened.

Presidential systems tend to facilitate two-party systems. However, presidentialism carries with it certain characteristic problems. For one, a presidential system tends to concentrate power in the executive branch, which may be unhealthy for nascent democracies where the separation of powers and checks and balances are not well established. In Sri Lanka, the shift to a presidential system in 1978 "has led to an increasing centralization of [executive] powers" and "a de facto devaluation of the . . . legislature and judiciary," with parliament being virtually transformed into "a rubber stamp institution."[31] This capacity for unfettered power may explain the shift from parliamentary to presidential forms of government in Ghana under Nkrumah and in Uganda under Obote, and the greater frequency with which presidential executives, like Marcos in the Philippines, have ended democracy by executive coup.

The advantages of a parliamentary system lie in its greater flexibility. An executive who has lost popular support can be turned out of office before his term is up. Coalitions can be formed to reach across significant political divisions, and these can be reformed in light of shifting political issues and fortunes, making for a less "zero-sum" game. Moreover, because they are associated with a greater number of parties, parliamentary systems are somewhat less conducive to the polarization of politics between two or three major political parties, each identified with major class or ethnic cleavage groups.

The theoretical case for these advantages lies largely with the experience of parliamentary democracy in Western Europe and the disastrous experience with presidentialism of some Latin American countries, such as Chile.[32] Unfortunately, our sample of Third World cases does not provide a sufficient range of experience with parliamentary systems to evaluate these arguments. One could argue that the parliamentary system has served to broaden the base of power in multi-ethnic, semi-democratic Malaysia, although it failed to do so in Nigeria's First Republic.

Our case studies suggest several other ways in which constitutional designs can have a tangible impact on democratic performance and viability. First, electoral systems do shape the party system. Systems of proportional representation, by allocating seats with minimal or lesser distortion of the popular vote, make it easier for minor parties to win representation. By contrast, the single-member district, plurality method of legislative election tends to enable a dominant party to muster a disproportionate share of seats. Certainly this has contributed to the relatively stable political dominance of the Congress party in India, which has rarely managed to win an absolute majority of the vote. At times, these distortions can have profound political implications by giving overwhelming legislative power to a party lacking any kind of equivalent electoral mandate. This was particularly apparent in Sri Lanka in 1970 and 1977. In the latter case, for example, the UNP (United Nationalist Party) won a bare majority of the popular vote (50.9%) but over 80% of the seats. Both times, and especially in 1977, this overwhelming power was turned to antidemocratic ends, eroding both the democratic character and the legitimacy and stability of the political system. (Perhaps significantly, Sri Lanka has since changed to proportional representation).

The overall strength of parties and party systems can profoundly affect the capacity of authoritarian regimes to establish themselves firmly. When parties are deeply rooted in the society, it is difficult for authoritarian rule to institutionalize its domination. In Colombia, the fact that the two political parties completely dominated the country's political landscape had much to do with General Rojas's failure to establish an authoritarian corporatist political movement to perpetuate his dictatorship in the 1950s. The depth of the traditional parties and of popular identification with them similarly frustrated efforts by the military to institutionalize authoritarian rule in Uruguay during the past decade. By contrast, the weakness of the parties in South Korea and Thailand has facilitated the perpetuation of military domination over the politics of those two countries. This, however, has been a circular phenomenon; frequent military intervention in South Korea has prevented any party from staying "around long enough to claim loyalty and support from the people."[33] This has been particularly debilitating to democratic development in Thailand, where only four parliaments in the past half-century have been able to complete their tenures. The lack of any continuous experience with party democracy in Thailand (given the deep-seated hostility of the bureaucracy and military to political parties) has led to a proliferation of parties, none of which has been able to develop organizational depth and internal discipline, or to establish effective linkages with politically active groups. Hence, when a chance at full democracy came in 1974, that brief experience "was close to anarchy."[34]

We also stress the importance to democracy of a strong and independent judiciary. A powerful judiciary can be the bulwark of a democratic constitution, defending both its integrity (and hence political freedom and due process) and also its preeminence as the source of democratic legitimacy. More generally, the judiciary is the ultimate guarantor of the rule of law, and thus of the accountability of rulers to the ruled, which is a basic premise of democracy.

In Sri Lanka, however, the constitution does not provide for court review after Parliament enacts legislation, and even an advance judicial ruling on the constitutionality of a pending bill can be waived by a two-thirds vote of parliament. This weakness, which has prevented the judiciary from overturning antidemocratic legislation, and the concerted efforts of the executive to erode judicial autonomy have been important factors in the authoritarian deterioration of the democratic system in recent years. By pointed contrast, during the authoritarian emergency in India, "a beleaguered and partially 'captured' Supreme Court still struck down a constitutional amendment, enacted by parliament, that would have destroyed an 'essential feature' of the constitution."[35] Similarly in Zimbabwe, an independent and sophisticated judiciary has played an important role in the defense of human rights and democracy as they have come under increasing pressure.[36]

Finally, the importance of creative institution-building should not be overlooked. A crucial factor in the record of honest and highly legitimate elections in Costa Rica—which in turn have been a major foundation of stable democracy there—has been the structure of electoral administration. The Constitution gives a powerful independent agency, the Supreme Electoral Tribunal (TSE) power not only to administer the voter registration, balloting and counting, but to investigate charges of political bias by public employees, file criminal charges against violators of electoral laws, control the police and other forces during election periods, monitor executive neutrality in campaigns, and allocate the governmental subvention of campaign costs. Botswana has been able to control political corruption relatively effectively in part because of institutional arrangements that include a "fairly rigorous system of accounting controls which allows quick tracing of misused funds" and "an independent and extremely aggressive audit under the supervision of the National Assembly."[37]

State and Society

The weakness of parties, interest groups and other input institutions in some countries reflects (and has helped to produce) the ascendance of bureaucratic state institutions. This raises the important and neglected question of the relationship between bureaucracy and democracy. Stable democracy requires that the bureaucracy should not assume the top policy-making positions in government, nor be the main source of recruitment of political elites, nor think that civil servant bureaucrats should undertake the task of organizing social and political participation. The case of Thailand shows the negative implications for the development of democratic institutions and processes of a bureaucratically oriented polity, in which paternalistic bureaucratic tutelage and control displaces the initiatives and conflicts of organized citizens. Democracy requires a division of labor between the state and society, between amateur or professional politicians and civil servants, and requires limits to the bureaucratic penetration and control of society. Democratic politicians and leaders have to establish such limits and controls over bureaucratic activities, and create a space in which conflicting interests can be articulated without bureaucratic interference.

On the other hand, we agree with Schumpeter that democratic stability depends on an efficient, cooperative but not subservient bureaucracy. The need for some measure of efficiency is obvious. Because stable democracy presumes a capacity for effective governance, it requires state structures that can produce economic growth, meet distributive demands, and maintain order without quashing liberty. The need for control of the bureaucracy by elected politicians does not mean that politicians should freely appoint civil servants (except to fill a limited number of policy-making and advisory roles), that the bureaucracy should serve as a widespread source of party or personal patronage, or that criteria of professional competence and standards of professional conduct should be ignored. Relative autonomy and continuity of the bureaucracy constitute an important check on the absolute and arbitrary power of the politicians, while its professional competence may limit the impact of their "amateur" and often poorly thought-out ideas. All of this helps to ensure citizens at least a minimum of neutrality in the application of the law and a minimum of probity in the conduct of administration, as well as a basic continuity in the functioning of the state that compensates for the instability of political leadership in many democracies.

The evidence from our case studies shows how bureaucratic competence and professionalism can buttress a democratic system. A significant case in this regard, despite the paternalism of its political elite, is Botswana. And even with its many flaws, the strength of the bureaucracy in India—often cited as the "steel frame" of the system—has been an important factor in that country's economic progress and relatively effective administration since independence.

By contrast, the appropriation by politicians—both democratic and authoritarian—of the bureaucracy, its conversion into a partisan or personalistic patronage resource, transforms it into a patrimonial bureaucracy, which becomes the tool for perpetuating the ruling group in power and advancing its interests by any means. This decay has been most stunning in Africa. In Ghana, for example, the relentless plundering and personalization of state structures have reached the point where society has disengaged itself from the state, whose capacity and authority have so deteriorated that the country has become virtually ungovernable.[38] But whether one talks of Ghana or Uganda, the Dominican Republic or the Philippines, Nigeria or Mexico, the effects are devastating. The extreme politicization and corruption of the bureaucracy undermines the democratic prospect by ruining development performance, alienating society, constricting free competition, and deepening the zero-sum character of politics, resulting in bitterness that further diminishes the possibility of free and fair electoral competition.

These consequences follow from the nature not just of the bureaucracy but of the entire relationship between state and society. Among the most important dimensions of that relationship is the strong tendency we find for state dominance over the economy and society to undermine democratic politics in developing countries. In the least developed region, Sub-Saharan Africa, this tendency has been most powerful because there the state's extensive economic ownership and mediation of social opportunities and rewards is not counterbalanced by private sources of economic accumulation and socioeconomic opportunity. Hence, upward social mobility and the accumulation of personal wealth depend on getting and maintaining control of, or at least access to, the state. This raises the premium on political power to the point where no competing party or candidate is willing to entertain the prospect of defeat. The result is a zero-sum game, the politics of intolerance, desperation, violence and fraud.

In Nigeria, where "most of the country's wealth continues to be mediated through government contracts, jobs, import licenses, development projects and so on," this has been a primary factor underlying the failure of both the First and Second Republics.[39] Ozbudun has noted a similar effect in Turkey, where public enterprises have proliferated to the point that they now produce about half of Turkey's industrial output. The ruling party's access to such immense resources in relation to the resource base of society, and the clientelistic traditions that give the political class wide scope in distributing state resources, make being out of power in Turkey very costly. This in turn has helped to generate the political polarization and unwillingness to compromise that have repeatedly destabilized democratic regimes. Similarly in Colombia, state expansion—and the consequent anxiety over the consequences of losing state control—heavily contributed to the "politicization, polarization and violence" that brought down the democratic regime and ushered in the devastating period of "la violencia" following the 1946 election.[40] State expansion may also intensify ethnic political conflict. The fact that the state is the biggest employer in Sri Lanka, for example, has heightened the stakes in the ethnic struggle and made accommodation (and so the reequilibration of democracy) more difficult.[41]

Excessive state control over the economy and society may also reduce democratic regime performance in two important respects. As we have already implied, it feeds corruption. And throughout the Third World, the evidence is accumulating that huge public sectors and pervasive state subsidies and controls have hampered economic efficiency and come to represent a major obstacle to vigorous economic growth. This has become increasingly apparent in recent years in India, where state ownership has led to higher waste of capital and labor, corruption, and a heavy drag of unprofitable, inefficient state enterprises, depressing growth potential. Similar problems exist in many other countries reported on in our study, including Turkey, Nigeria, Senegal, Ghana, the Philippines, Argentina and Mexico. Even in Costa Rica, where it has not had the political consequences that it has elsewhere, the extensive state regulation of the economy, numerous public sector monopolies, and heavy state investment in production are now increasingly under attack for stifling productive individuals and firms and fostering the growth of corruption.

One must be cautious, however, about drawing blanket conclusions. There are instances where extensive state economic ownership and control have not had obvious extensive deleterious consequences for democracy. Costa Rica, Botswana and perhaps Uruguay come to mind. Each of these countries has had mechanisms or traditions (like those in the European social democracies) that have tended to insulate the state from brazen partisan abuse and corrupt personal accumulation. We have noted earlier the administrative structures in Botswana that "keep the lid on corruption." In Costa Rica, the fact that state economic control and financial expenditures operate primarily through autonomous administrative agencies puts the bulk of this state power beyond the reach of politial patronage and partisan manipulation. In Uruguay, the fact that state economic ownership and control "emerged simultaneously with the achievement of democracy at the beginning of this century"[42] may have generated norms of separation between politics and state administration.

Another crucial dimension of state structure and its relationship to civil society involves the military. Where, as in Argentina, the military is large and politicized, with doctrines that appoint themselves "as the privileged definers and guardians of the national interest," repeated military intervention is more likely and democracy is more difficult to establish and maintain.[43] Where the military is either weak or socialized to democratic values and civilian control, democratic stability is more likely. The classic positive affirmation of this relationship is, of course, Costa Rica, which abolished its army after the 1948 civil war. Booth finds that "the absence of a standing army greatly strengthens the authority of civil government," frees fiscal resources and promotes both policy continuity and political flexibility.

However, the military variable is not necessarily independent of political ones. Typically, military role expansion is induced by the corruption, stagnation and malfunctioning of democratic institutions, to the point where the military is increasingly called upon to maintain order and comes to see itself as the only salvation of the country. In virtually every country in our study which has experienced democratic breakdown by military coup, these interventions have come in the wake of manifest political and often economic crisis. Indonesia reflects the general pattern. "The Army has not increased its political power by coups against legitimate governments, but rather has stepped in whenever vacuums needed to be filled. . . . It has come to see itself as the savior of the nation from rapacious and incompetent politicians as well as rightist and leftist extremists endangering the unity of the country . . ."[44] The size, autonomy and role conception of the military may determine their threshold for intervention, but they do not constitute a wholly independent cause of democratic breakdown.

Democracy: Factors in Development

This is not to say that factors external to the political process do not shape the military disposition to intervene. External communist threats, or perceptions of communist support for indigenous insurgencies, have heightened the military's readiness to intervene and rule on behalf of "national security" not only in much of Latin America, but in Thailand and especially in South Korea, where the "militarized" nature of society has been a major factor creating a political setting conducive to authoritarian rule.

International Factors

Under certain circumstances (including questionable or eroding internal legitimacy), democratic and authoritarian regimes in the Third World can be vulnerable to international political and military pressures. United States pressure alone cannot effect democratic change, but the potential for American influence should not be underestimated. One supporting factor in the consolidation of democracy in Venezuela was the fact that the Kennedy Administration "bet heavily on democracy in Venezuela, the kind of bet later administrations have taken only too rarely."[45] In Argentina, U.S. human rights pressure under the Carter Administration did not force the withdrawal of the military, but such pressure "saved many victims of indiscriminate repression in the late 1970s, and was a factor in the international isolation of the military regime."[46] By the same token, the absence of pressure can be taken as a sign of tacit support from which an authoritarian regime may draw strength. During the later 1960s and 1970s, the lack of U.S. pressure for democratization was an important "permissive" factor in the construction and consolidation of authoritatian rule in South Korea. Previously, "American pressure had been responsible, at least in part, for the re-introduction of the National Assembly and the holding of the presidential election in 1963."[47] Continuing U.S. support for multilateral loans to Chile—$2.2 billion worth since 1980—helps perpetuate the Pinochet regime. "Yet on the one occasion when substantive pressure was threatened—the 1985 multilateral loan abstentions—the dictator quickly lifted the state of seige."[48]

External military pressure or insecurity can affect the democratic prospect by strengthening the military establishment and its claim to power, as we have already noted in the case of South Korea. In Thailand, the communist insurgency heightened the military's fear of competitive politics, so that "any democratic movement which aimed at mobilizing and gaining support from the masses was usually suspected of being communist-inspired."[49] Recently, democracy in Costa Rica has been made less secure by increasing regional military instability and Nicaragua's growing military strength, and also by the presence of "contra" forces and the strengthening (with U.S. assistance) of the Costa Rican Civil Guard to the point where it could become "a new power contender in the Costa Rican polity."[50] Rising pressure from South Africa, in the form of cross-border commando raids, represents a growing threat to democracy in Botswana and Zimbabwe, which is also becoming entangled in an escalating war in neighboring Mozambique.

At the current time, however, and no doubt in many previous times, the most important international influences on the prospects for democracy in developing countries appear to be economic. We reject emphatically the simplistic argument that international economic dependence is incompatible with democracy, or that foreign investment and local capital accumulation in developing countries require political repression. We also reject the implication of many dependency theories that Third World or "peripheral" countries are somehow not responsible for their own political and economic failures. As we have indicated, even the degree and type of dependence of developing countries is significantly affected by their policy choices and implementation. Nevertheless, we cannot ignore the degree to which international economic constraints—severe indebtedness, weak or obstructed export markets, sluggish growth and demand in the industrialized countries, and steep balance of payments crises—may severely limit the maneuverability and damage the legitimacy of Third World democratic regimes.

To be sure, democratic legitimacy rests on other foundations than short-term economic performance, and the task of democratic consolidation is, to a substantial degree, a matter of what Linz and Stepan term "political crafting."[51] Thus, even in a recently established democracy such as Spain, the consolidation of democracy may proceed in the face of relatively weak economic performance and sharply declining belief in the socioeconomic efficacy of democracy.[52]   And recent evidence from Costa Rica demonstrates that where the legitimacy of the democratic system is already firmly established, democracy can remain stable even in the face of real and perceived crises of effectiveness.[53]

However, there is always some danger in extrapolating from one historical case to another. The Philippines is not Costa Rica, and Brazil, Argentina, and Peru are not Spain. These and other recently reestablished democracies appear to face even deeper economic crises and social tensions, with less working capital of system legitimacy and without the benefits of being part of the democratic community of Europe. Each of these new democracies is deeply threatened by grave and urgent economic crises the relief (not to mention resolution) of which depends on a host of factors in the world economy over which they can have only very limited if any influence—interest rates, growth rates, trade barriers, levels of economic assistance, and so on. Consolidating these and other new democracies will require skillful political crafting and courageous and wise policy choices by their leaders. It will further demand considerable patience and forbearance by their publics and interest groups. But it is also likely to depend on the flexibility and vision of powerful international economic actors, and especially the major industrialized democracies, in dealing with the critical issues of Third World debt and trade. The more hostile and inflexible is this international environment, the more heroic must be the performances and compromises of leaderships and the sacrifices and forbearance of publics. History suggests that heroism and sacrifice are not promising conditions on which to depend for the survival, much less consolidation, of new democratic regimes.

NOTES

1. The authors gratefully acknowledge the support of the National Endowment for Democracy and the Hoover Institution. This paper draws from the forthcoming four-volume publication we are editing, **Democracy in Developing Countries** (Boulder, Colorado: Lynne Rienner Publishers, 1988).

2. Our 26 cases are, in Africa (Volume 2): Nigeria, Ghana, Senegal, Botswana, Zimbabwe, and Uganda; in Asia (Volume 3): India, Pakistan, Sri Lanka, Turkey, the Philippines, South Korea, Thailand, Malaysia, Papua New Guinea, and Indonesia; and in Latin America (Volume 4): Argentina, Brazil, Chile, Uruguay, Venezuela, Colombia, Peru, Costa Rica, the Dominican Republic, and Mexico. Because of the limits of our resources and the lesser experience with and prospects for democracy in the Middle East, we reluctantly decided to exclude that region (save for Turkey). The logic of our selection of cases is discussed in the preface to our three regional volumes.

3. Robert Dahl, **Polyarchy: Participation and Opposition** (New Haven: Yale University Press, 1971), pages 3-20. See also Seymour Martin Lipset, **Political Man** (Baltimore: Johns Hopkins University Press, 1981), page 27, and Juan J. Linz,**The Breakdown of Democratic Regimes: Crisis, Breakdown and Reequilibration** (Baltimore: Johns Hopkins University Press, 1978), page 5.

4. For a full review, see Volume 1 of our forthcoming study, **Democracy in Developing Countries.** A more limited review may be found in our paper, "Developing and Sustaining Democratic Government in the Third World," presented to the 1986 Annual Meeting of the American Political Science Association, pages 9-32.

5. John D. Holm, "Botswana: A Paternalistic Democracy," in **Democracy in Developing Countries: Africa.**

6. Jyotirindra Das Gupta, "India: Democratic Becoming and Planned Development," in **Democracy in Developing Countries: Asia.**

7. World Bank, **World Development Report, 1987** (New York: Oxford University Press, 1987), Table 19, pages 238-9.

8. Jonathan Hartlyn, "Colombia: The Politics of Violence and Accommodation," in **Democracy in Developing Countries: Latin America.**

9. Daniel Levine, "Venezuela: The Nature, Sources and Future Prospects of Democracy," in **Democracy in Developing Countries: Latin America.**

10. John Booth, "Costa Rica: The Development of Stable Democracy," in **Democracy in Developing Countries: Latin America.**

11. Das Gupta, "India."

12. David M. Lipset, "Papua-New Guinea: The Melanesian Ethic and the Spirit of Capitalism," in **Democracy in Developing Countries: Asia.**

13. Cynthia McClintock, "Peru: Unstable Undemocratic Rule and the Possibilities of Democratic Consolidation," in **Democracy in Developing Countries: Latin America.**

14. Ergun Ozbudun, "Turkey: Crises, Interruptions and Reequilibrations of Democracy," in **Democracy in Developing Countries: Asia.**

15. Zakaria Haji Ahmad, "Malaysia: Semi-Democracy in a Divided Society," in **Democracy in Developing Countries: Asia.**

16. Chai-Anan Samudavanija, "Thailand: A Stable Semi-Democratic Regime," in **Democracy in Developing Countries: Asia.**

17. Masipula Sithole, "Zimbabwe: In Search of a Stable Democracy," in **Democracy in Developing Countries: Africa.**

18. Karl Jackson, "The Philippines: The Search for a Suitable Democratic Solution, 1946-1986," in **Democracy in Developing Countries: Asia.**

19. Charles Gillespie and Luis Eduardo Gonzales, "Uruguay: The Survival of Old and Autonomous Institutions," in **Democracy in Developing Countries: Latin America.**

20. Howard Wiarda, "The Dominican Republic: The Mirror Legacies of Democracy and Authoritarianism," in **Democracy in Developing Countries: Latin America.**

21. McClintock, "Peru."

22. Bolivar Lamounier, "Brazil: Inequality against Democracy," in **Democracy in Developing Countries: Latin America.**

23. Booth, "Costa Rica."

24. Levine, "Venezuela."

25. Naomi Chazan: "Ghana: Problems of Governance and the Emergence of Civil Society," in **Democracy in Developing Countries: Africa.**

26. Daniel Levy, "Mexico: Sustained Civilian Rule Without Democracy," in **Democracy in Developing Countries: Latin America.**

27. Leo Rose, "Pakistan: Experiments With Democracy Since 1947," in **Democracy in Developing Countries: Asia;** Omari Kokole and Ali Mazrui, "Uganda: The Dual Polity and the Plural Society," in **Democracy in Developing Countries: Africa.**

28. Larry Diamond, "Nigeria: Pluralism, Statism and the Struggle for Democracy," in **Democracy in Developing Countries: Africa.**

29. Christian Coulon, "Senegal: The Development and Fragility of Semi-Democracy," in **Democracy in Developing Countries: Africa.**

30. Levine, "Venezuela."

31. Urmila Phadnis, "Sri Lanka: Crises of Legitimacy and Integration," in **Democracy in Developing Countries: Asia.**

32. Arturo Valenzuela, "Chile: The Origins, Consolidation and Breakdown of a Democratic Regime," in **Democracy in Developing Countries: Latin America.**

33. Sung-joo Han, "South Korea: Politics in Transition," in **Democracy in Developing Countries: Asia.**

34. Samudavanija, "Thailand."

35. Richard L. Sklar, "Developmental Democracy." Paper presented to the 1985 Annual Meeting of the American Political Science Association, New Orleans; page 13.

36. Ibid., page 14.

37. Holm, "Botswana."

38. Chazan, "Ghana."

39. Diamond, "Nigeria."

40. Hartlyn, "Colombia."

41. Phadnis, "Sri Lanka."

42. Gillespie and Gonzales, "Uruguay," page 54.

43. Carlos Waisman, "Argentina: The Primacy of Politics," in **Democracy in Developing Countries: Latin America.**

44. Ulf Sundhausen, "Indonesia: Past and Present Encounters with Democracy," in **Democracy in Developing Countries: Asia.**

45. Levine, "Venezuela."

46. Waisman, "Argentina."

47. Han, "South Korea."

48. Pamela Constable and Arturo Valenzuela, "Is Chile Next?" **Foreign Policy,** number 63 (1986), pages 74-5.

49. Samudavanija, "Thailand."

50. Booth, "Costa Rica."

51. Juan Linz and Alfred Stepan, "Political Crafting of Democratic Consolidation or Destruction: European and South American Comparisons." Paper presented at the Conference on "Reinforcing Democracy in the Americas," The Carter Center of Emory University, November 1986.

52. Ibid., pages 4-12.

53. Mitchell A. Seligson and Edward N. Muller, "Democratic Stability and Economic Crisis: Costa Rica, 1978-1983," **International Studies Quarterly** 31, pages 301-326; and Booth, "Costa Rica."

PART V

Country Summaries

INTRODUCTION

The following country descriptions summarize the evidence that lies behind our ratings for each country. They first bring together for each country most of the tabular material of Part I. Then, political rights are considered in terms of the extent to which a country is ruled by a government elected by the majority at the national level, the division of power among levels of government, and the possible denial of self-determination to major subnationalities, if any. While decentralization and the denial of group rights are deemphasized in our rating system, these questions should not be ignored. The summaries also contain consideration of civil liberties, especially as these include freedom of the media and other forms of political expression, freedom from political imprisonment, torture, and other forms of government reprisal, and freedom from interference in nonpublic group or personal life. Equality of access to politically relevant expression is also considered, as well as economic conditions and organization in their relation to freedom. In some cases the summaries will touch on the relative degree of freedom from oppression outside the government arena, for example, through slavery, labor bosses, capitalist exploitation, or private terrorism: this area of analysis is little developed at present.

At the beginning of each summary statement the country is characterized by the forms of its economy and polity. The meanings of the terms used in this classification may be found in the discussion of the relation of political-economic systems to freedom and its accompanying Table 8. The classification is highly simplified, but it serves our concern with the developmental forms and biases that affect political controls. As in Table 8, the terms inclusive and noninclusive are used to distinguish between societies in which the economic activities of most people are organized in accordance with the dominant system and those dual societies in which they remain largely outside. The system should be assumed to be inclusive unless otherwise indicated.

Each state is categorized according to the political positions of the national or ethnic groups it contains. Since the modern political form is the "nation-state," it is not surprising that many states have a relatively homogeneous population. The over-whelming majority in these states belong to roughly the same ethnic group; people from this group naturally form the dominant group in the state. In relatively homogeneous states there is no large subnationality (that is, with more than one million people or twenty percent of the population) residing in a defined territory within the country: Austria, Costa Rica, Somalia, and West Germany are good examples. States in this category may be ethni-cally diverse (for example, Cuba or Colombia), but there are no sharp ethnic lines between major groups. These states should be distinguished from ethnically complex states, such as Guyana or Singapore, that have several ethnic groups, but no major group that has its historic homeland in a particular part of the country. Complex states may have large minorities that have suffered social, political, or economic discrimination in the recent past, but today the governments of such states treat all peoples as equals as a matter of policy. In this regard complex states are distinguishable from ethnic states with major nonterritorial subnationalities, for the governments of such states have a deliberate policy of giving preference to the dominant ethnic group at the expense of other major groups. Examples are Burundi or China (Taiwan).

Another large category of states is labeled ethnic states with (a) major territorial subnationalities(y). As in the homogeneous states there is a definite ruling people (or Staatsvolk) residing on its historic national territory within the state. But the state also incorporates other territories with other historic peoples that are now either without a state, or the state dominated by their people lies beyond the new border. As explained in Freedom in the World 1978 (pp. 180-218), to be considered a subnationality a territorial minority must have enough cohesion and publicity that their right to nationhood is acknowledged in some quarters. Often recent events have forged a quasi-unity among quite distinct groups—as among the peoples of Southern Sudan. Typical countries in this category are Burma and the USSR. Ethnic states with major potential territorial subnationalities fall into a closely related category. In such states—for example, Ecuador or Bolivia—many individuals in pre-national ethnic groups have merged, with little overt hostility, with the dominant ethnic strain. The assimilation process has gone on for centuries. Yet in these countries the new consciousness that accompanies the diffusion of nationalistic ideas through education may reverse the process of assimilation in the future, especially where the potential subnationality has preserved a more or less definable territorial base.

There are a few truly multinational states in which ethnic groups with territorial bases coexist in one state without an established ruling people. In such states the several "nations" normally have autonomous political rights, although these do not in law generally include the right to secession. India and Nigeria (when under civilian rule) are examples. One trinational and a few binational states complete the categories of those states in which several "nations" coexist.

The distinction between truly multinational states and ethnic states with territorial subnationalities may be made by comparing two major states that lie close to the margin between the categories—the ethnic Russian USSR and multinational India. In the USSR, Russian is in every way the dominant language. By contrast, in India Hindi speakers have not achieved dominance. English remains a unifying lingua franca, the languages of the several states have not been forced to change their script to accord with Hindi forms, and Hindi itself is not the distinctive language of a "ruling people"—it is a nationalized version of the popular language of a portion of the population of northern India. (The pre-British ruling class used a closely related language with Arabic, Persian, and Turkish infusions; it was generally written in Persian-Arabic script.) Unlike Russians in the non-Russian Soviet Republics, Hindi speakers from northern India do not have a special standing in their own eyes or those of other Indians. Calcutta, Bombay, and Madras are non-Hindi speaking cities, and their pride in their identities and cultures is an important aspect of Indian culture. By contrast, many Soviet Republics are dominated by Russian speakers, a situation developing even in Kiev, the largest non-Russian city.

Finally, transethnic heterogeneous states, primarily in Africa, are those in which independence found a large number of ethnically distinct peoples grouped more or less artificially within one political framework. The usual solution was for those taking over the reins of government to adopt the colonial approach of formally treating all local peoples as equal, but with the new objective of integrating all equally into a new national framework (and new national identity) as and when this would be possible. Rulers of states such as Senegal or Zaire may come from relatively small tribes, and it is in their interest to deemphasize tribalism. In some cases the tribes are so scattered and localistic that there is no short-term likelihood of secession resulting from tribalism. However, in other cases portions of the country have histories of separate nationhood making the transethnic solution hard to implement. In a few countries recent events have placed certain ethnic groups in opposition to one another or to ruling circles in such a way that the transethnic state remains only the formal principle of rule, replaced in practice by an ethnic hierarchy, as in Cameroon, Togo, or Zimbabwe.

The descriptive paragraphs for political and civil rights are largely self-explanatory. Subnationalities are generally discussed under a subheading for political rights, although the subject has obvious civil liberties aspects. Discussion of the existence or nonexistence of political parties may be arbitrarily placed in one or the other section. These paragraphs only touch on a few relevant issues, especially in the civil liberties discussion. An issue may be omitted for lack of information, because it does not seem important for the country addressed, or because a particular condition can be inferred from the general statement of a pattern. It should be noted that we have tried where possible to incorporate the distinction between a broad definition of political prisoners (including those detained for violent political crimes) and a narrow definition that includes those arrested only for nonviolent actions—-often labeled "prisoners of conscience." Obviously we are primarily concerned with the latter.

Under civil liberties there is often a sentence or two on the economy. However, this is primarily a survey of politically relevant freedoms and not economic freedoms. In addition our view of economic freedom depends less on the economic system than the way in which it is adopted and maintained. (See Lindsay M. Wright, "A Comparative Survey of Economic Freedoms," in Freedom in the World 1982, pages 51-90.)

At the end of each country summary we have included an overall comparative statement that places the country's ratings in relation to those of others. Countries chosen for comparison are often neighboring or similar ones, but juxtaposing very different countries is also necessary for tying together the system.

Human rights, in so far as they are not directly connected with political and civil liberties, are given little attention in the following summaries. Capital punishment, torture, denial of refugee status, or food and medical care are issues that are less emphasized in this treatment than they would be in a human rights report. The summaries take little account of the oppressions that occur within the social units of a society, such as family and religious groups, or that reflect variations in the nonpolitical aspects of culture. The reader will note few references in the following summaries to the relative freedom of women. Democracies today have almost universally opened political and civic participation to women on at least a formal basis of equality, while most nondemocratic societies that deny these equal rights to women also deny effective participation to most men. In such societies granting equal rights has limited meaning. There is little gain for political and most civil rights when women are granted equal participation in a totalitarian society.

AFGHANISTAN

Economy: noninclusive socialist
Polity: communist one-party
Population: 14,200,000 (est.)*

Political Rights: 7
Civil Liberties: 7
Status: not free

An ethnic state with major territorial subnationalities

Political Rights. Afghanistan's ruling communist party is under the tutelage and direct control of the Soviet Union. The rule of this very small party has no electoral or traditional legitimization. Soviet forces control the major cities but their control is contested by a variety of resistance movements throughout the country. In many areas local administration is in the hands of traditional or ad hoc resistance leaders. Subnationalities: The largest minority is the Tajik (thirty percent), the dominant people of the cities and the western part of the country. Essentially lowland Persians, their language remains the lingua franca of the country. The Persian speaking Hazaras constitute five to ten percent of the population. Another ten percent belong to Uzbek and other Turkish groups in the north.

Civil Liberties. The media are primarily government owned and under rigid control. Antigovernment organization or expression is forbidden. Conversation is guarded and travel is restricted. In a condition of civil war and foreign occupation, political imprisonment, torture and execution are common, in addition to war deaths and massacres. Resources have been diverted to the Soviet Union as payment for its military "assistance." Economic, educational, and cultural programs may be laying the basis for incorporation into the USSR. The modern sectors of the economy are controlled; much of the agricultural economy has been destroyed. The objectives of the state are totalitarian; their achievement is limited by the continuing struggle for control.

Comparatively: Afghanistan is as free as Mongolia, less free than Iran.

---

* Population estimates generally are derived from the 1987 World Population Data Sheet of the Population Reference Bureau, Washington, DC. Especially doubtful population totals, such as Afghanistan's, are followed by (est.). In this case, of the estimated total, several million Afghanistanis are refugees in Pakistan or Iran.

A L B A N I A

Economy: socialist
Polity: communist one-party
Population: 3,100,000

Political Rights: 7
Civil Liberties: 7
Status: not free

A relatively homogeneous population

Political Rights. Albania is a traditional Marxist-Leninist dictatorship. While there are a number of elected bodies, including an assembly, the parallel government of the communist party (4.5 percent of the people) is decisive at all levels; elections offer only one list of candidates. Candidates are officially designated by the Democratic Front, to which all Albanians are supposed to belong. In recent years extensive purges within the party have maintained the power of the top leaders.

Civil Liberties. Press, radio, and television are completely under government or party control, and communication with the outside world is minimal. Media are characterized by incessant propaganda, and open expression of opinion in private conversation may lead to long prison sentences. There is an explicit denial of the right to freedom of thought for those who disagree with the government. Imprisonment for reasons of conscience is common; torture is frequently reported, and execution is invoked for many reasons. All religious institutions were abolished in 1967; religion is outlawed; priests are regularly imprisoned. Apparently there are no private organizations independent of government or party. Only party leaders live well. Most people are required to work one month of each year in factories or on farms; there are no private cars. Attempting to leave the state is a major crime. Private economic choice is minimal.

Comparatively: Albania is as free as Cambodia, less free than Yugoslavia.

A L G E R I A

Economy: socialist
Polity: socialist one-party
Population: 23,500,000

Political Rights: 6
Civil Liberties: 6
Status: not free

An ethnic state with a potential subnationality

Political Rights. Algeria has combined military dictatorship with one-party socialist rule. Elections at both local and national levels are managed by the party; they allow little opposition to the system, although choice among individuals is encouraged. The pragmatic, puritanical military rulers may be supported by a fairly broad consensus. Subnationalities: Fifteen to twenty percent of the people are Berbers, who have demonstrated a desire for enhanced self-determination.

Civil Liberties. The media are governmental means for active indoctrination; opposition expression is controlled and foreign publications are closely watched. Private conversation appears relatively open. Although not fully independent, the regular judiciary has established a rule of law in some areas. Independent human rights organizations are not allowed to function. Many prisoners of conscience are detained for short periods; a few for longer terms. There are no appeals from the decisions of special courts for state security and economic crimes. Land reform has transformed former French plantations into collectives. Although the government is socialist, the private sector has received increasing emphasis. Travel is generally free. Eighty percent of the people are illiterate; many are still very poor, but extremes of wealth have been reduced. The right to association is limited; unions have slight freedom. Islam's continued strength provides a counterweight to governmental absolutism. There is freedom of religious worship.

Comparatively: Algeria is as free as Tanzania, freer than Iraq, less free than Morocco.

ANGOLA

Economy: noninclusive socialist
Polity: socialist one-party
Population: 8,000,000

Political Rights: 7
Civil Liberties: 7
Status: not free

A transethnic heterogeneous state with major subnationalities

Political Rights. Angola is ruled by a small, elitist, Marxist-Leninist party, relying heavily on Soviet equipment and Cuban troops to dominate the civil war and to stay in power. The parliament is elected but the party controls the selection of candidates. Subnationalities: The party is not tribalist, but is opposed by groups relying on particular tribes or regions—especially in Cabinda, the northeast, and the south-central areas. The UNITA movement, strongest among the Ovimbundu people, actively controls much of the south and east of the country.

Civil Liberties. The nation remains in a state of war, with power arbitrarily exercised, particularly in the countryside. The media in controlled areas are government owned and do not deviate from its line. Political imprisonment and execution are common; repression of religious activity has moderated, and church leaders speak out on political and social issues. Travel is tightly restricted. Private medical care has been abolished, as has much private property—especially in the modern sectors. Strikes are prohibited and unions tightly controlled. Agricultural production is held down by peasant opposition to socialization and lack of markets.

Comparatively: Angola is as free as Mongolia, less free than Zambia.

ANTIGUA AND BARBUDA

Economy: capitalist
Polity: centralized multiparty
Population: 81,000

Political Rights: 2
Civil Liberties: 3
Status: free

A relatively homogeneous population

Political Rights. Antigua is a parliamentary democracy with an elected house and appointed senate. The opposition's inability to compete may indicate deficiencies in the electoral or campaign system. Corruption or nepotism are problems of the government. The secessionist island of Barbuda has achieved special rights to limited self-government.

Civil Liberties. Newspapers are published by opposing political parties, but an opposition paper has been repeatedly harassed, especially by libel cases. Radio and television are either owned by the state or the prime minister's family—both have been charged with favoritism. The effectiveness of the rule of law is enhanced by an inter-island court of appeals for Antigua and five of the other small former British colonies in the Antilles. Rights to organization and demonstration are respected; unions are free, have the right to strike, and are politically influential.

Comparatively: Antigua and Barbuda is as free as India, freer than Guyana, less free than Dominica.

A R G E N T I N A

Economy: capitalist-statist
Polity: centralized multiparty
Population: 31,500,000

Political Rights: 2
Civil Liberties: 1
Status: free

A relatively homogeneous population

Political Rights. Argentina has a functioning constitutional democracy under a strong president. The president is elected by electors, but as in the United States it is essentially a direct election. Two successful elections and the well-publicized trials of the country's previous military junta leaders for murder and torture have exemplified democratic rule. Potentially, the military remains a threat to democracy. Elected provincial governments show increasing independence.

Civil Liberties. Private newspapers and both private and government broadcasting stations operate. The media freely express varying opinions. The government has used the broadcasting media to serve its purposes, but only in exceptional circumstances. Political parties organize dissent, and public demonstrations are frequent. Courts are independent. The church and trade unions play a strong political role. Human rights organizations are active. The economy includes a large government sector.

Comparatively: Argentina is as free as Finland, freer than Bolivia, less free than Costa Rica.

A U S T R A L I A

Economy: capitalist   Political Rights: 1
Polity: decentralized multiparty   Civil Liberties: 1
Population: 16,200,000   Status: free

A relatively homogeneous population with small aboriginal groups

Political Rights. Australia is a federal parliamentary democracy with strong powers retained by its component states. With equal representation from each state, the Senate provides a counterbalance to the House of Representatives. The British-appointed governor-general retains some power in constitutional deadlocks. Constitutional referendums add to the power of the voters. The states have separate parliaments and premiers, but appointed governors. The self-determination rights of the aborigines are recognized through limited self-administration and return of property.

Civil Liberties. All newspapers and most radio and television stations are privately owned. The Australian Broadcasting Commission operates government radio and television stations on a basis similar to BBC. Although Australia lacks many formal guarantees of civil liberties, the degree of protection of these liberties in the common law is similar to that in Britain and Canada. Freedom of assembly is generally respected, although it varies by region. Freedom of choice in education, travel, occupation, property, and private association are perhaps as complete as anywhere in the world. Relatively low taxes enhance this freedom.

Comparatively: Australia is as free as the United Kingdom, freer than France.

A U S T R I A

Economy: mixed capitalist
Polity: centralized multiparty
Population: 7,600,000

Political Rights: 1
Civil Liberties: 1
Status: free

A relatively homogeneous population

Political Rights. Austria's parliamentary system has a directly elected lower house and an upper (and less powerful) house elected by the provincial assemblies. The president is directly elected, but the chancellor (representing the majority party or parties in parliament) is the center of political power. The two major parties have alternated control since the 1950s, but the government often seeks broad consensus. In 1987 it was again governed by a "grand coalition" of the two major parties. The referendum is used on rare occasions. Provincial legislatures and governors are elective. Subnationalities: Fifty thousand Slovenes in the southern part of the country have rights to their own schools.

Civil Liberties. The press in Austria is free and varied, although foreign pressures have exceptionally led to interference. Radio and television are under a state-owned corporation that by law is supposed to be free of political control. Its geographical position and constitutionally defined neutral status places its media and government in a position analogous to Finland's, but the Soviets have put less pressure on Austria to conform to Soviet wishes than on Finland. The rule of law is secure, and there are no political prisoners. Banks and heavy industry are largely nationalized.

Comparatively: Austria is as free as Belgium, freer than Greece.

B A H A M A S

Economy: capitalist-statist
Polity: centralized multiparty
Population: 240,000

Political Rights: 2
Civil Liberties: 3
Status: free

A relatively homogeneous population

Political Rights. The Bahamas have a parliamentary system with a largely ceremonial British governor-general. The House is elective and the senate appointed. The ruling party has a large majority, but there is an opposition in parliament. Government power is maintained in part by discrimination in favor of supporters and control over the broadcast media. There has not been a change in government since independence. Most islands are administered by centrally appointed commissioners. There is no army.

Civil Liberties. Independent and outspoken newspapers are constrained by strict libel laws. The Speaker of the House has, on occasion, compelled the press not to print certain materials. Radio and television are government owned and often fail to disseminate opposition viewpoints. Labor and business organization are generally free; there is a right to strike. A program of Bahamianization is being promoted in several sectors of the economy. Rights of travel, occupation, education, and religion are secure. Corruption is widely alleged, and may reach the highest governmental levels.

Comparatively: Bahamas is as free as India, freer than Haiti, less free than Barbados.

B A H R A I N

Economy: capitalist-statist
Polity: traditional nonparty
Population: 430,000

Political Rights: 5
Civil Liberties: 5
Status: partly free

The citizenry is relatively homogeneous

Political Rights. Bahrain is a traditional shaikhdom with a modernized administration. A former British police officer still directs the security services. Direct access to the ruler is encouraged. The legislature is dissolved, but powerful merchant and religious families place a check on royal power. There are local councils. Subnationalities: The primary ethnic problem has been the struggle between the Iranians who once ruled and the Arabs who now rule; in part this is reflected in the opposition of the Sunni and majority Shi'a Muslim sects.

Civil Liberties. The largely private press seldom criticizes government policy. Radio and television are government owned. There is considerable freedom of expression in private, but informers are feared. Rights to assembly and demonstration are limited, but a human rights organization functions. The legal and educational systems are a mixture of traditional Islamic and British. Short-term arrest is used to discourage dissent, and there are long-term political prisoners. In security cases involving violence, fair and quick trials are delayed and torture occurs. Rights to travel, property, and religious choice are secured. There is a record of disturbances by worker groups, and union organization is restricted. Many free social services are provided. Citizenship is very hard to obtain; there is antipathy to foreign workers (but unlike neighboring shaikhdoms most people in the country are citizens).

Comparatively: Bahrain is as free as Guyana, freer than Saudi Arabia, less free than India.

B A N G L A D E S H

Economy: noninclusive
capitalist-statist

Polity: centralized dominant-party
(military dominated)

Population: 107,000,000

Political Rights: 4

Civil Liberties: 5

Status: partly free

An ethnically and religiously complex state

Political Rights. Bangladesh alternates between military and parliamentary rule. Political parties are active. Return to quasi-civilian rule through parliamentary and presidential elections in 1986 was seriously marred by violence, widespread abstention, and government interference. Local elective institutions are functioning, and have been expanded by well-contested subdistrict level elections. Subnationalities: Non-Muslim hill tribes have been driven from their lands, tortured, and killed.

Civil Liberties. The press is largely private and party. The papers are intermittently censored, and there is pervasive self-censorship through both government support and pressure. International news is closely controlled. Radio and television are government controlled, but are not actively used for mobilization. In a violent context, there have been recurrent executions and imprisonments, and considerable brutality. Opposition leaders are frequently detained, but there are few if any long-term prisoners of conscience. Political parties organize and mobilize the expression of opposition, and large rallies are frequently held—and as frequently banned. Civilian courts can decide against the government, but judicial tenure is insecure. In spite of considerable communal antipathy, religious freedom exists. Travel is generally unrestricted. Although they do not have the right to strike, labor unions are active and strikes occur. Over half of the rural population are laborers or tenant farmers; some illegal land confiscation by local groups has been reported. The country is plagued by continuing large-scale corruption and extreme poverty.

Comparatively: Bangladesh is as free as Morocco, freer than Burma, less free than Malaysia.

BARBADOS

Economy: capitalist
Polity: centralized multiparty
Population: 250,000

Political Rights: 1
Civil Liberties: 1
Status: free

A relatively homogeneous population

Political Rights. Barbados is governed by a parliamentary system, with a ceremonial British governor-general. Elections have been fair and well administered. Power alternates between the two major parties. Public opinion has a direct and powerful effect on policy. Local governments are also elected.

Civil Liberties. Newspapers are private and free of censorship. Both the private and government radio stations are largely free; the only television station is organized on the BBC model. There is an independent judiciary, and general freedom from arbitrary government action. Travel, residence, and religion are free. Although both major parties rely on the support of labor, private property is fully accepted.

Comparatively: Barbados is as free as Costa Rica, freer than Jamaica.

BELGIUM

Economy: capitalist
Polity: decentralized multiparty
Population: 9,900,000

Political Rights: 1
Civil Liberties: 1
Status: free

A binational state

Political Rights. Belgium is a constitutional monarchy with a bicameral parliament. Elections lead to coalition governments, generally of the center. Continual instability due to linguistic controversies has enhanced the power of the bureaucracy. Subnationalities: The rise of nationalism among the two major peoples—Flemish and Walloon—has led to increasing transfer of control over cultural affairs to the communal groups. However, provincial governors are appointed by the national government.

Civil Liberties. Newspapers are free and uncensored. Radio and television are government owned, but independent boards are responsible for programming. The full spectrum of private rights is respected; voting is compulsory. Property rights, worker rights, and religious freedom are guaranteed.

Comparatively: Belgium is as free as Switzerland, freer than France.

BELIZE

Economy: capitalist
Polity: centralized multiparty
Population: 163,000

Political Rights: 1
Civil Liberties: 1
Status: free

An ethnically complex state

Political Rights. Belize is a parliamentary democracy with an elected house and indirectly elected senate. The governor-general retains considerable power. Elections are competitive and fair; a recent election transferred power to the opposition. Competitive local elections are also a part of the system. However, the increasing identification of parties with the two main ethnic groups is bringing new bitterness to the political system. A small British military force remains because of non-recognition by Guatemala.

Civil Liberties. The press is free and varied. Radio is government controlled but presents opposition viewpoints. Television is private and very diverse. Organization and assembly are guaranteed, as is the rule of law. The opposition is well organized, and can win in the courts. Private cooperatives have been formed in several agricultural industries. Unions are independent and diverse; strikes have been used to gain benefits.

Comparatively: Belize is as free as Costa Rica, freer than Honduras.

B E N I N

Economy: noninclusive socialist
Polity: socialist one-party
     (military dominated)
Population: 4,300,000

Political Rights: 7
Civil Liberties: 7

Status: not free

A transethnic heterogeneous state

Political Rights. Benin is a military dictatorship buttressed by a one-party organization. Regional and tribal loyalties may be stronger than national. Elections are single list, with no opposition. Local assemblies are closely controlled.

Civil Liberties. All media are rigidly censored; most are owned by the government. Opposition is not tolerated; criticism of the government often leads to a few days of reeducation in military camps. There are few long-term political prisoners, but the rule of law is very weak. Detainees are mistreated. Private schools have been closed. Although there is general freedom of religion, some sects have been forbidden. Independent labor unions are banned. Permission to leave the country is closely controlled. Economically, the government's interventions have been in cash crops and external trade, and industries have been nationalized; control over the largely subsistence and small entrepreneur economy remains incomplete. Widespread corruption aggravates already large income disparities.

Comparatively: Benin is as free as Iraq, less free than Zimbabwe.

B H U T A N

Economy: preindustrial
Polity: traditional nonparty
Population: 1,500,000

Political Rights: 5
Civil Liberties: 5
Status: partly free

An ethnic state with a significant subnationality

Political Rights. Bhutan is a hereditary monarchy in which the king rules with the aid of a council and an indirectly elected National Assembly. There are no legal political parties, and the Assembly does little more than approve government actions. Villages are traditionally ruled by their own headmen, but districts are directly ruled from the center. The Buddhist hierarchy is still very important in the affairs of the country. In foreign policy Bhutan's dependence on India has been partially renounced; it is still dependent for defense. Subnationalities: The main political party operates outside the country, agitating in favor of the Nepalese and democracy. Although they may now be a majority, the Nepalese are restricted to one part of the country.

Civil Liberties. The only papers are government and private weeklies. There are many small broadcasting stations. Outside media are freely available. There are few if any prisoners of conscience. No organized opposition exists within the country. The legal structure exhibits a mixture of traditional and British forms. There is religious freedom and freedom to travel. Traditional agriculture, crafts, and trade dominate the economy.

Comparatively: Bhutan is as free as Bahrain, freer than Swaziland, less free than Nepal.

B O L I V I A

Economy: noninclusive
    capitalist-statist
Polity: centralized multiparty
Population: 6,500,000

Political Rights: 2

Civil Liberties: 3

Status: free

An ethnic state with major potential subnationalities

Political Rights. Bolivia is a parliamentary democracy with a directly elected president. The traditional power of the military and security services has been curtailed, but not eliminated. Union power expressed through massive strikes has become a major challenge. Provincial and local government is controlled from the center. Subnationalities: Over sixty percent of the people are Indians speaking Aymara or Quechua; these languages have been given official status alongside Spanish. The Indian peoples remain, however, more potential than actual subnationalities. The Spanish-speaking minority still controls the political process.

Civil Liberties. The press and most radio stations are private and are now largely free. But fear remains in the presence of private security forces and mob action; torture has occurred. The Catholic Church retains a powerful and critical role. The people are overwhelmingly post-land-reform, subsistence agriculturists. The major mines and much of industry are nationalized; the workers have a generous social welfare program, given the country's poverty. While union leaders are frequently ousted, this results more from the often violent political struggle of union and government than from the simple repression of dissent.

Comparatively: Bolivia is as free as India, freer than Guyana, less free than Venezuela.

B O T S W A N A

Economy: noninclusive capitalist
Polity: decentralized multiparty
Population: 1,200,000

Political Rights: 2
Civil Liberties: 3
Status: free

A relatively homogeneous population

Political Rights. The republican system of Botswana combines traditional and modern principles. The assembly is elected for a fixed term and appoints the president who rules. There is also an advisory House of Chiefs. Nine district councils, led either by chiefs or elected leaders, have independent power of taxation, as well as traditional control over land and agriculture. Elections continue to be won overwhelmingly by the ruling party, as they were before independence, yet there are opposition members in parliament and the opposition controls town councils. There is economic and political pressure from both black African and white neighbors. Subnationalities: The country is divided among several major tribes belonging to the Batswana people, as well as minor peoples on the margins. The latter include a few hundred relatively wealthy white farmers.

Civil Liberties. The radio and the daily paper are government owned; there are private and party papers. Opposition party and foreign publications are available. However, 1987 saw an opposition editor arrested on vague charges. Courts appear independent. Rights of assembly, religion, and travel are respected but regulated. Passport controls may be restrictive, and have been applied in the past to the opposition. Prisoners of conscience are not held. Unions are independent, but under pressure. In the modern society civil liberties appear to be guaranteed, but most people continue to live under traditional rules. (Government support is firmest in rural areas of great inequality.)

Comparatively: Botswana is as free as Cyprus (T), freer than Gambia, less free than Mauritius.

B R A Z I L

Economy: capitalist–statist
Polity: decentralized multiparty
Population: 141,500,000

Political Rights: 2
Civil Liberties: 2
Status: free

A complex but relatively homogeneous population with many very small, territorial subnationalities

Political Rights. Although still in a transitional stage, in which the president has not been directly elected, the fully open process by which he came to power was effectively democratic. The legislature is popularly elected. The military remains politically powerful. Political party activity is free, but political power depends on individuals. There are independently organized elected governments at both state and local levels. Subnationalities: The many small Indian groups of the interior are under both private and governmental pressure on their lands, culture, and even lives.

Civil Liberties. The media are private, except for a few broadcasting stations. The powerful and critical press is free of censorship, however government control of most industry, and thus advertising, limits freedom to criticize government. While radio and television are generally free, government control of access during campaigns has been criticized. Private concentration in the media, in the absence of a tradition of neutrality, may limit full freedom. Rights of assembly and organization are recognized, and prisoners of conscience are not held. Massive opposition demonstrations have become a recent feature of political life. Private violence against criminals, suspected communists, peasants, and Indians continues outside the law. The courts are beginning to move actively against officers and others accused of killing or corruption. Union organization is powerful and strikes are widespread, though sometimes repressed. In spite of large-scale government ownership of industry, rights to property are respected. Freedom of religion, travel, and education exists. Extreme regional, class, and racial differences in living standards continue to imperil democracy.

Comparatively: Brazil is as free as Israel, freer than Bolivia, less free than Argentina.

B R U N E I

Economy: capitalist-statist
Polity: monarchy
Population: 230,000

Political Rights: 6
Civil Liberties: 5
Status: partly free

An ethnic state with a major nonterritorial subnationality

Political Rights. Brunei is ruled in the traditional manner as an absolute monarchy with little delegation of authority. The cabinet is dominated by the Sultan and his relatives. Religious questions are decided by the government's religious department. Considerable reliance on the military forces and advice of the United Kingdom and Singapore continues.

Civil Liberties. Little or no dissent is allowed in the nation's media. Radio and television and a major paper are government owned. However, many students attend schools overseas, and foreign media of all kinds are widely available. Political parties calling for constitutional monarchy have been established. A few dissidents remain in jail. Formally the judicial system is patterned on the English model. The position of Chinese non-citizens (many long-term residents) has declined since independence. All land is government owned, as is most of the oil wealth.

Comparatively: Brunei is as free as Chile, freer than Burma, less free than Singapore.

B U L G A R I A

Economy: socialist
Polity: communist one-party
Population: 9,000,000

Political Rights: 7
Civil Liberties: 7
Status: not free

A relatively homogeneous population

Political Rights. Bulgaria is governed by its Communist Party, although the facade of a parallel government and two-party system is maintained. The same man has essentially ruled over the system since 1954; elections at both national and local levels have little meaning. Soviet influence in the security services is decisive. Subnationalities: The government has destroyed the cultural identity of Muslim and other minorities.

Civil Liberties. All media are under absolute control by the government or its Party branches. Citizens have few if any rights against the state. There are hundreds or thousands of prisoners of conscience, many living under severe conditions. Brutality and torture are common. Those accused of opposition to the system may also be banished to villages, denied their occupations, or confined in psychiatric hospitals. Believers are subject to discrimination. Hundreds have been killed in enforcing name changes. Citizens have little choice of occupation or residence. Political loyalty is required to secure many social benefits. The most common political crimes are illegally trying to leave the country, criticism of the government, and illegal contacts with foreigners. However, there have been openings through a new spirit of independence and attempts at deconcentration in the economic sphere.

Comparatively: Bulgaria is as free as Mongolia, less free than Hungary.

B U R K I N A   F A S O
(UPPER VOLTA)

Economy: noninclusive mixed
    socialist
Polity: military nonparty
Population: 7,300,000 (est.)

Political Rights: 7

Civil Liberties: 6
Status: not free

A transethnic heterogeneous state

Political Rights. The anarchic and dictatorial military government modeled on Libya's was upset by yet another military coup in 1987. The eventual form of the new government remains unclear.

Civil Liberties. The media have been government-controlled means of indoctrination. Censorship had become the rule, although private criticism remained common. By late 1986 most prisoners of conscience had been released. Freedom of assembly or political organization was denied and trade unions were under strong government pressure. Labor leaders were released from detention after the coup. External travel is restricted; internal movement is free. The economy remains dependent on subsistence agriculture, with the government playing the role of regulator and promoter of development.

Comparatively: Burkina Faso is as free as Mali, freer than Albania, less free than Sierra Leone.

B U R M A

Economy: noninclusive mixed
    socialist

Political Rights: 7

Polity: socialist one-party
    (military dominated)

Civil Liberties: 7

Population: 38,800,000

Status: not free

An ethnic state with major territorial subnationalities

Political Rights. Burma is governed by a small military elite as a one-party socialist state. The government's dependence on the army makes its strengths and weaknesses more those of a military dictatorship than those of a Marxist-Leninist regime. Elections are held at both national and local levels: the Party chooses the slate of candidates. **Subnationalities:** The government represents essentially the Burmese people that live in the heartland of the country. The Burmese are surrounded by millions of non-Burmese living in continuing disaffection or active revolt. Among the minorities on the periphery are the Karens, Shan, Kachins, Mon, and Chin. Many Muslims have been expelled, encouraged to leave, or imprisoned indefinitely.

Civil Liberties. All media are government owned, with alternative opinions expressed obliquely if at all; both domestic and foreign publications are censored. The media are expected to actively promote government policy. Organized dissent is forbidden; even private expression is dangerous. Massive arrests have brought the Buddhist hierarchy under control. Prisoners of conscience have been common, but few ethnic Burmans now seem to be detained for reasons of conscience. The regular court structure has been replaced by "people's courts." Racial discrimination has been incorporated in government policy. Emigration or even travel outside the country is very difficult. Living standards have progressively declined as the country falls into ruin. Although the eventual goal of the government is complete socialization, areas of private enterprise remain, subject to control by government marketing monopolies.

Comparatively: Burma is as free as Cambodia, less free than Bangladesh.

B U R U N D I

Economy: noninclusive mixed
    capitalist

Political Rights: 7

Polity: socialist one-party
    (military dominated)

Civil Liberties: 6

Population: 5,000,000

Status: not free

An ethnic state with a major, nonterritorial subnationality

Political Rights. Burundi's military president was overthrown by another military leader in 1987. More democracy was promised; at last report the government was still in the process of reorganization. Subnationalities: The rulers and nearly all military officers continue to be from the Tutsi ethnic group (fifteen percent) that has traditionally ruled; their dominance was reinforced by a massacre of Hutus (eighty-five percent) after an attempted revolt in the early 1970s.

Civil Liberties. The media are all government controlled and closely censored, as are often the foreign media. Lack of freedom of political speech or assembly is accompanied by political imprisonment and reports of brutality. Under current conditions there is little guarantee of individual rights, particularly for the Hutu majority. However, in recent years the exclusion of the Hutu from public services, the Party, and other advantages has been relaxed. There are no independent unions, but short wildcat strikes have been reported. Close regulation of religious activities has been relaxed after the coup. Traditional group and individual rights persist on the village level: Burundi is not a highly structured modern society. Travel is relatively unrestricted. Although officially socialist, private or traditional economic forms predominate.

Comparatively: Burundi is as free as Czechoslovakia, freer than Somalia, less free than Kenya.

C A M B O D I A

Economy: noninclusive socialist
Polity: communist one-party
Population: 6,500,000 (est.)

Political Rights: 7
Civil Liberties: 7
Status: not free

A relatively homogeneous population

Political Rights. Cambodia is divided between the remnants of
the Pol Pot tyranny and a less tyrannical, Marxist-Leninist regime
imposed by the Vietnamese. Although the Vietnamese have
reestablished a degree of civilized life, the people have little part
in either regime. More democratic rebel groups also exist.

Civil Liberties. The media continue to be completely controlled in both areas; outside publications are rigorously controlled,
and there are no daily papers. Political execution has been a
common function of government. Reeducation for war captives is
again practiced by the new government. There is no rule of law;
private freedoms are not guaranteed. Buddhist practices are again
allowed. Cambodians continue to be one of the world's most
tyrannized peoples. At least temporarily much of economic life has
been decollectivized.

Comparatively: Cambodia is as free as Mongolia, less free than
Indonesia.

C A M E R O O N

Economy: noninclusive capitalist
Polity: nationalist one-party
Population: 10,300,000

Political Rights: 6
Civil Liberties: 6
Status: not free

A transethnic heterogeneous state with a major subnationality

Political Rights. Cameroon is a one-party state ruled by the
same party since independence in 1960. The government has
steadily centralized power. Referendums and other elections have
little meaning; voters are given no alternatives, although a
legislative candidate may be rejected. Provincial governors are
appointed by the central government. Attempts have been made to

286

incorporate all elements in a government of broad consensus. A recent party election at several levels introduced a degree of democracy. Subnationalities: The most significant opposition has come from those opposing centralization. Politics is largely a struggle of regional and tribal factions.

Civil Liberties. The largely government-owned media are closely controlled; elaborate pre-publication censorship is the rule. Works of critical authors are prohibited, even university lectures are subject to government censorship. In addition, self-censorship is common in all media. A number of papers have been closed, and journalists arrested. Freedom of speech, assembly, and union organization are limited, but there is increasingly open discussion. Freedom of occupation, education, and property are respected. Prisoners of conscience are detained without trial and may be ill-treated. Many have recently been released. Internal travel and religious choice are relatively free; foreign travel may be difficult. Labor and business organizations are closely controlled. Although still relatively short on capital, private enterprise is encouraged wherever possible.

Comparatively: Cameroon is as free as Algeria, freer than Ethiopia, less free than South Africa.

CANADA

Economy: capitalist
Polity: decentralized multiparty
Population: 25,900,000

Political Rights: 1
Civil Liberties: 1
Status: free

A binational state

Political Rights. Canada is a parliamentary democracy with alternation of rule between leading parties. A great effort is made to register all eligible voters. The provinces have their own democratic institutions with a higher degree of autonomy than the American states. Subnationalities: French has linguistic equality, and French is the official language in Quebec. In addition, Quebec has been allowed to opt out of some national programs and maintains its own representatives abroad. Rights to self-determination for Indian and Eskimo groups in the North have been emphasized recently.

Civil Liberties. The media are free, although there is a government-related radio and television network. The full range of civil liberties is generally respected. The new Charter of Rights and Freedoms includes the right of judicial review. In Quebec rights to choose English education and language have been infringed. There has been evidence of the invasion of privacy by Canadian security forces in recent years, much as in the United States. Many judicial and legal structures have been borrowed from the United Kingdom or the United States, with consequent advantages and disadvantages. Some provinces limit employment opportunities for nonresidents.

Comparatively: Canada is as free as the United States of America, freer than France.

C A P E   V E R D E

Economy: noninclusive mixed socialist

Polity: socialist one-party

Population: 326,000

Political Rights: 5

Civil Liberties: 6

Status: partly free

An ethnically complex state

Political Rights. The single ruling party enlists no more than four percent of the population. Although elections are controlled, choice is allowed, and there are extensive consultations. Abstention and negative votes are common. The resulting assembly includes independents and has demonstrated considerable freedom.

Civil Liberties. Nearly all media are government owned; all are controlled to serve party purposes. Foreign print and broadcast media are freely available, and a Catholic publication exists. Rights to organize opposition, assembly, or political expression are not respected, but little political imprisonment or mistreatment takes place. The judiciary is weak. Drought and endemic unemployment continue to lead to emigration. Most professions, fishing, farming, and small enterprises are private. Land reform has emphasized land-to-the-tiller programs. Religion is relatively free, although under political pressure; labor unions are government controlled. Travel is relatively free.

Comparatively: Cape Verde is as free as Cote d'Ivoire, freer than Equatorial Guinea, less free than Gambia.

CENTRAL AFRICAN REPUBLIC

Economy: noninclusive
    capitalist-statist
Polity: nationalist one-party
    (military dominated)
Population: 2,700,000

Political Rights: 6

Civil Liberties: 6

Status: not free

A transethnic heterogeneous state

Political Rights. The Central African Republic is a military dictatorship with an elected one-party parliament. The loosely organized single party allows for choice. The current system has been approved by referendum. French-style prefects are appointed by the central government. Heavily dependent on French economic and military aid, France has influenced or determined recent changes of government, and French forces are still present.

Civil Liberties. All media are government owned or closely controlled, but some de facto free expression exists. There are prisoners of conscience. Party affiliation is voluntary. Religious freedom is generally respected. The judiciary is not independent. Movement is occasionally hampered by highway security checks. Most economic activity is private with limited government involvement; workers are not free to organize. Corruption is particularly widespread.

Comparatively: Central African Republic is as free as Tanzania, freer than Somalia, less free than Senegal.

CHAD

Economy: noninclusive capitalist
Polity: military nonparty
Population: 4,600,000 (est.)

Political Rights: 6
Civil Liberties: 7
Status: not free

A transitional collection of semi-autonomous ethnic groups

Political Rights. The central government is under control of a military-factional leader. However, the government now includes leaders from a variety of ethnic and factional groups. France's participation in the defense of the present government has reduced its independence in inter-state relations. Subnationalities: The primary ethnic cleavage is between the southern negroes (principally the Christian and animist Sara tribe) and a number of northern Muslim groups (principally nomadic Arabs). Political factionalism is only partly ethnic.

Civil Liberties. Media are government owned and controlled. There is little chance for free expression. In recent years many have been killed or imprisoned without due process. Labor and business organizations exist with some independence. Religion is relatively free. Not an ideological area, traditional law is still influential. The economy is predominantly subsistence agriculture with little protection of property rights.

Comparatively: Chad is as free as Ethiopia, freer than Somalia, less free than Tanzania.

CHILE

Economy: capitalist
Polity: military nonparty
Population: 12,400,000

Political Rights: 6
Civil Liberties: 5
Status: partly free

A relatively homogeneous population

Political Rights. The government of Chile is led by a self-appointed military dictator assisted by a junta of military officers. Although a 1980 plebiscite confirming government policy allowed an opposition vote of thirty percent, all power is concentrated at the center; there are no elective positions. Popular support for the system has declined.

Civil Liberties. All media have both public and private outlets; newspapers are primarily private. The media, although censored and often suspended, express a considerable range of opinion, occasionally including direct criticism of government policy. Limited party activity is tacitly allowed, and human rights organizations operate under pressure. Students, church leaders, and former political leaders regularly express dissent, sometimes massively and in the face of violent government repression. While one can win against the government, the courts are under government pressure. Prisoners of conscience are still commonly taken for short periods; torture, political expulsion, internal exile, and assassination of government opponents continue. Violent confrontations lead repeatedly to repressions, only to be followed by new periods of relaxation. Unions are restricted but have some rights, including a limited right to strike and organize at plant levels. Many nationalized enterprises have been resold to private investors, with government intervention in the economy now being limited to copper and petroleum.

Comparatively: Chile is as free as Iran, freer than Czechoslovakia, less free than Peru.

C H I N A (Mainland)

Economy: mixed socialist
Polity: communist one-party
Population: 1,062,000,000

Political Rights: 6
Civil Liberties: 6
Status: not free

An ethnic state with peripheral subnationalities

Political Rights. China is a one-party communist state under the collective leadership of the Politburo. A National People's Congress is indirectly elected within party guidelines, but its discussions are now much more open and competitive than is common in Marxist-Leninist states. Still, national policy struggles are obscured by secrecy, and choices are sharply limited. Some local elections have had limited competition. Party administration is decentralized. Subnationalities: There are several subordinated peripheral peoples such as the Tibetans, Uygurs, Mongols, and the much acculturated Zhuang. These are granted a limited degree of separate cultural life. Amounting to not more than six percent of the population, non-Chinese ethnic groups have tended to be diluted and obscured by Chinese settlement or sinification. However, minority peoples have been given a special dispensation to have more than the single child allowed most Han Chinese.

Civil Liberties. The mass media remain closely controlled tools for mobilizing the population. There is limited non-political cultural and scientific freedom. Many local papers not entirely under government control have developed recently. Although there is movement toward "socialist legality" on the Soviet model, court cases are often decided in political terms. There are unknown thousands of political prisoners, including those in labor-reform camps; the government has forced millions to live indefinitely in undesirable areas. Political executions are still reported. Millions of Chinese have been systematically discriminated against because of "bad class background," but such discrimination has recently been curtailed. Political-social controls at work are pervasive.

Compared to other communist states popular opinions and pressures play a considerable role. Occasional poster campaigns, demonstrations, and evidence of private conversation shows that pervasive factionalism has allowed elements of freedom and consensus into the system; recurrent repression, including imprisonment, equally shows the government's determination to keep dissent from becoming a threat to the system or its current leaders. Rights to travel and emigration are limited, as are religious freedoms. Rights to marry and have children are perhaps more closely controlled than in any other country in the world. Economic pressures have forced some, not wholly successful, rationalization of economic policy, including renunciation of guaranteed employment for youth. Introduction of private sector incentives has increased economic freedom, especially for small entrepreneurs and farmers. Small local strikes and slowdowns have been reported concerning wage increases and worker demands for greater control over choice of employment. Inequality derives from differences in political position and location rather than direct income.

Comparatively: China (Mainland) is as free as Algeria, freer than Mongolia, less free than China (Taiwan).

C H I N A (Taiwan)

Economy: capitalist-statist
Polity: centralized dominant party
Population: 19,600,000

Political Rights: 5
Civil Liberties: 4
Status: partly free

A quasi-ethnic state with a majority nonterritorial subnationality

Political Rights. Taiwan has been ruled by a single party organized according to a communist model (although anticommunist ideologically), and under strong military influence. Parliament includes some representatives from Taiwan, but most parliamentarians are still persons elected in 1947 as representatives of districts in China where elections could not be held subsequently because of communist control. Opposition legislators have been few and isolated. However, a new opposition party organized in late 1986, and its subsequent effective showing at the polls, marked a significant shift in the system. Campaigns have been limited, particularly because the media are overwhelmingly pro-government. The indirect presidential election is pro forma. Some local and regional positions are elective, including those in the provincial assembly that are held by Taiwanese. Subnationalities: The people are eighty-six percent native Taiwanese (speaking two Chinese dialects); opposition movements in favor of transferring control from the mainland immigrants to the Taiwanese are repressed. The vice-president is Taiwanese. Small indigenous ethnic groups are discriminated against.

Civil Liberties. The media include government or party organs, but are mostly in private hands. Newspapers and magazines are subject to censorship or suspension, and most practice self-censorship. Dissenting journals of independent editors and publishers were unable to publish in most of 1986. Martial law was ended in 1987, but replaced by a law that greatly reduced the meaning of its repeal. Government thought-police and their agents also operate overseas. Television is one-sided. Rights to assembly are limited, but are sporadically granted. Nearly all political prisoners have been released. Unions achieved increased independence in 1987. Private rights to property, education, and religion are generally respected. Rights to travel overseas, including mainland China, have been liberalized.

Comparatively: China (Taiwan) is as free as Hungary, freer than Burma, less free than South Korea.

COLOMBIA

Economy: capitalist
Polity: centralized multiparty
Population: 29,900,000

Political Rights: 2
Civil Liberties: 3
Status: free

A relatively homogeneous population with scattered minorities

Political Rights. Colombia is a constitutional democracy. The president is directly elected, as are both houses of the legislature. Power alternates between the two major parties. Both have well-defined factions. The largest guerrilla group now participates in electoral politics. The provinces are directly administered by the national government. The military and police are not firmly under government control.

Civil Liberties. The press is private, with most papers under party control, and quite free. Radio includes both government and private stations; television is a government monopoly. All media have been limited in their freedom to report subversive activity. Personal rights are generally respected; courts are relatively strong and independent. However, endemic violence curbs expression through fear of assassination by right or left—or gangsters more connected with the drug trade than ideology. Assemblies are often banned for fear of riots. In these conditions the security forces have infringed personal rights violently, especially those of leftist unions, peasants, and Amerindians in rural areas. Many persons are rounded up in antiguerrilla or antiterrorist campaigns, and may be tortured or killed. However, opponents are not given prison sentences simply for the nonviolent expression of political opinion, and the government and courts have attempted to control abuses. Human rights organizations are active. The government encourages private enterprise where possible; union activity and strikes for economic goals are legal.

Comparatively: Colombia is as free as India, freer than Guyana, less free than Venezuela.

C O M O R O S

Economy: noninclusive capitalist
Polity: nationalist one-party
Population: 445,000 (est.)

Political Rights: 6
Civil Liberties: 6
Status: not free

A relatively homogeneous population

Political Rights. The present Comoran dictator returned to power with the aid of mercenaries in 1978, and they continue to protect him. 1987 assembly elections were prefaced by consultations with the people on candidates for the ruling party. Although an opposition party participated in the subsequent election, the election was marked by massive judicial exclusion, widespread fraud, and hundreds of arrests. All, or nearly all, seats in the weak assembly are now controlled by the ruling party. Each island has an appointed governor and council. (The island of Mahore is formally a part of the Comoros, but it has chosen to be a French dependency.)

Civil Liberties. Radio is government owned and controlled. There is no independent press, but some outside publications and occasional underground dissident writings are available. People are detained for reasons of conscience, and there are many political prisoners. Pressure is reported against the opposition, but private criticism is allowed. There is a new emphasis on Islamic customs. The largely plantation economy has led to severe landlessness and concentrated wealth; emigration to the mainland for employment is very common. The concentration of wealth in a few hands closely connected to the government reduces choice.

Comparatively: Comoros is as free as Tanzania, freer than Mozambique, less free than Madagascar.

C O N G O

Economy: noninclusive mixed
    socialist

Polity: socialist one-party
    (military dominated)

Population: 2,100,000 (est.)

Political Rights: 7

Civil Liberties: 6

Status: not free

A formally transethnic heterogeneous state

Political Rights. Congo is an increasingly arbitrary military dictatorship with a very small ruling party based primarily in one section of the country. One-party elections allow little opposition, but criticism is aired in parliament. Two thousand Cuban troops help to maintain the regime.

Civil Liberties. The press and all publications are heavily censored. Broadcasting services and most of the press are government owned. Criticism may lead to imprisonment, yet there is some private discussion and limited dissent. Executions and imprisonment of political opponents have occurred, but conditions have improved. The only union is state sponsored; strikes are illegal. Religious organization is generally free; however, government and Party are officially atheist and some church functions or services have been abolished. There is little judicial protection; passports are difficult to obtain. At the local and small entrepreneur level private property is generally respected; most large-scale commerce and industry are either nationalized or controlled by expatriates. Literacy is high for the region.

Comparatively: Congo is as free as Syria, freer than Iraq, less free than Kenya.

C O S T A   R I C A

Economy: capitalist

Polity: centralized multiparty

Population: 2,800,000

Political Rights: 1

Civil Liberties: 1

Status: free

A relatively homogeneous population

Political Rights. A parliamentary democracy, Costa Rica has a directly elected president and several important parties. No parties are prohibited, and intraparty democracy is highly developed. Much of the society and economy is administered by a large and diffuse network of autonomous public institutions. This structure is supplemented by an independent tribunal for overseeing elections. Elections are fair; rule alternates between parties. Lacking a regular army, politics are not under military influence. Provinces are under the direction of the central government.

Civil Liberties. The media are notably free, private, and varied; they serve a society ninety percent literate. A surprisingly onerous licensing requirement for journalists is an isolated stain on the country's otherwise exemplary freedom. The courts are fair, and private rights, such as those to movement, occupation, education, religion, and union organization, are respected.

Comparatively: Costa Rica is as free as Australia, freer than Colombia.

C O T E   D ' I V O I R E
(IVORY COAST)

Economy: noninclusive capitalist
Polity: nationalist one-party
Population: 10,800,000

Political Rights: 6
Civil Liberties: 5
Status: partly free

A transethnic heterogeneous state

Political Rights. Cote d'Ivoire is ruled by a one-party, capitalist dictatorship in which a variety of political elements have been integrated. Assembly elections have recently allowed choice of individuals, including nonparty, but not policies. Rates of voter participation are quite low. Provinces are ruled directly from the center. Contested municipal elections occur. The French military, bureaucratic, and business presence remains powerful.

Civil Liberties. Although the legal press is party or government controlled, it presents a limited spectrum of opinion. Foreign publications are widely available. While opposition is discouraged, there is no ideological conformity. Radio and television are government controlled. Major events may go unreported. Short-term imprisonment and conscription are used to control opposition. Travel and religion are generally free. Rights to strike or organize unions are quite limited. All wage earners must contribute to the ruling party. Economically the country depends on small, private or traditional farms; in the modern sector private enterprise is encouraged.

Comparatively: Cote d'Ivoire is as free as Transkei, freer than Guinea, less free than Senegal.

C U B A

Economy: socialist
Polity: communist one-party
Population: 10,300,000

Political Rights: 6
Civil Liberties: 6
Status: not free

A complex but relatively homogeneous population

Political Rights. Cuba is a one-party communist state on the Soviet model. Real power lies, however, more in the person of Fidel Castro and in the Russian leaders upon whom he depends than is the case in other noncontiguous states adopting this model. Popular election at the municipal level is closely supervised. Provincial and national assemblies are elected by municipalities but can be recalled by popular vote. The whole system is largely a show: political opponents are excluded from nomination by law, many others are simply disqualified by Party fiat; no debate is allowed on major issues; once elected the assemblies do not oppose Party decisions.

Civil Liberties. All media are state controlled and express only what the government wishes. Although the population is literate, publications, foreign or domestic, are in very short supply. Cuba may have the longest serving prisoners of conscience in the world. Torture has been reported in the past; hundreds who have refused to recant their opposition to the system continue to be held in difficult conditions, and new arrests are frequent. There are hundreds of thousands of others who are formally discriminated against as opponents of the system. There is freedom to criticize policy administration through the press and the institutions of "popular democracy," but writing or speaking against the system, even in private is severely repressed. There are reports of psychiatric institutions also being used for incarceration. Independent human rights organizations are not allowed to function. Freedom to choose work, education, or residence is greatly restricted; new laws force people to work harder. It is generally illegal to leave Cuba, but some have been forced to leave.

Comparatively: Cuba is as free as Gabon, freer than Czechoslovakia, less free than Guyana.

C Y P R U S (G)

Economy: capitalist
Polity: centralized multiparty
Population: 500,000

Political Rights: 1
Civil Liberties: 2
Status: free

An ethnic state

Political Rights. The "Greek" portion of Cyprus is a fully functioning parliamentary democracy on the Westminster model. Elections have been fair and highly competitive. Recently, local elective government has been instituted. However, the community continues to be under considerable political influence from mainland Greece. The atmosphere of confrontation with the Turkish side of the island may restrict freedoms, especially for the small number of remaining citizens of Turkish background.

Civil Liberties. The newspapers are free and varied in both sectors, but generally support their respective governments. Radio and television are under the control of governmental or semigovernmental bodies. The usual rights of free peoples are respected, including occupation, labor organization, and religion. Because of communal strife and invasion, property has often been taken from members of one group by force (or abandoned from fear of force) and given to the other. Under these conditions rights to choose one's sector of residence or to travel between sectors have been greatly restricted.

Comparatively: Cyprus (G) is as free as Malta, freer than Brazil, less free than Denmark.

C Y P R U S (T)

Economy: capitalist
Polity: centralized multiparty
Population: 150,000

Political Rights: 2
Civil Liberties: 3
Status: free

An ethnic state

Political Rights. "Turkish" Cyprus was created after Turkish troops intervened to prevent a feared Greek takeover. A large section of the island, including much territory formerly in Greek hands, is protected by Turkish military power from the larger Greek portion of the island, as well as the much larger Greek population. In spite of this limitation, parliamentary forms are functioning in the Turkish sector: 1985 witnessed three elections that fully confirmed the popularity of the present government. However, the continuing confrontation restricts choice for some, particularly the few remaining Greek Cypriots in the Turkish sector.

Civil Liberties. Publications are free and varied. Radio and television are under governmental or semigovernmental control. The usual rights of free peoples are respected, including occupation, labor, organization, and religion. However, travel between the sectors and the removal of property is restricted. Many people formerly resident in the Turkish part of the island have lost their property.

Comparatively: Cyprus (T) is as free as Bahamas, freer than Turkey, less free than Greece.

C Z E C H O S L O V A K I A

Economy: socialist
Polity: communist one-party
Population: 15,550,000

Political Rights: 7
Civil Liberties: 6
Status: not free

A binational state

Political Rights. Czechoslovakia is a Soviet style, one-party communist state, reinforced by the presence of Soviet troops.

Elections are noncompetitive and there is essentially no legislative debate. Polls suggest passive opposition of the great majority of the people to the governing system. Subnationalities: The division of the state into separate Czech and Slovak socialist republics has only slight meaning since the Czechoslovak Communist Party continues to rule the country (under the guidance of the Soviet Communist Party). Although less numerous and poorer than the Czech people, the Slovaks are granted at least their rightful share of power within this framework.

Civil Liberties. Media are government or Party owned and rigidly censored. There is a general willingness to express dissent in private, and there are many serious, if small, underground publications. Freedoms of assembly, organization, and association are denied. Heavy pressures are placed on religious activities, especially through holding ministerial incomes at a very low level and curtailing religious education. There are a number of prisoners of conscience; exclusion of individuals from their chosen occupations and short detentions are more common sanctions. The beating of political suspects is common, and psychiatric detention is employed. Successful defense in political cases is possible, but lawyers may be arrested for overzealous defense. Human rights groups are persecuted. Travel to the West and emigration are restricted. Independent trade unions and strikes are forbidden. Rights to choice of occupation and to private property are restricted.

Comparatively: Czechoslovakia is as free as East Germany, freer than Bulgaria, less free than Poland.

D E N M A R K

Economy: mixed capitalist
Polity: centralized multiparty
Population: 5,100,000

Political Rights: 1
Civil Liberties: 1
Status: free

A relatively homogeneous population

Political Rights. Denmark is a constitutional monarchy with a unicameral parliament. Elections are fair. Since a wide variety of parties achieve success, resulting governments are based on

301

coalitions. Referendums may be used to decide major issues. Districts have governors appointed from the center and elected councils; local administration is under community control.

Civil Liberties. The press is free (and more conservative politically than the electorate). Radio and television are government owned but relatively free. Labor unions are powerful both socially and politically. All other rights are guaranteed. The very high tax level constitutes more than usual constraint on private property in a capitalist state, but has provided a fairly equitable distribution of social benefits. Religion is free but state supported.

Comparatively: Denmark is as free as Norway, freer than Finland.

D J I B O U T I

Economy: inclusive capitalist
Polity: nationalist one-party
Population: 360,000 (est.)

Political Rights: 6
Civil Liberties: 6
Status: not free

A binational state with subordination

Political Rights. Djibouti is formally a parliamentary democracy under French protection. Only one party is allowed, and in recent elections there has been little if any choice. The party is tightly controlled by a small elite. Although all ethnic groups are carefully included in the single-party lists, one group is clearly dominant. French influence, backed by a large French garrison, is critical.

Civil Liberties. The media are government owned and controlled and there is no right of assembly. However, some opposition literature is distributed. There have recently been prisoners of conscience and torture. Unions are under a degree of government control, but there is a right to strike. An extremely poor country, its market economy is still dominated by French interests.

Comparatively: Djibouti is as free as Tanzania, freer than Somalia, less free than North Yemen.

D O M I N I C A

Economy: capitalist
Polity: centralized multiparty
Population: 80,000 (est.)

Political Rights: 2
Civil Liberties: 2
Status: free

A relatively homogeneous population with a minority enclave

Political Rights. Dominica is a parliamentary democracy with competing political parties. An opposition party came to power in highly competitive 1980 elections. There have been several violent attempts to overthrow the government, and the military has subsequently been disbanded. The dissolution of the army has been accepted by the voters. There are local assemblies. Rights of the few remaining native Caribs may not be fully respected.

Civil Liberties. The press is private; radio is both private and public. The press is generally free and critical, and the radio presents alternative views. Rights of assembly and organization are guaranteed. There is rule of law and no prisoners of conscience. States of emergency have recurrently limited rights to a small extent. Personal rights to travel, residence, and property are secured, as are the union rights of workers.

Comparatively: Dominica is as free as Nauru, freer than Guyana, less free than Grenada.

D O M I N I C A N   R E P U B L I C

Economy: capitalist
Polity: centralized multiparty
Population: 6,500,000

Political Rights: 1
Civil Liberties: 3
Status: free

A complex but relatively homogeneous population

Political Rights. The Dominican Republic is a presidential democracy on the American model. Elections are free and competitive. Military influence is greatly reduced. Provinces are under national control, municipalities under local.

Civil Liberties. The media are generally privately owned, free, and diverse, but government advertising may be denied unfavored papers, and stations may be closed for defamation. Communist materials are restricted. Broadcasting is highly varied, but subject to government review. Public expression is generally free; the spokesmen of a wide range of parties quite openly express their opinions. There are no prisoners of conscience; the security services seem to have been responsible for disappearances and many arbitrary arrests in recent years. The courts appear relatively independent, and human rights groups are active. Labor unions operate under constraints and strikes have been repressed. Travel overseas is sometimes restricted. State-owned lands are slowly being redistributed.

Comparatively: Dominican Republic is as free as Uruguay, freer than Colombia, less free than Belize.

E C U A D O R

Economy: noninclusive capitalist
Polity: centralized multiparty
Population: 10,000,000

Political Rights: 2
Civil Liberties: 3
Status: free

An ethnic state with a potential subnationality

Political Rights. Ecuador is governed by an elected president and congress. 1984 witnessed a change of government by electoral process, an event rare in the country's history. There have been minor restrictions on party activity and nominations. Provinces and municipalities are directly administered, but local and provincial councils are elected. The struggle of an aggressive president with a hostile congress, rebellious military officers, and labor unions produced continuing instability in 1986-87. The government has openly ignored decisions of both congress and courts. Subnationalities: Forty percent of the population is Indian, most of whom speak Quechua. This population at present does not form a conscious subnationality in a distinct homeland.

Civil Liberties. Newspapers are under private or party control and quite outspoken. Radio and television are mostly under private control. However, programs have been cancelled, reporters fired, or advertising cancelled for falling out of government favor. In an atmosphere of intense political struggle and successive general strikes, the government has curtailed rights by "intervening" foundations and other emergency actions. There are no long-term prisoners of conscience, but persons are detained for criticizing government officials. Human rights organizations are active. Torture is alleged. The court system is not strongly independent. Land reform has been hampered by resistance from landed elites. Although there are state firms, particularly in major industries, Ecuador is essentially a capitalist and traditional state.

Comparatively: Ecuador is as free as India, freer than Panama, less free than Venezuela.

E G Y P T

Economy: mixed socialist
Polity: dominant-party
     (military dominated)
Population: 51,900,000

Political Rights: 5
Civil Liberties: 4

Status: partly free

A relatively homogeneous population with a communal religious minority

Political Rights. Egypt is a controlled democracy. Within limits political parties may organize: communist and religious extremist parties are forbidden. The ruling party makes sure of overwhelming election victories by excluding groups and individuals from the competition, harassment of opponents, limited campaigns, election period arrests, and general domination of the media. Participation rates are very low; electoral laws greatly favor the government party. The military is largely autonomous and self-sufficient. Neither house of parliament plays a powerful role. Subnationalities: Several million Coptic Christians live a distinct communal life.

Civil Liberties. The Egyptian press is mostly government owned, but presents critical discussions in many areas; weekly party papers are relatively free and increasingly influential. Radio and television are under governmental control. A fairly broad range of literary publications has recently developed. There is limited freedom of assembly. Severe riot laws and a variety of laws restricting dissent have led to large-scale imprisonment or banning from political or other organizational activity. Many prisoners of conscience have been held in the last few years, but very seldom for long periods. Women's rights have improved. In both agriculture and industry considerable diversity and choice exists within a mixed socialist framework. Unions have developed some independence from the government, but there is no right to strike. The predominance of state corporations contributes to the acquiescence of unions in official policy. Travel and other private rights are generally free. More substantial democratic development is retarded by corruption, poverty, population growth, and Islamic fundamentalism.

Comparatively: Egypt is as free as China (Taiwan), freer than Algeria, less free than Brazil.

EL SALVADOR

Economy: capitalist
Polity: centralized multiparty
(military influenced)
Population: 5,300,000 (est.)

Political Rights: 3
Civil Liberties: 4

Status: partly free

A relatively homogeneous population

Political Rights. El Salvador is ruled by an elected president and parliament. The 1984 election was fair, but the armed opposition did not participate. In the countryside a bloody struggle between government and guerrilla forces continues. On the government side, armed killers have prevented the establishment of normal political or civil relationships. Recent elections have legitimized the power of the civil, elected government and confirmed the political weakness of the guerrillas. But the army continues to operate outside government control, even in the area of rural development.

Civil Liberties. Newspapers and radio are largely in private hands. Under strong pressure from all sides, the media have been self-censored, but are showing more independence. Legal and illegal opposition papers and broadcasts appear, but no major critical voice on the left has developed comparable to the opposition voice offered by the La Prensas of Nicaragua and Panama (closed in late 1987). The right-wing, anti-government press is outspoken. The rule of law is weak and assassination common. Conscription by both sides has been a major rights problem. Atrocities are committed by both sides in the conflict, probably frequently without the authorization of leaders. On the government side, no military officer has yet been successfully tried for a human rights offense. Human rights organizations are active. The Catholic Church remains a force. The university has reopened, but faculty and students continue to live under threat. Union activities are common, and strikes, legal and illegal, have become a major means of political expression for groups on the left. Although still a heavily agricultural country, rural people are to a large extent involved in the wage and market economy. Banking and foreign trade of export crops have been nationalized; land reform has had limited but significant success.

Comparatively: El Salvador is as free as Nepal, freer than Nicaragua, less free than Dominican Republic.

E Q U A T O R I A L G U I N E A

Economy: noninclusive
         capitalist-statist
Polity: military nonparty
Population: 325,000 (est.)

Political Rights: 7

Civil Liberties: 7
Status: not free

An ethnic state with a territorial minority

Political Rights. Equatorial Guinea is a military dictatorship in which power has been concentrated in one family or clan. The coup that replaced the former dictator was popular, but the population as a whole played and plays little part. The partially elected assembly seems irrelevant. A five-hundred-man-Moroccan body-guard protects the incumbent. The local army is recruited from only one ethnic group.

Civil Liberties. The media are very limited, government owned, and do not report opposition viewpoints. Many live in fear. The rule of law is tenuous; there are political prisoners, but perhaps none of conscience. Police brutality is common, and execution casual. Compulsory recruitment for plantation and other

307

work occurs. Opposition parties are not tolerated, and there are no unions. Religious freedom was reestablished in 1979, and private property is recognized. Plantation and subsistence farming is still recovering from near destruction under the previous government.

Comparatively: Equatorial Guinea is as free as Iraq, less free than Tanzania.

E T H I O P I A

Economy: noninclusive socialist
Polity: communist one-party
    (military dominated)
Population: 46,000,000 (est.)

Political Rights: 6
Civil Liberties: 7

Status: not free

An ethnic state with major territorial subnationalities

Political Rights. Ethiopia is ruled by a Marxist-Leninist military committee that has successively slaughtered the leaders of the ancien regime and many of its own leaders. A spectrum of mass organizations has been established on the model of a one-party socialist state. Establishing locally elected village councils has been the primary effort to mobilize the people. Membership in the communist party remains secret. In 1987, extended open discussions of the proposed constitution before its enactment led to important changes (such as dropping a ban on polygamy). Subsequent assembly elections under the new constitution allowed a restricted choice of individuals.

Subnationalities. The heartland of Ethiopia is occupied by the traditionally dominant Amhara and acculturated subgroups of the diffuse Galla people. In the late nineteenth century Ethiopian rulers united what had been warring fragments of a former empire in this heartland, and proceeded to incorporate some entirely new areas. At that time the Somali of the south came under Ethiopian rule; Eritrea was incorporated as the result of a UN decision in 1952. Today Ethiopia is crosscut by linguistic and religious conflicts: most important is separatism due to historic allegiances to ancient provinces (especially Tigre), to different experiences (Eritrea), and to the population of a foreign nation (Somalia).

Perhaps one-third of the country remains outside government control.

Civil Liberties. The media are controlled, serving the mobilization needs of the government. Individual rights are unprotected under conditions of despotism and anarchy. Political imprisonment, forced confession, execution, disappearance, and torture are common. There are no rights to assembly. Many thousands have been killed aside from those that died in civil war. Education is totally controlled. What freedom there was under the Ethiopian monarchy has been largely lost. Initially, land reform benefited many, but the subsequent villagization policy seriously disrupted agriculture. Choice of residence and workplace is often made by the government; there have been reports of forced transport to state farms, and of the forced movement of ethnic groups. Religious groups have been persecuted, and religious freedom is limited. Peasant and worker organizations are closely controlled. Travel outside the country is strictly controlled; hostages or guarantors are often required before exit. The words and actions of the regime indicate little respect for private rights in property. The economy is under increasing government control through nationalizations, state-sponsored peasant cooperatives, and the regulation of business licenses. Starvation has been a recurrent theme, with government ineffectiveness playing a part both before and after the accession of the present regime. Starvation is also used as a tool in the struggle against dissident peoples.

Comparatively: Ethiopia is as free as South Yemen, freer than Somalia, less free than Sudan.

EUROPEAN COMMUNITY

Economy: capitalist-statist
Polity: decentralized multiparty
Population: 322,300,000

Political Rights: 2
Civil Liberties: 1
Status: free

An ethnically heterogeneous community of independent states

Political Rights. The Community has evolved a variety of institutions since World War II for the managing of economic and political affairs. As in most international organizations, major decision making is made through an international bureaucracy or commission representing the member countries, and through the periodic meeting of representatives of their respective governments—the Council of Ministers and European Council. However, the Community has also developed a directly elected parliament that is growing in influence, and a Community Court of Justice. Increasingly, the law made by these institutions is coming to be considered superior to the national law of member countries. In addition, other institutions in Western Europe reinforce the operation of a system of free institutions within the Community itself.

Civil Liberties. The availability of information to the publics of the Community is characteristic of the free nature of these societies. In addition, the Council of Europe's court of human rights has striven to raise the level of respect for civil liberties.

Comparatively: The European Community is as free as France, less free than Denmark, freer than Turkey.

F I J I

Economy: noninclusive capitalist
Polity: military nonparty
Population: 700,000 (est.)

Political Rights: 6
Civil Liberties: 5
Status: partly free

A binational state

Political Rights. A military leader overthrew the democratic political system in 1987. New institutions have not yet been established. Clearly, the power of the armed forces and the traditional council of chiefs have been enhanced. Local government is organized both by the central government and by a Fijian administration headed by the council of chiefs. Subnationalities: The Fiji Indian community, slightly larger than the native Fijian, has become economically dominant, even with sharp restrictions on the rights of its members to own land. Many native Fijians, dominant in the army, intend to prevent Indian political dominance by forcing through laws that rule out this eventuality.

Civil Liberties. The private press is now censored. All broadcasting is closely controlled. Freedom to assemble is not recognized. However, privately much of the open discussion of a free society continues. Judges have been arbitrarily dismissed; union and political party activity curtailed. There is still little political imprisonment. Rights to property have been sacrificed to guarantee special rights of inalienability of land granted the Fijians. The country may be about evenly divided between a subsistence economy, based on agriculture and fishing, and a modern market economy.

Comparatively: Fiji is as free as Indonesia, freer than Burma, less free than Vanuatu.

F I N L A N D

Economy: mixed capitalist Political Rights: 1
Polity: centralized multiparty Civil Liberties: 2
Population: 4,900,000 Status: free

An ethnic state with a small territorial subnationality

Political Rights. Finland has a parliamentary system with a strong, directly elected president. Since there are many relatively strong parties, government is almost always by coalition. Elections have resulted in shifts in coalition membership. By treaty foreign policy cannot be anti-Soviet, but recent elections suggest a weakening of the Soviet veto on the political process. The provinces have centrally appointed governors. Subnationalities: The rural Swedish minority (seven percent) has its own political party and strong cultural ties to Sweden. The Swedish-speaking Aland Islands have local autonomy and other special rights.

Civil Liberties. The press is private, diverse, and uncensored. Government-press relations can be so hostile as to restrict communications. Most of the radio service is government controlled, but there is an important commercial television station. The government network has been manipulated at times. Discussion in the media is controlled by a political consensus that criticism of the Soviet Union should be circumspect. There is a complete rule of law; private rights are secured, as is freedom of religion, business, and labor.

Comparatively: Finland is as free as France, freer than Turkey, less free than Sweden.

F R A N C E

Economy: mixed capitalist
Polity: centralized multiparty
Population: 55,600,000

Political Rights: 1
Civil Liberties: 2
Status: free

An ethnic state with major territorial subnationalities

Political Rights. France is a parliamentary democracy with many features of the American system, such as a strong presidency and a check and balance of several centers of power. Either the Senate or the more powerful Assembly can check the power of government. If the president's party does not control parliament, experience in 1986 suggested that the prime minister can exercise powers comparable to those of the president. The constitutional council oversees elections and passes on the constitutionality of assembly or executive actions on the model of the United States Supreme Court. Regional and local power has recently been greatly increased: communes, departments, and regions now have elected governments. Subnationalities: Territorial subnationalities continue to have limited rights as ethnic units, but the ethnic and self-determination rights of such groups as the Bretons, Corsicans, and Basques are increasingly observed.

Civil Liberties. The French press is generally free. There is government involvement in financing and registration of journalists; press laws restrict freedom more than in other Western states. Criticism of the president and top officials may be muted by government threats and court actions. The news agency is private. Radio is now free and plural; the government television monopoly has ended, but new owners seem equally intrusive. In spite of recent changes there is still an authoritarian attitude in government-citizen relations, publications may be banned at the behest of foreign governments, and arrest without explanation still occurs, particularly of members of subnationalities. Police brutality is commonly alleged. Information and organization about conscientious objection is restricted. France is, of course, under the rule of law, and rights to occupation, residence, religion, and property are secured. A new Secretary of State for Human Rights, concerned primarily with internal issues, should improve governmental performance. Both through extensive social programs and the creation of state enterprises France is quite far from a pure capitalist form.

Comparatively: France is as free as Spain, freer than India, less free than Italy.

GABON

Economy: noninclusive capitalist
Polity: nationalist one-party
Population: 1,200,000 (est.)

Political Rights: 6
Civil Liberties: 6
Status: not free

A transethnic heterogeneous state

Political Rights. Gabon is a moderate dictatorship operating in the guise of a one-party state, with controlled elections characteristic of this form. Candidates must be party approved, but there is limited competition, particularly at the local level. The system remains dependent on the French (French military garrison, French army officers in the army, and French bureaucrats in the government). The dictator attempts to incorporate potential opposition leaders and individuals from a variety of ethnic groups in successive cabinets.

Civil Liberties. All media are government owned and controlled; few legitimate opposition voices are raised; journalists may be arrested for expression. Some critical items appear in local or available foreign media. Prisoners of conscience are held and mistreatment is alleged. The right of political assembly is not respected; only one labor union is sanctioned. Membership in the governing party is compulsory. The authoritarian government generally does not care to interfere in private lives, and respects religious freedom, private property, and the right to travel. The government is taking a more active role in the economy and is gradually replacing foreign managers with Gabonese.

Comparatively: Gabon is as free as Libya, freer than Angola, less free than Sudan.

G A M B I A

Economy: noninclusive capitalist
Polity: dominant party
Population: 750,000 (est.)

Political Rights: 3
Civil Liberties: 3
Status: partly free

A transethnic heterogeneous state

Political Rights. This is a parliamentary democracy in which the same party and leader have been in power since independence in 1965; elections are won with substantial margins. In a recent election the opposition candidate campaigned from prison. There is local, mostly traditional autonomy, but not regional self-rule. The state is now in confederation with Senegal, and the system is protected by Senegalese troops.

Civil Liberties. The private and public newspapers and radio stations are generally free, but are subject to self-censorship. In campaigns, the government may misuse its control of the radio. Arrests for antigovernment pamphlets occur. However, opposition organizational expression is freely allowed, and the independent judiciary maintains the rule of law. A threatening law against treason was passed in 1986. Labor unions operate within limits. The agricultural economy remains traditionally organized and is largely dependent on peanuts, the export of which is a state monopoly. Internal travel is limited by document checkpoints.

Comparatively: Gambia is as free as Vanuatu, freer than Sierra Leone, less free than Botswana.

G E R M A N Y, E A S T

Economy: socialist
Polity: communist one-party
Population: 16,700,000

Political Rights: 7
Civil Liberties: 6
Status: not free

A relatively homogeneous population

Political Rights. East Germany is in practice a one-party communist dictatorship. No electoral competition is allowed that involves policy questions; all citizens are compelled to vote; the

314

government-selected list of candidates may offer limited choice. In addition, the presence of Soviet troops and direction from the Communist Party of the Soviet Union significantly reduces the sovereignty (or group freedom) of the East Germans.

Civil Liberties. Media are government-owned means of indoctrination. Dissidents are repressed by imprisonment and exclusion; the publication or importation of materials with opposing views is forbidden. One may be arrested for private criticism of the system, but complaints about policy implementation occur in all the media; a few favored dissidents have managed to exist and publish outside the country. Among the thousands of prisoners of conscience, the most common offenses are trying to leave the country illegally (or in some cases even seeking permission to leave), or propaganda against the state. Prisoners of conscience may be severely beaten or otherwise harmed. Political reeducation may be a condition of release. The average person is not allowed freedom of occupation or residence. Once defined as an enemy of the state, a person may be barred from his occupation and his children denied higher education. Particularly revealing has been the use of the "buying out scheme" by which West Germany has been able intermittently to obtain the release of prisoners in the East through cash payments and delivering goods such as bananas and coffee. There is considerable religious freedom, with the Catholic and Protestant hierarchies possessing some independence, as does the peace movement at times. Freedom exists within the family, although there is no right to privacy or the inviolability of the home, mail, or telephone. Agriculture is highly collectivized; virtually all industry is state controlled. Membership in unions, production cooperatives, and other associations is compulsory.

Comparatively: East Germany is as free as Saudi Arabia, freer than Bulgaria, less free than Poland.

G E R M A N Y, W E S T

Economy: capitalist
Polity: decentralized multiparty
Population: 61,000,000

Political Rights: 1
Civil Liberties: 2
Status: free

A relatively homogeneous population

Political Rights. West Germany is a parliamentary democracy with an indirectly elected and largely ceremonial president. Both major parties have ruled since the war. The weak Senate is elected by the assemblies of the constituent states and loyally defends states' rights. Successive national governments have been based on changing party balances in the powerful lower house. The recent success of the "Greens" at all levels suggests the openness of the system to change. The states have their own elected assemblies; they control education, internal security, and culture.

Civil Liberties. The papers are independent and free, with little governmental interference. Radio and television are organized in public corporations under the usually neutral direction of the state governments. Generally the rule of law has been carefully observed, and the full spectrum of private freedoms is available. Terrorist activities have led to tighter security regulations, invasions of privacy, and less acceptance of nonconformity. Arrests have been made for handling or producing inflammatory literature, for neo-Nazi propaganda, or for calling in question the courts or electoral system. Anti-census literature has been confiscated. Government participation in the economy is largely regulatory; in addition, complex social programs and mandated worker participation in management have limited certain private freedoms while possibly expanding others.

Comparatively: West Germany is as free as Portugal, freer than Greece, less free than the United States of America.

G H A N A

Economy: capitalist-statist
Polity: military nonparty
Population: 13,900,000

Political Rights: 7
Civil Liberties: 6
Status: not free

A transethnic heterogeneous state with subnationalities

Political Rights. A small military faction rules with the support of radical organizations. On the local level traditional sources of power are minimal. Local councils are elected, but are closely supervised where possible. Widespread violence suggests anarchy in many areas. Subnationalities: The country is composed of a variety of peoples, with those in the South most self-conscious. The latter are the descendants of a number of traditional kingdoms, of which the Ashanti are the most important. A north-south, Muslim-Christian opposition exists but is weakly developed, because of the numerical and economic weakness and incomplete hold of Islam in the north. In the south and center of the country a sense of Akan identity is developing among the Ashanti, Fanti, and others; since they include forty-five percent of the people, this amounts to strengthening the ethnic core of the nation. The one million Ewe in the southeast (a people divided between Ghana and Togo) play a major role in the new revolutionary government.

Civil Liberties. Radio and television and most of the press are government owned. All are under close government scrutiny. However, a degree of independence is suggested by the periodic suspension and banning of semi-independent publications. Private opinion is restrained. There have been hundreds of political arrests and political trials; many professionals have been murdered, apparently for "revolutionary" reasons. Soldiers are reported out of control. Papers and universities have been closed. Peoples' courts have been used to counter the previous judicial system. Government control is decisive in some areas of the economy—especially in cocoa production, on which the economy depends, and in modern capital-intensive industry. The assets of many businesses have been frozen. Some groups, including the strong women's marketing associations, have resisted government attempts to impose price ceilings on all goods. Labor unions are controlled, but union leaders have become outspoken critics of the government. Like Senegal, Ghana has a relatively highly developed industry and agriculture dependent on world markets. There is religious freedom; travel is controlled.

Comparatively: Ghana is as free as Niger, freer than Romania, less free than Cote d'Ivoire.

G R E E C E

Economy: mixed capitalist
Polity: centralized multiparty
Population: 10,000,000

Political Rights: 2
Civil Liberties: 2
Status: free

A relatively homogeneous state

Political Rights. Greece is a parliamentary democracy with an indirectly elected president. The development and extension of free institutions has proceeded rapidly, and recent elections have been competitive and open to the full spectrum of parties. However, governmental actions in elections and parliament have led to serious accusations of misuse of authority. Provincial administration is centrally controlled; there is local self-government.

Civil Liberties. Newspapers are private and the judiciary is independent. Most broadcast media are government owned and controlled, but private and opposition radio stations were established in 1987; television favors the government viewpoint. Government interference in journalism, broadcasting, and universities has recently been reported. There are no known prisoners of conscience. Because of the recent revolutionary situation, all views are not freely expressed (a situation similar to that in post-fascist Portugal). One can be imprisoned for insulting the authorities or religion. The courts are not entirely independent. Pressures have been reported against the Turkish population in Western Thrace, in regard to education, property, and free movement. Union activity is under government influence, particularly in the dominant public sector. Private rights are respected.

Comparatively: Greece is as free as Mauritius, freer than Turkey, less free than France.

G R E N A D A

Economy: capitalist-statist   Political Rights: 2
Polity: centralized multiparty   Civil Liberties: 1
Population: 112,000   Status: free

A relatively homogeneous population

Political Rights. Parliamentary rule has been effectively reestablished. The 1984 elections were free and fair, and included all major political forces. The legislature governs. There is no local government. Direct United States influence has been reduced to that characterizing the region as a whole.

Civil Liberties. The newspapers are independent, varied, and free. Radio is government controlled—the government has been accused of restricting the development of private radio. There are no prisoners of conscience. All groups have full rights of expression and organization. The judiciary and trade unions are strong and independent. The economy is largely private.

Comparatively: Grenada is as free as St. Lucia, freer than Panama, less free than Barbados.

GUATEMALA

Economy: noninclusive capitalist
Polity: centralized multiparty
    (military influenced)
Population: 8,400,000

Political Rights: 3
Civil Liberties: 3

Status: partly free

An ethnic state with a major potential territorial subnationality

Political Rights. Guatemala is in transition from military to civilian rule. Credible elections in November and December 1985 reestablished formal civilian rule. The executive and congress have moved slowly but steadily to reestablish civilian institutions. However, military and other security forces maintain extra-constitutional power at all levels. The provinces are centrally administered; local government under elected officials is important in some areas. Subnationalities: Various groups of Mayan and other Indians make up half the population; they do not yet have a subnationalist sense of unity, but are involved both forcibly and voluntarily in guerrilla and antiguerrilla activity.

Civil Liberties. The press and a large portion of radio and television are privately controlled. Until recently self-censorship has been common because of the threat of torture and murder by political opponents. Expression is now relatively free, although many killings continue to occur. The struggle against rural guerrillas has led to frequent attacks on recalcitrant peasants or Indians by security forces. Tens of thousands have been killed in the last few years, primarily by the security forces. Thousands have sought refuge internally and in border areas. The judiciary is under both leftist and governmental pressure in political or subver-

319

sive cases and has been relatively ineffective in these areas. Recent improvements in security have increased rights in many areas. Rights of assembly and demonstration are vigorously expressed. Political parties are active, and unions are reestablishing their strength.

Comparatively: Guatemala is as free as Thailand, freer than Mexico, less free than Ecuador.

G U I N E A

Economy: noninclusive
      mixed capitalist
Polity: military nonparty
Population: 6,400,000

Political Rights: 7

Civil Liberties: 6

Status: not free

A formally transethnic heterogeneous state

Political Rights. Guinea is under military rule. Local elective councils with very limited powers have been established.

Civil Liberties. The government controls all media; free expression is limited by fear of dismissal. However, critical foreign publications are available. Unions are under government direction, but some independence has been achieved. Many political detainees have been tortured and executed after secret political trials. Industry is heavily nationalized.

Comparatively: Guinea is as free as Mali, freer than Equatorial Guinea, less free than Cote d'Ivoire.

G U I N E A - B I S S A U

Economy: noninclusive socialist
Polity: socialist one-party
      (military dominated)
Population: 890,000

Political Rights: 6

Civil Liberties: 7

Status: not free

A transethnic heterogeneous state

Political Rights. Guinea-Bissau is administered by one party; other parties are illegal. Regional council elections lay the basis for indirect election of the assembly; party guidance is emphasized at all levels. Public pressure has caused the replacement of some local officials. Increasingly violent struggle among top leaders has resulted in many deaths.

Civil Liberties. The media are government controlled; criticism of the system is forbidden. Human rights is not protected by an adequate rule of law; many have been executed without adequate trial or died in detention. Union activity is government directed. Land ownership is public or communal. The small industrial sector remains mixed, but the continuing economic crisis has virtually halted all private sector activity. An additional block to further decollectivization is the Soviet and Cuban presence. Religion is relatively free, as are travel and other aspects of private life.

Comparatively: Guinea-Bissau is as free as Mozambique, freer than Somalia, less free than Libya.

G U Y A N A

Economy: mixed socialist
Polity: dominant party
Population: 800,000

Political Rights: 5
Civil Liberties: 5
Status: partly free

An ethnically complex state

Political Rights. Guyana is a parliamentary democracy with a strong executive and an increasingly dominant ruling party. In recent elections the government has been responsibly charged with irregularities that resulted in its victory. In the last election (December 1985), the opposition was often excluded from the polling stations both to vote and observe the process. Opposition parties are denied equal access to the media, and their supporters are discriminated against in employment. Administration is generally centralized but some local officials are elected.

Civil Liberties. Radio is government owned. Several opposition newspapers have been nationalized; the opposition press is under continuing pressure. However, a variety of foreign news media are still available. There is a right of assembly, but harassment occurs. Opposition parties remain well organized. There is an operating human rights organization. All private schools have been nationalized, and the government has interfered with university appointments. It is possible to win against the government in court; there are no prisoners of conscience, though torture of convicts may be practiced. Art and music are under considerable government control. The independence of unions has been greatly abridged. The private sector is stagnating under official intimidation and extensive state control of productive property, although a black market thrives. The opposition is terrorized by armed gangs and the police; the general public suffers under arbitrary and severe controls. Political patronage is extensive and some social benefits are allocated on a preferential basis. Internal exile has been used against political opponents.

Comparatively: Guyana is as free as Nicaragua, freer than Indonesia, less free than Guatemala.

H A I T I

Economy: noninclusive capitalist
Polity: military nonparty
Population: 6,200,000 (est.)

Political Rights: 6
Civil Liberties: 5
Status: partly free

A relatively homogeneous population

Political Rights. In 1986 Haiti came under the loose control of an initially popular military caretaker government. It has failed to move effectively toward establishing a legitimate democratic system. After ratifying by referendum a democratic constitution, the electoral commission was prevented by violence, and military indifference, from carrying out a democratic election. At the end of 1987 the country appeared to be sporadically under military, vigilante, gangster, and anarchic rule.

Civil Liberties. The media are private and public, highly varied and nominally free. The prisons have been emptied. The main human rights problems are those of anarchy—many have been killed or persecuted without trial. Fear has become a major control over expression or assembly. Union activity remains restricted. Corruption and extreme poverty has seriously infringed rights to political equality.

Comparatively: Haiti is as free as Lesotho, freer than Malawi, less free than Guyana.

HONDURAS

Economy: noninclusive capitalist
Polity: centralized multiparty
Population: 4,700,000

Political Rights: 2
Civil Liberties: 3
Status: free

A relatively homogeneous population

Political Rights. The government is a parliamentary democracy with an elected president. The relationships between the president, congress, the supreme court, and the military are still in question. Military leaders have retained influence, but civilian government has been able to assert its dominance. Provincial government is centrally administered; local government is elected.

Civil Liberties. The media are largely private and free of prior censorship. Licensing requirements for journalists can limit freedom. Human rights organizations are active. Militant peasant organizations are quite active, and the struggle of peasants for land often leads to violence. The spreading of guerrilla war from neighboring countries has led to repressions of refugees and others. Most private rights are respected—in so far as government power reaches. Private killings, especially of leftists and with the involvement of security forces, have often been reported. Labor unions have suffered oppression, but are relatively strong, especially in plantation areas. There is freedom of religion and movement.

Comparatively: Honduras is as free as Colombia, freer than Panama, less free than Uruguay.

H U N G A R Y

Economy: socialist
Polity: communist one-party
Population: 10,600,000

Political Rights: 5
Civil Liberties: 4
Status: partly free

A relatively homogeneous population

Political Rights. Hungary is ruled as a one-party communist dictatorship. Although there is an elective national assembly as well as local assemblies, all candidates must be approved by the party, and the decisions of the politburo are decisive. Within this framework recent elections have allowed choice among candidates. Independents have been elected and in many cases run-offs have been required. Parliament has come to take a more meaningful part in the political process. The group rights of the Hungarian people are diminished by the government's official acceptance of the right of the Soviet government to intervene in the domestic affairs of Hungary by force. A council to represent the special interests of the large gypsy community has been established.

Civil Liberties. Media are under government or party control. Basic criticism of top leaders, communism, human rights performance, or the Soviet presence is inadmissable, but some criticism is allowed; this is expressed through papers, plays, books, the importation of foreign publications, or listening to foreign broadcasts. Radio and television give relatively balanced presentations, even of news. Major public organizations such as the writers' union and the Academy of Sciences have defied the government. Opposition marches for democracy are held. Informally organized dissident groups are allowed to exist. Individuals are regularly detained for reasons of conscience, though usually for short periods. Control over religious affairs is more relaxed than in most communist states. Although private rights are not guaranteed, in practice there is considerable private property, and permission to travel into and out of the country is easier to obtain than in most of Eastern Europe. The border with Austria is essentially open. Unions are party directed and have no right to strike; however, workers have gained some control over enterprise management and operations.

Comparatively: Hungary is as free as China (Taiwan), freer than Czechoslovakia, less free than Mexico.

I C E L A N D

Economy: capitalist
Polity: centralized multiparty
Population: 230,000

Political Rights: 1
Civil Liberties: 1
Status: free

A relatively homogeneous population

Political Rights. Iceland is governed by a parliamentary democracy. Recent years have seen important shifts in voter sentiment, resulting successively in right- and left-wing coalitions. Although a small country, Iceland pursues an independent foreign policy. Provinces are ruled by central government appointees.

Civil Liberties. The press is private or party and free of censorship. Radio and television are state owned but supervised by a state board representing major parties and interests. There are no political prisoners and the judiciary is independent. Private rights are respected; few are poor or illiterate.

Comparatively: Iceland is as free as Norway, freer than Portugal.

I N D I A

Economy: noninclusive
        capitalist-statist
Polity: decentralized multiparty
Population: 800,000,000

Political Rights: 2
Civil Liberties: 3
Status: free

A multinational and complex state

Political Rights. India is a parliamentary democracy in which the opposition has an opportunity to rule. The strong powers retained by the component states have been compromised in recent years by the central government's frequent imposition of direct rule. However, control of the states by regional political parties

325

has increased. Use of criminal elements in politics in some local areas is a threat to fair participation. A 1985 law to prohibit change of party affiliation after election strengthened voter rights.

Subnationalities. India contains a diverse collection of mostly territorially distinct peoples united by historical experience and the predominance of Hinduism. India's dominant peoples are those of the north central area that speak as a first language either the official language, Hindi (Hindustani), or a very closely related dialect of Sanskrit origin. The other major subnational peoples of India may be divided into several groups: (1) peoples with separate states that are linguistically and historically only marginally distinct from the dominant Hindi speakers (for example, the Marathi, Gujerati, or Oriya); (2) peoples with separate states that are of Sanskrit background linguistically, but have a relatively strong sense of separate identity (for example, Bengalis or Kashmiris); (3) peoples with separate states that are linguistically and to some extent racially quite distinct (for example, Telegu or Malayalam); and (4) peoples that were not originally granted states of their own, and often still do not have them. These peoples, such as the Santali, Bhuti-Lepcha, or Mizo, may be survivors of India's pre-Aryan peoples. The Indian federal system accords a fair amount of democratic rights to its peoples. Several peoples from groups (2), (3), and (4) have shown through legal (especially votes) and illegal means a strong desire by a significant part of the population for independence or greater autonomy (notably Kashmiris, Nagas, and Gurkhas). In 1986, after a long struggle, the Mizos were granted a greater degree of self-determination. Sikh extremists continue to impede the successful reestablishment of elected state government in the Punjab. The Northeast is inflamed by hatred of encroaching Bengalis from both Indian Bengal and Bangladesh. This accounting leaves out many nonterritorial religious and caste minorities, although here again the system has granted relatively broad rights to such groups for reasonable self-determination.

Civil Liberties. The Indian press is diversified, independent, but often not strongly critical or investigative. Governmental pressure against a major paper through union activity and bureaucratic harassment became a critical issue for Indian democracy in late 1987. Radio and television are government controlled in this largely illiterate country, and they serve government interests. There is freedom of organization and assembly, but there have been illegal arrests, questionable killings, and reports of torture by the police, which have often been out of control. Journalism can be dangerous. There is a remarkable extent of private political organization at many social levels and for a variety of causes. The judiciary is generally responsive, fair, and independent. The frequent approach to anarchy in Indian society offers many examples of both freedom and repression. There are few if any prisoners of conscience, but hundreds are imprisoned for real or "proposed" political violence; demonstrations often lead to fatalities and massive detentions. Due to the decentralized political structure, operation of the security laws varies from region to region. Kashmir and Bihar have especially repressive security policies in relation to the press and political detention; Sikkim is treated as an Indian colony; the same might be said for some other border areas. Assam and the Punjab are necessarily under stricter supervision. Indians enjoy freedom to travel, to worship as they please, and to organize for mutual benefit, especially in unions and cooperatives. Lack of education, extreme poverty, and surviving traditional controls reduce the meaning of such liberties for large numbers.

Comparatively: India is as free as Peru, freer than Malaysia, less free than Japan.

INDONESIA

Economy:	noninclusive capitalist-statist	Political Rights:	5
Polity:	centralized dominant-party (military dominated)	Civil Liberties:	6
Population:	175,000,000	Status:	partly free

A transethnic complex state with active and potential subnationalities

Political Rights. Indonesia is a controlled parliamentary democracy under military direction. Recent parliamentary elections allowed some competition but severely restricted opposition campaigning and organization. The number and character of opposition

327

parties are carefully controlled, parties must refrain from criticizing one another, candidates of both government and opposition require government approval, and the opposition is not allowed to organize in rural areas. All parties must accept the broad outline of state policy and the state ideology. All civil servants are expected to vote for the government. In any event parliament does not have a great deal of power. Regional and local government is under central control, although there is limited autonomy in a few areas. Local and regional assemblies are elected. Military officers are included in most legislatures and play a major part in the economy as managers of both public and army corporations.

Subnationalities. Indonesia includes a variety of ethnic groups and is divided by crosscutting island identities. Although the island of Java is numerically dominant, the national language is not Javanese, and most groups or islands do not appear to have strong subnational identifications. There is discrimination against Chinese culture. Both civilian and military elites generally attempt to maintain religious, ethnic, and regional balance, but government-sponsored settlement of Javanese on outer islands results in the destruction of minority cultures and the denial of self-determination. Groups demanding independence exist in Sulawesi, the Moluccas, Timor, West Irian, and northern Sumatra. Today the most active movements are in West Irian and Timor—among peoples with little in common with Indonesians.

Civil Liberties. Most newspapers are private. All are subject to fairly close government supervision; there is heavy self-censorship and censorship. Criticism of the system is muted by periodic suppressions. Radio and television are government controlled, whether or not private. Freedom of assembly is restricted, but citizens are not compelled to attend meetings. All organizations must now conform to the official ideology. There are prisoners of conscience. Thousands of released prisoners remain in second-class status, especially in regard to residence and employment. In this area the army rather than the civilian judiciary is dominant. The army has been responsible for many thousands of unnecessary deaths in its suppression of revolt in, or conquest of, East Timor. Recently there have been many murders of nonpolitical criminals, apparently at the hands of "hit squads" allied to the security services. Union activity is closely regulated, but labor organization is widespread and strikes occur. Many people are not allowed to travel outside the country for political reasons. Movement, especially to the cities, is restricted; other private rights are generally respected. The Indonesian bureaucracy has an unenviable reputation for arbitrariness and corruption—practices that reduce the effective expression of human rights. The judiciary is not independent. There are many active human rights organizations. Much of industry and commercial agriculture is government owned; sharecropping and tenant farming are relatively common, particularly on Java.

Comparatively: Indonesia is as free as South Africa, freer than Burma, less free than Singapore.

I R A N

Economy: noninclusive capitalist-statist

Polity: quasi-dominant party

Population: 50,400,000

Political Rights: 5

Civil Liberties: 6

Status: partly free

An ethnic state with major territorial subnationalities

Political Rights. Iran has competitive elections, but the direction of the nonelective, theocratic leadership narrowly defines who may compete in the elections. Those who oppose the overall system on fundamentals are silenced or eliminated. Political parties are poorly defined. However, parliament is an open and disputatious body with considerable influence. Elections are increasingly important on the local level. Subnationalities: Among the most important non-Persian peoples are the Kurds, the Azerbaijani Turks, the Baluch, and a variety of other (primarily Turkish) tribes. Many of these have striven for independence in the recent past when the opportunity arose. The Kurds are in active revolt.

Civil Liberties. Newspapers are semi-private or factional, and all are closely controlled. However, strong criticisms of government leaders (other than Khomeini) appears in major publications. The other media are largely government-owned propaganda organs. Parliamentary debates are broadcast in full. The right of assembly is denied to those who do not approve of the new system. There are many prisoners of conscience, and executions

329

for political offenses—often nonviolent—have been frequent. Unions have been suppressed. Vigilante groups compete with the official security system; many private rights have become highly insecure, as the goal of the Islamic system is control over most aspects of life. This is especially so for the Bahais and other religious minorities. Legal emigration is quite difficult. Education is subject to religious restrictions; the freedom and equality of women is radically curtailed. However, privacy has recently been reemphasized and there appears to be a good deal of freedom in the home. Diversity and choice still characterize economic activity.

Comparatively: Iran is as free as Yugoslavia, freer than Iraq, less free than Egypt.

I R A Q

Economy: noninclusive socialist
Polity: socialist one-party
Population: 17,000,000

Political Rights: 7
Civil Liberties: 7
Status: not free

An ethnic state with a major territorial subnationality

Political Rights. Iraq is a one-party state under dictatorial leadership. Elections allow some choice of individuals, but all candidates are carefully selected, and no policy choices are involved in the process. Resulting parliaments have little if any power. Provinces are governed from the center. Subnationalities: Many Kurds remain in open war with the regime, in spite of institutions ostensibly developed for them.

Civil Rights. Newspapers are public or party and are closely controlled by the government; foreign and domestic books and movies are censored. Radio and television are government monopolies. The strident media are emphasized as governmental means for active indoctrination. Major events go unrecorded. Political imprisonment, brutality, and torture are common, and execution frequent. Poisoning on release from prison is reported. The families of suspects are often imprisoned. Rights are largely de facto or those deriving from traditional religious law. Religious freedom or freedom to organize for any purpose is very limited. Education is intended to serve the party's purposes. Iraq has a dual economy with a large traditional sector. The government has taken over much of the modern petroleum-based economy; land reform is, however, now expanding private choice.

Comparatively: Iraq is as free as Bulgaria, less free than Lebanon.

I R E L A N D

Economy: capitalist
Polity: centralized multiparty
Population: 3,500,000

Political Rights: 1
Civil Liberties: 1
Status: free

A relatively homogeneous population

Political Rights. Ireland is a parliamentary democracy that successively shifts national power among parties. The bicameral legislature has an appointive upper house with powers only of delay. Local government is not powerful, but is elective rather than appointive. Referendums are also used for national decisions.

Civil Liberties. The press is free and private, and radio and television are under an autonomous corporation. Strong censorship has always been exercised over both publishers and the press, but since this is for social rather than political content, it lies within that sphere of control permitted a majority in a free democracy. The rule of law is firmly established and private rights are guaranteed.

Comparatively: Ireland is as free as Canada, freer than France.

I S R A E L

Economy: mixed capitalist
Polity: centralized multiparty
Population: 4,400,000

Political Rights: 2
Civil Liberties: 2
Status: free

An ethnic state with microterritorial subnationalities

Political Rights. Israel is governed under a parliamentary system. Recent elections have resulted in increasingly uneasy or unstable coalitions. Provinces are ruled from the center, although important local offices in the cities are elective. Subnationalities: National elections do not involve the Arabs in the occupied territories, but Arabs in Israel proper participate in Israeli elections as a minority grouping. Arabs both in Israel and the occupied territories must live in their homeland under the cultural and political domination of twentieth century immigrants.

Civil Liberties. Newspapers are private or party, and free of censorship except for restrictions relating to the always precarious national security. Radio and television are governmentally owned. In general the rule of law is observed, although Arabs in Israel are not accorded the full rights of citizens, and the orthodox Jewish faith holds a special position in the country's religious, customary, and legal life. Detentions, house arrest, and brutality have been reported against Arabs opposing Israel's Palestine policy. Because of the war, the socialist-cooperative ideology of its founders, and dependence on outside support, the role of private enterprise in the economy has been less than in most of Euro-America. Arabs are, in effect, not allowed to buy land from Jews, while Arab land has been expropriated for Jewish settlement. Unions are economically and politically powerful and control over twenty-five percent of industry. The Survey's rating of Israel is based on its judgment of the situation in Israel proper and not that in the occupied territories.

Comparatively: Israel is as free as Uruguay, freer than Turkey, less free than Malta.

ITALY

Economy: capitalist-statist
Polity: centralized multiparty
Population: 57,400,000

Political Rights: 1
Civil Liberties: 1
Status: free

A relatively homogeneous population with small territorial subnationalities

Political Rights. Italy is a bicameral parliamentary democracy. Elections are free. Since the 1940s governments have been dominated by the Christian Democrats, with coalitions shifting between dependence on minor parties of the left or right. Recently premiers have often been from these smaller parties. At the same time, the major parties have improved their internal democracy and legitimacy. The fascist party is banned. Referendums are used increasingly to supplement parliamentary rule. Opposition parties gain local political power. Regional institutions are developing, and the judiciary's moves against mob influence at this level improves the legitimacy of the system.

Civil Liberties. Italian newspapers are free and cover a broad spectrum. Radio and television are both public and private and provide unusually diverse programming. Laws against defamation of the government and foreign and ecclesiastical officials exert a slight limiting effect on the media. Freedom of speech is inhibited in some areas and for many individuals by the violence of extremist groups or criminal organizations. Since the bureaucracy does not respond promptly to citizen desires, it represents, as in many countries, an additional impediment to full expression of the rule of law. The judiciary has recently shown strong independence and determination. Detention may last for years without trial. Unions are strong and independent. Catholicism is no longer a state religion but remains a favored religion. Major industries are managed by the government, and the government has undertaken extensive reallocations of land.

Comparatively: Italy is as free as Austria, freer than Greece.

J A M A I C A

Economy: capitalist-statist   Political Rights: 2
Polity: centralized multiparty   Civil Liberties: 2
Population: 2,300,000   Status: free

A relatively homogeneous population

Political Rights. Jamaica is a parliamentary democracy in which power changes from one party to another. However, political life is violent; election campaigns have been accompanied

333

by hundreds of deaths. The general neutrality of the civil service, police, and army preserves the system. Responses by both parties to the anomalous one-party parliament has been excellent (more open debate in parliament and a mock opposition parliament taking its arguments to the people). Public opinion polls are becoming an increasingly important part of the political process. Regional or local administrations have little independent power, but local elections have taken an increasing national significance.

Civil Liberties. The press is largely private; the broadcasting media largely public. Critical media are widely available to the public. Freedom of assembly and organization are generally respected. The judiciary and much of the bureaucracy retain independence, although the police and legal system have been accused of countenancing brutality and severe punishments. The number of criminals shot by the police is remarkably high. However, political violence has declined. Some foreign companies have been nationalized, but the economy remains largely in private hands. Labor is both politically and economically powerful.

Comparatively: Jamaica is as free as Mauritius, freer than Guatemala, less free than Barbados.

J A P A N

Economy: capitalist
Polity: centralized multiparty
Population: 122,200,000

Political Rights: 1
Civil Liberties: 1
Status: free

A relatively homogeneous population

Political Rights. Japan is a bicameral, constitutional monarchy with a relatively weak upper house. The conservative-to-centrist Liberal Democratic Party has ruled since the mid-1950s, either alone or in coalition with independents. Concentrated business interests have played a strong role in maintaining Liberal Party hegemony through the use of their money, influence, and prestige. In addition, weighting of representation in favor of rural areas tends to maintain the Liberal Party position. Opposition parties are fragmented. They have local control in some areas, but the power of local and regional assemblies and officials is limited. The

Supreme Court has the power of judicial review, but its voice is not yet powerful. Subnationalities: Many people in the Ryukyu Islands (including Okinawa) regard themselves as occupied by a foreign people.

Civil Liberties. News media are generally private and free, although many radio and television stations are served by a public broadcasting corporation. Television is excellent and quite free. Courts of law are not as important in Japanese society as in Europe and America. Although the courts and police appear to be relatively fair, nearly all of those arrested confess and are convicted. A high rate of involuntary admissions to mental hospitals is reported. Travel and change of residence are unrestricted. By tradition public expression and action are more restricted than in most modern democracies. Japanese style collectivism leads to strong social pressures, especially psychological pressures, in many spheres (unions, corporations, or religious-political groups, such as Soka Gakkai). Most unions are company unions. Human rights organizations are very active. Discrimination against Koreans and other minority groups remains a problem.

Comparatively: Japan is as free as Australia, freer than Argentina.

J O R D A N

Economy: capitalist
Polity: limited monarchy
Population: 3,700,000

Political Rights: 5
Civil Liberties: 5
Status: partly free

A relatively homogeneous population

Political Rights. Although formally a constitutional monarchy, Jordan has had few elections and a very weak parliament. Provinces are ruled from the center; elected local governments have limited autonomy. The king and his ministers are regularly petitioned by citizens.

Civil Liberties. Papers are mostly private, but self-censored and occasionally suspended. Television and radio are government controlled. Free private conversation and mild public criticism are allowed. Under a continuing state of martial law, normal legal guarantees for political suspects are suspended, and organized opposition is not permitted. There are prisoners of conscience and instances of torture. Labor has a limited right to organize and strike. Private rights such as those of property, travel, or religion appear to be respected. The government has partial control over many large corporations.

Comparatively: Jordan is as free as Bhutan, freer than South Yemen, less free than Egypt.

K E N Y A

Economy: noninclusive capitalist
Polity: nationalist one-party
Population: 22,400,000

Political Rights: 6
Civil Liberties: 6
Status: not free

A transethnic heterogeneous state with active and potential subnationalities

Political Rights. Kenya is a one-party nationalist state. Only members of the party can run for office, and political opponents are excluded or expelled. All civil servants have been ordered to join the party, which includes a large part of the population. Election results can express popular dissatisfaction, but candidates avoid discussion of basic policy or the president. Selection of top party and national leaders is by acclamation. In this increasingly dictatorial state both parliament and judiciary have become subservient to the president. The administration is centralized, but elements of tribal and communal government continue at the periphery. Subnationalities: Comprising twenty percent of the population, the Kikuyu are the largest tribal group. In a very heterogeneous society, the Luo are the second most important subnationality.

Civil Liberties. The press is private, but little criticism of major policies is allowed. Radio and television are under government control. Opposition statements are either ignored or declared treasonous. Rights of assembly, organization, and demonstration are severely limited, particularly for students and faculty. There are hundreds of prisoners of conscience, and torture is common. Defending them in court is itself dangerous. Unions are active but strikes are de facto illegal. Private rights are generally respected. Land is gradually coming under private rather than tribal control.

Comparatively: Kenya is as free as Tanzania, freer than Ethiopia, less free than Sudan.

K I R I B A T I

Economy: noninclusive capitalist-statist

Polity: decentralized nonparty

Population: 64,000

Political Rights: 1

Civil Liberties: 2

Status: free

A relatively homogeneous population with a territorial subnationality

Political Rights. Kiribati has a functioning parliamentary system. Although there are no formal parties, both the legislature and president are elected in a fully competitive system. In his attempt to retain the presidency, the incumbent has been charged with stretching the constitution. Local government is significant.

Civil Liberties. The press is private; radio government owned. Public expression appears to be free and the rule of law guaranteed. The modern economy is dominated by investments from the now virtually depleted government-run phosphate industry. A free union operates, and most agriculture is small, private subsistence; land cannot be alienated to non-natives.

Comparatively: Kiribati is as free as Portugal, freer than Western Samoa, less free than New Zealand.

K O R E A, N O R T H

Economy: socialist

Polity: quasi-communist one-party

Population: 21,400,000

Political Rights: 7

Civil Liberties: 7

Status: not free

A relatively homogeneous state

Political Rights. North Korea is a hard-line communist dictatorship in which the organs and assemblies of government are only a facade for party or individual rule. The communism and Marxism-Leninism on which the governing system is based seems to have been replaced by the ruler's personal ideology. National elections allow no choice. The politburo is under one-man rule; the dictator's son is the dictator's officially anointed successor. Military officers are very strong in top positions.

Civil Liberties. The media are all government controlled, with glorification of the leader a major responsibility. External publications are rigidly excluded, and those who listen to foreign broadcasts severely punished. No individual thoughts are advanced publicly or privately. Individual rights are minimal. Everyone is given a security rating that determines future success. Opponents are even kidnapped overseas. Rights to travel internally and externally are perhaps the most restricted in the world: tourism is unknown—even to communist countries. Social classes are politically defined in a rigidly controlled society; differences between the standard of living of the elite and the general public are extreme. Thousands are long-term prisoners of conscience; torture is reportedly common. There are also reeducation centers and internal exile. There is no private business or agriculture.

Comparatively: North Korea is as free as Albania, less free than South Korea.

K O R E A, S O U T H

Economy: capitalist-statist
Polity: centralized multiparty
Population: 42,100,000

Political Rights: 4
Civil Liberties: 4
Status: partly free

A relatively homogeneous state

Political Rights. South Korea is under a military regime with the support of a partly free legislature. Recent elections of both president and assembly have given the opposition a restricted right to compete. The opposition now controls a substantial bloc of legislators, but the legislature is relatively weak, and legislators have been arrested for their public statements. The method of allocating seats greatly favors the government party. Public campaigns can significantly affect government. In late 1987, after overwhelming public endorsement of a new constitution, the country awaited the emergence of a democratic government with much reduced military involvement. Local government is not independent.

Civil Liberties. Although most newspapers are private, as well as many radio stations and one television station, they have been reorganized by government fiat. Independent broadcasting almost ceased to exist. However, by late 1987 much had changed: statements in the print media and public assemblies were free of restraints on most topics. Most prisoners of conscience were also released. The courts have not been able to effectively protect the rights of political suspects or prisoners. Many political opponents have been denied travel permits, but freedom of internal and external travel is otherwise unabridged. There is religious freedom (but not freedom of religious groups to criticize the government). Human rights organizations are active, but have been under heavy pressure. Outside this arena, private rights have been generally respected. Rapid capitalistic economic growth has been combined with a relatively egalitarian income distribution. Government controls most heavy industry; other sectors are private. Union activity, severely curtailed under a 1980 labor law, has recently become much freer and significant strikes have occurred.

Comparatively: South Korea is as free as Mexico, freer than China (Mainland), less free than Thailand.

K U W A I T

Economy: mixed capitalist-statist
Polity: traditional nonparty
Population: 1,900,000

Political Rights: 6
Civil Liberties: 5
Status: partly free

The citizenry is relatively homogeneous

Political Rights. Kuwait's limited parliament was again dissolved in 1986 when its criticisms of the government became too threatening to the ruling family. Citizens have access to the monarch. More than half the population are immigrants: their political, economic, and social rights are inferior to those of natives; they very seldom achieve citizenship for themselves or their children.

Civil Liberties. Although the private press presents diverse opinions and ideological viewpoints, papers are subject to suspension for "spreading dissension," or for criticism of the monarch, Islam, or friendly foreign states. Radio and television are government controlled. Imported media are censored. Freedom of assembly is curtailed. Public critics may be detained, expelled, or have their passports confiscated. Formal political parties are not allowed. Private discussion is open, and few, if any, political prisoners are held. Most private freedoms are respected, and independent unions operate. However, many have been expelled or prevented from leaving for security reasons. There is a wide variety of enabling government activity in fields such as education, housing, and medicine that is not based on reducing choice through taxation.

Comparatively: Kuwait is as free as South Africa, freer than Oman, less free than Egypt.

L A O S

Economy: noninclusive socialist
Polity: communist one-party
Population: 3,800,000

Political Rights: 7
Civil Liberties: 7
Status: not free

An ethnic state with active or potential subnationalities

Political Rights. Laos has established a traditional communist party dictatorship in which the party is superior to the external government at all levels. The small cadre party enlists little more than one percent of the population. The government is subservient, in turn, to the desires of the Vietnamese communist party, upon which the present leaders must depend. Vietnam continues to maintain five divisions in the country; it is strongly represented in nearly every government ministry. Resistance continues in rural areas, where many groups have been violently suppressed. Subnationalities: Pressure on the Hmong people has caused the majority of them to flee the country.

Civil Liberties. The media are all government controlled. There are prisoners of conscience; thousands have spent as long as a decade in reeducation camps. Few private rights are accepted, but there is relaxed opposition to traditional ways, particularly Buddhism. Collectivization has been halted since 1979 because of peasant resistance; most farms continue to be small and individually owned. The limited industry is nationalized. Travel within and exit from the country are highly restricted.

Comparatively: Laos is as free as Benin, less free than China (Mainland).

L E B A N O N

Economy: capitalist
Polity: decentralized multiparty
Population: 3,000,000 (est.)

Political Rights: 6
Civil Liberties: 5
Status: partly free

A complex, multinational, microterritorial state

Political Rights. In theory Lebanon is a parliamentary democracy with a strong but indirectly elected president. After the calamities of the last decade, the constitutional government has almost ceased to exist. The parliament is elected, although the last general election was in 1972. Palestinians, local militias, Syrian and Israeli forces have erased national sovereignty in much of the country. Subnationalities: Leading administrative and parliamentary officials are allocated among the several religious or communal groups by complicated formulas. These groups have for years existed semi-autonomously within the state, although their territories are often intermixed.

Civil Liberties. Renowned for its independence, the press still offers a highly diverse selection to an attentive audience. Most censorship is now self-imposed, reflecting the views of locally dominant military forces. Radio is government and party; television is part government and now officially uncensored. Widespread killing in recent years has inhibited the nationwide expression of most freedoms and tightened communal controls on individuals. In many areas the courts cannot function effectively, but within its power the government secures most private rights. Few if any pri-

341

soners of conscience are detained by the government. Unions are government-supervised and subsidized, but have become increasingly active in the cause of peace. Government seldom intervenes in the predominantly service-oriented economy. There is an active human rights organization.

Comparatively: Lebanon is as free as Haiti, freer than Syria, less free than Jordan.

L E S O T H O

Economy: noninclusive capitalist
Polity: military nonparty
Population: 1,600,000

Political Rights: 5
Civil Liberties: 6
Status: partly free

A relatively homogeneous population

Political Rights. After an early 1986 coup, Lesotho has been ruled by a military leader with the apparent endorsement of the king. There is some local government, and the chiefs retain limited power at this level. Although there are frequent expressions of national independence, the country remains under considerable South African economic and political pressure. Lesotho is populated almost exclusively by Basotho people, and the land has never been alienated. A large percentage of the male citizenry works in South Africa.

Civil Liberties. The media are government and church; criticism is dangerous and muted. Political activity or assembly is repressed, but not eliminated; some members of the previous government have been detained—or killed under mysterious circumstances. The judiciary preserves considerable independence vis-a-vis the government: one can win against the government in political cases. Limited union activity is permitted; some strikes have occurred. Most private rights are respected, but political opponents may be denied foreign travel.

Comparatively: Lesotho is as free as South Africa, freer than Angola, less free than Madagascar.

L I B E R I A

Economy: noninclusive capitalist
Polity: dominant party
(military dominated)
Population: 2,400,000

Political Rights: 5
Civil Liberties: 5

Status: partly free

A transethnic heterogeneous state

Political Rights. Liberia's election of president and assembly in 1985 was marred by the exclusion of important candidates and parties from the process. Credible accusation of falsification led to an attempted coup in the aftermath and the subsequent detention of opposition leaders. However, opposition parties continue to operate in and out of parliament, and parliament has successfully opposed government bills. There is some traditional local government.

Civil Liberties. The press is private, exercises self-censorship, but represents a variety of positions. Papers may be suspended or closed. Radio and television are largely government controlled. Lack of legal protection continues to characterize the country; anarchical conditions are common. Executions, coups, and accusations of coups are frequent. Disappearances and torture are reported. Prisoners of conscience are detained. Travel and other private rights are generally respected. Only blacks can become citizens. Religion is free. Union organization is partly free; illegal strikes have occurred, often without government interference. Most industry is government or foreign owned.

Comparatively: Liberia is as free as Sierra Leone, freer than Togo, less free than Senegal.

L I B Y A

Economy: mixed socialist
Polity: socialist quasi one-party
(military dominated)
Population: 3,800,000

Political Rights: 6
Civil Liberties: 6

Status: not free

A relatively homogeneous state

343

Political Rights. Libya is a military dictatorship effectively under the control of one person. Although officially there is no party, the effort to mobilize and organize the entire population for state purposes follows the socialist one-party model. The place of a legislature is taken by the direct democracy of large congresses. Elections held at local levels reflect local interests and are relatively fair; some have been nullified by the central government on the basis that they too closely reflected "outworn" tribal loyalties. Whatever the form, no opposition is allowed on the larger questions of society. Institutional self-management has been widely introduced in the schools, hospitals, and factories. Sometimes the system works well enough to provide a meaningful degree of decentralized self-determination.

Civil Liberties. The media are government-controlled means for active indoctrination. Political discussion at local and private levels may be relatively open. There are many political prisoners; the use of military and people's courts for political cases suggests little respect for the rule of law, yet acquittals in political cases occur. All lawyers must work for the state. Torture and mistreatment are frequent; executions for crimes of conscience occur—even in foreign countries through assassination. Although ideologically socialist some of the press remains in private hands. Oil and oil-related industries are the major areas of government enterprise. Socialization tends to be announced at the top and imposed rather anarchically and sporadically at the bottom. Most private associations and trade organizations are being integrated into or replaced by state organizations. Employment is increasingly dependent on political loyalty. Respect for Islam provides some check on arbitrary government.

Comparatively: Libya is as free as Rwanda, freer than Afghanistan, less free than Tunisia.

L U X E M B O U R G

Economy: capitalist
Polity: centralized multiparty
Population: 366,000

Political Rights: 1
Civil Liberties: 1
Status: free

A relatively homogeneous state

Political Rights. Luxembourg is a constitutional monarchy on the Belgian model, in which the monarchy is somewhat more powerful than in the United Kingdom or Scandinavia. The legislature is bicameral with the appointive upper house having only a delaying function. Recent votes have resulted in important shifts in the nature of the dominant coalition.

Civil Liberties. The media are private and free. The rule of law is thoroughly accepted in both public and private realms. Rights of assembly, organization, travel, property, and religion are protected.

Comparatively. Luxembourg is as free as Iceland, freer than France.

M A D A G A S C A R

Economy: noninclusive mixed socialist

Polity: dominant party (military dominated)

Population: 10,600,000

Political Rights: 5

Civil Liberties: 5

Status: partly free

A transethnic heterogeneous state

Political Rights. Madagascar is essentially a military dictatorship with a very weak legislature. Legislative elections have been restricted to candidates selected by the former political parties on the left grouped in a "national front"; resulting parliaments have played a small part in government. The presidential election in late 1982 allowed vigorous opposition. Although the opposition candidate was later arrested, he subsequently won a seat in the 1983 parliamentary elections. Emphasis has been put on developing the autonomy of local Malagasy governmental institutions. The restriction of local elections to approved "front" candidates belies this emphasis, but contests are genuine. 1987 saw a breakup of the national front—with unpredictable consequences. Opposition party organization remains vigorous. Although tribal rivalries are very important, all groups speak the same language.

Civil Liberties. There is a private press, but papers are carefully censored and may be suspended. Broadcasting is government controlled. Movie theaters have been nationalized. There is no right of assembly; still, election processes allow periods of intense criticism, and vocal, organized opposition persists. There are few long-term prisoners of conscience; short-term political detentions are common, often combined with ill-treatment. The rule of law is weak, but political prisoners may be acquitted. Labor unions are not strong and most are party-affiliated. Religion is free, and most private rights are respected. Public security is very weak. Overseas travel is restricted. While still encouraging private investment, most businesses and large farms are nationalized. Corruption is widespread.

Comparatively: Madagascar is as free as Liberia, freer than Mozambique, less free than Morocco.

M A L A W I

Economy: noninclusive capitalist
Polity: nationalist one-party
Population: 7,400,000

Political Rights: 6
Civil Liberties: 7
Status: not free

A transethnic heterogeneous state

Political Rights. Malawi is a one-man dictatorship with party and parliamentary forms. Elections allow some choice among individuals. Administration is centralized, but there are both traditional and modern local governments.

Civil Liberties. The private and religious press is under strict government control, as is the government-owned radio service. Even private criticism of the administration remains dangerous. Foreign publications are carefully screened. The country has been notable for the persecution of political opponents, including execution and torture. There are prisoners of conscience, and even slight criticism can lead to severe penalties. Asians suffer discrimination. Corruption and economic inequality are characteristic. The comparatively limited interests of the government offer considerable scope for individual rights. There is some protection by law in the modernized sector. Small-scale subsistence farming is dominant, with much of the labor force employed in southern Africa.

Comparatively: Malawi is as free as Burkino Faso, freer than Somalia, less free than Zambia.

MALAYSIA

Economy: capitalist
Polity: decentralized
     dominant-party
Population: 16,100,000

Political Rights: 3
Civil Liberties: 5

Status: partly free

An ethnic state with major nonterritorial subnationalities

Political Rights. Malaysia is a parliamentary democracy with a weak, indirectly elected and appointed senate and a powerful lower house. The relatively powerless head of state is a monarch; the position rotates among the traditional monarchs of the constituent states. A multinational front has dominated electoral and parliamentary politics. By such devices as imprisonment, the banning of demonstrations, and very short campaigns, the opposition is not given an equal opportunity to compete in elections. However, the ruling front incorporates a variety of parties and interests. For example, in 1985-86 a regional opposition party won its state elections. It was eventually allowed both to rule in the state and to displace the former ruling party in the front. The states of Malaysia have their own rulers, parliaments, and institutions, but it is doubtful if any state has the power to leave the federation. Elected local governments have limited power. Subnationalities: Political, economic, linguistic, and educational policies have favored the Malays (forty-four percent) over the Chinese (thirty-six percent), Indians (ten percent), and others. Malays dominate the army. Traditionally the Chinese had been the wealthier and better-educated people. Although there are Chinese in the ruling front, they are not allowed to question the policy of communal preference. Increasingly, Chinese voters are voting for the opposition.

Civil Liberties. The press is private and highly varied. However, nothing that might affect communal relations negatively can be printed, and editors are constrained to follow government advice on many issues by the need to renew their publishing licenses annually. "Undesirable" publications, defined in the broadest terms, may not be printed or distributed. Foreign journalists are closely controlled. Radio is mostly government owned, television entirely so: both present primarily the government's viewpoint. Academics are restrained from discussing sensitive issues. In many areas discrimination against non-Malays is official policy. The atmosphere of fear in academic, opposition, and minority political circles worsened in late 1987 when over 90 political and intellectual leaders were arrested on vague charges of fomenting disorder. These joined, at least briefly, the three hundred political suspects that had been detained without trial for years, generally on suspicion of communist activity. Some are clearly prisoners of conscience; several have held responsible political positions. Confessions are often forcibly extracted. Nevertheless, significant criticism appears in the media and in parliament. The government regularly interferes with Muslim religious expression, restricting both those too modernist and too fundamentalist. Christians cannot proselytize. Chinese must convert to Islam before marrying a Muslim. Unions are permitted to strike and have successfully opposed restrictive legislation. Although the government has begun to assume control of strategic sectors of the economy, economic activity is generally free, except for government favoritism to the Malays.

Comparatively: Malaysia is as free as Mexico, freer than Indonesia, less free than India.

M A L D I V E S

Economy: noninclusive capitalist
Polity: traditional nonparty
Population: 190,000

Political Rights: 5
Civil Liberties: 6
Status: partly free

A relatively homogeneous population

Political Rights. The Maldives have a parliamentary government in which a president (elected by parliament and confirmed by the people) is predominant. The elected parliament has gained some freedom of discussion. Regional leaders are presidentially appointed, but there are elected councils. Both economic and political power are concentrated in the hands of a very small, wealthy elite. Islam places a check on absolutism.

Civil Liberties. Newspapers are private, but writers are subject to prosecution for expressing even modest criticism. The radio station is owned by the government. Foreign publications are received; political discussion is limited. Several persons have been arrested for their political associations since a coup attempt. The legal system is based on traditional Islamic law. There is no freedom of religion. No unions have been formed. Most of the people rely on a subsistence economy; the small elite has developed commercial fishing and tourism.

Comparatively: Maldives is as free as Brunei, freer than Seychelles, less free than Mauritius.

M A L I

Economy: noninclusive mixed socialist	Political Rights: 7
Polity: nationalist one-party (military dominated)	Civil Liberties: 6
Population: 8,400,000	Status: not free

A transethnic heterogeneous state

Political Rights. Mali is a military dictatorship with a recently constructed political party to lend support. The regime appears to function without broad popular consensus. Assembly and presidential elections allow no choice, though there is some at the local level. Military officers have a direct role in the assembly. Subnationalities: Although the government is ostensibly transethnic, repression of northern peoples has been reported.

Civil Liberties. The media are nearly all government owned and closely controlled. Antigovernment demonstrations are forbidden. Private conversation is relatively free, and foreign publications enter freely. There are prisoners of conscience, and reeducation centers are brutal. Student protests are controlled by conscription and detention. Religion is free; unions are controlled; travelers must submit to frequent police checks. There have been reports of slavery and forced labor. Private economic rights in the modern sector are minimal, but collectivization has recently been deemphasized for subsistence agriculturists—the majority of the people. Corruption, particularly in state enterprises, is widespread and costly.

Comparatively: Mali is as free as Ghana, freer than Burundi, less free than Liberia.

M A L T A

Economy: mixed capitalist-statist
Polity: centralized multiparty
Population: 350,000 (est.)

Political Rights: 1
Civil Liberties: 2
Status: free

A relatively homogeneous population

Political Rights. Malta is a parliamentary democracy in which power alternates between the two major parties. There is little local government. A major party agreement and subsequent election in 1987 established the power of the majority to rule, but also introduced an element of broad consensus into major decisions.

Civil Liberties: The press is free and highly partisan. Radio and television are government controlled. In an often enflamed and partisan atmosphere, individuals are likely to have felt constrained by those about them. Rights to assembly and organization are fully respected. Rights to personal and religious freedom now appear fully guaranteed. The unions are free and diverse.

Comparatively: Malta is as free as France, freer than Turkey, less free than Italy.

M A U R I T A N I A

Economy: noninclusive
capitalist-statist

Polity: military nonparty

Population: 1,900,000

Political Rights: 6

Civil Liberties: 6

Status: not free

An ethnic state with a major territorial subnationality

Political Rights. Mauritania has been ruled by a succession of military leaders without formal popular or traditional legitimation. Local elections provide an authentic competitive opportunity for a variety of political groupings. Subnationalities: There is a subnational movement, in the non-Arab, southern part of the country.

Civil Liberties. The media are government owned and censored, but foreign publications and broadcasts are freely available. There are few if any long-term prisoners of conscience. Arrests are common, particularly for voicing opposition to Arabicization. Conversation is free; no ideology is imposed, but no opposition organizations or assemblies are allowed. Travel may be restricted for political reasons. Internal exile has been imposed on some former officials. Union activity is government controlled. There is religious freedom within the limits of an Islamic country. The government controls much of industry and mining, as well as wholesale trade, but there have been recent moves to reduce government involvement. The large rural sector remains under tribal or family control. Only in 1980 was there a move to abolish slavery.

Comparatively: Mauritania is as free as Tanzania, freer than Niger, less free than Kuwait.

M A U R I T I U S

Economy: capitalist

Polity: centralized multiparty

Population: 1,100,000

Political Rights: 2

Civil Liberties: 2

Status: free

An ethnically complex state

351

Political Rights. Mauritius is a parliamentary democracy. Recent elections have shifted control from one party to another. However, the weakness of parties and political allegiances inhibits the development of stable and thoroughly legitimate government. A variety of different racial and religious communities are active in politics. There are guarantees in the electoral system to make sure no major group is unrepresented in parliament. Elected local governing bodies are important.

Civil Liberties. The press is private or party, pluralistic and uncensored. Nevertheless, there has been a struggle between journalists and the government over the imposition of restrictions, and rights of reply on television. Broadcasting is government owned; opposition views are aired. Opposition parties campaign freely and most rights are guaranteed under a rule of law. The security services have been accused of violating the privacy of dissenters. The labor union movement is quite strong, as are a variety of communal organizations. Strikes are common, but restrictive laws make most strikes both illegal and costly to the participants. There is religious and economic freedom; social services are financed through relatively high taxes.

Comparatively: Mauritius is as free as Papua New Guinea, freer than Honduras, less free than Portugal.

M E X I C O

Economy: capitalist-statist
Polity: decentralized
    dominant-party
Population: 81,900,000

Political Rights: 4
Civil Liberties: 4

Status: partly free

An ethnic state with potential subnationalities

Political Rights. Mexico is ruled by a governmental system formally modeled on that of the United States; in practice the president is much stronger and the legislative and judicial branches much weaker. The states have independent governors and legislatures, as do local municipalities. The ruling party has had a near monopoly of power on all levels since the 1920s. Political competition has been largely confined to factional struggles within the ruling party. Party conventions are controlled from the top down. Progress in opening the system to other parties has been reflected in recent elections, but 1985 elections were marred by irregularities. Plausible accusations include adding fictitious names, stuffing the ballot boxes, excluding opposition observers, and fraudulent counting. Government pressure on the bureaucracy and media for support is overwhelming. The clergy are not allowed to participate in the political process. Subnationalities: There is a large Mayan area in Yucatan that has formerly been restive; there are also other smaller Indian areas.

Civil Liberties. The media are mostly private, but operate under a variety of direct and indirect government controls (including subsidies and take-overs). Free of overt censorship, papers are subject to government "guidance." Literature and the arts are free. The judicial system is not strong. However, decisions can go against the government; it is possible to win a judicial decision that a law is unconstitutional in a particular application. Religion is free. Widespread bribery and lack of control over the behavior of security forces greatly limits freedom, especially in rural areas. Disappearances occur, detention is prolonged, torture and brutality have been common. Private economic rights are respected; government ownership predominates in major industries, graft is legendary. Access to land continues to be a problem despite reform efforts. Nearly all labor unions are associated with the ruling party. Their purpose is as much to control workers for the system as to represent them. There is a right to strike. Some union and student activity has been repressed. Critical human rights organizations exist.

Comparatively: Mexico is as free as Suriname, freer than Nicaragua, less free than Colombia.

M O N G O L I A

Economy: socialist
Polity: communist one-party
Population: 1,900,000

Political Rights: 7
Civil Liberties: 7
Status: not free

A relatively homogeneous population

Political Rights. A one-party communist dictatorship, Mongolia has recently experienced a change of leader through a mysterious politburo shift of power. Power is organized at all levels through the party apparatus. Those who oppose the government cannot run for office. Parliamentary elections offer no choice and result in 99.9% victories. Mongolia has a subordinate relationship to the Soviet Union; 25,000 Soviet troops are maintained in the country. It must use the USSR as an outlet for nearly all of its trade, and its finances are under close Soviet supervision.

Civil Liberties. All media are government controlled. Religion is restricted; Lamaism is nearly wiped out. Freedom of travel, residence, and other civil liberties are denied. As in many communist countries, all typewriting and duplicating machines must be registered annually. Employment is assigned; workers committees are extensions of the party.

Comparatively. Mongolia is as free as Bulgaria, less free than China (Mainland).

M O R O C C O

Economy: noninclusive capitalist-statist

Polity: centralized multiparty

Population: 24,400,000

Political Rights: 4

Civil Liberties: 5

Status: partly free

An ethnic state with active and potential subnationalities

Political Rights. Morocco is a constitutional monarchy in which the king has retained major executive powers. Parliament is active and competitive, but not powerful. Referendums have been used to support the king's policies. Recent elections at both local and national levels have been well contested. Many parties participated; the moderate center was the chief victor. The autonomy of local and regional elected governments is limited.

Subnationalities. Although people in the newly acquired land of the Western Sahara participate in the electoral process, it has an important resistance movement—mostly in exile. In the rest of the country the large Berber minority is a subnationality whose self-expression is restricted.

Civil Liberties. Newspapers are private or party, and quite diverse. Recently there has been no formal censorship, but government guidance is common, and backed up with the confiscation of particular issues and the closing of publications. Monarchical power must not be criticized. Broadcasting stations are under government control, although they have recently been opened to the parties for campaign statements. In the past the use of torture has been quite common and may continue; the rule of law has also been weakened by the frequent use of prolonged detention without trial. There are many political prisoners; some are prisoners of conscience. Private organizational activity is vigorous and includes student, party, business, farmer, and human rights groups. There are strong independent labor unions in all sectors; religious and other private rights are respected. State intervention in the economy is increasing, particularly in agriculture and foreign trade.

Comparatively: Morocco is as free as Sudan, freer than Algeria, less free than Spain.

M O Z A M B I Q U E

Economy: noninclusive socialist
Polity: socialist one-party
Population: 14,000,000 (est.)

Political Rights: 6
Civil Liberties: 7
Status: not free

A transethnic heterogeneous state

Political Rights. Mozambique is a one-party communist dictatorship in which all power resides in the "vanguard party." All candidates are selected by the party at all levels, but there is some popular control of selection at local levels. Discussion in party congresses and other meetings can be quite critical. Regional administration is controlled from the center. Southerners and non-Africans dominate the government. Much of the country is under guerrilla control.

Civil Liberties. All media are rigidly controlled. Rights of assembly and foreign travel do not exist. There are no private lawyers. Secret police are powerful; thousands are in reeducation camps, and executions occur. Police brutality is common. Unions

355

are prohibited. Pressure has been put on several religious groups, especially the Catholic clergy and Jehovah's Witnesses, although there has been some recent relaxation. Villagers are being forced into communes, leading to revolts in some areas. However, the socialization of private entrepreneurs has been partially reversed. The emigration of citizens is restricted, although seasonal movement of workers across borders is unrecorded.

Comparatively: Mozambique is as free as Malawi, freer than Equatorial Guinea, less free than Gabon.

N A U R U

Economy: mixed capitalist-statist
Polity: traditional nonparty
Population: 8,400

Political Rights: 2
Civil Liberties: 2
Status: free

An ethnically complex state

Political Rights. Nauru is a parliamentary democracy in which governments change by elective and parliamentary means. All MP's have been elected as independents, although parties are forming. The country is under Australian influence.

Civil Liberties. The media are free of censorship but little developed. The island's major industry is controlled by the government under a complex system of royalties and profit-sharing. No taxes are levied; phosphate revenues finance a wide range of social services. The major cooperative and union are independent.

Comparatively: Nauru is as free as Mauritius, freer than Tonga, less free than New Zealand.

N E P A L

Economy: noninclusive capitalist
Polity: traditional nonparty
Population: 17,800,000

Political Rights: 3
Civil Liberties: 4
Status: partly free

An ethnic state with active and potential subnationalities

Political Rights. Nepal is a constitutional monarchy in which the king is dominant. A relatively free referendum held in 1980 rejected a move toward party government, but the new constitution opened the system to direct elections for most members of parliament. Although neither king nor government determines who is elected, the king appoints many MPs. Although parliament acts independently, and is able to change governments, as in Morocco the king has almost unlimited power to make final decisions. Recently, local elections have gained in significance.

Subnationalities. There are a variety of different peoples, with only fifty percent of the people speaking Nepali as their first language. Hinduism is a unifying force for the majority. Historically powerful Hindu castes continue to dominate.

Civil Liberties. Principal newspapers are public and print only what the government wishes; private journals carry criticism of the government but not the king. Some offending publications have been suspended in the recent past. Radio is government owned. Private contacts are relatively open. Political detention is common, sometimes probably for little more than expression of opinion. Parties are banned as the result of the referendum, but human rights organizations function. Union organization is under government control. The judiciary is not independent. Religious proselytizing and conversion is prohibited, and the emigration of those with valuable skills or education is restricted. The population is nearly all engaged in traditional occupations; sharecropping and tenant farming is common. Illiteracy levels are very high.

Comparatively: Nepal is as free as Sri Lanka, freer than Bhutan, less free than Thailand.

NETHERLANDS

Economy: mixed capitalist
Polity: centralized multiparty
Population: 14,600,000

Political Rights: 1
Civil Liberties: 1
Status: free

A relatively homogeneous population

Political Rights. Netherlands is a constitutional monarchy in which nearly all the power is vested in a directly elected legislature. The results of elections have periodically transferred power to coalitions of the left and right. There is some diffusion of political power below this level, but not a great deal. The monarch retains more power than in the United Kingdom through the activity of appointing governments in frequently stalemated situations, and through the advisory Council of State.

Civil Liberties. The press is free and private. Radio and television are provided by private associations under state ownership. Commercial services have been introduced. A wide range of views is broadcast. The courts are independent, and the full spectrum of private rights guaranteed. Non-European immigrants are not well accepted by the society. The burden of exceptionally heavy taxes limits some economic choice, but benefits offer the opportunity to choose not to work.

Comparatively: The Netherlands is as free as Belgium, freer than Portugal.

NEW ZEALAND

Economy: capitalist
Polity: centralized multiparty
Population: 3,300,000

Political Rights: 1
Civil Liberties: 1
Status: free

A relatively homogeneous state with a native subnationality

Political Liberties. New Zealand is a parliamentary democracy in which power alternates between the two major parties. There is elected local government, but it is not independently powerful. Subnationalities: About ten percent of the population are Maori, the original inhabitants. Their rights are now a growing concern; the seriousness with which they are taken is suggested by the growing impediment to development presented by Maori land claims.

Civil Liberties. The press is private and free. Television and most radio stations are government owned, but without reducing their independence significantly. The rule of law and private rights are thoroughly respected. Since taxes (a direct restriction on choice) are not exceptionally high, and industry is not government owned, we label New Zealand capitalist. Others, emphasizing the government's highly developed social programs and penchant for controlling prices, wages, and credit, might place New Zealand further toward the socialist end of the economic spectrum.

Comparatively: New Zealand is as free as the United States, freer than Argentina.

N I C A R A G U A

Economy: mixed capitalist	Political Rights: 5
Polity: dominant-party	Civil Liberties: 5
Population: 3,400,000	Status: partly free

A relatively homogeneous population

Political Rights. Government is in the hands of the Sandinista political-military movement. Major opposition parties chose not to participate in the November 1984 elections, because of Sandinista controls on the media and harassment of the opposition campaigns. Detailed Sandinista controls over livelihood makes a free vote impossible. Still, there is a small, legal, elected opposition in the legislature. The legislature has little significance in the political system; in the Marxist-Leninist style, the government is controlled by the Party rather than the legislature. Subnationalities: Miskito and related Indian groups struggle for greater autonomy with limited success.

Civil Liberties. Most newspapers and radio stations are under direct or indirect government control; private television is not allowed. However, a major opposition newspaper and a religious radio station have been reopened—the latter with only limited freedom. Government gangs regularly break up opposition rallies. Political activity by parties outside the Sandinista movement is restricted. Recent releases of political prisoners may still leave hundreds or thousands incarcerated. Neighborhood watch committees have been established. Killing and intimidation occur, especially in rural areas. Thousand of disappearances have been reported. The independence of the judiciary is not well developed, although the government does not always win in court. A parallel judiciary has constricted the rule of law. Foreign travel is restricted for some political opponents. Internal travel is restricted in much of the country. Nongovernment labor unions are restricted. A private human rights organization is active, but its publications have been censored and then suspended. The Catholic Church retains its critical independence, as do many individuals and small groups. Some enterprises and farms have been national-ized; much of the economy remains formally private, though supplies must generally be bought from, and products sold to, the government.

Comparatively: Nicaragua is as free as Liberia, freer than Cuba, less free than El Salvador.

NIGER

Economy: noninclusive capitalist
Polity: military nonparty
Population: 7,000,000

Political Rights: 7
Civil Liberties: 6
Status: not free

A transethnic heterogeneous state

Political Rights. Niger is a military dictatorship with no elected assembly or legal parties. New institutions were approved in an unopposed referendum in 1987, but at last report they had not been implemented. All districts are administered from the center.

Civil Liberties. Niger's very limited media are government owned and operated, and are used to mobilize the population. Dis-sent is seldom tolerated, although ideological conformity is not demanded, and foreign publications are available. There is little overt censorship, but also no barrier to censorship. A military court has taken the place of a suspended Supreme Court; a few political prisoners are held under severe conditions. Unions and religious organizations are relatively independent but nonpolitical. Foreign travel is relatively open; outside of politics the government does not regulate individual behavior. The economy is largely subsistence farming based on communal tenure; direct taxes on the poor have been abolished; agriculture has been honestly supported.

Comparatively: Niger is as free as Mali, freer than North Korea, less free than Mauritania.

N I G E R I A

Economy: capitalist-statist
Polity: military nonparty
Population: 108,000,000 (est.)

Political Rights: 6
Civil Liberties: 5
Status: partly free

A multinational state

Political Rights. After successive coups, Nigeria is under the direct rule of the military. The full spectrum of political positions has been replaced by the military command. However, a complex plan to return the country to democracy has been widely accepted in this relatively open and consensual society. Local elections are to be held in December, 1987. Subnationalities: Nigeria is made up of a number of powerful subnational groupings. The numerical dominance of Muslims, and agitation for an Islamic state, makes full majoritarian democracy unattractive to many non-Muslims. Speaking mainly Hausa, the people of the north are Muslim. The highly urbanized southwest is dominated by the Yoruba; and the east by the Ibo. Within each of these areas and along their borders there are other peoples, some of which are conscious of their identity and number more than one million persons. Strong loyalties to traditional political units—lineages or kingdoms—throughout the country further complicate the regional picture.

Civil Liberties. The status of civil liberties remains in flux. Television and radio are now wholly federal or state owned, as are all but two of the major papers, in part as the result of a Nigerianization program. Still, the media have limited editorial independence, and, between clampdowns, express diverse and critical opinions. Political organization, assembly, and publication are largely eliminated. The universities, secondary schools, and trade unions are under close government control or reorganization in the last few years. The national student association has been banned. The courts have demonstrated their independence on occasion. Police are often brutal, and military riot control has led to many deaths. There is freedom of religion and travel, but rights of

361

married women are quite restricted. The country is in the process of moving from a subsistence to industrial economy—largely on the basis of government-controlled oil and oil-related industry. Government intervention elsewhere in agriculture (cooperatives and plantations) and industry has been considerable. Since private business and industry are also encouraged, this is still far from a program of massive redistribution. General corruption in political and economic life has frequently diminished the rule of law. Freedom is respected in most other areas of life.

Comparatively: Nigeria is as free as Cote d'Ivoire, freer than Benin, less free than Sierra Leone.

N O R W A Y

Economy: mixed capitalist
Polity: centralized multiparty
Population: 4,200,000

Political Rights: 1
Civil Liberties: 1
Status: free

A relatively homogeneous population with a small Lapp minority

Political Rights. Norway is a centralized, constitutional monarchy. Labor remains the strongest party, but other parties have formed several governments since the mid-1960s. Norway appears to lead the world in the acceptance of women in high government position. There is relatively little separation of powers. Regional governments have appointed governors, and cities and towns their own elected officials.

Civil Liberties. Newspapers are privately or party owned; radio and television are state monopolies, but are not used for propaganda. This is a pluralistic state with independent power in the churches and labor unions. Relatively strong family structures have also been preserved. Norway is capitalistic, yet the government's control over the new oil resource and general reliance on centralized economic plans reduce the freedom of economic activity. Wages are equalized to an unusual degree; private hospitals are all but forbidden.

Comparatively: Norway is as free as the United Kingdom, freer than West Germany.

O M A N

Economy: noninclusive
    capitalist-statist
Polity: centralized nonparty
Population: 1,200,000 (est.)

Political Rights: 6

Civil Liberties: 6

Status: not free

An ethnic state with a territorial subnationality

Political Rights. Oman is an absolute monarchy with no political parties or elected assemblies. There is an appointed consultative assembly. Regional rule is by centrally appointed governors, but the remaining tribal structure at the local and regional level gives a measure of local autonomy. British influence remains strong. Subnationalities: The people of Dhofar constitute a small regional subnationality.

Civil Liberties. Broadcasting is government owned; the daily papers are government owned, weeklies are subsidized. There is little or no criticism. Foreign publications are censored regularly. Although the preservation of traditional institutions provides a check on arbitrary action, the right to a fair trial is not guaranteed in political cases. Freedom of assembly is curtailed, and there are no independent unions. With all this, there are few if any prisoners of conscience. Travel is not restricted; private property is respected. Proselytizing for non-Muslim faiths is illegal. The population is largely involved in subsistence agriculture.

Comparatively: Oman is as free as Algeria, freer than Saudi Arabia, less free than the United Arab Emirates.

P A K I S T A N

Economy: noninclusive
    capitalist-statist
Polity: quasi-multiparty
    (military dominated)
Population: 104,000,000

Political Rights: 4

Civil Liberties: 5

Status: partly free

A multinational state

Political Rights. Pakistan is under mixed military and civilian rule. A December 1984 referendum on the President's rule and Islam was a farce—it was almost impossible to vote against it. However, in 1985 nonparty assembly elections created a parliament that has increasingly shown its independence. Although the established political parties did not compete, many of their individual members did. Campaigning for a boycott was illegal. Local elections of increasing significance have been held. Military officers have positions throughout the bureaucracy and private industry.

Subnationalities. Millions of Pathans, Baluch, and Sindis have a long record of struggle for greater regional autonomy or independence. Provincial organization has sporadically offered a measure of self-determination, but at least the Baluch and Sindis continue to feel oppressed.

Civil Liberties. Newspapers are censored; the frequent detention of journalists and closing of papers lead to self-censorship. Radio and television are government controlled; movies are closely controlled for political content. For ordinary crimes punishments are often severe; torture is alleged, and executions have been common. Thousands of members of the opposition have been imprisoned or flogged in the violent political climate. Although political party activity is again legal, and pro- and anti-government parties are very active, rights of assembly are limited, as well as travel for political persons. Courts preserve some independence. Union activity is restricted but strikes and demonstrations occur; student unions are banned. Emphasis on Islamic conservatism curtails private rights, especially freedom of religion and women's rights: religious minorities suffer discrimination. Prayer wardens attempt to ensure general observance of five prayers a day. Teaching must conform to Islam. Private property is respected; some basic industries have been nationalized. Over half the rural population consists of sharecroppers and tenant farmers.

Comparatively: Pakistan is as free as Bangladesh, freer than Iran, less free than India.

P A N A M A

Economy: capitalist-statist
Polity: centralized multiparty
(military dominated)
Population: 2,300,000

Political Rights: 5
Civil Liberties: 5

Status: partly free

A relatively homogeneous population with small subnationalities

Political Rights. Panama is formally organized as a democracy on the American model. The 1984 election that was to return power to a civilian government was influenced by the military. In 1985 the military forced the resignation of the president they had chosen, replacing him with the relatively unknown vice-president. In most respects the legislature and civilian government continues to function. The provinces are administered by presidential appointees, with elected councils; there is considerable local power in Indian areas.

Civil Liberties. The major opposition paper closed in 1987; censorship and self-censorship greatly restricts all other media. Through regulation, sanctions, threats, and special arrangements, the government ensures a preponderance of pro-government reporting. Occasional opposition announcements or publications appear—including those of the church. In 1987 political activities and demonstrations were restricted in an atmosphere of confrontation between the civilian opposition and often violent security forces. Detentions are frequent, but generally last for only a few days. The judiciary is not independent; the rule of law is weak in both political and nonpolitical areas. There are few if any prisoners of conscience, but individuals dangerous to the military's interests may be eliminated. Labor unions are under some restrictions. There is freedom of religion, although foreign priests are not allowed. In general, travel is free and private property respected. Major firms are state owned; land reform has been largely ineffective in reducing inequities in land ownership.

Comparatively: Panama is as free as Guyana, freer than Brunei, less free than Colombia.

P A P U A   N E W   G U I N E A

Economy: noninclusive capitalist
Polity: decentralized multiparty
Population: 3,600,000

Political Rights: 2
Civil Liberties: 2
Status: free

A transethnic heterogeneous state with many subnationalities

Political Rights. Papua New Guinea is an independent parliamentary democracy, although it remains partially dependent on Australia economically, technically, and militarily. In spite of many irregularities, elections are broadly fair and seats are divided among a number of major and minor parties. With a very large number of candidates in many single-member districts, some candidates are elected with less than 10% of the vote. Since party allegiances are still fluid, there is considerable party-switching after elections. Parties are weakened by the overwhelming desire of politicians for government positions and their perquisites. Because of its dispersed and tribal nature, local government is in some ways quite decentralized. Elected provincial governments with extensive powers have been established, but only a few have firm public support. Subnationalities: The nation is being created from an amalgam of small tribal peoples with similar racial and cultural backgrounds. Development of provincial governments has quieted secessionist sentiments in Bougainville, Papua, and elsewhere.

Civil Liberties. The press is free, but not highly developed. Radio is government controlled but presents critical views; Australian stations are also received. There are no political prisoners. Rights to travel, organize, demonstrate, and practice religion are secure. The legal system adapted from Australia is operational, but a large proportion of the population lives in a preindustrial world with traditional controls, including violence, that limit freedom of speech, travel, occupation, and other private rights. In the cities wide disparities in income and violent crime are major social issues; in the country, continued tribal warfare. Land ownership is widely distributed.

Comparatively: Papua New Guinea is as free as Philippines, freer than Vanuatu, less free than Australia.

PARAGUAY

Economy: noninclusive capitalist-statist	Political Rights: 5
Polity: centralized dominant-party (military dominated)	Civil Liberties: 6
Population: 4,300,000	Status: partly free

A relatively homogeneous state with small Indian groups

Political Rights. Paraguay has been ruled as a modified dictatorship since 1954. In addition to an elected president, there is a parliament that includes members of opposition parties. Presidential election results determine parliamentary representation. Elections are regularly held, but they have limited meaning: the ruling party receives about ninety percent of the vote, a result guaranteed by direct and indirect pressures on the media, massive government pressure on voters, especially in the countryside, interference with opposition party organization, and perhaps electoral fraud. The most important regional and local officials are appointed by the president. Subnationalities: The population represents a mixture of Indian (Guarani) and Spanish peoples; ninety percent continue to speak Guarani as well as Spanish—a bilingualism the government has promoted. Several small tribes of primitive forest people are under heavy pressure from both the government and the public.

Civil Liberties. The government closely controls both press and broadcasting; nongovernmental stations and papers have very limited editorial independence. Dissenting opinion is expressed, especially by the church hierarchy. Opposition political organization continues, as do human rights organizations, but there is open discrimination in favor of members of the ruling party in education, government, business, and other areas. A limited right of assembly and demonstration is exercised. Imprisonment, torture, and execution of political opponents, particularly peasants, have been and, to a limited extent, still are an important part of a sociopolitical situation that includes general corruption and anarchy. Mobs are often used by the government to intimidate the opposition. Political opponents or dissident writers may also be refused passports or exiled. There are now few if any long-term prisoners of conscience, but the rule of law is very weak. Most unions are dominated by the ruling party, but some demonstrate independence. Beyond the subsistence sector, private economic rights are restricted by government intervention, control, and favoritism. A large proportion of peasants work their own land, partly as a result of government land reform.

Comparatively: Paraguay is as free as Kuwait, freer than Cuba, less free than Guatemala.

P E R U

Economy: noninclusive capitalist-statist	Political Rights: 2
Polity: centralized multiparty	Civil Liberties: 3
Population: 20,700,000	Status: free

An ethnic state with a major potential territorial subnationality

Political Rights. Peru is ruled by an elected multiparty par-liamentary system. Won by the opposition, 1985 elections have led to strong assertion of civilian control over security forces. Provincial administration is not independent, but local elections are significant. Subnationalities: Several million people speak Quechua in the highlands, and it is now an official language. There are other important Indian groups.

Civil Liberties. The media are largely private. Censorship has been abolished. Essentially all positions are freely expressed, but there is still the shadow of the military and the recent past. There is little if any imprisonment for conscience, but many are killed or imprisoned in the course of antiguerrilla and antiterrorist campaigns; torture occurs. However, thousands of members of the security forces have been censored or arrested for excesses, and even generals have been held responsible. Periodic states of emergency reduce freedoms, especially in certain areas. Travel is not restrained, and rights to religion and occupation are generally respected. Labor is independent and politically active; strikes are common. The public sector remains dominant; except in banking, private property has regained governmental acceptance.

Comparatively: Peru is as free as Ecuador, freer than Mexico, less free than Venezuela.

P H I L I P P I N E S

Economy: noninclusive
capitalist-statist
Polity: centralized multiparty
Population: 61,500,000 (est.)

Political Rights: 2

Civil Liberties: 2
Status: free

A transethnic heterogeneous state with active and potential subnationalities

Political Rights. In 1987 a constitutional referendum and subsequent legislative elections confirmed the legitimacy of the new presidential system and incumbent. Although there were minor problems in both elections, the results were broadly reflective of popular sentiment. Threats to the system from the armed forces continue, but for now civilian control appears to have been reestablished. Subnationalities: The Philippines includes a variety of different peoples of which the Tagalog speaking are the most important (although a minority). A portion of the Muslim (Moro) subnationality is in active revolt along the front of Christian-Muslim opposition. There are several major potential subnationalities that may request autonomy in the future on the basis of both territorial and linguistic identity.
Civil Liberties. Newspapers and broadcasting are largely private, free, and pluralistic. Diverse foreign publications are available. Radio is free and varied, but television seems to continue under more government influence. Demonstrations by groups from the far right to the far left have been massive. Unions are again developing independence, and strikes occur. Military actions against insurgents have led to many arrests and deaths in a violent atmosphere of struggle with both urban and rural guerrillas. The Catholic Church maintains its independence. The private economy is marginally capitalist, but rapid growth in government intervention, favoritism, and direct ownership of industries by government and government favorites brings the economy closer to capitalist-statist.

Comparatively: Philippines is as free as Uruguay, freer than Singapore, less free than New Zealand.

P O L A N D

Economy: mixed socialist
Polity: communist one-party
    (military dominated)
Population: 37,800,000

Political Rights: 5
Civil Liberties: 5

Status: partly free

A relatively homogeneous population

Political Rights. Poland is a one-party communist and military dictatorship. Assembly elections in 1985 allowed some competition. All candidates must support the system. More generally, in recent years a few nonparty persons have gained election to the assembly, and some sessions have evidenced more than pro forma debate. Remarkably, in 1987 the government allowed itself to be defeated on a major referendum. There are elected councils at provincial levels. Although party and military hierarchies operating from the top down are the loci of power, the Catholic Church, academics, peasants, and workers must be considered by any government. The Soviet Union's claim to a right of interference and continual pressure diminishes Poland's independence.

Civil Liberties. The Polish newspapers are both private and government; broadcasting is government owned. Censorship is pervasive, but legal media have opened their discussion to a wide range of opinions. Underground publication on a massive scale exists in a variety of fields. Private expression is relatively free. Although, there are no formal rights of assembly or organization, the government has accepted tacitly the concept of a legitimate opposition. The courts have also begun to accept the concept of the accountability of government officials to the courts. The Church remains a major independent voice, as do the leaders of the formally disallowed Solidarity. Detention, beating, and harassment are common means of restricting opposition. Illegal attempts to leave Poland have frequently led to arrest, but opponents have been forced into exile. For most people passports are now relatively easy to obtain. Most agriculture and considerable commerce remain in private hands; industry is fully nationalized.

Comparatively: Poland is as free as Panama, freer than Czechoslovakia, less free than Mexico.

P O R T U G A L

Economy: mixed capitalist
Polity: centralized multiparty
Population: 10,300,000

Political Rights: 1
Civil Liberties: 2
Status: free

A relatively homogeneous population

Political Rights. Portugal is a parliamentary democracy with a more powerful president than is common in Europe. There is vigorous party competition over most of the spectrum (except the far right), and fair elections. The overwhelming majority of voters are centrist. Elections are competitive and power is shared by several groups. Provincial government is centrally directed.

Civil Liberties. In spite of government or party ownership of most major papers, journalism is now quite free. Radio and television are government owned, except for one Catholic station. They are both relatively free editorially. The government has restored the rule of law. There are few if any prisoners of conscience, yet one can be imprisoned for insult to the military or government. Long periods of detention without trial occur in isolated instances. Imprisonment for "fascist" organization or discussion was promulgated in 1978. The Catholic Church, unions, peasant organizations, and military services remain alternative institutions of power. Although there is a large nationalized sector, capitalism is the accepted form for much of the economy.

Comparatively: Portugal is as free as France, freer than Brazil, less free than United Kingdom.

Q A T A R

Economy: mixed capitalist-statist
Polity: traditional nonparty
Population: 315,000

Political Rights: 5
Civil Liberties: 5
Status: partly free

A relatively homogeneous citizenry

Political Rights. Qatar is a traditional monarchy. The majority of the residents are recently arrived foreigners; of the native population perhaps one-fourth are members of the ruling family. Open receptions are regularly held for the public to present grievances. Consensus plays an important role in the system.

Civil Liberties. The media are public or subsidized private, and loyalist. Discussion is fairly open; foreign publications are controlled. Political parties are forbidden. This is a traditional state still responsive to Islamic and tribal laws that moderate the absolutism of government. The family government controls the nation's wealth through control over oil, but there are also independently powerful merchant and religious classes. There are no income taxes, and many public services are free. There are no organized unions or strikes. The rights of women and religious minorities are quite limited: only native Muslim males have the full rights of citizens.

Comparatively: Qatar is as free as the United Arab Emirates, freer than Saudi Arabia, less free than Morocco.

R O M A N I A

Economy: socialist
Polity: communist one-party
Population: 22,900,000

Political Rights: 7
Civil Liberties: 7
Status: not free

An ethnic state with territorial subnationalities

Political Rights. Romania is a traditional communist state. Assemblies at national and regional levels are subservient to the party hierarchy. Although the party is not large, all decisions are made by a small elite and especially the dictator. Elections involve only candidates or issues chosen by the party or dictator; for some assembly positions the party may propose several candidates. Soviet influence is relatively slight. Subnationalities: The Magyar and German minorities are territorially based. If offered self-determination, one Magyar area would surely opt for rejoining neighboring Hungary; many of the Germans evidently wish to migrate to Germany, and many have. In Romania the cultural rights of both groups are narrowly limited.

Civil Liberties. The media include only government or party organs; self-censorship committees replace centralized censorship. Private discussion is guarded; police are omnipresent. Dissenters are frequently imprisoned. Forced confessions, false charges, and psychiatric incarceration are characteristic. Treatment may be brutal; physical threats are common. Many arrests have been made for attempting to leave the country or importing foreign literature (especially Bibles and publications in minority languages). Contacts with foreigners must be reported if not given prior approval. Religious and other personal freedoms, such as the right not to have children, are quite restricted. Outside travel and emigration are not considered rights; potential emigrants may suffer economic discrimination, but many have been allowed to leave the country. Private museums have been closed. Independent labor and management rights are essentially nonexistent. Attempts to form a trade union in 1979 were crushed, as was a major coal strike in 1981. Pressure on workers and consumers to provide a greater surplus is heavy. Central planning is pervasive throughout the highly nationalized economy.

Comparatively: Romania is as free as Albania, less free than the USSR.

R W A N D A

Economy: noninclusive mixed
    socialist
Polity: nationalist one-party
    (military dominated)
Population: 6,800,000

Political Rights: 6

Civil Liberties: 6

Status: not free

An ethnic state with a minor nonterritorial subnationality

Political Rights. Rwanda is a military dictatorship with an auxiliary party organization. Elections are not free and candidates are pre-selected, but voters have some choice. Districts are administered by the central government. Everyone must belong to the party, but party elections and deliberations have some competitive and critical aspects. There are elected local councils and officials. Subnationalities: The former ruling people, the Tutsi, have been persecuted and heavily discriminated against, but the situation has improved.

Civil Liberties. The weak media are governmental or religious; Only the mildest criticism is voiced; there is no right of assembly. Political prisoners are held. The courts have some independence. Hundreds of followers of religious sects were sentenced in 1986 for crimes such as failing to salute or to pay mandatory party contributions. Travel is restricted both within the country and across its borders. Labor unions are very weak. There are no great extremes of wealth. The government is socialist in intent, but missionary cooperatives dominate trade, and private business is active in the small nonsubsistence sector. Traditional ways of life rather than government orders regulate the lives of most.

Comparatively: Rwanda is as free as Tanzania, freer than Burundi, less free than Zambia.

S T. K I T T S — N E V I S
(S T. C H R I S T O P H E R   A N D   N E V I S)

Economy: capitalist
Polity: decentralized multiparty
Population: 46,000

Political Rights: 1
Civil Liberties: 2
Status: free

A relatively homogeneous state

Political Rights. St. Kitts-Nevis has a fully functioning parliamentary system in which the smaller Nevis has a relatively large share of power, internal self-government, and an open option to secede. Both unicameral parliaments include several appointed senators.

Civil Liberties. Although television is government owned, the media are free. There is a constitutional rule of law with the full spectrum of democratic rights. However, recently a libel suit and accusation of sedition against a opposition leader raised a question as to the willingness of the government to freely allow the full spectrum of expression.

Comparatively: St. Kitts-Nevis is as free as Costa Rica, freer than Jamaica.

S T. L U C I A

Economy: capitalist   Political Rights: 1
Polity: centralized multiparty   Civil Liberties: 2
Population: 140,000   Status: free

A relatively homogeneous state

Political Rights. This is a functioning parliamentary democracy in which power alternates between parties, most recently in 1982. Elections are extremely close. There are also elected local governments.

Civil Liberties. The papers are largely private or party controlled, and uncensored. Radio is government and private; television private. Organization and assembly are free, but harassment and violence accompany their expression. There are strong business, labor, and religious organizations. Massive strikes played a role in forcing the resignation of the prime minister in early 1982. Personal rights generally are secured, although travel to Libya has been limited for potential dissidents.

Comparatively: St. Lucia is as free as Venezuela, freer than Solomon Islands, less free than the United States.

S T. V I N C E N T A N D T H E G R E N A D I N E S

Economy: capitalist   Political Rights: 1
Polity: centralized multiparty   Civil Liberties: 2
Population: 111,000   Status: free

A relatively homogeneous state

375

Political Rights. St. Vincent is an operating multiparty state. In a 1984 election the ruling party was defeated.

Civil Liberties. Weekly papers present a variety of uncensored opinion, although there may be some government favoritism. Radio is government owned and has been accused of bias. Foreign media are readily available. There is a full right to assembly and organization; effective opposition to government policies is easily organized and often successful. There is a rule of law, but accusations of police brutality. Much of economic activity is based on agriculture.

Comparatively: St. Vincent is as free as Finland, freer than Colombia, less free than Barbados.

SAO TOME AND PRINCIPE

Economy: socialist
Polity: socialist one-party
Population: 110,000

Political Rights: 7
Civil Liberties: 7
Status: not free

A relatively homogeneous population

Political Rights. Sao Tome and Principe are governed under strongman leadership by the revolutionary party that led the country to independence. There is an indirectly elected assembly. Popular dissatisfaction and factional struggles occasionally appear, but no public opposition is allowed. A liberalization of the system is expected in the near future. Local elections allow greater freedom. Angolan and other foreign troops have been used to maintain the regime.

Civil Liberties. The media are government owned and controlled; opposition voices are not heard; there is no effective right of political assembly. Labor unions are not independent. The rule of law does not extend to political questions; persons are detained for expression of wrong opinions; many opponents are in exile. There is little evidence of brutality or torture. Union activity is minimal and controlled. The largely plantation agriculture has been socialized, as has most of the economy. Illiteracy is particularly high.

Comparatively: Sao Tome and Principe appear to be as free as Angola, less free than Comoros.

S A U D I   A R A B I A

Economy: capitalist-statist
Polity: traditional nonparty
Population: 14,000,000 (est.)

Political Rights: 6
Civil Liberties: 7
Status: not free

A relatively homogeneous population

Political Rights. Saudi Arabia is a traditional family monarchy ruling without representative assemblies. Political parties are prohibited. The right of petition is guaranteed, and religious leaders provide a check on arbitrary government. Ten thousand Bangladeshi contract soldiers help support the system. Regional government is by appointive officers; there are some local elective assemblies.

Civil Liberties. The press is both private and governmental; strict self-censorship is expected. Radio and television are mostly government owned, although ARAMCO also has stations. Private conversation is relatively free; there is no right of political assembly or political organization. Islamic law limits arbitrary government, but the rule of law is not fully institutionalized. There are political prisoners, and torture is reported; there may be prisoners of conscience. Citizens have no freeaom of religion—all must be Muslims, and must observe Muslim rites. Strikes and unions are forbidden. Private rights in areas such as occupation or residence are generally respected, but marriage to a non-Muslim or non-Saudi is closely controlled. Women may not marry non-Muslims, and suffer other special disabilities, particularly in the right to travel. The economy is overwhelmingly dominated by petroleum or petroleum-related industry, which is directly or indirectly under government control. The commercial and agricultural sectors are private, but connection to the royal family may be critical for success. Extreme economic inequality is maintained by the political system.

Comparatively: Saudi Arabia is as free as Ethiopia, freer than Iraq, less free than Bahrain.

S E N E G A L

Economy: mixed capitalist	Political Rights: 3
Polity: centralized	Civil Liberties: 4
dominant-party	
Population: 7,100,000	Status: partly free

A transethnic heterogeneous state

Political Rights. Although elections are fairly open and parties represent a variety of positions, one party continues to dominate elections, and not without help from the government. Opposition parties have not been allowed to form coalitions—a regulation that is frequently tested—and election regulations do not provide for adequate supervision. Contested elections occur on the local level. Subnationalities: Ethnically eighty percent are Muslims; the Wolof people represent thirty-six percent of the population, including most of the elite, the urban population, and the more prosperous farmers. However, regional loyalties, both within and outside of this linguistic grouping, seem to be at least as important as communal groupings in defining potential subnationalities. Rapid assimilation of rural migrants in the cities to Wolof culture has reduced the tendency toward ethnic cleavage, but a separatist movement in the far south has shown increasing activity.

Civil Liberties. The press is predominantly public; the independence of private publications is somewhat constrained, although opposition papers and journals appear. Radio and television are under an autonomous government body, but not fully impartial. Rights of assembly and demonstration are often denied. There are at least separatist prisoners of conscience. Unions have gained increasing independence. Religion, travel, occupation, and other private rights are respected. The government sometimes loses in the courts. Although much of the land remains tribally owned, government-organized cooperatives, a strong internal private market, and dependence on external markets have transformed the preindustrial society. Many inefficient and corrupt state and quasi-public enterprises are now being dismantled.

Comparatively: Senegal is as free as El Salvador, freer than Cote d'Ivoire, less free than Botswana.

S E Y C H E L L E S

Economy: mixed socialist
Polity: socialist one-party
Population: 70,000 (est.)

Political Rights: 6
Civil Liberties: 6
Status: not free

A relatively homogeneous population

Political Rights. Seychelles is a one-party state allowing little political competition for parliament and none for president. The former ruling party is said to have "simply disappeared." Tanzanian military support has largely been replaced by North Korean. There is no local government.

Civil Liberties. Aside from an occasional, mildly critical Catholic publication, there is no independent opinion press; radio is government owned. No opposition in publication or even conversation is legal. Individuals have little judicial protection. There is no right of political assembly, and the security services have broad powers of arrest. Opposition party activities are banned; people have frequently been arrested on political charges. Critics are often urged to leave, exiled, or refused permission to leave. Labor and government are interconnected. Private rights, including private property, are generally respected. Religious institutions maintain some independence. Quasi-government enterprises are being established; state monopolies control the marketing of all export crops. Government services in this largely impoverished country are extensive.

Comparatively: Seychelles is as free as Djibouti, freer than Vietnam, less free than Maldives.

S I E R R A   L E O N E

Economy: noninclusive capitalist
Polity: socialist one-party
    (military dominated)
Population: 3,900,000

Political Rights: 5
Civil Liberties: 5

Status: partly free

A formally transethnic heterogeneous state

Political Rights. Sierra Leone's one-party system has coopted many members of the previous opposition. The 1985 presidential election allowed no choices; participation was suspiciously high. The 1986 parliamentary election allowed choice, but many candidates were arbitrarily excluded. Military influence in government is critical. There are some elected and traditional local governments.

Civil Liberties. The press is private and governmental. Radio is government controlled. There is occasional independence in the press, but it is under pressure; still there is considerable freedom of private speech. The courts do not appear to be very powerful or independent. Special emergency powers have sporadically given the government untrammeled powers of detention, censorship, restriction of assembly, and search. There may now be no prisoners of conscience. Identity cards have recently been required of all citizens. Labor unions are relatively independent, and travel is freely permitted. The largely subsistence economy has an essentially capitalist modern sector. Corruption is pervasive and costly.

Comparatively: Sierra Leone is as free as Jordan, freer than Gabon, less free than Senegal.

SINGAPORE

Economy: mixed capitalist
Polity: centralized dominant-party
Population: 2,600,000

Political Rights: 4
Civil Liberties: 5
Status: partly free

An ethnically complex state

Political Rights. Singapore is a parliamentary democracy in which the ruling party traditionally wins all legislative seats. Economic and other pressures against all opposition groups (exerted in part through control of the media) make elections very unfair. Opposition leaders have been sentenced and bankrupted for such crimes as defaming the prime minister during the campaign. The opposition still obtains thirty percent of the vote. In December 1984 the opposition won two seats and greatly improved its vote. Alarmed, the government continued to bring actions against one MP until he was jailed and expelled from parliament. There is no local government.

Civil Liberties. The press is nominally free, but owners of shares with policy-making power must be officially approved—in some cases the government owns the shares. By closing papers and imprisoning editors and reporters, the press is kept under close control. Government argues that the press has a duty to support government positions. Letters to the editors do express opposition opinion. Broadcasting is largely a government monopoly and completely controlled. The prime minister has publicly pressed the law society to expel members of which he disapproves. University faculties are under pressure to conform. Rights of assembly are restricted. Most opposition is treated as a communist threat and, therefore, treasonable. Prisoners of conscience are held; in internal security cases the protection of the law is weak—prosecution's main task appears to be obtaining forced confessions of communist activity. Torture is alleged. Trade union freedom is inhibited by the close association of government and union. Private rights of religion, occupation, or property are generally observed, although a large and increasing percentage of manufacturing and service companies are government owned. Natalist policy favors better educated. Many youths have reportedly been forcibly drafted into construction brigades.

Comparatively: Singapore is as free as China (Taiwan), freer than Indonesia, less free than Malaysia.

S O L O M O N   I S L A N D S

Economy: noninclusive capitalist
Polity: decentralized multiparty
Population: 275,000

Political Rights: 2
Civil Liberties: 2
Status: free

A relatively homogeneous state with subnational strains

Political Rights. The Solomon Islands are a parliamentary democracy under the British monarch. Elections are intensely contested; party discipline is weak. There is some decentralization of power at the local level; further decentralization to the provincial level is planned.

Civil Liberties. Radio is government controlled; the limited press is both private and governmental. There is no censorship. Although some pressures against journalists have been reported, discussion in both media is varied and critical. The rule of law is maintained in the British manner alongside traditional ideas of justice. Published incitement to inter-island conflict has led to banishment for several persons. Union activity is free, and strikes occur. The government is involved in major businesses. Most land is held communally but farmed individually.

Comparatively: The Solomon Islands are as free as Mauritius, freer than Vanuatu, less free than New Zealand.

S O M A L I A

Economy: noninclusive mixed socialist

Polity: socialist one-party (military dominated)

Population: 7,000,000 (est.)

Political Rights: 7

Civil Liberties: 7

Status: not free

A relatively homogeneous state

Political Rights. The Somali Republic is under one-man military rule combining glorification of the ruler with one-party socialist legitimization. Elections with ninety-nine percent approval allow no choice. Ethnically the state is homogeneous, although until the military coup in 1969 the six main clan groupings and their subdivisions were the major means of organizing loyalty and power. While politics is still understood in lineage terms, in its centralizing drive the government has tried to eliminate both tribal and religious power. Opposition guerrilla activity is frequently reported.

Civil Liberties. The media are under strict government control, private conversation is controlled, and those who do not follow the government are considered to be against it. There are many political prisoners, including prisoners of conscience. There have been jailings for strikes and executions for reasons of conscience. Travel is restricted. Some state farms and industries have been established beyond the dominant subsistence economy.

A large black market circumvents official distribution channels; corruption is widespread in government and business.

Comparatively: Somalia is as free as Cambodia, less free than Kenya.

S O U T H   A F R I C A

Economy: capitalist-statist
Polity: centralized multiparty
Population: 27,000,000 (est.)

Political Rights: 5
Civil Liberties: 6
Status: partly free

An ethnic state with major territorial and nonterritorial subnationalities

Political Rights. South Africa is a parliamentary democracy in which the black majority is excluded from participation in the national political process because of race. Recent constitutional changes add over ten percent more to the politically accepted population; the great majority black population remains excluded. For the nonblack population elections appear fair and open. There is a limited scope for blacks to influence affairs within their own communities. Subnationalities: Most of the black majority is ascribed to a variety of "homelands" that they may or may not live in, although thousands have been forced to move to these limited areas. Several of these have become independent states in the eyes of South Africa, but they have not received such recognition elsewhere. (Except for Transkei, we see these as dependent territories; because of their close integration into South Africa politically and economically we treat these states as part of South Africa for most purposes. The dependent governments of these states are generally unpopular and tyrannical, although this is less so in Bophuthatswana. Geographically and historically Transkei has a reasonable claim to statehood, in spite of the purposes for which it was brought into being. Its dependency is comparable to that of Lesotho, Swaziland, or, further afield, states such as Bhutan or Mongolia.) In the homelands that have not yet separated from the country officially, black leaders have some power and support from their people. Most black political parties are banned, but operating political parties among Indians and people of mixed blood

383

represent the interests of their peoples. Regionally, government within the white community includes both central government officials and elected councils.

Civil Liberties. The white South African press is private and quite outspoken, although censored and restricted. Restrictions apply more to reportage and access to information than to expression of opinion. The nonwhite press is closely restricted, but nevertheless shows critical independence on occasion. Broadcasting is under government control. The courts are independent on many issues, including apartheid, but have not effectively controlled the security forces. There are political prisoners and torture—especially for black activists, who live in an atmosphere of terror. Nevertheless, black organizations regularly denounce the government's racial and economic policies, hold conferences, and issue statements. Academic groups publish highly critical well-publicized studies of the system. Private rights are generally respected for whites. Blacks have rights to labor organization, although political activity is restricted. Legal separation of the races remains, but has been relaxed in a number of ways. Rights to choice of residence and occupation have improved for nonwhites, but hundreds of thousands have been forcibly moved, and such expulsions continue. Human rights organizations are active in both white and black communities. Church organizations have become centers of opposition to apartheid. Escalating violence and counterviolence, and the emergency powers that accompany the violence, obscure these gains.

Comparatively: South Africa is as free as Zimbabwe, freer than Congo, less free than Morocco.

S P A I N

Economy: capitalist
Polity: centralized multiparty
Population: 38,800,000

Political Rights: 1
Civil Liberties: 2
Status: free

An ethnic state with major territorial subnationalities

Political Rights. Spain is a constitutional monarchy with a fully functioning democratic system. In the last few years it has managed to largely overcome or pacify military, far right, and Basque dissidence. Elected regional and local governments are of increasing importance. Referendums are also used for major issues. Subnationalities: The Basque and Catalan territorial subnationalities have had their rights greatly expanded in recent years.

Civil Liberties. The press is private and is now largely free. The television network and some radio stations are government owned. National television is controlled by an all-party committee, but there are autonomous regional channels. There are few prisoners of conscience; imprisonment still threatens those who insult the security services, the courts, the state, or the flag. Short detention periods are often used with little legal redress. Police brutality and torture still occur, and the government has been slow to punish the civil guardsmen often responsible. Criticism of the government and of suspected human rights violators are quite freely expressed both publicly and privately. Private freedoms are respected. Continued terrorism and reactions to terrorism affect some areas. Union organization is free and independent.

Comparatively: Spain is as free as France, freer than Uruguay, less free than Netherlands.

S R I   L A N K A

Economy: mixed capitalist-statist
Polity: centralized multiparty
Population: 16,300,000

Political Rights: 3
Civil Liberties: 4
Status: partly free

An ethnic state with a major subnationality

Political Rights. Sri Lanka is a parliamentary democracy in which opposition groups have been partially excluded. In late 1982 the government used its then current popularity to guarantee by referendum a six-year extension of its rule. The referendum was held under a state of emergency restricting opposition campaigning. Regional government is centrally controlled; local government is by elected councils. Indian troops now operate in the northeast against guerrilla Tamil forces. Subnationalities: Receiving a large vote in the most recent election, the Tamil minority constitutes a serious secessionist tendency. Recent agreements grant the Tamils major regional authority in the east and north.

Civil Liberties. The government-owned press is dominant and under strong pressure to follow the governmental line. However, a broad range of independent journals is also available. Government-controlled broadcasting presents a narrow range of views. The rule of law has been threatened by communal violence, as well as by the use and misuse of state-of-emergency powers to detain political opponents. Courts remain independent of the government; an important human rights movement supports their independence. However, their decisions can be overruled by parliament. A few prisoners of conscience have been arrested, usually for advocating Tamil independence; torture and brutality is alleged. There is freedom of assembly but not demonstration. Private rights to movement, residence, religion, and occupation are respected in theory; in practice, nationalist and leftist gangs and the army have denied these rights to many through widespread looting, destruction, and killing, especially in Tamil areas. Strikes in public services are restricted, but unions are well developed and politically influential. Extensive land reform has occurred, and the state has nationalized a number of enterprises in this largely plantation economy. The system has done an excellent job in providing for the people's basic nutrition, health, and educational needs.

Comparatively: Sri Lanka is as free as El Salvador, freer than Indonesia, less free than India.

S U D A N

Economy: noninclusive mixed capitalist	Political Rights: 4
Polity: multiparty	Civil Liberties: 5
Population: 23,000,000 (est.)	Status: partly free

An ethnic state with major but highly diverse subnationalities

Political Rights. Elected, multiparty parliamentary government functions more or less adequately for the northern two-thirds of the country. The unstable system is beset by periodic breakdowns and continual threats. Much of the south is effectively under rebel or military control. Subnationalities: The peoples of the south are ethnically and religiously distinct. The national government remains overwhelmingly northern. A war for southern independence is again underway with atrocities on both sides—southerners on both sides. Other major ethnic groups are also interested in regional autonomy.

Civil Liberties. The press is being privatized. Radio and television are government controlled. There is considerable independence of expression, at least in the capital city. Arrests for expression still occur, however, and violence or its threat limits expression elsewhere. Worker and professional organizations are politically effective.

Comparatively: Sudan is as free as Egypt, freer than Ethiopia, less free than Turkey.

S U R I N A M E

Economy: capitalist
Polity: multiparty
    (military dominated)
Population: 380,000

Political Rights: 4
Civil Liberties: 4

Status: partly free

An ethnically complex state

Political Rights. Nineteen eighty-seven saw a gradual return toward democratic rule. The bureaucracy, former political parties, business, and labor played an increasing part in the militarily ruled system as the year progressed. A somewhat vague, but ostensibly democratic constitution was overwhelmingly approved by the people. Then, on November 25 a legislative election showed that the people rejected military parties in favor of the old democratic parties. The assembly is to elect the president. However, the willingness of the military to actually relinquish power to the new system, and the constitutional division of power still remained in doubt.

Civil Liberties. Although press and radio are largely private and varied, they have been under strong government pressure to conform. Political organization and assembly was allowed with increasing freedom as the year progressed. Several leaders of

387

major opposition groups (political parties, unions, journalists, and academia) were executed without trial in late 1982. Until recently prisoners of conscience were detained and treated brutally. During the military oppression the courts and unions retained surprising independence. In rural areas many have been senselessly gunned down in the course of antiguerrilla operations.

Comparatively: Suriname is as free as South Korea, freer than Albania, less free than Western Samoa.

S W A Z I L A N D

Economy: noninclusive capitalist
Polity: traditional nonparty
Population: 670,000 (est.)

Political Rights: 5
Civil Liberties: 6
Status: partly free

A relatively homogeneous population

Political Rights. Swaziland is ruled by a king. Indirect elections for part of an advisory legislature are held, but only one party is allowed. Local councils invite popular participation. South African political and economic influence is pervasive.

Civil Liberties. Private media exist alongside the dominant government media; little criticism is allowed; South African and other foreign media provide an alternative. Opposition leaders have been repeatedly detained, and partisan activity is forbidden. Criticism is common in parliament and other councils, but public assemblies are restricted, unions limited, emigration difficult. The rule of law is very insecure. Religious, economic, and other private rights are maintained. The traditional way of life is continued, especially on the local level. Several thousand whites in the country and in neighboring Transvaal own the most productive land and business.

Comparatively: Swaziland is as free as South Africa, freer than Mozambique, less free than Botswana.

S W E D E N

Economy: mixed capitalist
Polity: centralized multiparty
Population: 8,400,000

Political Rights: 1
Civil Liberties: 1
Status: free

A relatively homogeneous population

Political Rights. Sweden is a parliamentary democracy in which no party monopolizes power, and the king's power has been all but extinguished. Referendums are held. Although there are some representative institutions at regional and local levels, the system is relatively centralized. Resident aliens have a right to vote in local elections. The tendency of modern bureaucracies to regard issues as technical rather than political has progressed further in Sweden than elsewhere.

Civil Liberties. The press is private or party; broadcasting is by state-licensed monopolies. Although free of censorship; the media are accused of presenting a narrow range of views, but this may be changing as politics become polarized. There is the rule of law. The defense of those accused by the government may not be as spirited as elsewhere, but, on the other hand, the ombudsman office gives special means of redress against administrative arbitrariness. Most private rights are respected. State interference in family life is unusually strong, with many children unjustly taken from their parents. The national church has a special position. In many areas, such as housing, individual choice is restricted more than in other capitalist states—as it is of course by the very high tax load. Unions are a powerful part of the system. The state intervenes in the economy mainly through extensive business regulation rather than direct ownership.

Comparatively: Sweden is as free as Italy, freer than West Germany.

S W I T Z E R L A N D

Economy: capitalist
Polity: decentralized multiparty
Population: 6,500,000

Political Rights: 1
Civil Liberties: 1
Status: free

A trinational state

Political Rights. Switzerland is a parliamentary democracy in which all major parties are given cabinet positions on the basis of the size of the vote for each party. The president and vice-president are elected on a rotating basis from this cabinet. Parties that increase their vote above a certain level are invited to join the government, although such changes in party strength rarely occur. The lack of a decisive shift in power from one party to another in the last fifty years is a major limitation on the democratic effectiveness of the Swiss system. However, its dependence on the grand coalition style of government is a partial substitute, and the Swiss grant political rights in other ways that compensate for the lack of a transfer of power. Many issues are decided by the citizenry through national referendums or popular initiatives. After referendums, in keeping with the Swiss attitude, even the losing side is given part of what it wants if its vote is sufficiently large. Subnationalities: The three major linguistic groups have separate areas under their partial control. Their regional and local elected governments have autonomous rights and determine directly much of the country's business. National governments try to balance the representatives of the primary religious and linguistic groups; this is accomplished in another way by the upper house that directly represents the cantons (regions) on an equal basis.

Civil Liberties. The high-quality press is private and independent. Broadcasting is government operated, although with the considerable independence of comparable West European systems. Unions are free. Strikes are few because of a 1937 labor peace agreement requiring arbitration. The rule of law is strongly upheld; as in Germany it is against the law to question the intentions of judges. 1985 saw a major extension of women's rights. Private rights are thoroughly respected.

Comparatively: Switzerland is as free as the United States, freer than West Germany.

S Y R I A

Economy: mixed socialist
Polity: centralized dominant-party
(military dominated)
Population: 11,000,000 (est.)

Political Rights: 6
Civil Liberties: 7

Status: not free

A relatively homogeneous population

Political Rights. Syria is a military dictatorship assisted by an elected parliament. The election of the military president is largely pro forma; in assembly elections a variety of parties and independents compete within and without the National Front, organized under the leadership of the governing party. Many "independents" serve in the cabinet, but their independence is minimal. Because of its control of the army, the Alawite minority (ten percent) has a very unequal share of national power. Provinces have little separate power, but local elections are contested.

Civil Liberties. The media are in the hands of government or party. Broadcasting services are government owned. The media are used as governmental means for active indoctrination. Medical, bar, and engineering associations have been dissolved. Thousands have been arrested and many executed. Other thousands have been killed in punitive expeditions. The courts are neither strongly independent nor effective in political cases where long-term detention without trial occurs. Political prisoners are often arrested following violence, but there are also prisoners of conscience. Political opponents may even be killed overseas. Torture has frequently been employed in interrogation. Religious freedom is restricted. Rights to choice of occupation or residence are generally respected; foreign travel and emigration are closely controlled for certain groups. Much of industry has been nationalized; the commercial sector remains private. Land reform has successfully expanded private ownership. There is no independent labor movement.

Comparatively: Syria is as free as South Yemen, freer than Somalia, less free than Kuwait.

T A N Z A N I A

Economy: noninclusive socialist
Polity: socialist one-party
Population: 23,000,000

Political Rights: 6
Civil Liberties: 6
Status: not free

A transethnic heterogeneous nation in union with Zanzibar

Political Rights. Tanzania is an unequal union of two states. The single parties of each state have joined to form one all-Tanzanian party. Elections offer choice between individuals, but no issues are to be discussed in campaigns; all decisions come down from above, including the choice of candidates. Over half of the MP's are appointed. The resulting parliament is not, however, simply a rubber stamp. Local government is an extension of party government. Subnationalities: Ethnically, the country is divided into a large number of peoples (none larger than thirteen percent); most are not yet at the subnational level. The use of English and Swahili as national languages enhances national unity. Recent resistance by some Zanzibar leaders to continued association with the mainland has been defused by the appointment of a Zanzibari as president.

Civil Liberties. Civil liberties are subordinated to the goals of the socialist leadership. No contradiction of official policy is allowed to appear in the media, nearly all of which is government owned, or in educational institutions; private and limited criticism of implementation appears. The people learn only of those events the government wishes them to know. There is no right of assembly or organization. Millions of people have been forced into communal villages; people from the cities have been abruptly transported to the countryside; forced labor on the farms is still a problem. Thousands have been detained for political crimes. There are prisoners of conscience. Lack of respect for the independence of the judiciary and individual rights is especially apparent in Zanzibar. Union activity is government controlled. Neither labor nor capital have legally recognized rights—strikes are illegal. Most business and trade and much of agriculture are nationalized. Religion is free, at least on the mainland; overseas travel is restricted.

Comparatively: Tanzania is as free as Algeria, freer than Malawi, less free than Zambia.

T H A I L A N D

Economy: noninclusive capitalist
Polity: centralized multiparty
(military dominated)
Population: 53,600,000

Political Rights: 3
Civil Liberties: 3

Status: partly free

An ethnic state with a major territorial subnationality

Political Rights. Thailand is a constitutional monarchy with continuing military influence. Both parties and parliament are, however, significant. The politics are those of consensus. Provincial government is under national control; there are elected and traditional institutions at the local level. Subnationalities: There is a Muslim Malay community in the far south, and other small ethnic enclaves in the north.

Civil Liberties. The press is private, but periodic suppressions and warnings lead to limited self-censorship. Casting doubt on the monarchy is illegal. Most broadcasting is government or military controlled. Some books are banned as subversive. There are few long-term prisoners of conscience, but many are periodically detained for communist activity. Human rights and other public interest organizations are active. Labor activity is relatively free. Private rights to property, choice of religion, or residence are secure; foreign travel or emigration is not restricted. However, corruption limits the expression of all rights. Government enterprise is quite important in the basically capitalist modern economy.

Comparatively: Thailand is as free as Turkey, freer than Malaysia, less free than India.

T O G O

Economy: noninclusive mixed socialist	Political Rights: 6
Polity: nationalist one-party (military dominated)	Civil Liberties: 6
Population: 3,200,000	Status: not free

A transethnic heterogeneous state

Political Rights. Attaining power by military coup, Togo's dictator now rules in the name of a one-party state. In this spirit there is a deliberate denial of the rights of separate branches of government, including a separate judiciary, or even of private groups. National elections allow choice among party-approved candidates. Campaigns allow no policy discussion. Essentially everyone can join the party and there is some discussion in parliament and party organs. An effort has been made to include a variety of ethnic groups and former leaders in policy discussion. Local elections allow a more open expression of popular desires. The government depends on French troops to protect it against internal enemies. Subnationalities: The southern Ewe are culturally dominant and the largest group (twenty percent), but militant northerners now rule.

Civil Liberties. No criticism of the government is allowed in the government or church media, and foreign publications may be confiscated. There are prisoners of conscience, and torture occurs. Jehovah's Witnesses are banned. There is occasional restriction of foreign travel. Union organization is closely regulated. It is yet to be seen whether the establishment of a government-sponsored human rights organization will have a positive effect. In this largely subsistence economy the government is heavily involved in trade, production, and the provision of services. All wage earners must contribute to the ruling party.

Comparatively: Togo is as free as Gabon, freer than Ethiopia, less free than Zambia.

TONGA

Economy: noninclusive capitalist
Polity: traditional nonparty
Population: 109,000

Political Rights: 5
Civil Liberties: 3
Status: partly free

A relatively homogeneous population

Political Rights. Tonga is a constitutional monarchy in which the king and nobles retain power. Only a minority of the members of the legislative assembly are elected directly by the people; but the veto power of the assembly can be effectively expressed. Corruption of political leaders has been alleged. Regional administration is centralized; there are some elected local officials.

Civil Liberties. The main paper is a government weekly; radio is under government control. Other foreign and local media are available, and recently, a critical monthly has gained an attentive readership. There is a rule of law, but the king's decision is still a very important part of the system. Private rights within the traditional Tonga context seem guaranteed.

Comparatively: Tonga is as free as Mexico, freer than Seychelles, less free than Western Samoa.

TRANSKEI

Economy: noninclusive capitalist
Polity: centralized
    dominant-party
Population: 2,600,000 (est.)

Political Rights: 5
Civil Liberties: 6

Status: partly free

A relatively homogeneous population

Political Rights. In form Transkei is a multiparty parliamentary democracy; in fact it has been under the rule of powerful chiefs in the name of their dominant political party. The meaning of recent elections has been partly nullified by governmental interference, including the jailing of some opposition leaders. Chiefs form half of the assembly by appointment. The balancing of tribal interests remains very important in the system, but beyond that there is little decentralization of power. Corruption charges led to a change of government in 1987; the resulting party selection of a new prime minister may signal the emergence of a more open system. South Africa has de facto power over the state, both because of its massive budgetary support and the large number of nationals that work in South Africa. However, Transkei is at least as independent as several Soviet satellites; it has had continuing public disputes with South Africa.

Civil Liberties. The press is private, but under strong government pressure. Broadcasting is government controlled. Many members of the opposition have been imprisoned; new retroactive laws render it illegal to criticize Transkei or its rulers. Freedom of organization is very limited, although an opposition party still exists. Private rights are respected within the limits of South African and Transkei custom. Capitalist and traditional economic rights are diminished by the necessity of a large portion of the labor force to work in South Africa.

Comparatively: Transkei is as free as Swaziland, freer than Mozambique, less free than Sierra Leone.

T R I N I D A D   A N D   T O B A G O

Economy: capitalist-statist
Polity: decentralized multiparty
Population: 1,300,000

Political Rights: 1
Civil Liberties: 1
Status: free

An ethnically complex state

Political Rights. Trinidad and Tobago is a parliamentary democracy in which the ruling party was replaced in a landslide election in December, 1986. There has been a decentralization of power, and elections are vigorously contested by a variety of parties. Local government is elected. Tobago has an elected regional government with significant independent power.

Civil Liberties. The private or party press is generally free of restriction; broadcasting is under both government and private control. Opposition is regularly and effectively voiced. There is a full spectrum of private rights. Violence and communal feeling reduce the effectiveness of such rights for some, as does police violence. Many sectors of the economy are government owned. Human rights organizations are active. Labor is powerful and strikes frequent.

Comparatively: Trinidad and Tobago is as free as Costa Rica, freer than Grenada.

T U N I S I A

Economy: mixed capitalist
Polity: dominant party
Population: 7,200,000

Political Rights: 6
Civil Liberties: 5
Status: partly free

A relatively homogeneous population

Political Rights. Tunisia has a dominant party system. Its increasingly senile and erratic ruler was replaced in 1987 through a palace coup. The step was generally approved by opposition and government elites. Elections to the assembly are contested primarily within the one-party framework; opposition parties and opposition factions in the ruling party were forced outside the process by increasingly authoritarian rule. Regional government is centrally directed; there is elected local government.

Civil Liberties. The private, party, and government press is under government pressure. Frequently banned or fined, opposition papers have almost ceased to exist after government suspensions. Broadcasting is government controlled. Distribution of cassettes and video tapes give a modest dimension of freedom. Private conversation is relatively free, but there is no right of assembly. Organizational activity is restricted. The courts demonstrate only a limited independence, but it is possible to win against the government. Unions have been relatively independent despite periods of repression. There are few if any long-term prisoners of conscience, but arrests for unauthorized political activity or expression occur. The unemployed young are drafted for government work. Overseas travel is occasionally blocked. Most private rights seem to be respected, including economic freedoms since doctrinaire socialism was abandoned and much of agriculture returned to private hands.

Comparatively: Tunisia is as free as Kuwait, freer than Algeria, less free than Egypt.

T U R K E Y

Economy: capitalist-statist
Polity: multiparty
Population: 51,400,000

Political Rights: 2
Civil Liberties: 4

Status: partly free

An ethnic state with a major territorial subnationality

Political Rights.   Power is divided between a military president and a civilian prime minister. The current president was confirmed in power on a questionable adjunct to a constitutional referendum in late 1982. Opposition campaigning was restricted and the vote not entirely secret. However, power is now in the hands of a freely elected parliamentary government. A 1987 referendum and subsequent legislative election further strengthened democracy. Military power to influence government has been reduced but not eliminated. Power is centralized, but local and provincial elections are significant. Subnationalities: Denied the least self-determination or cultural existence, several million Kurds support a violent, leftish movement in eastern Turkey.

Civil Liberties.   The press is private; the government controls the broadcasting system directly or indirectly. In spite of suspensions and arrests, the press has become increasingly outspoken. Kurds and Armenians remain prohibited topics, even in books. Religious expression is free only if religion is not related to law and way of life.   There remain many prisoners of conscience under martial law, and petitioners to expand rights have been detained. Torture has been common, but the government has made arrests of some accused torturers. The courts exhibit some independence in political decisions. Human rights organizations are active. Independent union activity has been curtailed; but strikes are now permitted. Nearly fifty percent of the people are subsistence agriculturists. State enterprises make up more than half of Turkey's industry.

Comparatively: Turkey is as free as Thailand, freer than Yugoslavia, less free than Greece.

T U V A L U

Economy: noninclusive capitalist
Polity: traditional nonparty
Population: 8,200

Political Rights: 1
Civil Liberties: 1
Status: free

A relatively homogeneous state

Political Rights. Tuvalu is a parliamentary democracy under the British monarch. Each island is represented; seats are contested individually. Opposition blocs have been formed in the assembly and have been able to achieve power. There are local councils for each island. Continued dependence on the United Kingdom is self-chosen and economically unavoidable.

Civil Liberties. Media are government owned but little developed. The rule of law is maintained in the British manner, alongside traditional ideals of justice. The economy is largely subsistence farming; much of the labor force is employed overseas.

Comparatively: Tuvalu is as free as New Zealand, freer than Mauritius.

U G A N D A

Economy: noninclusive
    capitalist-statist
Polity: transitional military
Population: 16,000,000 (est.)

Political Rights: 5

Civil Liberties: 4
Status: partly free

A transethnic heterogeneous state with major subnationalities

Political Rights. A rebel movement representing ethnically the majority of the population attained power by military victory in 1986. The announced goal is to build a democratic society; the inclusion of a variety of former political leaders in government reenforces this presumption. Subnationalities: The population is divided among a wide variety of peoples, some of which are subnationalities based on kingdoms that preceded the present state. The most important of these was Buganda.

Civil Liberties. Newspapers are private, party, or government; radio and television are government owned. In 1986 the new regime banned an obstreperous newspaper. Free discussion has again emerged. Assembly and travel are restricted within the country. Unions are weak and government influenced. The murder of opposition politicians has declined, and over 1,000 political prisoners have been released. The courts have some independence. A human rights organization is active, but its leaders remain in prison. Religious freedom has been partially reestablished, and the churches play a balancing role to a limited extent. The economy has suffered severe dislocation: property is not secure, the black market flourishes.

Comparatively: Uganda is as free as Hungary, freer than Lesotho, less free than Suriname.

UNION OF
SOVIET SOCIALIST REPUBLICS

Economy: socialist
Polity: communist one-party
Population: 284,000,000

Political Rights: 7
Civil Liberties: 6
Status: not free

A complex ethnic state with major territorial subnationalities

Political Rights. The Soviet Union is ruled by parallel party and governmental systems: the party system is dominant. Elections are held for both systems, but in neither is it possible for the rank and file to determine policy. Candidacy and voting are closely controlled, and the resulting assemblies do not seriously question the policies developed by party leaders (varying by time or issue from one individual to twenty-five). Experiments with democracy at local party and communal levels are beginning. The Soviet Union is in theory elaborately divided into subnational units, but in fact the all-embracing party structure renders local power minimal.

Subnationalities. Russians account for half the Soviet population. The rest belong to a variety of subnational groupings ranging down in size from the forty million Ukrainians. Most groups are territorial, with a developed sense of subnational identity. The political rights of all of these to self-determination, either within the USSR or through secession, is effectively denied. In many cases Russians or other non-native peoples have been settled in subnational territories in such numbers as to make the native people a minority in their own land (for example, Kazakhstan). Expression of opinion in favor of increased self-determination is repressed at least as much as anticommunist opinion. Most of these peoples have had independence movements or movements for enhanced self-determination since the founding of the USSR. Several movements have been quite strong since World War II (for example, in the Ukraine or Lithuania); the blockage of communication by the Soviet government makes it very difficult to estimate either the overt or latent support such movements might have. In 1978 popular movements in Georgia and Armenia led to the retention of the official status of local languages in the Republics of the Caucasus; freedoms, such as that to move in and out of the country, are notable in Armenia. In 1987 demonstrations by Crimean Tatars and other nationalities were allowed, or repressed with less severity than in the past.

Civil Liberties. The media are totally owned by the government or party and are, in addition, regularly censored. Major deviations from the party line are found primarily in unofficial underground publications. Arrest and exile have silenced nearly all dissident criticism. However, official discussion of policy issues has become more diversified and critical among writers, economists, and others. Crimes against the state, including insanity (demonstrated by perverse willingness to oppose the state), are broadly defined; as a result, political prisoners are present both in jails and insane asylums. Nearly all imprisonment and mistreatment of prisoners in the Soviet Union are carried out in accordance with Soviet security laws—even though these laws conflict with other Soviet laws written to accord with international standards. Since the Bolshevik Revolution there has never been an acquittal in a major political trial. Insofar as private rights, such as those to religion, education, or choice of occupation, exist, they are de facto rights that may be denied at any time. Travel within and outside of the USSR is highly controlled; many areas of the country are still off-limits to foreigners—especially those used as areal prisons for dissidents. Some private entrepreneurial activity has now been legalized; there are rights to nonproductive personal property. In nonsensitive areas private organizational activity has increased. Other rights, such as those to organize independent labor unions, are strictly denied. Literacy is high, few starve, and private oppression is no more.

Comparatively: The USSR is as free as East Germany, freer than Romania, less free than Hungary.

U N I T E D   A R A B   E M I R A T E S

Economy: capitalist-statist
Polity: decentralized nonparty
Population: 1,400,000

Political Rights: 5
Civil Liberties: 5
Status: partly free

A relatively homogeneous citizenry

Political Rights. The UAE is a confederation of seven shaikhdoms in which the larger are given the greater power both in the appointed assembly and the administrative hierarchy. There is a great deal of consultation in the traditional pattern. Below the confederation level there are no electoral procedures or parties. Each shaikhdom is relatively autonomous in its internal affairs. The majority of the people are recent immigrants and noncitizens. Most officers and enlisted men in the army are foreign.

Civil Liberties. The press is private or governmental. There is self-censorship, but some criticism is expressed. Broadcasting is under federal or shaikhdom control. There are no political assemblies, but there are also few, if any, prisoners of conscience. The courts dispense a combination of British, tribal, and Islamic law. Labor unions are prohibited, but illegal strikes have occurred. Private rights are generally respected; there is freedom of travel. As in most Muslim countries there is freedom of worship for established religions, but only the favored Muslims may proselytize. Many persons may still accept the feudal privileges and restraints of their tribal position. The rights of the alien majority are less secure: "troublemakers" are deported. Private economic activity exists alongside the dominance of government petroleum and petroleum-related activities.

Comparatively: United Arab Emirates are as free as Bahrain, freer than Saudi Arabia, less free than Sudan.

UNITED KINGDOM

Economy: mixed capitalist
Polity: centralized multiparty
Population: 56,800,000

Political Rights: 1
Civil Liberties: 1
Status: free

An ethnic state with major subnationalities

Political Rights. The United Kingdom is a parliamentary democracy with a symbolic monarch. Plurality elections from single-member districts on the basis of party affiliation rather than personal record lead to strong parties and political stability. Fair elections are open to all parties, including those advocating secession. Unchecked by a written constitution or judicial review, parliament is restrained only by tradition. Between elections this means potentially great powers for the prime minister. There are elected local and regional governments, and their limited powers are gradually being increased. Subnationalities: Scots, Welsh, Ulster Scots, and Ulster Irish are significant and highly self-conscious territorial minorities. In 1978 parliament approved home rule for Scotland and Wales, but the Welsh and (more ambiguously) the Scots voters rejected this opportunity in 1979. Northern Ireland's home rule has been in abeyance because of an ethnic impasse. Ulster Scot and Irish live in intermixed territories in Northern Ireland. Both want more self-determination—the majority Ulster Scots as an autonomous part of the United Kingdom, the minority Ulster Irish as an area within Ireland.

Civil Liberties. The press is private and powerful; broadcasting has statutory independence although it is indirectly under government control. British media are comparatively restrained because of strict libel and national security laws, and a tradition of accepting government suggestions for the handling of sensitive news. In Northern Ireland a severe security situation has led to the curtailment of private rights, to imprisonment, and on occasion to torture and brutality. However, these conditions have been relatively limited, thoroughly investigated by the government, and improved as a result. Elsewhere the rule of law is entrenched, and private rights generally respected. Unions are independent and powerful. In certain areas, such as medicine, housing, inheritance, and general disposability of income, socialist government policies have limited choice for some while improving opportunities for others.

Comparatively: The United Kingdom is as free as the United States, freer than West Germany.

U N I T E D   S T A T E S   O F   A M E R I C A

Economy: capitalist
Polity: decentralized multiparty
Population: 243,800,000

Political Rights: 1
Civil Liberties: 1
Status: free

An ethnically complex state with minor territorial subnationalities

Political Rights. The United States is a constitutional democracy with three strong but separate centers of power: president, congress, and judiciary. Elections are fair and competitive, but voter participation is frequently less than fifty percent. Parties are remarkably weak: in some areas they are little more than temporary means of organizing primary elections. States, and to a less extent cities, have powers in their own rights; they often successfully oppose the desires of national administrations. Each state has equal representation in the upper house, which in the USA is the more powerful half of parliament.

Subnationalities. There are many significant ethnic groups, but the only clearly territorial subnationalities are the native peoples. The largest Indian tribes, the Navaho and Sioux, number 100,000 or more each. About 150,000 Hawaiians still reside on their native islands, intermingled with a much larger white and oriental population. Spanish-speaking Americans number in the millions; except for a few thousand residing in an area of northern New Mexico, they are mostly twentieth-century immigrants living among English-speaking Americans, particularly in the large cities. Black Americans make up over one-tenth of the U.S. population; residing primarily in large cities, they have no major territorial base. In spite of this, Black and Hispanic political power has been steadily growing in recent years. Black and Spanish-speaking Americans are of special concern because of their relative poverty; their ethnic status is comparable to that of many other groups in America, including Chinese, Japanese, Filipinos, Italians, or Jews.

Civil Liberties. The press is private and free; both private and public radio and television are government regulated. There are virtually no government controls on the content of the printed media (except in nonpolitical areas such as pornography) and few on broadcasting. There are no prisoners of conscience or sanctioned uses of torture; some regional miscarriages of justice and police brutality have political and social overtones. Widespread use of surveillance techniques and clandestine interference with radical groups or groups thought to be radical have occurred sporadically; as a reduction of liberties the threat has remained largely potential. A new threat is control over the expression of former government employees. Wherever and whenever publicity penetrates, the rule of law is generally secure, even against the most powerful. The government often loses in the courts. Private rights in most spheres are respected, but rights to travel to particular places, such as Cuba, are circumscribed. Unions are independent and politically influential. Although a relatively capitalistic country, the combination of tax loads and the decisive government role in agriculture, energy, defense, and other industries restricts individual choice as it increases majority power.

Comparatively: The United States is as free as Australia, freer than Spain.

U R U G U A Y

Economy: mixed capitalist
Polity: centralized multiparty
Population: 3,100,000

Political Rights: 2
Civil Liberties: 2
Status: free

A relatively homogeneous population

Political Rights. Uruguay has a democratically elected president and parliament. All parties have been legalized; the former guerrilla movement has joined the political process. Since the military is not completely under civilian control, trials of military officers implicated in human rights offenses have been delayed.

Civil Liberties. The press is private, and broadcasting private and public. Both are free, as are books and journals. Foreign media are widely available. Rights of assembly and organization as well as the independence of the judiciary and the civil service have been reestablished. All prisoners of conscience have been released. Private rights are generally respected. The tax load of an overbuilt bureaucracy and emphasis on private and government monopolies in major sectors still restrict choice in this now impoverished welfare state.

Comparatively: Uruguay is as free as Greece, freer than Ecuador, less free than Venezuela.

V A N U A T U

Economy: noninclusive capitalist-statist	Political Rights: 2
Polity: decentralized multiparty	Civil Liberties: 4
Population: 135,000	Status: partly free

A relatively homogeneous society with geographical subnationalities

Political Rights. Vanuatu has a parliamentary system with an indirectly elected president. Elections have been freely contested by multiple parties. Opposition exists between islands and between the French- and English-educated. Local government is elected; a decentralized federal system of regional government is being developed.

Civil Liberties. Government controls both print and broadcast media; the only critical paper was closed by government order in 1983. The full spectrum of civil freedoms is observed, but in the aftermath of the suppression of a secessionist (largely French supported) movement at independence, many political arrests and trials occurred; mistreatment was reported. The judiciary is independent. Rights to political, economic, and union organization are observed, but unions have been under pressure. There is a general right to travel.

Comparatively: Vanuatu is as free as Turkey, freer than Tonga, less free than Solomon Islands.

V E N E Z U E L A

Economy: capitalist-statist
Polity: centralized multiparty
Population: 18,300,000

Political Rights: 1
Civil Liberties: 2
Status: free

A relatively homogeneous population

Political Rights. Venezuela is a constitutional democracy in which power has alternated between major parties in recent years. Campaigns and voting are fair and open. Regional and local assemblies are relatively powerful, but governors are centrally appointed. Each state has equal representation in the upper house.

Civil Liberties. The press is private and generally free; most broadcasting is also in private hands. Censorship occurs only in emergencies, but television scripts on certain subjects must be approved in advance; journalists have been warned or arrested, and programs suspended, for normal reportage. The rule of law is generally secure, but police brutality is commonly reported in poorer areas. However, there are no prisoners of conscience, and the government has taken steps to prevent torture. The court can rule against the government, and charges are brought against the security forces. Most private rights are respected; government involvement in the petroleum industry has given it a predominant economic role. Human rights organizations are very active. Unions are well organized and powerful.

Comparatively: Venezuela is as free as France, freer than Ecuador, less free than Costa Rica.

VIETNAM

Economy: socialist
Polity: communist one-party
Population: 62,200,000

Political Rights: 6
Civil Liberties: 7
Status: not free

An ethnic state with subnationalities

Political Rights. Vietnam is a traditional communist dictatorship with the forms of parliamentary democracy. Actual power is in the hands of the communist party; this is, in turn, dominated by a small group at the top. Officially there is a ruling national front, as in several other communist states, but the noncommunist parties are facades. However, recent elections have allowed a semblance of choice and campaigning. Government has become more open. Administration is highly centralized, with provincial boundaries arbitrarily determined by the central government. The flow of refugees and other evidence suggest that the present regime is very unpopular, especially in the South which is treated as an occupied country. Subnationalities: Continued fighting has been reported in the Montagnard areas in the South. Combined with new resettlement schemes, non-Vietnamese peoples are under pressure in both North and South Vietnam. Many Chinese have been driven out of the country.

Civil Liberties. The media are under direct government, party, or army control; only the approved line is presented. While the people have essentially no rights against the state, there is occasional public criticism and passive resistance, especially in the South. Newspaper letter columns have begun to offer an outlet for alternative opinion. Arbitrary arrest is frequent. Repression of religious groups has eased, at least in the South. Perhaps one-half million persons have been put through reeducation camps, hundreds of thousands have been forced to move into new areas, or to change occupations; thousands are prisoners of conscience or in internal exile. Former anticommunist and other groups are regularly discriminated against in employment, health care, and travel. There are no independent labor union rights, rights to travel, or choice of education; many have been forced into collectives.

Comparatively: Vietnam is as free as USSR, freer than Mongolia, less free than China (Mainland).

WESTERN SAMOA

Economy: noninclusive capitalist
Polity: centralized multiparty
Population: 160,000

Political Rights: 4
Civil Liberties: 3
Status: partly free

A relatively homogeneous population

Political Rights. Western Samoa is a constitutional monarchy in which the assembly is elected by 16,000 "family heads." There have been important shifts of power among parties in the assembly as the result of elections, or the shift of allegiance of factions without elections. A recent election was voided in the courts on a corruption issue. Campaigning by lavish distribution of gifts is common. Village government has preserved traditional forms and considerable autonomy; it is also based on rule by "family heads."

Civil Liberties. The press is private and government; radio is government owned; television is received only from outside. Government media have limited independence. There is general freedom of expression, organization, and assembly. The judiciary is independent and the rule of law and private rights are respected within the limits set by the traditional system. Most arable land is held in customary tenure. Health and literacy standards are very high for a poor country.

Comparatively: Western Samoa is as free as Senegal, freer than Indonesia, less free than Nauru.

YEMEN, NORTH

Economy: noninclusive capitalist
Polity: military nonparty
Population: 6,500,000

Political Rights: 5
Civil Liberties: 5
Status: partly free

A complex but relatively homogeneous population

Political Rights. North Yemen is a military dictatorship supplemented by an appointive and elected advisory assembly. Leaders are frequently assassinated. The tribal and religious structures still retain considerable authority, and the government must rely on a wide variety of different groups in an essentially nonideological consensual regime. Local elections allow meaningful competition. Political parties are forbidden. The country is divided between city and country, a variety of tribes, and two major religious groupings, and faces a major revolutionary challenge.

Civil Liberties. The weak media are largely government owned; the papers have occasional criticisms—the broadcast media have none. Foreign publications are routinely censored. Yet proponents of both royalist and far left persuasions are openly accepted in a society with few known prisoners of conscience. There is no right of assembly. Politically active opponents may be encouraged to go into exile. The traditional Islamic courts give some protection; many private rights are respected. There is no right to strike or to engage in religious proselytizing. Unions and professional associations are government sponsored. Economically the government has concentrated on improving the infrastructure of Yemen's still overwhelmingly traditional economy. Most farmers are tenants; half the labor force is employed abroad.

Comparatively: North Yemen is as free as Bhutan, freer than South Yemen, less free than Egypt.

Y E M E N, S O U T H

Economy: noninclusive socialist
Polity: socialist one-party
     (military influenced)
Population: 2,300,000

Political Rights: 6
Civil Liberties: 7

Status: not free

A relatively homogeneous population

Political Rights. South Yemen is formally organized according to the Marxist-Leninist one-party model. In practice, it is government of tribal factions by coup and violence. Elections follow the one-party model; there is some choice among individuals, particularly on the local level. Soviet influence in internal and external affairs is powerful.

Civil Liberties. The media are government owned or controlled, and employed actively as means of indoctrination. Even conversation with foreigners is highly restricted. In the political and security areas the rule of law hardly applies. Political imprisonments, torture, and "disappearances" have instilled a pervasive fear in those who would speak up. Death sentences against protesting farmers have been handed down by people's courts. Independent private rights are few, although some traditional law and institutions remain. Unions are under government control. Industry and commerce have been nationalized, some of the land collectivized.

Comparatively: South Yemen is as free as Malawi, freer than Somalia, less free than Oman.

Y U G O S L A V I A

Economy: mixed socialist
Polity: communist one-party
Population: 23,400,000

Political Rights: 6
Civil Liberties: 5
Status: partly free

A multinational state

Political Rights. Yugoslavia is governed on the model of the USSR, but with the addition of unique elements. These include: the greater role given the governments of the constituent republics; and the greater power given the managers and workers of the self-managed communities and industrial enterprises. The Federal Assembly is elected indirectly by those successful in lower level elections. The country has been directed by a small elite of the communist party, but measures to increase in-party democracy seem genuine. No opposition member is elected to state or national position, nor is there public opposition in the assemblies to government policy on the national level.

Subnationalities. The several peoples of Yugoslavia live largely in their historical homelands. The population consists of forty percent Serbs, twenty-two percent Croats, eight percent Slovenes, eight percent Bosnian Muslims, six percent Macedonians, six percent Albanians, two percent Montenegrins, and many others. The Croats have an especially active independence movement; Albanians have agitated for more self-determination. Republics and autonomous areas are accumulating more and more power. For

411

example, both politically and economically Slovenia is developing western rather than eastern-bloc traditions—while remaining within the official limits of the system.

Civil Liberties. The media in Yugoslavia are controlled directly or indirectly by the government, although there is ostensible worker control. The range of ideas and criticism of government policy in domestic and available foreign publications is greater than in most communist states: there is no prepublication censorship. There is no right of assembly, but some assemblies are allowed outside of government direction. Hundreds have been imprisoned for ideas expressed verbally or in print that deviated from the official line (primarily through subnationalist enthusiasm, anticommunism, or communist deviationism). Dissidents are even pursued overseas. Torture and brutality occur; psychiatric hospitals are also used to confine prisoners of conscience. As long as the issue is not political, however, the courts have some independence; there is a realm of de facto individual freedom that includes the right to seek employment outside the country. Travel outside Yugoslavia is often denied to dissidents; religious proselytizing is forbidden, but sanctioned religious activity is increasing. Labor is not independent, but has rights through the working of the "self-management" system; local strikes are common, but illegal. Although the economy is socialist or communalist in most respects, agriculture in this most agricultural of European countries remains overwhelmingly private.

Comparatively: Yugoslavia is as free as Cape Verde, freer than Romania, less free than Hungary.

Z A I R E

Economy: noninclusive
    capitalist-statist
Polity: nationalist one-party
    (military dominated)
Population: 32,000,000 (est.)

Political Rights: 6

Civil Liberties: 7

Status: not free

A transethnic heterogeneous state with subnationalities

Political Rights. Zaire is under one-man military rule, with the ruling party essentially an extension of the ruler's personality. Presidential elections are farces. Elections at both local and parliamentary levels are restricted to one party, but allow for extensive choice among individuals. Elections in 1987 evidenced an intention to improve electoral procedures. Parliament has little if any power. Regions are deliberately organized to avoid ethnic identity: regional officers all are appointed from the center, generally from outside the area, as are officers of the ruling party. The president's personal exploitation of the system delegitimizes it.

Subnationalities. There are such a variety of tribes or linguistic groups in Zaire that no one group has as much as twenty percent of the population. The fact that French remains the dominant language reflects the degree of this dispersion. Until recently most Zaire citizens have seen themselves only in local terms without broader ethnic identification. The revolts and wars of the early 1960s saw continually shifting patterns of affiliation, with the European provincial, but not ethnic, realities of Katanga and South Kasai being most important. The most self-conscious ethnic groups are the Kongo people living in the west (and Congo and Angola) and the Luba in the center of the country. In both cases ethnicity goes back to important ancient kingdoms. There is continuing disaffection among the Lunda and other ethnic groups.

Civil Liberties. Private newspaper ownership remains only in name. Broadcasting is government owned and directed. Censorship and self-censorship are pervasive. There is no right of assembly, and union organization is controlled. Government has been arbitrary and capricious. The judiciary is not independent; prisoners of conscience are numerous, and execution and torture common. Ethnic organizations are closely restricted. Arrested conspirators have been forbidden their own lawyers. There is relative religious freedom; the Catholic church retains some power. Through the misuse of government power, the extravagance and business dealings of those in high places reduces economic freedom. Nationalization of land has often been a prelude to private development by powerful bureaucrats. Pervasive corruption and anarchy reduce human rights. There is also considerable government enterprise.

Comparatively: Zaire is as free as Vietnam, freer than Angola, less free than Rwanda.

413

Z A M B I A

Economy: noninclusive
         mixed socialist
Polity: socialist one-party
Population: 7,100,000

Political Rights: 5

Civil Liberties: 5

Status: partly free

A transethnic heterogeneous state

Political Rights. Zambia is ruled as a one-party dictatorship, although there have been elements of freedom within that party. Government and party strive for ethnic balance. Party organs are constitutionally more important than governmental ministries. Although elections have some meaning within this framework, the government has suppressed opposition movements within the party. Perhaps uniquely, parliament managed to block a government bill in 1985. Expression of dissent is possible through abstention or negative votes. There are some town councils with elected members.

Civil Liberties. All media are government controlled. A considerable variety of opinion is expressed, but it is a crime to criticize the president, the parliament, or the ideology. Foreign publications are censored. There is a rule of law and the courts have some independence; political cases are won against the government. Political opponents are often detained, and occasionally tortured, yet most people talk without fear. Traditional life continues. The government does not fully accept private or traditional rights in property or religion; important parts of the economy, especially copper mining, have been nationalized. Union, business, and professional organizations are under government pressure but retain significant independence.

Comparatively: Zambia is as free as Guyana, freer than South Africa, less free than Morocco.

Z I M B A B W E

Economy: noninclusive
capitalist-statist

Political Rights: 5

Polity: centralized
dominant party

Civil Liberties: 6

Population: 9,400,000

Status: partly free

An ethnically complex state with a territorial subnationality

Political Rights. Zimbabwe is a parliamentary democracy. The ruling party has achieved power through elections marked by coercion of the electorate both before and after the actual process. All military forces are still not controlled. Opposition parties have been all but banned as the country moves violently toward one-party rule. Subnationalities: The formerly dominant white, Indian, and colored populations (five percent altogether) are largely urban. The emerging dominant people are the majority Shona-speaking groups (seventy-four percent). The Ndebele (eighteen percent) are territorially distinct and politically self-conscious. Their allegiance to a minority party is being violently reduced.

Civil Liberties. The major papers are indirectly government owned and follow the government line, except occasionally in the letters columns. The government-owned broadcast media are active organs of government propaganda. The rule of law is increasingly threatened; opposition politicians have seen their rallies banned, and been personally forced into exile or imprisoned. Acquittals in political cases are often followed by rearrests. Racial discrimination is officially outlawed, especially in residence, occupation, and conscription. Many citizens live in fear of the nationalist parties and their former guerrilla forces. Many have been killed or beaten in an attempt to force change of party allegiance. Unions and private associations retain some independence, but are increasingly being unified under government direction. The economy has capitalist, socialist, and statist aspects. The white population still wields disproportionate economic power.

Comparatively: Zimbabwe is as free as Indonesia, freer than Mozambique, less free than Senegal.

415

PART VI

Related Territory Summaries

RELATED TERRITORY SUMMARIES

Using the same format as the Country Summaries, the dependent territories of each superordinate country are discussed below as a group. Exceptions to the general pattern are pointed out. It is often unclear whether a political unit should be regarded as a territory or an integral unit of its ruling state. For example, only the history of the Survey explains why the "independent" homelands of South Africa are considered dependent territories while the Republics of the USSR are not. Depending on the historical background, geographical separation—as by water and distance— often leads to the political unit being defined as a related territory. Many additional separated islands, such as those of India or Indonesia, could well be defined as dependent territories rather than as an integral part of the state. In general, if a unit is considered a full equal of the units of the superordinate state, it is not a territory.

A U S T R A L I A

CHRISTMAS ISLAND

Economy: capitalist-statist
Polity: agent
Population: 3,300

Political Rights: 4
Civil Liberties: 2
Status: partly free

An ethnically complex territory

COCOS ISLANDS

Economy: capitalist-statist   Political Rights: 4
Polity: agent and council   Civil Liberties: 2
Population: 600   Status: partly free

A relatively homogeneous population (nonwhite)

NORFOLK ISLAND

Economy: capitalist   Political Rights: 4
Polity: council & administrator   Civil Liberties: 2
Population: 2,200   Status: partly free

A relatively homogeneous population

Australia apparently follows democratic practices in so far as possible. Christmas Island is economically based on a state-run phosphate mine, which is soon to be depleted. The population is Chinese and Malay. Formerly a personal fiefdom, Cocos Islands has been placed under Australian administration, with the assistance of a local council. In 1984 the people voted in a UN supervised referendum to be integrated with Australia. Yet distance, the Malay population, and the plantation economy may make this difficult in more than theory. There appears to be free expression and a rule of law, but in neither are communications media developed.

Norfolk Island has a freely elected legislative assembly. It is in large measure self-governing; the wish of some residents for more independence is currently under consideration. An Australian "administrator" remains appointed. At least one lively free newspaper is published—in spite of threats and arson against the editor. Other rights of organization and law appear to be guaranteed.

C H I L E

EASTER ISLAND

Economy: capitalist-statist
Polity: governor
Population: 2,000

Political Rights: 5
Civil Liberties: 5
Status: partly free

A relatively homogeneous population (nonwhite)

The Island is granted limited autonomy within the generally repressive Chilean context. In 1984 the appointed governor was for the first time a native of the island. Discussion of local problems is quite open, and local elective institutions function. However, ninety-five percent of the land is controlled by the Chilean government.

D E N M A R K

FAROE ISLANDS

Economy: mixed capitalist
Polity: multiparty
Population: 44,000

Political Rights: 1
Civil Liberties: 1
Status: free

A relatively homogeneous population

GREENLAND

Economy: mixed capitalist
Polity: multiparty
Population: 51,000

Political Rights: 1
Civil Liberties: 1
Status: free

An ethnically complex population (nonwhite majority)

Both territories have elected parliamentary governments responsible for internal administration, and free to discuss their relationship to Denmark. In addition they elect representatives to the Danish parliament. They also have considerable freedom in international affairs—such as Greenland's ability to opt out of the European Economic Community in 1985. On major issues referendums are also held. Full freedoms of expression and organization are recognized. The local languages are dominant in both territories. The majority Inuit population is now politically in charge of Greenland.

F R A N C E

FRENCH GUIANA

Economy: noninclusive capitalist-statist	Political Rights: 3
Polity: dependent multiparty (limited)	Civil Liberties: 2
Population: 73,000	Status: partly free

An ethnically complex state (nonwhite majority)

FRENCH POLYNESIA

Economy: capitalist-statist	Political Rights: 3
Polity: dependent multiparty	Civil Liberties: 2
Population: 170,000	Status: partly free

A relatively homogeneous population (few French)

GUADELOUPE

Economy: capitalist-statist	Political Rights: 3
Polity: dependent multiparty (limited)	Civil Liberties: 2
Population: 324,000	Status: partly free

Relatively homogeneous with a small, dominant French minority

MAHORE (formerly MAYOTTE)

Economy: noninclusive capitalist	Political Rights: 2
Polity: dependent multiparty (limited)	Civil Liberties: 2
Population: 47,000	Status: free

A relatively homogeneous population (non-French)

MARTINIQUE

Economy: capitalist-statist	Political Rights: 3
Polity: dependent multiparty (limited)	Civil Liberties: 2
Population: 342,000	Status: partly free

Relatively homogeneous with a small, dominant French minority

MONACO

Economy: capitalist-statist	Political Rights: 4
Polity: dependent constitutional monarchy (limited)	Civil Liberties: 2
Population: 26,000	Status: partly free

An ethnically heterogeneous population

NEW CALEDONIA

Economy: capitalist-statist
Polity: dependent multiparty
Population: 150,000

Political Rights: 2
Civil Liberties: 2
Status: free

An ethnically complex territory (large French component)

REUNION

Economy: capitalist-statist
Polity: dependent multiparty
    (limited)
Population: 495,000

Political Rights: 3
Civil Liberties: 2

Status: partly free

An ethnically complex territory (few French)

ST. PIERRE AND MIQUELON

Economy: capitalist
Polity: dependent multiparty
    (limited)
Population: 6,260

Political Rights: 2
Civil Liberties: 2

Status: free

A relatively homogeneous territory (French)

WALLIS AND FUTUNA

Economy: capitalist-statist
Polity: dependent assembly
Population: 12,300

Political Rights: 4
Civil Liberties: 3
Status: partly free

A relatively homogeneous population (non-French)

The territories of French Guiana, Guadeloupe, Martinique, and Reunion are considered overseas departments of France. They have elected representatives in the French parliament (who need not be from the territory) and local councils. However, French law applies; a French administrator is the chief executive; both French subsidies and numbers of French bureaucrats, and sometimes troops or police are substantial. Open advocacy of independence in such integral parts of France is often repressed. Nevertheless, small independence movements exist in at least Guadeloupe and Martinique. Local elected governments have little power. The governance of the "collectivities" of Mahore (Mayotte) and St. Pierre and Miquelon is similar. In the latter, mainland French bureaucrats are numerous and dominant. Two recent referendums in Mahore have confirmed the desire of the people for their island to remain a part of France (because the Christian population would otherwise be ruled by the Muslim Comoros). Women are especially active in the anti-Comoros movement. Beyond the special colonial position, French law and its civil guarantees are maintained in the group.

The overseas territories of French Polynesia, New Caledonia, and Wallis and Futuna in the South Pacific are more traditional colonies in theory. In practice, the administrative structure is similar to that of the overseas departments. Assemblies have limited powers, although in the large territories perhaps as great as those in the overseas departments since the automatic application of French law does not apply to the territories. Independence is a lively and accepted issue, especially in New Caledonia. A 1987 referendum confirmed the desire of the majority of the inhabitants of New Caledonia to stay with France. The native people, the Kanaks (about forty percent), are highly organized and pro-independence—if the post-independence system could guarantee their control. Knowing they would lose, pro-independence Kanaks boycotted the 1987 referendum. Wallis and Futuna chose territorial status by referendum in 1959.

Monaco is not normally considered a dependent territory. However, by treaty with France, Monacan policy must conform to French security, political, and economic interests; the head minister must be chosen from a list submitted by the French government, and France controls foreign relations. The hereditary ruler appoints the government, but shares legislative power with an elected council. There is also elected local government. Foreign publications are freely available. Civil freedoms approximate those in France. The government owns the casino and major hotels.

425

Of the traditional colonial powers only France retains a grip on its colonies that seems to be resented by important segments of their populations. In particular, independence movements in Guadeloupe and Martinique have not had the opportunity for fair electoral tests of their desires that those in American and British colonies have had. France does not allow such electoral tests of independence sentiment in its overseas departments, and seldom elsewhere.

I S R A E L

OCCUPIED AREAS

Economy: capitalist	Political Rights: 5
Polity: external administration; local government	Civil Liberties: 5
Population: 1,150,000	Status: partly free

A complex population with a dominant minority

The Gaza Strip and the West Bank have had some elected local government; the decisive power is in the hands of the occupying force. Opposition to the occupation is expressed through demonstrations, local elections, and the media, but heavy pressure against any organized opposition is applied in an atmosphere of violence on both sides. There is censorship as well as other controls on the media and on movement. Settlement by the occupying people has steadily infringed upon the rights of the Arab majority.

I T A L Y

SAN MARINO

Economy: capitalist
Polity: dependent multiparty
Population: 19,380

Political Rights: 1
Civil Liberties: 1
Status: free

A relatively homogeneous state

VATICAN

Economy: statist
Polity: elected monarchy
Population: 860

Political Rights: 6
Civil Liberties: 4
Status: partly free

A relatively homogeneous population

San Marino is ruled by a multiparty parliamentary government with active elected local governments. The media are independent; in addition, Italian media are available. Although often considered independent, the influence of Italy is overwhelming. Defense and many foreign-relations areas are handled by the Italian government; major court cases are tried in Italian courts; the political parties are essentially branches of the respective Italian parties. Citizenship was recently extended to long-term residents for the first time.

The political situation of the Vatican is anomalous. On the one hand, the Vatican is ostensibly an independent state under absolutist rule, with the ruler chosen for life by a small international elite, which also has advisory functions. On the other hand, the international relations of the state are actually based on its ruler's status as head of a church rather than as head of a state. The people of the Vatican live more as Italian citizens than as citizens of the Vatican, regardless of their formal status. Vatican media represent the views of the church, yet Italian media and avenues of expression are fully available, and the dissatisfied can leave the context of the Vatican with minimal effort.

NETHERLANDS

ARUBA

Economy: mixed capitalist
Polity: multiparty internal
Population: 65,000

Political Rights: 1
Civil Liberties: 1
Status: free

An ethnically complex territory (few Dutch)

NETHERLANDS ANTILLES

Economy: mixed capitalist
Polity: multiparty internal
Population: 190,000

Political Rights: 1
Civil Liberties: 1
Status: free

An ethnically complex territory (few Dutch)

The Netherlands Antilles consist of two groups of islands in the Caribbean. Although the governor is appointed, the islands are largely self-governing at both the territory and island levels. The parliament is freely elected. The Netherlands has been urging the islands to accept independence, but the smaller islands have resisted independence in federation with the dominant island, Curacao. Full freedom of party organization, expression, and abstention are fully recognized. The press, radio, and television are private, free, and highly varied.

Aruba achieved autonomy in 1986 and is expected to attain full independence in 1996. The pattern of government is similar to that of the Netherlands Antilles.

NEW ZEALAND

COOK ISLANDS

Economy: capitalist-statist
Polity: multiparty internal
Population: 18,000

Political Rights: 2
Civil Liberties: 2
Status: free

A relatively homogeneous population (nonwhite)

NIUE

Economy: capitalist-statist
Polity: internal parliamentary
Population: 3,000

Political Rights: 2
Civil Liberties: 2
Status: free

A relatively homogeneous population (nonwhite)

TOKELAU ISLANDS

Economy: capitalist-statist
Polity: limited assembly
Population: 1,600

Political Rights: 4
Civil Liberties: 2
Status: partly free

A relatively homogeneous population (nonwhite)

The Cook Islands and Niue are largely self-governing territories with elected parliaments. There is continuing oversight by New Zealand, particularly in defense, foreign affairs, and justice. Niue has been unable to arrest a steady decline in population. Tokelau is administered by appointed officials with the help of the assembly. The assembly's powers have been growing, and it is becoming less aristocratic. Tokelau's assembly has informed the United Nations of satisfaction with its current relationship with New Zealand. Elsewhere, political life, particularly in the Cook Islands, has been vigorous and free.

P O R T U G A L

AZORES

Economy: capitalist-statist
Polity: internal multiparty
Population: 292,000

Political Rights: 2
Civil Liberties: 2
Status: free

A relatively homogeneous population

MACAO

Economy: capitalist-statist
Polity: limited internal assembly
Population: 400,000

Political Rights: 3
Civil Liberties: 4
Status: partly free

An ethnically complex population (majority Chinese)

MADEIRA

Economy: capitalist-statist
Polity: internal multiparty
Population: 266,000

Political Rights: 2
Civil Liberties: 2
Status: free

An ethnically complex but relatively homogeneous population

The Azores and Madeira are considered "autonomous regions," whose multiparty governments have a large degree of internal self-rule, including the right to issue their own stamps. The islands also have elected representatives in the Portuguese parliament. They have the same civil freedoms as on the mainland. Both regions have independence movements. Land holding has traditionally been very concentrated on Madeira. With populations made up largely of Portuguese settlers of past centuries, neither island group has been seen as a colony. Macao is administered by a Lisbon-appointed governor with the help of an elected local assembly. Peking and its supporters affect all levels of government and constrain the news media, as well as rights of assembly and organization. However, democratic institutions are more developed here than in Hong Kong.

SOUTH AFRICA

BOPHUTHATSWANA

Economy: capitalist-statist
Polity: dependent dominant party
Population: 1,400,000

Political Rights: 6
Civil Liberties: 5
Status: partly free

An ethnically complex population

CISKEI

Economy: capitalist-statist
Polity: dependent dominant party
Population: 740,000

Political Rights: 6
Civil Liberties: 6
Status: not free

An ethnically homogeneous territory

SOUTH WEST AFRICA (NAMIBIA)

Economy: capitalist-traditional
Polity: appointed multiparty-
     traditional
Population: 1,100,000

Political Rights: 6
Civil Liberties: 5

Status: partly free

An ethnically heterogeneous territory

VENDA

Economy: capitalist-statist
Polity: dependent multiparty
Population: 550,000

Political Rights: 6
Civil Liberties: 6
Status: not free

A relatively homogeneous territory

South West Africa, or Namibia, is ruled as a colony of South Africa, with the help of a multiparty government appointed in 1985. There is considerable freedom of the press, of discussion, and organization—although with occasional interventions. The judiciary is relatively independent and quite authoritative. Native chiefs and councils play political and judicial roles in their home areas. The northern or Ovambo half of the country is under police rule in a guerrilla war setting.

The other territories are homelands that have accepted formal independence—except for Transkei, which the Survey accepts as independent. Characteristically, most wage earners ascribed to these states work in South Africa proper; the states receive extensive South African aid, and they are not viable units geographically. South Africa exerts considerable control over their foreign affairs and security, although there are often disputes. Formally governed by parliamentary systems, the control of political organization and expression, the large number of appointed parliamentarians, and the violent atmosphere makes them more dictatorial than democratic. Expression of opinion in regard to the existence of the state is especially perilous. There are arrests for reasons of conscience and reports of torture. Nevertheless, these territories protect their peoples from many of the worst insults of apartheid, and, in Bophuthatswana, a much closer approximation to justice exists for blacks than in South Africa itself.

S P A I N

CANARY ISLANDS

Economy: capitalist
Polity: centralized multiparty
Population: 1,500,000

Political Rights: 1
Civil Liberties: 2
Status: free

A complex but relatively homogeneous population

C E U T A

Economy: capitalist-statist
Polity: dependent, unrecognized
Population: 78,000 (including
              12,000 soldiers)
An ethnically homogeneous population

Political Rights: 2
Civil Liberties: 3
Status: free

M E L I L L A

Economy: capitalist-statist
Polity: dependent, unrecognized
Population: 63,000

Political Rights: 2
Civil Liberties: 3
Status: free

An ethnically complex population

Spain has no official colonies. Its outposts in North Africa, Ceuta and Melilla, ruled as parts of the Spanish provinces across from them, remain anomalies. Both have been Spanish for centuries. Only after demonstrations in Melilla in 1986 did the government move to give most Muslims citizenship—but the process will evidently be very slow.

The Canary Islands are governed as two provinces. Although the people are of diverse origins and preserve many pre-Spanish customs, the culture today is largely Hispanic. There is an independence movement, but the development of internal self-determination on a regional basis may help to reduce the desire for separation. Spanish law guarantees rights as in Spain itself.

S W I T Z E R L A N D

LIECHTENSTEIN

Economy: capitalist-statist
Polity: constitutional monarchy
Population: 124,000

Political Rights: 3
Civil Liberties: 1
Status: free

A relatively homogeneous population

Foreign affairs, defense, and some economic regulations are controlled by Switzerland. Swiss money is used, as is the Swiss postal service. The government is responsible both to the hereditary monarch and an elected parliament. Referendums supplement parliamentary rule. There is local government. Women have recently attained the right to vote and have entered parliament. The media are mostly Swiss, although there are local papers.

U N I T E D   K I N G D O M

ANGUILLA

Economy: mixed capitalist
Polity: dependent limited
      assembly
Population: 6,500

Political Rights: 2
Civil Liberties: 2

Status: free

A relatively homogeneous population (nonwhite)

BERMUDA

Economy: mixed capitalist
Polity: multiparty
Population: 55,000

Political Rights: 2
Civil Liberties: 1
Status: free

An ethnically complex state (largely nonwhite)

434

BRITISH VIRGIN ISLANDS

Economy: mixed socialist
Polity: limited internal
       assembly
Population: 11,000

Political Rights: 2
Civil Liberties: 1

Status: free

A relatively homogeneous population (nonwhite)

CAYMAN ISLANDS

Economy: capitalist
Polity: limited internal
       assembly
Population: 17,000

Political Rights: 2
Civil Liberties: 2

Status: free

An ethnically mixed population (largely white)

CHANNEL ISLANDS

Economy: capitalist
Polity: traditional
       parliamentary
Population: 132,000

Political Rights: 2
Civil Liberties: 2

Status: free

An ethnically mixed population (white)

FALKLAND ISLANDS

Economy: capitalist-statist
Polity: limited representative
Population: 1,800

Political Rights: 2
Civil Liberties: 2
Status: free

A relatively homogeneous population (white)

GIBRALTAR

Economy: capitalist-statist
Polity: internal parliamentary
Population: 30,000

Political Rights: 1
Civil Liberties: 2
Status: free

An ethnically complex population

HONG KONG

Economy: capitalist
Polity: colonial
Population: 5,700,000

Political Rights: 4
Civil Liberties: 2
Status: partly free

A relatively homogeneous population (Chinese)

ISLE OF MAN

Economy: capitalist
Polity: parliamentary
Population: 65,000

Political Rights: 1
Civil Liberties: 1
Status: free

A relatively homogeneous population (white)

MONTSERRAT

Economy: capitalist
Polity: colonial legislative
Population: 12,000

Political Rights: 2
Civil Liberties: 2
Status: free

A relatively homogeneous population (nonwhite)

ST. HELENA

Economy: capitalist-statist
Polity: colonial legislative
Population: 5,200

Political Rights: 2
Civil Liberties: 2
Status: free

A relatively homogeneous population (white)

TURKS AND CAICOS

Economy: capitalist
Polity: colonial legislative
Population: 7,400

Political Rights: 2
Civil Liberties: 2
Status: free

A relatively homogeneous population (nonwhite)

The dependencies of the United Kingdom all have the civil rights common to the homeland. Nearly all have expressed, through elections, elected representatives, or simply lack of controversy in a free atmosphere, a desire to stay a dependency of the United Kingdom under present arrangements. For example, the party winning decisively in 1984 in Turks and Caicos ran on an anti-independence stand. The people of Gibraltar have often affirmed their desire to remain a colony. For the other colonies, there is little evidence of a significant denial of political or civil liberties. An exception may be the Channel Island of Guernsey, with a not fully representative parliament, exceptional lack of separation of powers, and an uncritical local media.

Constitutionally, the dependencies may be divided into three groups. The first consists of those units with essentially full internal autonomy, expressed through freely elected parliaments. The second group is administered by a strong appointed governor and a largely elected assembly or council. The third group consists of colonies with little if any power in elected assemblies or officials. The first group includes the Channel Islands, the Isle of Man, and possibly Bermuda. Midway between the first and second groups are the British Virgin Islands, Cayman Islands, Gibraltar, and possibly Montserrat. In the second group are Anguilla, Falkland Islands, St. Helena, and Turks and Caicos. The last group consists only of Hong Kong, whose political development, and to some extent even civil liberties have been arrested by the presence of communist China. In preparation for the turning back of sovereignty to China in 1997, legislative institutions are being developed, and political consciousness is growing. To date the suffrage is very limited. At the same time the self-censorship of the press is increasing.

U N I T E D   S T A T E S   O F   A M E R I C A

AMERICAN SAMOA

Economy: capitalist-communal
Polity: parliamentary self-
    governing
Population: 32,000

Political Rights: 2
Civil Liberties: 2

Status: free

A relatively homogeneous population (nonwhite)

BELAU

Economy: capitalist-communal
Polity: parliamentary self-
    governing
Population: 12,000

Political Rights: 2
Civil Liberties: 2

Status: free

A relatively homogeneous population (nonwhite)

GUAM

Economy: capitalist-statist
Polity: parliamentary self-
    governing
Population: 106,000

Political Rights: 2
Civil Liberties: 2

Status: free

An ethnically complex population (mostly nonwhite)

MARSHALL ISLANDS

Economy: capitalist-statist   Political Rights: 2
Polity: parliamentary self-   Civil Liberties: 2
    governing
Population: 31,000   Status: free

A relatively homogeneous population (nonwhite)

MICRONESIA, FEDERATED STATES OF

Economy: capitalist-communal   Political Rights: 2
Polity: parliamentary self-   Civil Liberties: 2
    governing
Population: 74,000   Status: free

A relatively homogeneous population (nonwhite)

NORTHERN MARIANAS

Economy: capitalist   Political Rights: 1
Polity: parliamentary self-   Civil Liberties: 2
    governing
Population: 17,000   Status: free

A relatively homogeneous population (nonwhite)

PUERTO RICO

Economy: capitalist   Political Rights: 2
Polity: self governing quasi-state   Civil Liberties: 1
Population: 3,300,000   Status: free

A relatively homogeneous population (Spanish speaking)

VIRGIN ISLANDS

Economy: capitalist
Polity: appointed governorship
Population: 97,000

Political Rights: 2
Civil Liberties: 2
Status: free

A complex population (mostly nonwhite)

Puerto Rico is an internally self-governing commonwealth with a political system modeled on that of the states of the United States. Control alternates between the major regional parties. Both directly and indirectly the Puerto Ricans have voted to remain related to the United States. (Independence parties have never received more than a small fraction of the vote.) There is full freedom of discussion and organization. The press and broadcast media are highly varied and critical. There are political prisoners, and instances of brutality and unnecessary killings, but no good evidence of imprisonment or killing simply for expression of opinion.

The rest of America's dependent territories are now either internally self-governing or have accepted in free referenda their present status. The territories have elective institutions including in most cases an elected governor or chief administrator. There have been a number of recent referendums approving free association with the United States in the Micronesian territories. However, except for the commonwealth of Northern Marianas, the agreements are not yet fully approved by the American Congress. Full independence was not discussed extensively by either the United States or the islanders. In Belau, dispute over the compact with the U.S. has led to violent deaths, doubtful judicial verdicts, and fear among some who disagree. Political activity on Guam is increasingly mature and independent. Guamanians also may soon wish to achieve commonwealth status similar to that of the Northern Marianas. Traditional chiefs have special powers in most other Pacific territories. Island groupings, such as the Marshalls or Micronesia (Federated States), are loose federations with strong local governments on the separate islands. Overdependence on American largesse is arguably the greatest hindrance to complete freedom in the Pacific territories. Freedom of expression, assembly, and organization are recognized in all territories.

FRANCE-SPAIN CONDOMINIUM

ANDORRA

Economy: capitalist
Polity: limited multiparty
Population: 31,000

Political Rights: 3
Civil Liberties: 3
Status: partly free

A relatively homogeneous population (Catalan)

Andorra has a parliamentary government overseen by the representatives of the French President and the Bishop of Urgel. Formal parties are not permitted, but "groupings" contest the elections in their stead. There has been agitation for more self-determination. External relations are handled primarily by France, a responsibility France has insisted on in recent discussions with the EEC. An independent weekly is supplemented by French and Spanish publications. Only recently has the Andorra Council been able to regulate its own radio stations.

INDEX

See also Country and Related Territory Summaries, as well as page vii.

Index

446